ENGLAND EXPECTS THAT EVERY MAN WILL DO HIS DUTY

VICTORY

ENGAGE THE ENEMY MORE CLOSELY

C000089185

Above: Sir Thomas Slade (c. 1703–71), innovative and far-sighted ship designer, and most notably the architect of HMS *Victory* in 1758/9. Though *Victory* is his most memorable memorial, he also created many other ships for the Navy. At the Nile in 1798, for example, eight out of thirteen British ships of the line were built to Slade designs. A later surveyor Sir John Henslow declared: 'He was truly a great man in the line he trod, such a one I believe never went before him, and … I may venture to say will hardly follow him'. Detail from an anonymous oil. Courtesy National Maritime Museum.

Frontispiece: HMS *Victory*, published in J.K. Laughton's, *Nelson and His Companions in Arms* (London, 1896). Not only is this an appropriate visual emblem to this edition of *The Trafalgar Chronicle*, which celebrates her 250th anniversary, there also remains something very apposite in Laughton's preface: 'Very many lives of Nelson have been written from almost as many points of view. With these the present work does not enter into competition ... but while dwelling on the principal incidents in Nelson's life and on the glories of his achievements, [the author] has endeavoured to describe some of the influences which tended to form Nelson's character; some of the men, second only to himself, from whom he derived his inspiration; some of those who so nobly worked with him in securing the liberty and establishing the greatness of England'.

THE
TRAFALGAR CHRONICLE

Yearbook
of
THE 1805 CLUB
No. 19, 2009

Shipwright, hand-coloured etching, published c. 1810.
Courtesy Warwick Leadlay Gallery.

Cover Illustration: HMS *Victory* in her final berth at Portsmouth,
from an original drawing by Hanslip Fletcher, 1932.
Courtesy Michael A. Nash Archive.

Published by The 1805 Club, 2009, Cranbrook, Kent, TN17 2QD.

Publication Design by Bumblebee *www.bumblebeedesign.net*
Printed by B D&H, Litho and Screen Printers, Norwich.

ISBN: 978-1-902392-19-6

THE
TRAFALGAR CHRONICLE
Yearbook of The 1805 Club. No.19, 2009

Membership of The 1805 Club

The 1805 Club is a non-profit-making voluntary association dedicated for the benefit of the public to the preservation and maintenance of Nelson-related graves and monuments. The 1805 Club also publishes original Nelson-related research, reprints, rare Nelson-related documents and organizes events of interest to students of the Royal Navy in the age of sail. Membership of The 1805 Club is open to all and is by direct application to, or special invitation from, its governing Council. Subscriptions are due on 1 January each year. All members receive, post-free, the Club's news magazine, the Club's Yearbook *The Trafalgar Chronicle* and the Club's occasional papers. A charge may be made for other special publications.

A prospectus is available on request from the Membership Secretary or the North American Secretary. For economy of administration, members are encouraged to pay their subscriptions by Standing Order.

Editorial

See you the ferny ride that steals
Into the oak-woods far?
O that was whence they hewed the keels
That rolled to Trafalgar.
                    Rudyard Kipling, *Puck's Song*, 1906.

This, the nineteenth edition of *The Trafalgar Chronicle*, once again takes as its keynote a birthday, though this year of a different sort. 23 July 2009 marked the 250th anniversary of the laying down of *Victory's* keel at His Majesty's dockyard at Chatham in Kent. Thus began the building of a vessel that would grow to become the oldest commissioned warship, and perhaps the most famous in the world.

Victory will always be linked with the name and memory of Lord Nelson and the Battle of Trafalgar, and that, of course, has been key to her survival into the present day. That she has survived 250 years, over 150 of them in the 'oggin', is remarkable but what is extraordinary is the dual role she nowadays enjoys. Not only is she a living museum of the Georgian navy, she also serves as the flagship of the Commander-in-Chief Naval Home Command. Proof that her heart beats yet – if proof were needed – is evident in the salute she fired on 18 September this year at the formal launch of the National Museum of the Royal Navy. *Victory* let go rolling broadsides and, pleasing to HM Treasury no doubt, this was done at the expense of less powder than gunners at Trafalgar would have used for a single shot. Never fear, HMS *Victory's* heart still beats strong.

In honour of her birth and longevity, we might do well to take as our metaphor for this issue the construction of a ship. A vessel floats, or sinks, according to the result of the cooperation of the skilled hands that go into her building. And in eighteenth-century Britain, the dockyard was the most complex industrial operation then known. It has been estimated that something like twenty-six different trades went into the building of a wooden-hulled, sail-powered warship. We hope the rough similarity of this figure and our complement of contributors this year is obvious. However, it would be inappropriate to stretch this comparison beyond its bounds and differentiate in order of importance between the master craftsmen who laid the keel and the lads who caulked the deck. Each plays a crucial part. Without due recognition of all hands, 'ships are but boards, sailors but men'.

The coordination of many people offering different, but complimentary, talents would have greatly cheered our friend, the late Dr Colin White. In addition to making a generous contribution himself, Colin would no doubt have given us encouragement in like measure, often as not in a practical form of guidance and critical suggestion. To see that spirit still manifest here is a warm reassurance.

As in previous years, it is our particular pleasure to see this *Trafalgar Chronicle* as the result of genuine team effort. All manner of disciplines, skills and trades have been brought to bear in the making of this journal. The common ambition of all the authors found in these pages appears to be the desire to volunteer one's very best. Never mind therefore whether it comes as the result of the professorial pen, the student's laptop, or the painstaking notes of the amateur historian. Each has its merits and all deserve a place here. Let us rejoice in this admixture and savour the result. Each essay widens and deepens our understanding, especially so in that solving a question very likely leads to raising many more. If this is so, then we look forward to their address in future issues.

Therefore, our thanks are due to each and all who have contributed to this edition. We hope you will find both enjoyment and edification in your *Trafalgar Chronicle*. On this note of celebration, in *Victory's* 'wonderful year', let us remind the reader of that enduringly good advice: 'if you have trouble opening your bottle of champagne, try hitting it with a ship!'

Anthony Cross   Huw Lewis-Jones

The Chairman's Dispatch:
Victory, Remembrance, and Daring

Peter Warwick

Over Time's misty tide-stream sailing,
Stirring the heart like the throbbing of the drums,
Banners of conquest and bravery trailing,
Out of the past she comes.
How shall we honour her? How shall we name her?
What shall her blazon be?
FLAGSHIP OF NELSON,
FLAGSHIP OF ENGLAND,
VICTORY'S 'VICTORY'
      Anon.

This year with the successful celebration of the 250th anniversary of Admiral Lord Nelson's birthday fresh in our minds, we celebrated the 250th anniversary of the laying down of the keel of HMS *Victory*. However, we also said mournful farewells to Lt Cdr David Harris MBE RN and Dr Colin White, two leading lights of The 1805 Club and the naval history community generally. Meanwhile, we have all been shocked by the grim financial climate – an economic crisis so severe that it has set the scene for public spending cuts that may affect the future of the Royal Navy.

Concurrently, we are on the threshold of commemorating the death, in March 1810, of another great figure from the era of the Georgian sailing navy, Admiral Lord Collingwood. This is very likely to be the last great naval bicentenary of the French Revolutionary and Napoleonic Wars that will be remembered in a major way. Will future generations look back and see the years immediately following the Trafalgar bicentenary as some kind of symbolic watershed marking a time when the allure of Britain's naval history and heritage had reached a highpoint, while the simple lessons 'out of the past' were misunderstood or even ignored? What shall *Victory's* blazon be now?

In the mid-nineteenth century William Thackeray penned, 'The bones of the *Victory* ought to be sacred relics for Englishmen to worship almost'. Today, there is still no more illustrious a warship name in British naval history than

HMS *Victory*, inextricably linked as it is with Admiral Lord Nelson, the Battle of Trafalgar and today's Royal Navy – the oldest commissioned warship in the world and flagship of the Second Sea Lord and Commander-in-Chief Naval Home Command. It is an amazing coincidence that this ship, which is forever associated with Nelson, was ordered in the year of his birth, and that her construction was begun before his first birthday.

Victory's keel was laid on 23 July 1759 in the Old Single Dock (Number 2) at Chatham Royal Dockyard, with construction continuing for six years. Designed by Sir Thomas Slade, the Senior Surveyor of the Navy (1755-71), she was the biggest warship ever built for the British fleet. Carrying 100 guns on three decks and with a length of 69.34 metres and a beam of 15.8 metres, she displaced 3,556 tonnes and drew 7.44 metres of water 'at mean load'. Some 6,000 oak and elm trees from the depleted Wealden forests of Kent and Sussex and oak and fir from the Baltic were used in her construction. The reason she enjoyed such a long fighting career was that much of this timber was more than a century old. It had been deliberately stockpiled to create a new first rate at a future date. This also accounts, in part, for why she has survived to this day.

In January 1922, thanks to the efforts of the Society for Nautical Research, *Victory* was permanently dry-docked in Number 2 Dock, HM Naval Base, Portsmouth, where she has been variously restored, repaired and lovingly preserved ever since. The 1805 Club is honoured to be among the organisations that are officially regarded by the Royal Navy as 'stakeholders'. Under its developing Naval Heritage Strategy the Royal Navy is demonstrating its duty of care for this magnificent ship at a difficult time. *Victory* is part of an over-stretched defence budget and it is clearly a challenge to justify monies for the preservation of her 'wood and tar' when sailors and marines requiring adequate kit are at risk of their lives in operational theatres. Last winter up to 40 per cent of Britain's forces in Afghanistan were from the Royal Navy and Royal Marines. Nevertheless, there is no doubt about the flagship's enduring significance. Lord West of Spithead, when First Sea Lord, believed, 'she should act as a reminder that the reasons for her being created in the first place still stand, that today and into the future, Britain needs to understand the worth of its Navy and its vital role in securing the nation'.

The late and lamented Dr Colin White expressed this belief more succinctly when he simply described her as 'the beating heart' of the Royal Navy, its standards and traditions: an icon for all those who have served and continue to serve. She is indeed a potent reminder that Britain is a maritime country and as such we should never lose sight of the worth of our Navy in securing the nation's freedoms and democracy. She reminds us that the sea should be at the heart of our defence. The standards can be damaged when, as Nelson once wrote to Lady Hamilton, 'Government don't care much for us'.

'Ladies and gentlemen, imagine that you are sitting with Nelson in the Great Cabin of Victory on the eve of Trafalgar …' Drawing by John Gwyther, 2009.

Like Nelson, whom he championed in such an inimitable way, Colin White's death in December 2008 tore a hole in the naval historical fabric. Like his hero, he died prematurely depriving the world of an undoubted talent. Admired and respected internationally – by royalty, the Royal Navy, historians and enthusiasts of Nelson and naval history alike – Colin was the right man in the right place at the right time. His apogee was the Trafalgar bicentenary, which he steered with considerable success. In the wake of his extensive research, which identified new sources (which he was happy to share with others, a rarity) and 'revealed new insights' (a favourite phrase), he launched a fleet of Nelson books culminating in the landmark *Nelson: The New Letters*, fired a broadside of spell-binding lectures and justly earned the description of being the admiral's 'representative on earth'.

It helped that he was a marvellous communicator with a vivid historical imagination and a fantastic theatrical ability to bring history to life. Many will recall how he would often say, 'Ladies and gentlemen, imagine that you are sitting with Nelson in the Great Cabin of *Victory* on the eve of Trafalgar ...' and then find themselves transported there by his magic. At the The1805 Club's Trafalgar Dinner at Newhouse in 2003 he had the guests in tears as he took them back, with the lights dimmed and candles burning, to St Paul's Cathedral and Nelson's funeral on that wintry afternoon of 9 January 1806.

The 1805 Club owes Colin White an immense debt of gratitude for his vision and leadership and for his utter dedication to our cause. We treasured his support, enthusiasm and loyalty to the Club, and we were always thrilled when he took part in our activities, which he did frequently. The most visible and lasting legacy of his work for the Club is The Trafalgar Captains' Memorial, which found and surveyed the graves and memorials of the British commanding officers at Trafalgar, conserved those at risk, and published their stories in the highly successful *The Trafalgar Captains: Their Monuments and Memorials*. The 1805 Club is preparing to venerate his outstanding contribution with The Colin White Memorial.

During the 1990s Colin was able to look directly out of his office window at HMS *Victory* and for three of those years her Commanding Officer was Lieutenant Commander David Harris MBE. On leaving the Navy, David became a solid supporter of The 1805 Club and edited *The Trafalgar Chronicle* for two years before taking on the role of Treasurer, which he managed with real aplomb. As with Colin White, the White Ensign was worn at half-mast at HM Naval Base Portsmouth on the day of his funeral as an exceptional mark of respect. Such was the measure of the man.

Close to HMS *Victory's* berth lies another warship. Her formidable and futuristic slab-sided stealth profile is topped by a radar tower as tall as an electricity pylon. She is as impressive as the wooden walls and towering masts of her antecedent. Her name is HMS *Daring*, the Royal Navy's latest asset and the first of a new class (Type 45), described as 'the most advanced surface warship in the world'. She weighs 7,500 tons and is 152.5 metres in length, which is a lot larger than the Navy's existing Type 42 Sheffield Class. Powered by an integrated electric propulsion system, driven by Rolls Royce WR21 gas turbines, her twin 100-ton electric shaft motors allow her to exceed 30 knots. At 18 knots, *Daring* can cruise across the Atlantic, from Portsmouth to New York, and back without stopping. Another advantage is her high-speed manoeuvrability, which is unmatched by any of the Royal Navy's previous warships. Her armament includes Sea Viper missiles, a 4.5in medium calibre main gun, and a flight deck large enough for a twin-rotor Chinook helicopter, although her typical helicopter aircraft is either the AgustaWestland Merlin or the modified Westland (Future Lynx).

Whether or not *Daring* is 'the most advanced surface warship in the world', one is tempted to speculate what Nelson would make of her? I believe he would be excited at the progress of technology and amazed at *Daring's* capabilities, which would have been unimaginable in his era, although he could reflect on how *Victory* was the super weapon of his day. He would surely regret that the original order for the Daring Class has been halved to six. Ultimately however, we know that Nelson would focus on the values, standards and traditions of the service itself: the quality of leadership, the practice of 'mission command', of which he was a master, and the professionalism and 'can do' attitude of an RN ships' company. I am sure he would also derive some satisfaction from the fact that every warship, including *Daring*, still salutes his old flagship as they pass her berth! In this way the ethos of the Royal Navy is like a golden thread connecting the past with the present and the future.

'How shall we honour her?' The Club's conservation work is linked to this thread and there is much it wishes to do in the future. This year we are between two major memorial projects: the completion of the *Trafalgar Captains* and the launch of *Nelson's Nile and Copenhagen Captains*. A considerable amount of background research has been undertaken on the latter by members of the Club. We are now close to preparing applications for funding.

Fundraising generally is an issue on which the Club is concentrating because it is one of the highest hurdles it has to jump if it is to not only undertake major projects but also increase the energy of its conservation activity. Meanwhile, the Club has initiated and launched a groundbreaking Website Educational Programme with students at Admiral Lord Nelson School, Portsmouth, which allows them to inform their peer groups through the Internet about Nelson and the sailing navy, thus stimulating their potential interest in a modern way. This exciting Programme has been dedicated to the Club's Past-President Lily McCarthy CBE.

It is with much pleasure that I welcome two new, and very distinguished, Vice-Presidents to the Club: Rear Admiral Joe Callo and Dr Agustin

Guiméra. They are both recognised naval historians and living in the United States and Spain respectively reinforce the Club's influence and reputation in those countries.

In the opinion of all great commanders and leaders, not least Nelson and Collingwood, the focus is always on people since they provide the capability, zest and enthusiasm to get things done. As an admiral once said, 'It's not the ships, it's the men in them'. This viewpoint is certainly true of The 1805 Club. Our vice-presidents and members of Council are unbelievably hard working and are always at the ready to add yet more lustre to the reputation of the Club. As Chairman I have always found it a pleasure to highlight their endeavour and commitment and to convey the sense of gratitude that our loyal membership must feel about their efforts. This year is no different, and on your behalf as well as for myself, I should like to pay a genuine and heartfelt tribute by offering a huge 'Thank you! To them all'.

May I also express thanks to our joint editors for another wonderful issue of *The Trafalgar Chronicle*. For many members of the Club this yearbook and *The Kedge Anchor* are the most tangible benefits of their membership. I am confident that this attractive and stimulating edition of the *Chronicle* is one everyone will enjoy.

P. Warwick

Peter Warwick

In Search of Nelson's Spy:
A Research Case Study

Justin Reay

In 2004, an historian in the Catalan town of Roses asked me if I knew of the 'English merchant' who had lived there during the Napoleonic Wars, in the context of research I was undertaking into the Royal Navy on the coast of Catalonia. I had not heard of such a person but promised to look into it. At that time I did not even have a name for this mysterious Englishman who apparently had been a big wheel in business affairs in what, 200 years ago, was a prosperous port engaged in the export of wine, olives, anchovies, honey and lemons.[1]

During a conversation with the late Dr Colin White I mentioned this unknown merchant. Within a day or so he emailed me pages from the proofs of his then impending volume *Nelson, the New Letters* in which Colin quoted from a letter written in 1804 to Admiral Lord Nelson as commander-in-chief Mediterranean, with a note that the correspondent, Edward Gayner, may be the man in question. Now I had a name, proper research could begin and from the first day the link to Nelson was strong. This article briefly tells Gayner's story, and traces my continuing research into his life and his relationship with Nelson and the Royal Navy.

Paper silhouette of Edward Gayner as a young man, made by his sister Mary. Kind permission of the Heydon-Gayner Collection.

'The Virtuous Quaker'

Born in Bristol in 1764, Edward Gayner was the youngest child of a middling merchant's family, members of the local Quaker community.[2] His father was a broker selling cargoes of rice, sugar and indigo from the dockside, and Edward's mother was Mabel Mace

Fry, one of the Quaker Fry dynasty who introduced the mechanised production of chocolate. Following the Iberian custom, when Edward lived in Spain he incorporated his mother's family name into his surname, and in Catalan documents he is usually called Edward Gayner i Fry.

Edward left the family home in his twenties to work in France buying for a Bristol wine merchant. By 1790 Edward was living in Montpellier, the centre of the important wine trade exporting to Britain from southern France, where there was also a Quaker 'Meeting' (community of the Religious Society of Friends), formed in 1788 by French Protestants. Gayner also dealt with wine exporters in Spain, such as the Guernsey merchants Gregory & Guille in Barcelona; a letter from George Guille to Gayner of April 1791, is the earliest document we have concerning Gayner.[4] Two letters from Gayner

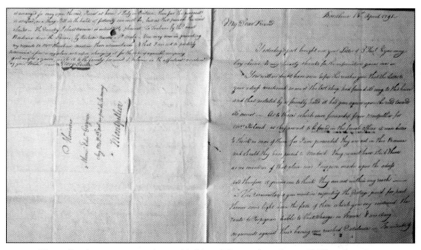

The earliest known correspondence with Edward Gayner, from George Guille at Barcelona, dating Gayner in France before April 1791. Courtesy the author.

in the early 1790s show a desire to visit England, but there is no evidence that he ever did return.[5] However, he became a partner in two Bristol business houses, Ames, Wright, Clayfield and Co, sugar merchants and Wright, Clayfield & Co, wine importers; those partnerships were dissolved and re-formed without Gayner in 1809, although they continued to trade with him for many years afterwards.[6]

Within a few weeks of Guille's letter, Gayner moved to the fortified town of Mont Louis in the Pyrenees. On the outbreak of the French Revolutionary

War in 1793, Mont Louis was captured by Spanish forces but retaken a year later, and Edward went to La Selva, a port just across the border. By 1803 Gayner was well established in Roses where he was dealing in the local wine, in French and Spanish brandy and also in honey, which he exported to England. He had become a *negociante*, trading internationally in his own name, with business partners in Roses and agents as far as Andalucía.

Both Britain and France considered Roses to be strategically very important. It was one of Spain's closest deep-water havens to France, less than a day's good sail from Toulon and half a day from Barcelona, protected from the harsh winter winds of this region by the mountains of the Pyrenees towering above the town, guarded by a large citadel and by a fortress on a headland commanding the seaward approach, well served by roads to the interior, with good fishing grounds offshore and many productive farms, vineyards and olive groves in its hinterland.

Second page of Gayner's letter to John Scott regarding a consignment of sheep for Lord Nelson's personal use shipped aboard the Fisgard, *undated but probably early September 1804. Kind permission Ben Burgess Collection, Norfolk Nelson Museum.*

Admiral Lord Nelson used the southern end of the long Gulf of Roses as one of three preferred stations for his large ships-of-the line (Rendezvous 97, 'under Cape San Sebastian'), while his frigates kept a loose blockade on Toulon for two years from the summer of 1803.[7] At the northern end, Roses itself was one of the Royal Navy's most important supply ports, and the Admiralty and Victualling Board records show that Nelson's ships frequently called there. Until Richard Ford was appointed Fleet Victualler at Sea, Nelson managed the victualling of his fleet himself and quickly made Gayner's acquaintance on arriving in the western Mediterranean in July 1803.[8] From February 1804 Ford dealt with the local suppliers, often going ashore with Nelson's secretary John Scott, and they also came to know Gayner.[9]

In the pre-phylloxera era the red wine and brandy of Catalonia was well regarded, being shipped to London and Bristol, some destined for the Royal Navy's warehouses.[10] Nelson bought from Gayner several consignments of 'good Rosas wine' for his own table on the *Victory* and to send home to Merton, and he also praised the health-giving efficacy of the excellent local

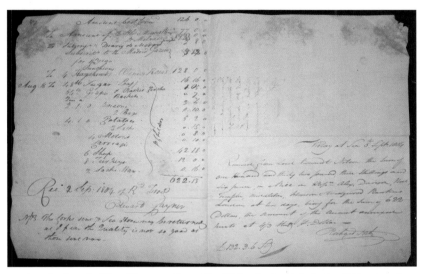

An order drawn by Edward Gayner on Viscount Lord Nelson for June to September 1804, endorsed by Richard Ford as paid in full by Nelson, 5th September 1804; showing subscriptions to Spanish newspapers and 4 puncheons of "Wines of Rosas" amongst fruit, vegetables, sugar loaves and livestock shipped aboard the Childers. *(Detail). Courtesy the author.*

honey.[11] Nelson's letters to Emma Hamilton, other personal correspondence and packages of valuables were often sent through Gayner for onward despatch via his business house in Bristol; several of Nelson's letters mention Gayner as the trusted intermediary, and his orders frequently require frigate commanders to collect letters and official documents at Roses.[12]

In April 1804 the large armed supply ship *Hindostan*, laden with spars, sails, medical supplies and several tons of gunpowder for the fleet, caught fire thirteen leagues (about 40 miles) off the Gulf of Roses, and the ship was in danger of exploding. Several men were injured and five died of asphyxia in the attempt to empty the gunpowder magazines. The ship was sailed inshore a mile south of Roses, before all hands had to be taken off. As the last boat reached the shore, bearing the *Hindostan's* commander, Captain John Le Gros and her second Lieutenant John Tailour (later to be the hero of an important cutting-out action at Roses in 1809), the vessel exploded and sank in 20 fathoms. Gayner arranged for the ship's company to be fed, clothed and housed, and hired sponge divers from Naples to salvage what remained of the ship and its vital stores, but all that was left were a few charred spars.

A silver Patriotic Fund vase (known as the 'Trafalgar Vase') made by Rundell & Bridge, hall-marked for 1805-06; the '100-guinea cup' ordered by the Admiralty in 1804 for presentation to Edward Gayner, made by the same goldsmiths, was probably very similar. Kind permission the Victoria and Albert Museum, London.

At Nelson's suggestion, towards the end of 1804 the Admiralty awarded Gayner a 'silver cup' valued at 100 guineas, which may have been one of the handsome Lloyds Patriotic Fund vases awarded from 1803 to mark 'successful exertions of valour or merit'.[13] It may be the item listed as 'una urna labrada' amongst Gayner's property inherited by his Catalan business partner in Minorca.[14] Important though Gayner's assistance was to the people of the *Hindostan*, it did not aid the re-supply of the fleet and was hardly more than one would expect of a well-connected compatriot in a neutral country. The award of a valuable silver vase from the public purse speaks of greater services to Britain.

With the regular consignments of supplies Gayner also provided Nelson with French and Spanish newspapers, which Nelson thought were so important that he instructed Gayner to make sure there was no delay in sending the latest editions. Such newspapers reported shipping movements from which the loading of a French supply convoy or the movements of military *materiel* could be detected. In the *Victory* was Nelson's "confidential" secretary, Dr Alexander John Scott (not to be confused with his clerical secretary, John Scott); he and Nelson would spend many hours analysing such reports and also documents from captured vessels. Gayner also passed information of strategic importance to Nelson; this is discussed below. On 5 October 1804 the ambush of a Spanish treasure fleet by a British squadron off Ferrol forced Spain to throw in her lot with the French. News of the action reached Catalonia a month later, and Gayner's letter to Nelson of 5 November, written in haste, mentions reports of the incident, which he regards as improbable. This is the last known letter from Gayner to Nelson.

War with Britain was not declared by Spain until December 1804 but before the end of November Nelson knew from his frigate commanders that their boats were being prevented from landing at Roses, and that something was wrong with his contacts ashore.[15] Gayner had been arrested on a charge of spying and incarcerated in the great Citadel. We know nothing about the merchant's imprisonment, but he may have been set at liberty before the Spanish uprising in May 1808; he had certainly left Roses before the siege by the French Armée de Catalogne in the winter of 1808, when the Royal Navy assisted the defence of the town.

Minorca was now again open to the British and Gayner moved there to set up another successful business. He lived in a large villa in the centre of Port Mahón, with warehouses in the commercial quarter, and was buying and selling cargoes of wine, wheat and olive oil and shipping lavender oil to London. From the end of the Peninsular War he again traded with Roses, becoming the largest exporter of wine from northern Catalonia.[16] He was well respected and appointed British Vice-Consul in the late 1830s.[17]

In 1840 Gayner produced a secret report for the British government, sent directly to Viscount Palmerston (the 'Prime Minister' in all but name), about growing French influence in the Balearic Islands during the Anglo-French naval arms race of that decade.[18] Writing that report must have given him wry amusement as he recalled his earlier and more dangerous confidential work for Lord Nelson. Edward Gayner died in Port Mahón in January 1846 at the age of 81, and was buried in the English cemetery overlooking the port, where his weathered headstone can still be seen marking the grave of 'the virtuous Quaker'.

Seeking Gayner: Research and Analysis

I was surprised that I had not heard of Edward Gayner before Colin White's helpful lead; with Gayner's connection to Nelson, I thought surely there must be much published about him. In fact, there was very little and my research became a long and sometimes frustrating journey, utilising all the resources available to modern historians.

Armed with Gayner's name I discovered three articles about his life as a merchant in Minorca after the end of the Napoleonic Wars, published in *The Nelson Dispatch* in the 1990s, a revised version in Spanish of one of those articles, and an entirely fanciful mention in an article of the 1920s in Barcelona about Nelson's 'battle-cane'.[19] The exegetical paragraph and quotations from relevant letters in Colin's volume of Nelson's 'new' letters gave more insight into his confidential intelligence work. Janet MacDonald discovered Gayner's name amongst the accounts and returns in Victualling Board papers in the Wellcome Institute collection, and in her excellent study of the supply of the Navy at this period she mentioned his supply of victuals and wine to Nelson's fleet and his imprisonment, as did Roger Knight in a biography of Nelson.[20] But when their works were in press, White, MacDonald and Knight knew nothing more about him than their brief notes.[21]

Ben Burgess had been misled in researching his short *Nelson Dispatch* article of 1991, and the pseudonymous piece by 'Trident' that followed offered nothing new. However, Burgess' notion that Gayner was Nelson's spy was not wrong, and his analysis of Nelson's correspondence published in Sir Nicholas Harris Nicolas' edition of Nelson's *Dispatches and Letters* was useful. The 50 or so letters in Nicolas mentioning Roses, some to or about Gayner, indicated that he may have been more than just a purveyor of supplies to the British. David Donaldson rebutted Burgess' theory in his own analytical article in the same journal in 1996; however, Dr Donaldson was writing from the evidence then available and in the last few years new research has proved that Gayner was passing covert information to Nelson. This was discussed in my articles in recent editions of *The Nelson Dispatch*.[22]

At the same time as I discovered Burgess' article, I also found a privately-published history of 'one Gayner family', by entering the name 'Gayner' in search fields of OLIS, the online catalogue of the Bodleian Library. Calling up Margaret Gayner's slim book from the bowels of our Offsite Repository, I was delighted to find it was the right family and to read a whole page about Edward Gayner. Miss Gayner's history included recent generations and I was able to contact her nephew, who now owns the image of Edward Gayner and his aunt's research papers; this enabled me to get in touch with Dr Donaldson, who was most generous in sharing his meticulous notes with me.

Primary Evidence

The French and Spanish newspapers Gayner supplied to Nelson – subscriptions appear in the invoices raised to Nelson's private account – were good sources of information, but do not constitute the type of intelligence which earns Gayner the sobriquet of 'spy'; other evidence is needed to prove Gayner was an active confidential agent. For historians, the best evidence is that produced at the time by the people concerned, as 'unwitting' testimony – to use the late Professor Arthur Marwick's useful distinction – made without a 'witting' eye to posterity's opinion. In naval history, ships' logs, muster books, supply orders, dispatches between officers as well as personal cor-

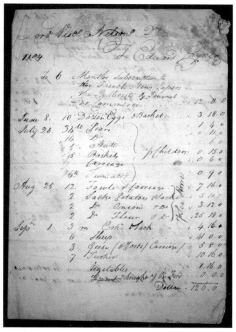

An order drawn on Nelson, endorsed by Gayner as paid by Richard Ford, 2 September 1804; this opening shows subscriptions to French newspapers and various livestock and vegetables for the fleet shipped aboard the Childers *and the* Sea Horse. *(Detail). Courtesy the author.*

respondence are valuable primary sources, but their contents and context need to be interpreted to uncover useful evidence which otherwise might remain hidden.

Gayner's visit to Nelson off Toulon in the winter of 1803, recorded in a letter from Nelson to Emma Hamilton, has been dismissed as just a courtesy call, but study of the primary material shows that the weather at the time was particularly bad, and also that there was a flurry of orders from Nelson requiring his outlying frigates to join the battle squadron off Toulon in expectation of a break-out from the French naval base.[23] Would Gayner risk his life to sail across hostile territory in a storm on a mere whim? The increase in the fleet's communications traffic at the same time raises the question as to whether Gayner had information about French naval and military movements which he felt could not be entrusted to anyone else to put in Nelson's hands as quickly as possible.

Throughout 1804 Gayner's letters to Nelson often include his own analysis of political affairs, and reports of the French fleet at Toulon or military matters in Spain. Gayner distinguishes between information that Nelson can trust and mere rumours, which he terms 'flying reports'. In January 1804 Gayner wrote an intelligence report, which he had mentioned in a previous letter (neither documents have yet been located); this was entrusted to Captain Ross Donnelly of the *Narcissus* anchored in Roses Bay, who in his own dispatch (13 January 1804, published in Nicolas) also mentions Spain's difficult relationship with Britain:

> *Mr Gayner came this forenoon... [and] has helped between the Governor and myself. I enclose his account of the intelligence alluded to in his former account... They [the Spanish] do not affect to deny the subsidy of three millions allowed to France & I see no very conciliatory conduct observed by Spain towards us.*

Nelson's orders regarding Roses clearly show that Gayner was giving the Admiral confidential information on a regular basis.[24] Ships-of-the-line and frigates were frequently ordered to Roses to 'wood and water' and allow their men to have some recreation ashore, but several orders contain specific instructions to 'wait upon Mr Gayner' for intelligence, or 'to take from Mr Gayner or his agent whatever information he may have', and return with it immediately to Nelson's current station. The gathering of information was often undertaken in a clandestine manner which approaches that of a spy's contacts; this order of 23 January 1804 takes Captain Donnelly back to Roses: '...proceed into the Bay of Rosas, and endeavour to communicate with the shore for the purpose of discovering the latest and most correct information of what is passing in France'. The Captain's Log for the following day records that the *Narcissus* anchored four miles southwest of the town and 'sent an officer on shore'.

Nelson's order to Captain Thomas Staines, commander of the sloop *Cameleon*, is typical of such instructions regarding information from Gayner:

> *Victory, off Cape St. Sebastians, 25th February, 1804*
>
> *You are hereby required and directed to proceed immediately with His Majesty's Sloop Cameleon, under your command, to the Bay of Rosas, and communicate with Mr. Edward Gayner of that place, or*

his partner in his absence, for the purpose of obtaining any intelligence of the Enemy's Fleet at Toulon, or of the line of conduct which Spain is likely to pursue, with any other information which you may deem necessary, and join with me an account thereof, on the present intended station of the Squadron (herewith transmitted) with the utmost dispatch, bringing with you any letters, &c., which Mr. Gayner may have for me.

Nelson and Bronte

Nelson constantly complained that he did not have enough frigates during the long blockade of Toulon. He had created what Colin White referred to as a 'finely-balanced chain of ships' with his small and extended fleet, and to take such precious assets as the *Cameleon* and the *Narcissus* away from this carefully orchestrated schedule indicates that Nelson regarded Gayner as a valuable source of strategic intelligence.

Such intelligence must have come from somewhere. In two letters to Nelson, Gayner mentions 'the Person who I alluded to' as being of service to the British and a reliable source of information; this eminence grise was probably the local shipping owner Narciso Mares. Gayner's other sources included Catalan merchants trading in southern France, and the French-speaking Guernsey *negociantes* in the wine and brandy trade, all of whom would observe the activities of the French.

During Spain's neutrality Gayner bribed or cajoled local officials to cast a blind eye to his illegal supply of the British Navy. In one of his letters to Nelson he refers to the usefulness of a 'douceur' – a sweetener – for the Collector of Customs. But with the new war from the end of 1804 Gayner was an alien trading with the enemy; however, his arrest was on a charge of spying. The *Exeter Morning Chronicle* printed on 12 February 1805 the first report of this:[25]

> *Mr Gayner, of Bristol, who resided at La Selva, and afterwards at the bay of Rosas, and two others, are taken up and confined in the citadel, having had their property and papers seized. They are charged with giving information to the English.*

On hearing of this Edward Rolle Clayfield, a partner in the Ames, Wright, Clayfield business house in Bristol, wrote to Nelson in January 1805. Nelson's reply was characteristically brief:[26]

Victory, March 30th 1805

Sir

I have received your letter of Jany 21st respecting Mr Gayner although I have not heard of him since the War with Spain, I have not the smallest idea of his being put in prison, and his conduct creates such an universal esteem that I have no doubt but that he is both at liberty and respected.

I am Sir Your
Most Obedient Servant,
Nelson and Bronte

However, Nelson already knew of his confidante's arrest; two days before his letter to Clayfield, Nelson had written to Henry Stanyford Blankley, the British Consul-General for the Balearic Islands then en route to Malta, including a reference to Gayner's 'hard fate'.[27] This shows that 'witting' evidence – in this case worded to protect Gayner should unfriendly eyes read Nelson's reply to Clayfield – must be treated with caution.

Digital Resources

Amongst the tools used by the modern historian, digitised documents and archives are very valuable, and the Internet has become commonly employed – if not often cited by 'serious' authors; those of us trained in the pre-Web era are amazed by its power to shorten research time, but cautious of its over-use. In my research into Gayner, three attributes of the digital revolution – the ability to search within digitised documents; access to online catalogues and digital archives; and the ease of communication with other scholars – led me to important information.

For example, the Caird Library at the National Maritime Museum recently added the Phillips-Croker Papers to its online indices, and from this I located six letters from or about Gayner whose existence was not previously recorded.[28] Using Web search engines I discovered Dr Donaldson's article in the Minorquine journal *Revista de Minorca*, which led to direct contact with him, via the Gayner Family papers, and sight of his notes for his earlier unreferenced article in the *Nelson Dispatch*. Accessing the digitised French National Archives from my study in Oxford saved me much time and expense in ascertaining whether Gayner appears in police records for his time in France or occupied Catalonia. However, there is no substitute for touching, reading and validating original primary material in hard copy, and the greatest single example of good evidence about Gayner has come from previously ignored manuscripts in the British Library.

The New Letters

That Gayner did more than just communicate gossip to Nelson is shown in his letters amongst that large set of Nelsonian documents at the British Library re-discovered and evaluated by Colin White, which had lain unregarded in the Bridport Papers and were assumed to be copies of correspondence already published by Clarke and McArthur in 1809 and subsequently in Nicolas.[29] Colin saw that most had never been published or had been poorly edited, and he transcribed many of the pressed-copy out-letters as part of the Nelson Letters Project, publishing them with exegetical chapter openings in the now-indispensable *Nelson, the New Letters*.[30] The lines he quoted from Gayner had started me on my journey but I thought that was all there was to be had from that source.

I was fortunate that Colin had been a mentor to me at the beginning of my 'third-age' career as a naval historian. He had not forgotten that I was researching the 'English merchant', and in his last illness late in 2008 he contacted me saying he had not closely studied all the in-letters in Bridport, and thought there may be 'a couple' of other letters by Gayner to Nelson, and suggested I should examine the collection.

Amongst the hundreds of folios I found 23 letters from Edward Gayner to Nelson (and one from Richard Ford written at Roses), only two of which had been published before. There are also a few unpublished pressed-copy out-letters from Nelson to Gayner, most now too faded to read; continuing study of these may decipher them for publication shortly.[31] In the letter from which Colin extracted two lines for the *New Letters*, Gayner analyses information, verifies it and assesses its military value; key aspects of espionage work:[32]

Rosas 10 February 1804

Respected Friend Lord Nelson

… Our accounts from France agree that the French are manning the Fleets I apprehend in part with Genoese. It is said they have nine Sail

of the Line & altogether 23 Sail of Vessels at Toulon. I suppose when they consider their Physical forces much exceed that of the English they will come out.

I could wish someone from the Fleet was to touch in here as soon as convenient as it might be useful in every Ten or Fifteen days.

I am very respectfully

Edward Gayner

Other letters cover business matters, but several touch upon politics; Gayner mentions Dr Scott in this context, stating that he carries a detailed account created by Gayner for Nelson.

Colin's thoughtfulness gave me a valuable source, and was a generous intellectual gift. Another occurred as I was drafting this article. In the summer of 2009 I was contacted by Dr Gregory Stevens Cox, the author of *The Guernsey Merchants and their World.* He had a letter from a partner in the Gregory & Guille trading house at Barcelona to Edward Gayner, then living in Montpellier; having seen a reference to my recently published articles on Gayner he thought I might be interested. George Guille's letter, the earliest document relating to Gayner yet found, gives us a firm date and an address for him in France, and indicates that Gayner dealt with the Guernsey wine *negociantes* in France and Spain as well as his own business houses in Bristol, a promising new line of research.

And so my search continues. Edward Gayner deserves wider recognition and research is continuing, especially into his relationship with Lord Nelson. There are many lacunae in the information known about Gayner – for example, his early years in France; who else in the Royal Navy's Mediterranean Fleet he had dealings with other than Nelson, Dr Scott and Richard Ford; the nature and duration of his imprisonment; and the date he left Roses for Port Mahón. Gayner's known correspondence, including a letter to Emma Hamilton, will be published in Spain and Britain in 2010, in my monograph on his life. Gayner was a competent, complex and likeable man who set aside his moral scruples inculcated by his Quaker upbringing, and put his own life in danger to serve his country at a time of great peril, a country he had left as a young man and would never see again.

1 For a detailed description of Roses and its strategic importance to French and British military interests at this period, see Justin Reay, 'A Place of Considerable Importance: Lord Cochrane and the Siege of Roses 1808' in *Mariner's Mirror*, 95:4 (2009), pp. 400-28, and Justin Reay, 'The Royal Navy in the Bay of Rosas 1808-1809' in Carlos Díaz Capmany, Robin Pedler and Justin Reay, *El Setge de Roses: Tres Visions de Guerra del Frances* (Roses, 2008).

2 Margaret Gayner, *From Smithy to Computer: A History of One Gayner Family*, 1582-1983 (Privately published, 1985).

3 In his will written in Català, Gayner states his occupation as 'negociante', the senior partner of an international merchant house. See Will of Edward Gayner i Fry, Port Mahon, 1845, Archivo de Mahón, Protocols Notorials U537 toma 9 f336, quoted in David Donaldson, 'Edward Gayner y la Leyenda de Nelson en Menorca', *Revista de Minorca* (1998).

4 George Guille letter to Edward Gayner, 13 April 1791 (Justin Reay Collection); the Guernsey merchant's important trade with France and Spain is discussed in Gregory Stevens Cox, *The Guernsey Merchants and their World* (Les Vauxbelets, 2009), a fascinating and well-researched monograph on a little-known area of European maritime history.

5 Margaret Gayner, *From Smithy to Computer*, p. 21.

6 Notice of dissolution of partnerships 30 June 1809, *The London Gazette* 30 April 1811.

7 See for example Nelson's order to Captain Frank Sotheron, of HMS *Excellent*, 28 April 1804, Sir Nicholas Harris Nicolas, *Dispatches and Letters of Vice-Admiral Lord Viscount Nelson*, (London, 1844-46), v, p. 521; other records of Royal Navy frigates at Roses are found in Admiralty *Journals of Proceedings of H M Ships*, The National Archives of England and Wales (TNA) ADM 51 (Captains' Logs) 1467, 1482, 1498, 4514, 1508 for 1803-1805.

8 Colin White, 'A Man of Business', *Mariner's Mirror*, (2005), gives a detailed account of Nelson's administrative management of the Mediterranean Fleet between 1803 and 1805.

9 *Victualling Order by Edward Gayner on Viscount Lord Nelson*, June to September 1804 with account settled by Richard Ford on 2 September and by Nelson three days later, private collection.

10 'Parliamentary Committee into Customs Revenue from Spain', Hansard, June 1865; see also Stevens Cox, *The Guernsey Merchants*, regarding the export of wine from Spain to England.

11 Nelson to Lady Hamilton, 19 April 1804, in Nicolas, v, p. 505.

12 'Friend Gayner... has taken charge of a letter for you', Nelson to Lady Hamilton, 7 December 1803, M. Eyre Matcham, *The Nelsons of Burnham Thorpe* (London, 1911).

13 70 silver urns of various values from 30 guineas upwards were awarded by the Lloyds Patriotic Fund between 1803 and 1815, in addition to 100 of the better-known Patriotic Fund swords, Christopher Hartop, *Royal Goldsmiths: The Art of Rundell & Bridge 1797-1843* (Cambridge, 2005), pp. 31-33; the completion of Gayner's vase by Rundell & Bridge was reported in *The Times* for 13 February 1805.

14 Recorded in Donaldson, 'Edward Gayner and the Nelson Legend in Minorca', *The Nelson Dispatch*, 5:12 (1996).

15 Dispatches from Royal Navy frigate commanders June 1804 to May 1805 in 'Phillips-Croker Papers' Caird Library, National Maritime Museum, CRK 6 / 9-11.

16 Letter from Richard Floris to his parents, Port Mahón, 24 December 1834, private collection.

17 Foreign Office *Archives re Consular Officials 1839-41*, TNA FO 72/537; 558; 587 and *Letters of the Consulate-General of the Balearic Islands* TNA FO 214/3, 11-13.

18 'Extract of a Despatch from Mr Gayner... to Viscount Palmerston, 16 January 1840' in *Parliamentary Papers Relative to the Temporary Occupation by the French Government of*

'*King's Islet*' *in the Port of Mahon*, February 1840, Parliamentary Papers subscriber digital alternate at: *Parlipapers.chadwyck.co.uk* (subscriber digital alternate) accessed May 2008.

[19] Ben Burgess, 'Edward Gayner – Spy for England', *Nelson Dispatch*, 3:4 (1991), pp. 65-67, and letter in *Nelson Dispatch*, 4:1 (1992), p. 95; Donaldson, *Nelson Dispatch* (1996) and *Revista de Menorca* (1998); Santiago Masferrer, 'Una Reliquia de Nelson, en Barcelona: El Bastón de Campaña, Favorito del Gran Almirante', in *El Mundo en Auto*, Barcelona (1926).

[20] Letters and Returns of Vessels under Admiral Lord Nelson's command 1780 to 1801, and as Commander-in-Chief Mediterranean 1803-05, Wellcome Institute Library, London, Western MSS 3667-3681.

[21] Colin White, *Nelson, the New Letters* (Woodbridge, 2005); Janet MacDonald, *Feeding Nelson's Navy* (Chatham, 2006); Roger Knight, *The Pursuit of Victory: A Life of Nelson* (London, 2005).

[22] Justin Reay, 'Edward Gayner, the Royal Navy's Man at Rosas', *Nelson Dispatch,* 9:12, 10:1 and 10:2 (2008-09).

[23] Captain's Log of the *Victory*, Sunday 4 December 1803, TNA ADM 51/1498, and squadron orders in Nicolas, 1 to 9 December 1804.

[24] Nelson, orders to frigate commanders June 1804 to May 1805 in Caird Library CRK 6 / 9-11, and also in Nicolas, passim.

[25] *Exeter Morning Chronicle*, 'Letters from Spain', 12 February 1805, in British Library 19th Century Newspapers Online subscriber digital alternate at: *Infotrac.galegroup.com* last accessed 10 August 2009.

[26] Nelson, letter to Edward Rolle Clayfield, 30 March 1805, private collection.

[27] Nelson, letter to Henry Stanyford Blankley, 28 March 1805, Adelaide University.

[28] Edward Gayner, letters to Nelson June-July 1804, in Caird Library CRK 6 / 9-11, and Gayner to Lady Hamilton, 17 August 1804 CRK 22/66.

[29] Edward Gayner, letters to Lord Nelson January to November 1804 in 'Nelson Papers, General Correspondence' (Bridport Papers) British Library Add Mss 34922-34926.

[30] Colin White, 'Most Secret and Confidential: the pressed-copy out-letters of Admiral Lord Nelson', *British Journal of History*, subscriber digital alternate 2006, accessed July 2008.

[31] Nelson, letters to Edward Gayner, BL Add Mss 34955, various folios.

[32] Edward Gayner to Nelson, 10 February 1804, BL Add Mss 34922 ff235-6.

Dedication: This article is dedicated to the memory of Dr Colin White FSA, whose untimely death in December 2008 is recorded elsewhere in this volume. Colin was always generous to other historians with his knowledge and support, and even during his final illness he found time to encourage me to continue the research described here.

Acknowledgements: For their support or help during the research this article describes, the author wishes to thank: Señor Salvador Guerra i Salamó, Fundació Roses Història i Natura; Katy Reay and Xavier Vaz Rodríguez of Roses; the late Dr Colin White FSA; Neil Heydon-Gayner; Dr David Donaldson; Dr Gregory Stevens Cox; Martyn Downer; Dr Peter Hicks, Fondation Napoléon, Paris; colleagues at the Bodleian Library, Oxford; and staff of the National Archives at Kew, the British Library, the Wellcome Institute Library, London, the Norfolk Nelson Museum, Great Yarmouth, the Caird Library, Greenwich, and the Museu Ciutadela de Roses.

The Battle of Santa Cruz: A Critical Transition

Joseph F. Callo

The Battle of Santa Cruz de Tenerife in July 1797 was a crushing defeat for Admiral Lord Nelson. The 'butcher's bill' for the action told the story: 251 British sailors and Marines killed, wounded, drowned, or missing and the cutter HMS *Fox* sunk. In addition, Nelson lost his right arm and very nearly his life. Following his defeat at Santa Cruz, Nelson took his squadron northeast from the Canary Islands, toward Cadiz and the main British fleet. He was sure his career was over. Yet when one gets beyond the basic narrative of the events, the Battle of Santa Cruz emerges as a paradoxically affirmative turning point for the man who shaped history from the quarterdecks of his ships.

Rear Admiral Horatio Nelson, Mezzotint engraving after Lemuel Abbott. The town of Santa Cruz, Tenerife is seen in flames in the background. Courtesy Warwick Leadlay Gallery.

On the Crest of a Wave

The first seven months of 1797 had been good for Nelson. In February while commanding the 74-gun HMS *Captain* at the Battle of Cape St. Vincent, he demonstrated his exceptional physical courage and tactical skills. At a crucial point in the engagement, he unhesitatingly risked his life and his career with a bold maneuver that was not specifically ordered by his commander-in-chief, Admiral Sir John Jervis. He turned out of the British line-ahead formation and sailed directly into the Spanish fleet that Jervis was seeking to engage. In so doing Nelson blocked the escape of the Spanish and precipitated the action Jervis sought.

As a result of his initiative and courage in the close combat, plus his own efforts at self-promotion that followed the Battle, the unique popularity among the British public that helped support Nelson's career was launched. Of equal importance he gained a powerful mentor in Jervis, who understood and appreciated Nelson's achievements as a warfighter at Cape St. Vincent. In writing about Nelson's initial action at the Battle, which has been consistently described by naval historians as disobedience to his commander's orders, noted author and historian Colin White chose to focus on the important relationship between Nelson and Jervis. He wrote: 'So, "disobedience" is not an appropriate word to describe Nelson's action: it is more helpful to see it as another demonstration of the remarkable degree of understanding and trust which had been established between the two men'.[1]

Shortly after the Battle of Cape St. Vincent, Nelson was knighted and advanced to rear admiral. Then in May he was ordered to shift his rear admiral's flag to HMS *Theseus*, like *Captain* a 74-gun ship-of-the-line. In *Theseus* Nelson commanded the British inshore squadron blockading the port of Cadiz. Like many British blockades at the time, there were dual objectives: applying economic pressure and driving the enemy's naval forces out of their anchorage and into battle.

Rear Admiral Nelson's Conflict in a Barge off Cadiz, July 1797. Copper engraving after William Westall. Courtesy the author.

Although blockade duty seldom provided opportunities for the building of a public image, the hero of the Battle of Cape St. Vincent managed to generate at least one such opportunity on 4 July. The incident that enhanced his burgeoning reputation with the British public, the

Admiralty, and Whitehall was a boat action off Cadiz that involved hand-to-hand fighting. Nelson had been in his barge, helping to position a bomb vessel within range of Cadiz harbor, when Spanish gunboats attempted to thwart the British effort. A melee ensued, during which he came close to being cut down by a sword on several occasions. Two years later he described the event to one of his first biographers John McArthur as 'a service hand-to-hand with swords, in which my coxswain, John Sykes, now no more, twice saved my life'.[2] Eventually the British succeeded in bombarding the town and harbor with considerable effect, but by mid-July, it was clear that the Spanish fleet was not coming out of Cadiz at any point soon. Nelson's inshore squadron was returned to Admiral Jervis' main fleet.

For Honour and More

The serious idea for an attack on Santa Cruz probably began to surface in early March, when Nelson was detached for a short period with a small squadron to intercept a Spanish ship carrying gold from Cuba to Spain. Nothing came of the search for the treasure ship, but British scouting frigates reported the presence in Santa Cruz of a vessel that could have been the one for which Nelson and his squadron had been searching. In addition, Royal Navy frigates had recently succeeded in cutting out individual ships in Santa Cruz harbor, the most recent being a French corvette *La Mutine*.

In a letter to Admiral Jervis of 12 April, Nelson mentioned a discussion the previous night with his friend of many years Captain Thomas Troubridge and went on to say: 'I have endeavoured to make myself master of the situation and means of approach by sea and land'.[3] He then launched into the details that would be involved in an attack on Santa Cruz. The plan Nelson was developing was an eighteenth-century version of modern expeditionary warfare, and its potential strategic benefits were too tempting to resist.

A successful assault from the sea against Santa Cruz would roil an important Spanish colony and threaten one of her crucial sea lines of communication. In the process a considerable amount of national wealth would be diverted from Spain to Great Britain. The latter factor also had immense personal implications for those who might successfully carry out the plan, since the prize money from such an achievement would make them extraordinarily wealthy. The letter of 12 April to Admiral Jervis discussed the terrain, how the Spanish moored their ships, the naval force, troops and special equipment that would be necessary, previous successful assaults against Santa Cruz, problems that could be faced, and even the economic impact of redirecting such a large amount of Spanish treasure to Great Britain. On the latter point Nelson suggested to his commander that the proposed attack 'has every prospect of raising our Country to a higher pitch of wealth than she ever yet attained'.[4] And at the end of the letter he added an interesting protestation: 'But I know with you, and I can lay my hand on my heart and say the same- it is the honour and prosperity of our Country that we wish to extend'.[5]

Like many plans, Nelson's looked good in theory. Admiral Jervis approved, and on 14 July he gave Nelson orders to take Santa Cruz and negotiate for the treasure presumed to be there. For good measure, Jervis also ordered him 'to take, sink, burn, or otherwise destroy, all Vessels of every description, even those employed in the Fishery, on the coast of Africa, unless a just contribution is made for their preservation by the inhabitants of the Canary Islands'.[6]

Based on the significant potential of the plan, Jervis provided Nelson with a powerful squadron consisting of three 74-gun ships-of-the-line (HMS *Theseus*, HMS *Culloden*, and HMS *Zealous*), three frigates (HMS *Emerald*, HMS *Seahorse*, and HMS *Terpsichore*), a cutter (HMS *Fox*) and a mortar vessel. As far as the ships were concerned, Nelson could not have asked for more, but the ground force was another matter. His plan anticipated a need for several thousand troops, but unfortunately neither British Army commander in the theater was willing to join the project. At that point Nelson made his first and perhaps most egregious mistake; he convinced Jervis that, lacking the army troops, he could carry out his plan with a naval force, augmented by a relatively small number of Royal Marines.

Nelson's overconfidence was a mistake born in his overestimation of his own and his fellow captains' abilities, and it was magnified by an equally serious underestimation of the Spanish General he would face at Santa Cruz, Don Antonio Gutiérrez. In the latter case, he was acting contrary to the wisdom of the German writer Johann Wolfgang von Goethe: 'The fortunes of war flow this way and that, and no prudent fighter holds his enemy in contempt'.[7] Nelson's hubris oozes from between the lines of a letter he wrote to his wife Fanny on 11 July:

> *My Late Affair here (the Battle of Cape St. Vincent) will not, I believe, lower me in the opinion of the world. I have had flattery enough to make me vain, and success enough to make me confident.*[8]

On several other occasions his correspondence reflected the unmistakable conviction that his plan could not fail.

On 21 July Nelson's squadron hove to as it neared the Canary Islands, and he gathered his captains for a final conference. Approximately 900 sailors and Marines in the landing force were transferred by small boats to the three frigates, and the frigates were then sent ahead for the initial landing, which was planned for the early hours of the following day. Nelson gave the frigates a three-hour start and then followed with the rest of his force, which would support the troops ashore with bombardment.

The First Attacks

Nelson arrived off Santa Cruz at about 04:30 on the 22nd, and he found that nature had already intervened in his meticulous planning. The landing party, led by Captain Troubridge, was confronting extremely rough seas and the strong offshore winds of the seasonal 'alisios' that blow in the Canary Islands during the spring and summer. The boats carrying the assault force should have been ashore and the troops deployed by that time, but they were still more than a mile from the beach. The benefit of surprise had been lost and General Gutiérrez had time to begin deploying his forces, which consisted of 400 regular army soldiers, 110 French sailors who had been left behind when *La Mutine* was cut out, and 700 local militiamen who rallied to meet the emergency. The General also had somewhat fewer than 400 gunners, about half the number needed to serve the artillery he had in the area.

Nelson's original plan was to take the fort at the Castillo de Paso Alto, which was about five miles along the coast and to the north of Santa Cruz, rather than the heavily defended port itself. From that position he planned to threaten to attack and raze Santa Cruz, unless the town's defenders met his terms. The principal elements of those terms were 'the immediate surrender of the Ship El Principe d'Asturias ... together with her whole and entire cargo; and also such other cargoes and such property as may have been landed in the Island of Teneriffe, and not intended for the consumption of its Inhabitants'.[9]

Unfortunately by the time Troubridge had struggled ashore, organized his forces, traversed the extremely difficult terrain, and attacked the Castillo, Gutiérrez had been able to begin reinforcing its defenders. It was the first indication of the General's ability to manoeuvre his forces to meet the British at their points of attack. The action was heavy, but a determined assault might have taken the fort. At that point, however, Troubridge withdrew the assault force and returned the men and equipment to the ships.

After another conference aboard *Theseus*, a modified plan was formulated: seize the high ground behind the Castillo and then attack it from the rear. The boats landed for a second time and after struggling through extremely difficult terrain, the assault force, again led by Captain Troubridge, reached a position behind the Castillo But the artillery fire from the fort made the British position untenable, and once again Troubridge led the landing force back to the ships. By then his force had been mauled by the Spanish guns and exhausted by the terrain, heat, and debilitating thirst.

After the two unsuccessful attacks on the Castillo de Paso Alto the weather again intervened, and on 23 July gale winds forced Nelson to devote his full attention to keeping his squadron from being scattered or driven ashore. As the weather subsided, yet another captains' conference was called. By now reality had set in, and just before the final attack on 24 July Nelson wrote to Jervis:

> [A]ll has hitherto been done which was possible, but without effect: this night I, humble as I am, command the whole, destined to land under the batteries of the Town, and to-morrow my head will probably be crowned either with laurel or cypress.[11]

Two factors contributed to the decision to make a final, all-or-nothing try. The first was Nelson's pride, which at this point had displaced his confidence. In his after-action report, he said: 'I considered it for the honour of our King and Country not to give over the attempt to possess ourselves of the Town, that our enemies might be convinced there is nothing which Englishmen are not equal to'. The second was false intelligence brought to the squadron by a deserter from Santa Cruz. The deserter claimed that the city's defenses were weak and disorganized.

The defenses were in fact the opposite, and despite the fact that he was fighting a defensive battle, General Gutiérrez was able to anticipate each attack made by Nelson. The way in which the British attacks were met by the defenders illuminates Nelson's lack of accurate, real-time intelligence. It was a planning flaw that negated his audacity and the courage of his men. It would turn out to be the tipping point in the Battle.

The Final Attack

The third and final attack was aimed directly at the centre of the enemy's strength. The assault force would attack at or close to the mole that extended into the harbor from the center of the town, take that position and the Castillo San Cristóbal at the landward end of the mole and proceed from there. It was a bold plan, influenced no doubt by Nelson's belief, which was applied successfully on numerous occasions during his later career, that the boldest measures are also the safest measures.

Nelson divided his landing force into six units; he led one, and each of the other units was led by one of his captains, including Troubridge, Miller, Waller, Hood, and Thompson. A reserve of 200 men in *Fox* was to remain just off shore. Once again Nelson lacked the advantage of surprise and by the time the boats neared shore they were exposed to deadly cannon and musket fire from strategically placed positions along the shore. Nelson's and Thompson's units landed on a small beach a few yards to the north of the mole. The units led by Troubridge, Miller, Waller, and Hood all struggled ashore somewhat to the south of the mole on rocky and otherwise awkward bits of shoreline that made debarking troops and equipment extremely difficult.

From the start the British were in desperate straits. Those from Nelson's and Thompson's units who managed to reach the mole were decimated by withering fire, and one of the early casualties was Nelson, whose right elbow was shattered by a musket ball as he was stepping out of his boat.[12] Nelson's stepson, Josiah Nisbet, was one of the junior officers in Nelson's unit and he undoubtedly saved his stepfather's life by quickly applying a tourniquet to the shattered arm and then getting him back to *Theseus*. There the ship's surgeon amputated Nelson's right arm above the elbow.

Shortly after Nelson was wounded, *Fox*, with the British reserve force still on board, was holed at the waterline by cannon fire and sank. Nelson, who was at that point being rowed back to *Theseus*, insisted that the boat pick up survivors from *Fox*. At the mole, things continued to go badly, and with the sinking of *Fox* there would be no reserve force to influence the outcome.

The units led by Captains Troubridge, Miller, Waller, and Hood had with great difficulty made it to shore south of the town. As they moved through the narrow streets, they were continuously confronted by defenders, who seemed to be able to constantly position themselves in front of the attackers. The fragmented British force eventually managed to come together perhaps a half mile inland from the mole, at the Convento de Santo Domingo, a large, square structure that provided a strong defensive position for the now besieged attackers.

Under the leadership of Captain Troubridge, a final, desperate tactic was formulated, and with a flag of truce, a message was sent to General Gutiérrez with a demand: surrender the town or it will be put to the torch. The General called Troubridge's bluff, and by the morning of 25 July the action was over. Gutiérrez was generous in his surrender terms: the British must leave without further threats against any of the Canary Islands; the attackers could leave with full military honours, including their arms.

In the Battle's immediate aftermath, the British were treated as worthy adversaries by General Gutiérrez and the entire town. Bread and wine were provided to the assault force, the wounded were treated in local hospitals, and boats were provided to return the British to their ships. In an interesting sidelight to the Battle, Gutiérrez, with the intention of discouraging future attacks, planted a bit of disinformation with the British captains by leading them to believe that there were 8,000 Spanish troops on Tenerife. Many historical accounts of the Battle actually use that erroneous figure in describing the Spanish order of battle.

The Aftermath

It's hard to imagine how troubled Nelson's state of mind was on 26 July. He was confronted with 'the world turned upside down'. After the remarkable surges in his self-esteem after the Battle of Cape St. Vincent and the actions off Cadiz, he was coping with a stunning defeat and a near-fatal wound. One of the first mitigating factors for Nelson was General Gutiérrez, who treated those he had defeated with both respect and compassion. In the times of conflict between Great Britain and Spain that followed, Nelson invariably dealt with the Spanish as honourable adversaries, a sharp contrast with his contempt for Napoleon and the French republican forces led by the Emperor.

Before leaving Santa Cruz, Nelson exchanged notes with General Gutiérrez. There was no arrogance on the Spaniard's part, and Nelson's note reflected his gratitude for the treatment of his men. It was an exchange between warfighters, both of whom understood the need for humanity in the aftermath of combat, despite the violence of their profession. And the hours immediately after the Battle of Santa Cruz constituted a time for such humanity. On 27 July, Nelson and his squadron departed Santa Cruz, and on 16 August they were back at Cadiz and under the direct control of their commander-in-chief. During the period of the Santa Cruz operation, Jervis had been created Earl St. Vincent.

Nelson was in considerable pain and was deeply depressed. There was, however, some consolation. Despite the fact that the defeat at Santa Cruz reflected negatively on his own judgment, the Earl never tried to shift the blame for the debacle onto Nelson. And when Nelson wrote despondently to the Earl reporting the details of his defeat, his commander-in-chief struck exactly the right note. He didn't lecture Nelson, but he also provided no excuse for self-pity. The tone was that of one naval officer to another:

Brave Admiral Jervis, mezzotint engraving, circa 1797. Courtesy Warwick Leadlay Gallery.

> *Mortals cannot command success; you and your Companions have certainly deserved it, by the greatest degree of heroism and perseverance that ever was exhibited.*[13]

The letter went on to talk of the preliminaries of peace with Spain and the progress of Nelson's stepson Josiah and then included regards for Betsy Fremantle who was embarked in her husband's ship HMS *Seahorse*. Lord St. Vincent ended his letter with a light note and a bit of grotesque black humour that would have forced a wry smile to Nelson's face: 'I will salute her and bow to your stump to-morrow morning, if you will give me leave'.[14] The admiral's tone would have provided a necessary brake on Nelson's depression. It was a noteworthy example of the importance of an admiral's *behavior*, a classic instance of not just doing the right thing, but of doing it in a manner that strengthens the impact of the action.

Healing the Body and the Spirit

On 20 August, Nelson struck his flag in *Theseus* and transferred to *Seahorse* for his return to England, along with many of the wounded from Santa Cruz. Foul winds and pain from his amputation were his constant companions, and the Nelson who stepped ashore in Portsmouth on 1 September was a very different man from the one who had covered himself with glory at Cape St. Vincent and the boat action off Cadiz. His cheeks were sunken, his hair had turned white, and of course he was missing his right arm. But in terms of spirit, Nelson was already on the way back from the despair of his defeat.

If his liberal treatment at the hands of General Gutiérrez had been the first step in his recovery process and the reaction of the Earl St. Vincent had been the second, a third was provided by the people of Portsmouth. Nelson wrote to St. Vincent about how his countrymen had welcomed him: 'My general reception from John Bull has been just what I wished for'.[15] During September and October, Nelson, in the constant care of his wife Fanny, sought medical attention. His wound did not seem to be healing and his pain was incessant. Finally in December nature took its course; the ligature that had been used by *Theseus'* surgeon to bind the wound came free and the pain dissipated.

The Final Reckoning

There were some surprising results of the events of 21-24 July 1797 at Santa Cruz. Nelson had proposed the mission to his commander-in-chief, done the planning, and led the operation. Yet no one seemed to blame him for the disaster, not St. Vincent, not the King, and certainly not the British public. In fact Nelson's career momentum not only didn't suffer, it actually accelerated. Even the citizens of Santa Cruz accorded him a startling exoneration by naming a boulevard in their city, not in honour of General Gutiérrez, the victor at the Battle of Santa Cruz, but in honour of the man who had attacked them and been defeated: Admiral Lord Nelson!

There was also a uniquely personal by-product of the Battle for Nelson. The period during his recovery was probably the happiest period of his marriage. Fanny was needed by her husband, and he was quite free in expressing genuine gratitude for her care. In addition, he was with her rather than at sea performing the acts of daring that kept her in desperate fear of being widowed.

Arguably the most important result of the Battle was, however, that Nelson was cured of the dangerous overconfidence that infected his judgement leading up to Santa Cruz. He was not yet forty years old, although he looked older, and the most important years of his career were ahead. In fact, he would soon be selected for a most important assignment as commander-in-chief of Britain's Mediterranean Fleet. Ahead of him lay the history-shaping Battles of the Nile in 1798, Copenhagen in 1801, and his final triumph at Trafalgar in 1805.

Coinciding with Nelson's sudden recovery from the loss of his arm, an anonymous note was delivered to St. George's Church on South Audley Street, Hanover Square, London, a few steps from Nelson's and Fanny's lodging on Bond Street. The unsigned note read: 'An Officer desires to return Thanks to Almighty God for his perfect recovery from a severe Wound, and also for the many mercies bestowed on him'.[16] There was no sign of hubris in that succinct communication.

---

[1] Colin White, *1799 Nelson's Year of Destiny* (Phoenix Mill: Sutton Publishing, 1998) special note, 'The Significance of Nelson's action', p. 58.

[2] *The Dispatches and Letters of Vice Admiral Lord Viscount Nelson*, edited by Sir Nicholas Harris Nicolas (London: Chatham Publishing, 1997), ii, p. 405, note 6.

[3] Ibid., p. 379.

[4] Ibid., p. 380.

[5] Ibid., p. 381.

[6] Ibid., p. 413, note 2.

[7] Colonel Robert Debs Heinl, Jr., *Dictionary of Military and Naval Quotations* (Annapolis: United States Naval Institute Press, 1966), p. 123.

[8] *The Dispatches and Letters of Vice Admiral Lord Viscount Nelson*, edited by Sir Nicholas Harris Nicolas (London: Chatham Publishing, 1997), ii, p. 412.

[9] Ibid. , p. 419.

[10] Ibid., p. 421.

[11] Ibid., p. 425.

[12] The British were sure that it was a musket ball that struck Nelson, but the Spanish attributed Nelson wound to grapeshot from a cannon nicknamed 'El Tigre'. The cannon is exhibited in Tenerife's naval museum, along with captured battle flags and other artifacts from the Battle of Santa Cruz.

[13] *The Dispatches and Letters of Vice Admiral Lord Viscount Nelson*, edited by Sir Nicholas Harris Nicolas (London: Chatham Publishing, 1997), ii, p. 435, note 7.

[14] Ibid., p. 436, note 7.

[15] Ibid., pp. 445-46.

[16] Ibid., p. 455.

British Blockades in the Great Wars, 1793-1815

N.A.M. Rodger

The general idea of blockade held by non-specialist historians is a very simple one; that it was a strategy of keeping squadrons permanently on station off the enemy's ports in order to prevent his forces from putting to sea. This sort of blockade is generally supposed to have been a traditional British strategy, applied throughout the wars of the 'long eighteenth century'. In reality, blockade was only one of a wide range of strategies that might be applied according to circumstances. Moreover close blockade, which is what the word is most often understood to mean, was only one sort of blockade, and by some way the rarest and most difficult. In reality the word was applied to a variety of strategies designed to block, watch, mask or observe an enemy port more or less closely.

John Bull Peeping Into Brest, etching signed '[Piercy] Roberts. Middle Row', 1803.
Courtesy Warwick Leadlay Gallery.

A 'blockading' fleet might be kept permanently at sea, permanently in port, or cruising more or less frequently. It might be a mile from the enemy, or five hundred miles. Its objectives might be military or economic, and were often some mixture of the two. Blockades might be designed to stop the enemy fleet from sailing, or to encourage it to do so, and they might equally face outward towards inward-bound enemy ships. What sort of blockade was possible varied very much from port to port, depending on the facts of geography. What sort was desirable varied very much from time to time, for every kind of blockade had costs as well as benefits, and what costs it was possible or rational to undertake depended greatly on the nature of the threat the enemy presented. Finally, there was no standard British naval doctrine on blockade, but a range of opinions, which generated debate and often controversy among admirals and statesmen. For all these reasons the history of blockade during the Great Wars against France is more complex than the popular stereotype suggests.

The Western Squadron

Blockade is as old as naval warfare itself, but for the British officers of the French Revolutionary and Napoleonic Wars, blockade was closely linked with the rise of the Western Squadron in the late 1740s, and again during the Seven Years' War. This was the period when senior officers had first experienced blockades, and it was these wars to which they referred for guidance and encouragement. The more recent American War, in which the Royal Navy had been unable to set up a regular blockade of French or Spanish ports, offered few helpful precedents, for the available forces were too widely dispersed to allow an effective blockade of either French or American ports.[1] The Western Squadron, as it had been set up by Anson in 1747, did not attempt anything like a close blockade. It was a cruising force patrolling the Western Approaches, coming into port every few weeks for supplies and orders. It was intended to make it difficult and dangerous for the enemy to use the Atlantic ports – meaning Brest, Rochefort and to an extent Ferrol among naval ports; St.Malo, Lorient, Nantes and Bordeaux among the commercial ports. It was only able to do so if reliable advance intelligence of enemy movements could be obtained, for the Western Squadron did not pretend to be permanently on station, and the 'station' in any case covered upwards of ten thousand square miles of sea stretching from Fastnet to Finisterre.

The limitations of contemporary navigation helped it. French shipping inward-bound from the Atlantic was more or less forced to run in on the parallel of a safe landfall, and the only obvious choices for the Bay ports were Belle Île or Cape Ortegal. Ships outward-bound would be constrained by whatever wind was blowing when they sailed; French convoys almost always assembled in Aix Roads, the only convenient anchorage accessible from all the major naval or commercial ports of the Atlantic coast, from which in the prevailing westerlies a convoy would usually be obliged to stretch north-westerly for Ushant, or south-westerly for Finisterre. Intelligent analysis of all these factors allowed first Anson and then Hawke to intercept outward-bound French convoys in 1747. The strategy of the Western Squadron was thus successful, but considered as a blockade it was very loose and open, and blockade was only one of several functions which it fulfilled. Its tasks of covering the Channel against possible invasion attempts, and protecting the movements of British convoys in and out of the Channel, were equally or more important.

In the opening years of the Seven Years' War the Western Squadron was revived in a very similar form. Initially it cruised to the westward as it had done in previous wars, sweeping up a rich harvest of French merchant ships. Then the development of a French invasion scheme in 1758 and 1759 forced the Squadron to adopt a closer blockade of Brest, where the main French fleet lay. As a result, of course, it ceased to cover other French ports, except to the extent that the squadron could watch the parallel of Belle Île just to the south, and cruising frigates could threaten trade. In order to watch the port continuously, Hawke sent his ships in for supplies in rotation, until in 1759 a system of replenishment at sea was established, with convoys of victuallers sent from England.

A close blockade of Brest is greatly affected by the geography of the port, which has three widely separated entrances. The only approximately safe blockading station is north-west of Ushant with the Channel open to leeward, but from there the Raz de Sein, the southern and (for the French) most useful entrance and exit, is out of sight. Hawke's solution was to keep a small inshore squadron at the head of the Iroise close in with the Goulet, the single entrance to the inner roads, ready to warn him if the enemy should stir – but this station was extremely dangerous, and even an outstanding officer like Captain Augustus Hervey could not maintain it in all weathers. Nor could Hawke hold his; from mid-October to mid-November 1759 he was off his station half the time,[2] and when Conflans finally sailed in November 1759 the British squadron had taken refuge from a westerly gale in Torbay. When the wind veered both squadrons were able to sail, but the French had twenty-four hours' start. Had they been bound overseas they would almost certainly have been able to escape, but since it was known that the French army and its transports were assembled at Quiberon Bay, Hawke could tell where Conflans was going and was able to intercept him. After the great victory of Quiberon Bay, Brest was more or less empty and no longer required close watching, but a squadron was established in Quiberon Bay itself to blockade the French ships trapped up the River Vilaine. This was a blockade in relative luxury, in an excellent anchorage, with water, fish and vegetables available from the local islanders.

Thus the Seven Years' War extended the Royal Navy's experience of blockade, and provided further useful precedents. It also offered an oustanding example of an opportunity foregone, for when Vice-Admiral Byng arrived to relieve the British garrison of Minorca in 1756 he found a French besieging army ashore, dependent on unescorted merchant shipping for food, ammunition and even water. He did not need to win a victory over the French squadron to cut these supplies, for even a loose and distant blockade of the island would have put the French in acute difficulties. Instead he abandoned the Mediterranean altogether, and left them in tranquil command of a sea which he had the means of contesting.

The Revolutionary War

In the 1790s different officers drew different lessons from the experience of the Seven Years' War. Captain Philip Patton argued for close blockade:

> *This measure may be made more clearly essential by reverting to what was actually done from the year 1757 to the year 1762; for although several [British] expeditions were undertaken during that period, they were subservient to blocking up and opposing the enemy at home, which were the first considerations, and which were truly the foundation of our success through the whole war, when the fleet were kept off Brest and in Quiberon Bay. It consists with my own knowledge, that the ships were relieved alternately, and were supplied with fresh provisions, corned beef, potatoes, onions, greens, and beer, during the summer; and Sir Edward Hawke and Admiral Boscawen relieved each other.*[3]

The majority of admirals were more cautious. Close blockade was arduous and dangerous, it was almost impossible to make it fully effective in wintertime, and many of them thought it better policy not to shut the enemy in port but to allow him to sail to be intercepted and defeated. Blockade was at best a costly palliative; victory would solve the problem for good. Lords Howe, Hood and Bridport, the leading British admirals of the opening years of the French Revolutionary War, were all of this opinion, though the brothers Hood and Bridport stood for distant cruising in the manner of the Western Squadron, whereas Howe preferred to await intelligence of enemy movements in the relative comfort of a safe anchorage. Hood advised Cornwallis, when he took command of the Channel Fleet in 1801, that his highest priority should be to bring on a battle with the enemy fleet:

> *Therefore cease blocking the port, and tempt it out. I have ever held that opinion, and am persuaded that the war has been prolonged by the blockade. A temporary one, under particular circumstances, may not only be prudent but perfectly wise; but a perpetual one must bear us down, which the French know as well as we.*[4]

His younger contemporary Cuthbert Collingwood was of the same opinion:

> *While we lie in this bay [Torbay] we are much more ready than if we were at sea. They can scarce come out without the wind is easterly, and we cannot lie here with that wind. I know the people on shore think we are too much in port, but they do not know that it would be impossible to keep this fleet in a condition to meet the enemy if we were exposed to the buffetings of these gales.*[5]

Howe, commanding the Channel Fleet from 1793 to 1797, thought the French squadron in Brest too much weakened by the turmoil of the Revolution to pose any threat, and lay at anchor for long periods. When the French sailed in 1794 he was taken by surprise, and only intercepted them by chance, far out in the Atlantic. The result was a victory, but the French were not eliminated. On the last day of 1794 they got to sea again for a cruise of 34 days in which they took over one hundred prizes including a ship of the line.[6] Two years later, in December 1796, General Hoche's expedition to Ireland successfully got out of Brest in fog. Sir Edward Pellew with his one frigate sighted them and disrupted their sailing, but Vice-Admiral Colpoys with part of the Channel Fleet was off his station and not to be found, and Howe with the remainder of the fleet was far away at Spithead. The French expedition disintegrated through bad weather and incompetence, but on the British side only Pellew emerged with any credit.[7] Then in May and June 1797 the Channel Fleet was immobilized by the great mutinies, which did not improve the admirals' standing. Howe had finally retired, and Lord Spencer's Admiralty Board now subjected his successor Lord Bridport to much closer scrutiny, dissatisfied with his slack control of the blockade and his poor handling of his subordinates.[8] In May 1798 a squadron under Sir Roger Curtis was detached to join Lord St. Vincent's Mediterranean Squadron: 'a lamentable specimen of the state of your fleet at home', St. Vincent commented.

> *There is a dreadful licentiousness in the conversation of the officers which is very soon conveyed to the men ... unless you have an officer at the head who has the vigour and disposition to lay the axe to the root of this evil and you give him the most unequivocal support there will very soon be an end to all activity or energy in the natural defence of the country.*[9]

This was the way St. Vincent usually talked, but Spencer was not yet ready to take the hint and appoint him. Then in April 1799 there was another fiasco when Admiral Bruix sailed from Brest, again in fog. Bridport had allowed several of his frigates to go off on cruises, the inexperienced captain on station off Brest failed to keep in touch, and the French disappeared. Before the Admiralty found out where they had gone, they had been in the Mediterranean a week, where the scattered British squadrons would have been highly vulnerable to an officer of more energy and initiative than Bruix. In early August Bruix was back, now accompanied by the Spanish Cadiz squadron making a total of 45 sail, almost double the remaining strength of the Channel Fleet after reinforcements had been sent to the Mediterranean. For a week the Franco-Spanish fleet had a great victory within their grasp, until Lord Keith arrived from the Mediterranean in pursuit.[10] With the combined enemy fleet at the mouth of the Channel, conveniently but also dangerously close to home, the Admiralty urged Bridport to tighten the watch on Brest. They particularly wanted him to use his frigates to intercept the coastal convoys essential to feed the allied fleet.[11]

Finally in April 1800 Bridport retired, aged 73, and St. Vincent had his chance. What the Admiralty wanted from him now was a really close blockade, to make sure the large and dangerous enemy fleet could not escape at all. St. Vincent agreed: 'On the whole it appears to me that the combined fleets are better in Brest, than at sea with forty-eight hours' start of us.'[12] What he also wanted was to terrorize his own officers, using this exceptionally arduous and perilous service to tighten up the seamanship and discipline of the fleet. Even so Ganteaume escaped from Brest in January 1801 and got away to the Mediterranean, though he made nothing of his opportunities there. One month later St.Vincent was called to become First Lord of the Admiralty, leaving Cornwallis to continue the close blockade, but without St.Vincent's unconcealed pleasure in imposing discomfort and danger on his subordinates.

The Napoleonic War

With the renewal of the war in 1804 Cornwallis took up his old command, but the strategic situation was now different. Without the Spanish ships the enemy in Brest was less formidable – but so was the British fleet after the depredations of St.Vincent's 'reform' programme. Napoleon was known to be preparing an invasion attempt, but there was no margin to spare now for the inevitable casualties of close blockade, especially in winter. In September 1804 Lord Melville, St.Vincent's successor as First Lord, calculated that he had 70 ships of the line available in home waters, of which Cornwallis had 44, which sufficed to keep seven on station off Rochefort, another seven off Ferrol, and sixteen off Brest – to watch 21 inside. 'You have not the means of sustaining the necessary extent of naval force,' Melville reminded him,

> *if your ships are to be torn to pieces by an eternal conflict with the elements during the tempestuous months of winter, and allow me to remind you that the occasions when we have been able to bring our enemy to battle and our fleets to victory have generally been when we were at a distance from the blockading station.*[13]

The Trafalgar campaign perfectly illustrated how the Channel Fleet off Brest served not only to blockade the port, but as the central strategic reserve of Britain's naval defences. When the enemy fleets got to sea from Toulon and Cadiz, Orde, Calder, Nelson and Stirling each in turn fell back to join Cornwallis at the strategic point. 'In bringing to England the large ships under my command,' Orde wrote to the Admiralty, 'I shall afford an opportunity to dispose of them anew: by which little can be risked, and much might be gained if the enemy's blow is aimed at England or Ireland.'[14]

After Trafalgar Lord Barham the new First Lord relaxed the winter blockade: 'It is to little purpose for us to harass our officers and men and wear out the ships in a fruitless blockade during the winter.'[15] He even revived the name as well as the policy of the 1750s. 'I send you a short sketch for a disposition of the Western Squadron for the winter,' he wrote to William Pitt in December, 'and which with cruising squads will be more likely to reduce the Brest fleet than a fruitless endeavour of keeping them in port.'[16] Less than a fortnight before, as if to demonstrate the impossibility of shutting Brest off in winter, two French squadrons had got to sea, under Willaumez and Leissègues. In the ten war years from 1796 to 1806 seven French squadrons had got out of Brest and three from Rochefort, all but three of the ten in wintertime.[17]

Brest was the nearest enemy naval base to Britain, both the most dangerous and the easiest to blockade, but even here the meaning of blockade varied greatly according to the strategic situation and the judgement of the admirals. Only at certain periods was a genuine close blockade, meant to stop enemy ships entering or leaving the port, even attempted, and it was never possible to make it completely watertight. The object of blockade was to allow the uninterrupted use of the sea, for military and naval operations and for trade, and for long periods a more or less open blockade, with the possibility of intercepting and defeating the enemy at sea, offered better and cheaper prospects than trying to block the port up. The facts of geography, the situation of Britain's enemies and the prevailing wind, meant that the Western Approaches, near to Brest or further out, was the strategic centre of Britain's naval defences.

Distant Ports

The blockade of other, more distant, ports was never as easy, and seldom as important. The Texel and the Scheldt represented a real danger only at those periods when an enemy fleet lay there ready for sea, and in such cases the same choices of open or close blockade presented themselves as at Brest. Duncan, watching the Dutch fleet in the Texel with the North Sea Squadron in October 1797, thought that,

> *A fleet kept together in readiness to go wherever it may be wanted must be more formidable to an enemy (particularly at this season) than at sea, subject to spearation and disaster, and cannot go nearer to the enemy's port than where we now are [off Yarmouth], may also be drove out of their station as not to be found when wanted.*[18]

Rochefort and the other French ports in the Bay of Biscay could be blockaded, if at all, only as a subsidiary part of a blockade of Brest, otherwise the squadrons would have been far too vulnerable to being trapped by enemy ships from Brest. Ferrol, remote from any British base, might be loosely watched, but was only ever closely blockaded in 1803 and 1804 when Spain was neutral and it was a French squadron which was shut up in the port. In these circumstances Pellew's skilful diplomacy secured the use of Betanzos Bay from which a real blockade could be maintained. In 1805 Calder's squadron was detached from the Channel Fleet, not so much to blockade Ferrol but to cruise off Cape Ortegal to intercept inward as well as outward movement.[19] Cadiz could be blockaded, at least if sufficient force could be spared from home, and if supplies could be drawn from Lisbon and Morocco, but the object of keeping a British squadron there was only partly to do with the port itself. This station off the Straits of Gibraltar was an alternative to Gibraltar itself (an only marginally better anchorage) as a position to control movement into and out of the Mediterranean. In British organisation it was part of the Mediterranean station, which extended to Cape St.Vincent, and the blockade of Cadiz served indirectly to cover Cartagena and even Toulon as well.[20]

The French Toulon squadron was always a strategic danger to Britain, but it was only possible to blockade it directly if a substantial surplus of force was available to detach so far from home, and it was extremely difficult if Spain was hostile. With no base or anchorage available nearer than Mahon or Gibraltar, only a loose observation of the port was possible. Frequent winter gales blew ships off the coast, and from the mountain behind the town it was easy to observe where, or whether the enemy was cruising, and consequently when the port was open (a very different situation from Brest, where it was only possible to discover the blockaders' whereabouts if they came very close in). Nelson for one insisted that 'my system is the very contrary of blockading', and aimed to tempt the French out to fight them.[21] Collingwood in his turn found the same: 'You know how impossible it is to blockade Toulon; if we can keep a station near there it is well, but it is not a blockade.'[22] The only British admiral who found it possible to mount even a close observation of Toulon was Mathews in 1743 and 1744, when France was neutral and he could use Hyères Bay as an anchorage from which to watch the Spanish fleet in port.[23]

Economic Blockades

All this is considering only the military aspects of blockade, but it usually served as an instrument of economic warfare as well. Enemy trade was prevented from sailing by direct blockade, or intercepted by the cruising forces of a looser blockade. British trade was protected against direct attack, while naval action countered enemy attempts at economic warfare. The best known examples of this are the two 'Armed Neutralities' of 1780 and 1800, and the name warns us that economic blockade was the weapon of the neutral as well as the belligerent. Under Jefferson and Madison the U.S.A. adopted embargo or self-blockade as a weapon of economic warfare by a neutral trading nation against the belligerents, though the latest study concludes that the attempt was a total failure.[24] The most celebrated example of economic blockade during the Great Wars is of course Napoleon's Continental System, which however combined a number of different objectives. It was meant to deny Britain strategic imports, to shut off her export markets, to worsen her terms of trade and to promote French industry at the expense of the non-French parts of Napoleon's empire. These contradictory objectives were probably unattainable, and seem to have damaged France more than Britain.[25]

Naval blockade in most of its forms required ships to remain at sea for long periods. It imposed great strains on the officers and men, the ships (and consequently the dockyards), and on the victualling systems.[26] It was only possible for Britain because of long-term heavy investment in the infrastructure of sea power. It is best understood not as a single strategy but as a range of options designed to limit, control or prevent the enemy use of the sea, and therefore to promote and safeguard British use of the sea. Blockades were flexible and adaptable according to circumstances, and usually served a number of purposes simultaneously, but they were also limited by geography. They might be imposed on enemy or neutral ports almost anywhere in the world, but the most comprehensive examples come usually from the waters around or near the British Isles, where the bulk of British naval strength was maintained, and from places not too distant from British bases and supplies. Blockade was never easy, or simple, or automatic, but the study of the American War of Independence shows us, and showed to the British naval men who had fought in it, how much Britain risked by a failure to establish some sort of blockade of the ports of its European enemies. This lesson they applied in the Great Wars to make blockade in its various forms essential components of survival, and eventually of victory.

[1] *Cf British Naval Documents 1204-1960,* edited by John B. Hattendorf and others (Aldershot: Scolar Press for the Navy Records Society, 1993), pp. 399-401 for Howe's comments on the difficulties of blockading the American coast in 1777.

[2] Julian S. Corbett, *Some Principles of Maritime Strategy* (London: Longmans, 1911), p. 194.

[3] *Letters and Papers of Charles, Lord Barham ... 1758-1813,* edited by Sir J.K. Laughton (London: Navy Record Society, 1907-11) ii, pp. 392-93, to Sir Charles Middleton, 27 June 1794.

[4] George Cornwallis-West, *The Life and Letters of Admiral Cornwallis* (London: Holden, 1927), pp. 368-69.

[5] *The Private Correspondence of Admiral Lord Collingwood,* edited by Edward Hughes (London: Navy Record Society, 1957), p. 105, to Dr Alexander Carlyle, 6 November 1799.

[6] *The Channel Fleet and the Blockade of Brest*, 1793-1801, edited by Roger Morriss and Richard Saxby (London: Navy Records Society, 2001), pp. 11-28.

[7] *Private Papers of George, Second Earl Spencer*, edited by Julian S. Corbett and H.W. Richmond (London: Navy Records Society, 1913-24) i, pp. 374-77; G.E. Cooper, 'Pellew and the Departure of the Bantry Expedition, December 1796', *Mariner's Mirror*, 6 (1920), pp. 178-83; Morriss and Saxby, *Channel Fleet*, pp. 163-64.

[8] Morriss and Saxby, *Channel Fleet*, pp. 165-90 and pp. 239-91.

[9] Morriss and Saxby, *Channel Fleet*, p. 305, to Spencer, 28 May 1798.

[10] R.C. Saxby, 'The Escape of Admiral Bruix from Brest', *Mariner's Mirror*, 46 (1960), pp. 113-19; Corbett and Richmond, *Spencer Papers*, iii, pp. 43-53; Piers Mackesy, *Statesmen at War: The Strategy of Overthrow 1798-1799* (London: Longman, 1974), pp. 97-101 and p. 168; Morriss and Saxby, *Channel Fleet*, p. 347.

[11] Morriss and Saxby, *Channel Fleet*, pp. 350-448.

[12] Corbett and Richmond, *Spencer Papers*, iii, p. 341, to Spencer 15 June 1800.

[13] Cornwallis-West, *Cornwallis*, pp. 453-54.

[14] Julian S. Corbett, *The Campaign of Trafalgar* (London: Longmans, 1919), i, p. 71.

[15] Laughton, *Barham Papers*, iii, p. 296, to Cornwallis, 27 December 1805.

[16] Laughton, Barham Papers, iii, p. 297, 27 December 1805.

[17] M.A. Rae, 'The Blockade of Brest and the French Atlantic Ports, including Ferrol, in the Revolutionary and Napoleonic Wars, 1796-1806, together with the use of Torbay as a Port of Refuge' (Exeter: Unpublished MA thesis, 2000), p.15.

[18] Corbett and Richmond, *Spencer Papers*, ii, p. 192, to Spencer, 2 October 1797.

[19] *Despatches and Letters Relating to the Blockade of Brest*, 1803-1805, edited by John Leyland (London: Navy Records Society, 1899-1902), i, pp. 263-64 and p. 315. Cornwallis-West, *Cornwallis*, pp. 408-09.

[20] Piers Mackesy, *The War in the Mediterranean, 1803-1810* (London: Longmans, 1957), pp. 113-14.

[21] *The Despatches and Letters of Vice Admiral Lord Viscount Nelson*, edited by Sir N.H. Nicolas (London: Colburn, 1844-45), vii, Add.ccxxxiii, to Sir C.M. Pole, 25 May 1804.

[22] Hughes, *Collingwood Correspondence*, p. 254, to Rear Admiral J.C. Purvis, 5 October 1808.

[23] H.W. Richmond, *The Navy in the War of 1739-48* (Cambridge: Cambridge University Press, 1920), i, pp. 221-25 and ii, pp. 7-8.

[24] Lance E. Davis and Stanley L. Engerman, *Naval Blockades in Peace and War: An Economic History since 1750* (Cambridge: Cambridge University Press, 2006), pp. 77-94.

[25] Davis and Engerman, *Naval Blockades*, pp. 39-52. See also Francois Crouzet, 'Wars, Blockade and Economic Change in Europe, 1792-1815', *Journal of Economic History*, 24 (1964), pp. 567-88; Francois Crouzet, 'Blocus Mercantile et Blocus Offensif: L'Orde en Conseil du 26 Avril 1809', in *État, Marine et Société: Hommage à Jean Meyer*, edited by Martine Acerra and others (Paris: Presses de l'Université Paris-Sorbonne, 1995), pp. 163-76; Silva Marzagalli, *Les Boulevards de la Fraude: Le Négoce Maritime et le Blocus Continental, 1806-1813* (Villeneuve d'Ascq: Presses Universitaires du Septentrion, 1999); Mancur Olson, *The Economics of the Wartime Shortage: A History of British Food Supplies in the Napoleonic Wars and in World Wars I and II* (Durham, N.C.: Duke University Press, 1963), pp. 49-71; Nicholas Tracy, *Attack on Maritime Trade* (London: Macmillan, 1991), pp. 71-80.

[26] Roger Morriss, *The Royal Dockyards During the Revolutionary and Napoleonic Wars* (Leicester: Leicester University Press, 1983), p. 13; Michael Steer, 'The Blockade of Brest and the Victualling of the Western Squadron, 1793-1805', *Mariner's Mirror*, 76 (1990), pp. 307-16.

Terror in the Countryside:
HM Schooner *Whiting*
in Southern Nova Scotia in 1805

Keith Mercer

Nova Scotia, (Detail), c. 1810. Courtesy Warwick Leadlay Gallery.

In the summer of 1805, HM Schooner *Whiting* participated in one of the most shocking impressment cases in Nova Scotia's history. Led by Commander John Orkney, the *Whiting* raised men along the south coast for the North American squadron based at Halifax. First in Liverpool and then in Shelburne, municipal officials were outraged by the impressment of inhabitants and by the duplicity of Orkney and his naval party. With the help of magistrate John Hames, the latter terrorized the Shelburne countryside. Initially, Hames assisted the Navy in its search for deserters, but this quickly disintegrated into a series of unprovoked threats, violence, and impressments. The party forced its way into homes with axes and it physically assaulted a number of residents. Families fled into the forest and stayed there for more than a week to avoid the *Whiting*. Although a special court of sessions was held in Shelburne to identify the guilty parties, Hames, Orkney, and the *Whiting's* seamen were never brought to justice. Nor is there evidence that they were reported to the naval hierarchy in Halifax or that the Nova Scotia government discussed this case. In fact, if not for the papers left by Gideon White, the Shelburne magistrate who led the investigation, there would be no record of the *Whiting's* reign of terror on the south shore at all. Nevertheless, this case study sheds new light on impressment in Nova Scotia. It shows that press gangs often generated violence and resistance on shore, even in the Canadian colonies, and it foreshadows impressment's role in the deterioration of civil-naval relations in Nova Scotia during the Napoleonic Wars.[1]

The North American squadron was desperate for sailors in 1805. Beset by high desertion rates and short-handed crews, Vice-Admiral Andrew Mitchell grew increasingly frustrated about the manning problem in Nova Scotia. On the eve of Lord Nelson's victory over the combined French and Spanish fleet at the Battle of Trafalgar, the British government worried about Napoleon's invasion plans and the Admiralty was concerned with the European theatre of operations. North America was not a priority and no reinforcements of seamen were sent across the Atlantic. The squadron also suffered from its own successes: for example, Mitchell commissioned the recently-captured French warship *Ville de Milan* into the fleet that February but the local manning situation was so dire that it lay idle for several months without a crew. The Admiralty suggested to Mitchell that he send two warships to Newfoundland to enter as many volunteers as possible, and then to press the rest into the service.[2] Newfoundland was known as a productive source of sailors, but it speaks volumes about recruitment problems in the Halifax area that the squadron resorted to pillaging the labour market of a neighbouring and much smaller naval station.[3] The Halifax merchant community also offered generous bounties to volunteers that spring, in addition to those awarded by the Navy, but this did little to alleviate the squadron's deficiency of sailors.[4]

Mitchell was also handicapped by local impressment regulations and protections. From 1793 to 1805, the Nova Scotia government issued at least thirteen warrants to the Navy to send press gangs into Halifax. Most of these warrants had time and quota restrictions, and naval parties were supervised by magistrates on shore.[5] Although press gangs occasionally took dozens of

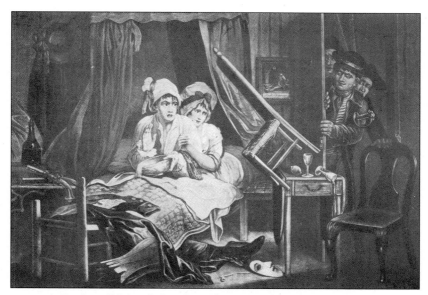

An Unwelcome Visit from the Press Gang. Photo-gravure, 1913 after an original c. 1800. Courtesy the author.

men in the Halifax area, many of them were released just as quickly because of residency protections and other claims. Press gangs from HMS *Leander*, for instance, conscripted thirty-three men in Halifax in December 1803 only to have Mitchell discharge twenty-two of them immediately because they were inhabitants of the town, while six others were relieved of naval duty because they were apprentices.[6] With few other options at his disposal, Mitchell petitioned Lieutenant-Governor John Wentworth for a press warrant in May 1805. The ensuing warrant lasted for a fortnight and permitted the squadron to enter an unlimited number of sailors, but Mitchell was still unhappy and demanded multiple warrants for six months a piece, which was rejected by the provincial government.[7] Even though warships such as HMS *Cambrian* pressed large numbers of men in Halifax that spring, this did not meet Mitchell's expectations and the following October he allowed press gangs from HMS *Cleopatra* to storm the streets of Halifax.[8] With his warrant expired and no backing from colonial or municipal authorities, a major riot took place in which one man was killed and several others injured. Wentworth lashed out at the admiral and ordered the solicitor general to prosecute the guilty parties, but in the end neither Mitchell nor the gangsmen were criminally charged.[9]

The fallout from this incident curbed impressment on shore, but most sailors had always been taken on the water in Nova Scotia. Guard boats in Halifax provided a steady source of recruits. Guided by a series of port orders, naval captains took turns launching cutters and other boats to perform harbour duty. They boarded incoming and outgoing vessels, inspected them for deserters and illicit goods, and reported intelligence to the admiral. They also served as floating press gangs, routinely conscripting nervous sailors who never knew if they were on harbour patrol or the impress service. The Admiralty issued warrants to captains and commanders that allowed them to press at sea without colonial permission. These warrants were used throughout the Atlantic Canadian region. Admirals dispatched small warships to Nova Scotia's outports and shipping lanes to recruit generally for the North American squadron. These vessels served as tenders for the larger men-of-war at Halifax. During the War of 1812, at least four sloops and schooners recruited along the south coast of Nova Scotia, while guard boats were active in Halifax harbour and other naval cruisers pressed men in the Bay of Fundy and the Northumberland Strait.[10] Vice-Admiral George Berkeley reported to the Admiralty in 1806 that unless he sent these small warships on the impress service there was no chance of keeping the Navy manned in Nova Scotia.[11]

Entrance into Halifax Harbour, aquatint engraving, published in The Naval Chronicle, 1803.
Courtesy of the author.

Intimidation and Injury

It was in this capacity that Mitchell sent the *Whiting* to southern Nova Scotia in the summer of 1805. From June to September, it pressed nearly thirty men, most of whom were turned over to the *Cleopatra* at Halifax.[12] Built in Bermuda in 1804, the *Whiting* was among the dozens of naval sloops, cutters, and schooners that were launched from that island during the 1790s and early nineteenth century, most of which stayed in North American waters. It was typical of the small warships that patrolled the Nova Scotia coastline in this period: it displaced seventy-five tons, mounted four twelve-pound carronades, and had a complement of eighteen men and boys.[13] Lieutenant John Orkney was its first commander. The *Whiting* spent one year on the North American station; afterwards, it served in the Channel Fleet, the North Sea, and the Mediterranean before being captured by an American privateer near Hampton Roads, Virginia, at the beginning of the War of 1812. Orkney was a young officer, having only been commissioned as a first lieutenant in 1804. The *Whiting* turned out to be his first and only command. After spending the summer of 1805 in Halifax and recruiting along the south shore, he was ordered to Bermuda for the rest of the year. Orkney commanded the *Whiting* for two more years, first in home waters and then in the North Sea. He did not make the rank of post captain and died at a relatively young age in 1813.[14]

The *Whiting* may not seem intimidating today, but to Nova Scotians in the early nineteenth century it was an impressive British warship. Small naval vessels such as the *Whiting* visited Liverpool and other south shore villages regularly in this period, and that is how most colonial residents encountered the Royal Navy. These cruises were significant for several reasons: naval vessels showed the flag throughout the region, which demonstrated their role in maritime defence and symbolized the imperial authority of the squadron at Halifax; these were social events in which the officers met with leading citizens of the town and participated in celebrations in their honour; and naval visits often resulted in people being pressed into the service. Like elsewhere in the British Atlantic world, merchants and mariners in Nova Scotia were terrified of impressment and followed the Navy's activities closely. The Liverpool trader Simeon Perkins learned from the arrival of a vessel in that port in May 1805 about Vice-Admiral Mitchell's intense recruitment drive in Halifax. Therefore, when the *Whiting* appeared off Liverpool harbour on 27 June, Perkins noted its movements with great interest: 'One of the Kings Cutters arrives from Halifax. She did not Shew

Colours till She got within half a mile then hoisted a Blue Ensign & Red pennant. The officers came on Shore but did not call on [the leading] men. Mr. [John] Power saw them at the Battery & waited on them to his House. He Says the officer Commanding is Lieu. Orkney'.[15]

Liverpool was the *Whiting's* first port of call in southern Nova Scotia and it quickly created a panic in the town. When one of its boats rowed ashore the people were so apprehensive of the press that it caused a 'rumpus' in the community. Three Black inhabitants took shelter in Perkins's home, after being 'chased by the men of war's people'. The *Whiting's* crew were insulted in the street; one of them was injured with a cutlass because it was feared that the 'Men of war's men were about to Impress'. Orkney complained about the mistreatment of his seamen and stated that he had no intention of pressing men in Liverpool. A much relieved Perkins took the commander at his word and apologized for the misunderstanding. But Orkney was not true to his word. A

Simeon Perkins, anon. watercolour, c. 1785. Courtesy Nova Scotia Archives and Records Management.

few days later he sent a naval party into town that pressed a settler named Lovelace Moc. This stemmed from a domestic dispute in which Moc's wife, in a rage at her husband, asked the *Whiting's* seamen to take him onboard the naval vessel, but she then 'made a great ado about it, and went hallowing thro the Street'. Over the next few days Orkney pressed several more men in Liverpool, including Anthony Smith and John Keaser. Municipal authorities applied to Orkney to get Smith released, and while the commander confirmed that Smith's impressment had been a mistake and that he would be set free, when the *Whiting* sailed on 4 July Smith was still onboard, as were both Moc and Keaser.[16] Indeed, Perkins was still trying to get Smith discharged from the Navy about a year later. In a letter to the attorney general's office, he described Orkney's actions in Liverpool as unlawful and unconstitutional, but the provincial government stayed out of this affair.[17]

The *Whiting* also pressed a sailor from an American ship on the way out of Liverpool. It then headed west to the fishing village of Port Mouton, where it anchored for a couple of days. Perkins learned from a Halifax constable that the *Whiting* had sailed in pursuit of a smuggler, and that Orkney refused to land Anthony Smith at Port Mouton. Liverpool feared another visit from the *Whiting* and watched the harbour intently, just in case the alarm needed to be sounded for its sailors to hide from the Navy. Perkins noted on 8 July that the '*Whiting* went by to the Westward Last evening'.[18] This was not the last that Liverpool heard from the naval schooner. The town had a large seafaring community and many of its young men worked in merchantmen and fishing schooners. These vessels were routinely boarded by British warships. In fact, the *Whiting* pressed the Liverpool teenager Prince Snow about a week or two after it had left his home port. Snow was on voyage to Boston when the *Whiting* boarded his vessel at Cape Negro. Snow was turned over to the *Cleopatra*, but Perkins and other Liverpool officials used their political influence, and the Snow family's desperate situation, to secure his release the following September. He seems to have been the only Liverpool resident who was pressed by the *Whiting* and subsequently discharged.[19] Although the *Whiting* only stayed in Liverpool for about a week, impressment threatened its mariners throughout the summer of 1805. Even this, however, paled in comparison to the *Whiting's* activities in Shelburne.

Word of the *Whiting's* recruitment campaign in Liverpool preceded its arrival in Shelburne. Fishermen had spread the alarm throughout southern Nova Scotia. Fear of impressment was so widespread that Orkney posted a notice at the Shelburne customs house on 10 July, which stated that he was not there to press fishermen or farmers into the Navy. This was against Vice-Admiral Mitchell's orders, he declared, and they should continue to follow their occupations in peace and safety.[20] Again, however, Orkney was not true to his word: only a few days later he sparked mass hysteria in Shelburne by allowing seamen from the *Whiting* to tear through the countryside. Dozens of people were awoken in the middle of the night, forced to open their doors or the naval party would knock them down with axes. Other inhabitants, both young and old, were threatened with cutlasses and pistols. Several of them suffered serious injuries. As a result, dozens of families in the Shelburne area, particularly Sandy Point, abandoned their homes and took refuge in the woods. A special court of sessions was convened on 22 July to hear complaints about the *Whiting's* press gang, as well as John Hames, the Shelburne customs collector and magistrate who played a key role in terrorizing the constituents that he was supposed to protect. Consisting of four magistrates, the court sat until 1 August and heard from more than fifteen victims and witnesses.

The Shelburne Sessions

Among the witnesses was sixty-seven-year-old Joseph Mangham, a twenty-five year veteran of the British Army. He had been a weaver and farmer in Shelburne County for two decades and was a freeholder at the time of this incident. He was also a surveyor of roads in his home district of Sandy Point. Mangham testified that his family, consisting of an elderly wife and two orphan children, was accosted by a party from the *Whiting* in his potato garden on the afternoon of 18 July. The garden was located near the Mangham home, and the family was working there when Mangham's wife noticed one of the *Whiting's* officers, likely the master's mate named Lawrence Hollows, approaching the house. Finding the door locked, Hollows threatened to break it down with an axe before she reluctantly agreed to open it. The naval party searched every inch of the dwelling but refused to give an explanation for doing so; however, three sailors had deserted from the *Whiting* a few days earlier, and it is likely that the seamen were looking for them, or at least for evidence that they had been in the area. Meanwhile, Mangham saw magistrate Hames standing in the road a little way off and asked him to intervene on his behalf and to stop the ransacking. To his surprise, not only did Hames refuse this request but he treated the old man with contempt. Fearing more violence, Mangham lodged his family in the forest until the court proceedings began several days later.[21]

More than a dozen families feared the Navy's intrusions to such an extent that they lived in the woods for extended periods of time. Many of the victims were elderly couples with young children. These families likely worked together to survive. Few had it as bad as Andrew Goodick, who lived in the forest with his wife and eight children for more than a week. Goodick was a fisherman and freeholder and he too had spent time in the Army.[22] A handful of male victims served in the British armed forces for large sections of their lives – twenty years in the Royal Artillery in the case of the seventy-nine-year-old farmer Casper Grassman. One father had a son serving in the Navy, while another had three sons in the Shelburne militia. Most of the male victims were freeholders and members of farming, fishing, and artisanal families with roots in the community. Several of them served as jurors in 1805 or occupied other municipal posts. When young or middle aged men were accosted by the naval party, some of them were forced onboard the *Whiting*. For example, the fisherman Conrad Buchanan testified that the naval party 'presented a Pistol at his Breast and Swore they would shoot him unless he went with them'.[23] Buchanan escaped and fled with his family into the forest. Faced with the same predicament – one naval seaman swearing

Shelburne Harbour, watercolour drawing, c. 1818.
Courtesy Dalhousie University Library, Special Collections.

that he 'would tie him Neck and heel if he did not go with him on board' the *Whiting* – the farmer Daniel Cormick also got clear and took to the woods. He was desperate to do so, as he had a daughter and a deranged wife to care for, and impressment threatened his family's very existence.[24]

As the naval party moved from house to house, the actions of its leaders, Hames and Hollows, moved beyond the criminal to border on the sadistic. Hollows had volunteered for the *Whiting* in Bermuda, his native island, just months before. Only twenty-one-years-old, his youth and inexperience likely played a role in the violence that unfolded at Shelburne. Near midnight one evening Hames barged through Henry Echlin's door with a sword in one hand and a pistol in the other, tore him away from his wife, threatened to 'blow his brains out', and confined him on the trumped-up charge of harbouring deserters. Hames even pressed the pistol up against Echlin's head. The magistrate then demanded twenty pounds from Echlin, a farmer and part-time school teacher, 'saying that was the Law for People who Harboured Deserters'. Echlin denied the charge, and having no money, Hames told him that he would take the place of one deserter and that a press gang was coming to 'sweep them all' into the Navy, especially his son when he returned from a fishing voyage. On the road outside, Hames called Echlin a 'Damned Rascall' and promised to flog him with a horse whip if he was saucy. To his wife's horror, the naval party marched Echlin to Shelburne and put him onboard the *Whiting*. She was left with six young children to care for, and in her words, not a 'morsel of Bread' nor the money or credit to obtain the 'necessarys of life'. When she appeared in court on 1 August, Anna Echlin had been living in the forest for more than two weeks and her husband was still onboard the *Whiting*. Unfortunately, there is no record of Echlin in the latter's muster book and it is unclear what became of him. He may have been regarded as a supernumerary and released, or he may have been turned over to another warship at Halifax and remained in the Navy. Hames repeated these outrages elsewhere, and what is worse, they seem to have been endorsed by Orkney, who watched the Echlin incident and did not intervene.[25]

The naval party's mission in the Shelburne countryside was to investigate desertion from its schooner, but it used that as an excuse to force several men onboard the *Whiting*, likely for interrogation or to frighten them. The fisherman Daniel Moore was taken onboard and released from the *Whiting* on the same day, after which he and his wife abandoned their home to live in the forest. Similarly, the sixty-year-old farmer Nathaniel Turner watched helplessly as the naval party roughed up his family, likely with the intention of pressing his two sons into the service. Hollis wounded both of them with a cutlass before the family escaped into the brush. Hollis was taken onboard the *Whiting* for three days before he was released, after which he also took refuge in the wilderness. Neither Moore nor Hollis was entered into the *Whiting's* books and they were not intended to serve in the Navy. Turner was exempt because of old age and would never have been cleared for naval service.[26]

Other Shelburne residents, such as the carpenter John Fell, were not as fortunate. Fell was in bed with his wife when he heard someone knocking at the door. Initially, the couple refused to open it, but relented when the naval party threatened to beat it down. In came two sailors who told Fell to come with them; when he declined, Hames entered the house with a pistol and, according to Fell's wife, threatened to 'blow her husbands brains out'. Unlike Moore and Turner, he was pressed into the *Whiting* and entered into its books, but managed to desert at Cape Forchu (near Yarmouth) less than a fortnight later. He likely opted for the safer route of returning home overland.[27] The *Whiting's* records are vague with respect to its movements at this time, but it is clear that Orkney entered more than a dozen men in southwestern Nova Scotia in late July and early August. Several of them were pressed at Shelburne. For instance, the Shelburne Sessions recommended the eight-man crew of the fishing vessel *Four Johns* 'for Protection to His Majesty's Officers of the Navy', because they were all freeholders or members of the Shelburne militia. Orkney left Shelburne and sailed to the southwest, where the *Whiting* harassed Barrington and

Yarmouth. These towns likely heard of the *Whiting's* exploits at Liverpool and Shelburne and took appropriate precautions.[28]

Gideon White, anon. watercolour, c. 1800. Courtesy Nova Scotia Archives and Records Management.

Once the witnesses recorded their depositions, the Shelburne Sessions drafted a petition to Chief Justice Sampson Salter Blowers. Gideon White and three other magistrates demanded satisfaction for the violent and unlawful conduct of Hames and the *Whiting's* seamen. They maintained that the depositions 'Convey but a faint Idea of the distress of the Inhabitants of this Town and Coast'. The magistrates stated that the damage caused by impressment extended beyond Shelburne to much of coastal Nova Scotia. 'We Cannot for a moment suppose', they declared, that Vice-Admiral Mitchell gave orders to press fishermen, farmers, and freeholders of the province. Orkney had posted a notice that this was against Mitchell's orders, which was signed by Hames in his capacity as customs collector, but Orkney broke that promise several days later when 'both Farmers and Fishermen were not only pressed but two [were] Cruelly wounded'. The 'Unnamed Citizens of Shelburne' requested Blowers to lay the case before Lieutenant-Governor Wentworth and the executive council to prevent such 'Outrageous and destructive Conduct' in the future. They also offered a warning: if this behaviour was allowed to continue, the young fishermen of the south shore, the most valuable part of their communities, would immigrate to the United States to escape impressment. Their fathers would likely go there as well, 'unless justice is done them'.[29]

The Shelburne magistrates also argued that Hames was the main cause of their distress. He was in town during the court proceedings, knew why it was sitting (he even lurked about the courthouse), but refused to testify. His fellow magistrates condemned Hames's conduct as tending to 'destroy that peace, Harmony, Good order and Governing which every Civil Magistrate under the British Government is sworn to Support'. Gideon White argued that Hames should be held responsible for his behaviour, especially his mistreatment of Joseph Mangham, one of the town's most respected inhabitants. White also highlighted Hames's influence with Orkney and the fact that he blatantly disobeyed the order against impressment at the customs house. Apparently,

Hames accused Mangham of resisting the naval party and of raising a mob. White dismissed the mob suggestion entirely, and declared that it was natural for British subjects to resist violent and unlawful intrusions into their homes and personal lives – what would you expect from an old man who had been 'wounded, abused, impressed and drove from' his house? The magistrates also educated the chief justice on Shelburne County's legal deficiencies. If anyone in the town could have issued writs of habeas corpus, for instance, neither Echlin nor Fell would have been pressed into the *Whiting*.[30]

In the end, not only did Hames avoid the Shelburne Sessions, but there is no indication that Orkney and the *Whiting's* seamen acknowledged its existence, let alone suffer a reprimand. There is also no evidence that Blowers took legal action or that the case was presented to Wentworth and the provincial government. It must have been a slap in the face for many Shelburne residents that Hames did not receive discipline of any kind either – he continued to serve as a magistrate in Shelburne, and a year later Wentworth granted him a leave of absence to travel to England on personal business, even expressing satisfaction with Hames's conduct in his 'Offices of the Revenue and Magistracy'.[30] Gideon White and other Shelburne officials did not record why the government refused to take an interest in this case. Had the incident occurred in Halifax, the outrages would have been laid bare for all to see – naval authorities, colonial officials, the merchant community, as well as the newspaper press. It is possible that the *Whiting's* impressments were overshadowed by the press gang riot that took place in Halifax several months later. Unfortunately, there remain important questions about this case that are unlikely to be answered by further research: for example, how could White and his fellow magistrates continue to work with Hames in the Shelburne courthouse, and how was Orkney's role in this affair not reported to Mitchell or the Admiralty? Given the outrages committed in the Shelburne countryside, it is difficult to believe that the magistrates did not present the town's petition to Blowers or the attorney general.[32]

Civil-Naval Animosity

What is clear, however, is that impressment disturbances in Shelburne and Halifax in 1805 tarnished the Navy's reputation in Nova Scotia. Provincial authorities stopped cooperating with the Navy after this, particularly with respect to the manning problem. They did not issue another press warrant until the War of 1812. Wentworth and his officials also seized upon the

Navy's violence in 1805 to regulate impressment more closely. Fishermen were formally protected from the press the following year, and exemptions were issued to merchant vessels, privateers, mast ships, and other craft in government service. Freeholders and militiamen, or people carrying papers to that effect, were off-limits to the Navy, and in most cases a man only needed to prove that he was a resident of Nova Scotia to escape impressment. After 1805, therefore, civil-naval relations deteriorated sharply in Nova Scotia because of impressment abuses. By the War of 1812, warships were normally short-handed in the colony and high desertion rates exacerbated an already tumultuous situation. Provincial impressment regulations prevented captains from filling many of these vacancies, and tensions inevitably spilled over into Halifax, where press gangs operated illegally on shore. Civilians clashed with naval parties in the streets, which sometimes ended up in court, and the North American squadron was attacked for its press gang abuses by the government, Halifax magistracy, and the merchant community. The *Whiting's* impressment campaign in southern Nova Scotia in the summer of 1805 marked the beginning of this period of civil-naval animosity.[33]

The social history of the Royal Navy has come a long way in recent years, but this case study demonstrates that the violent image of impressment in folklore and traditional literature is sometimes rooted in historical fact. Resistance to press gangs was one of the most violent and common forms of protest in Britain and colonial America in the eighteenth century.[34] The same was true of British North America – impressment was contested vigorously in Newfoundland, Quebec, and Nova Scotia between 1775 and 1815.[35] Although the *Whiting's* actions in Shelburne in 1805 were particularly hostile, impressment violence was not unusual in Nova Scotia. Naval parties were also resisted when they searched for deserters, since it was common to use these missions as a disguise to press men into the fleet. The strangest part of this episode is Hames's active role in the search for deserters and the impressment of settlers, and his mistreatment of the citizens he was paid to protect. Magistrates were normally hostile to the armed forces and the main protectors of their communities. Like Hames, Orkney was fortunate to escape punishment in this affair, but junior officers on the make often ran into trouble on the impress service. Feeling pressure from Mitchell, who sent the *Whiting* to the south coast to help man the squadron, Orkney likely turned a blind eye to the atrocities in Shelburne to impress the admiral and to advance his own career. In the process, he allowed the *Whiting* to terrorize southern Nova Scotia in the summer of 1805, which signaled a decline in civil-naval relations in the colony that lasted for the duration of the Napoleonic Wars.

1. The *Whiting's* activities in Shelburne in 1805 are absent from local histories and from the naval historiography. Marion Robertson, *King's Bounty: A History of Early Shelburne, Nova Scotia* (Halifax: Nova Scotia Museum, 1983); Julian Gwyn, *Frigates and Foremasts: The North American Squadron in Nova Scotia Waters, 1745-1815* (Vancouver: University of British Columbia Press, 2003). They are discussed briefly in Patricia L. Rogers, '"Unprincipled Men who are One Day British Subjects and the next Citizens of the United States": The Nova Scotian Merchant Community and Colonial Identity Formation, c. 1780-1820' (Michigan State University, Ph.D. Thesis, 2001), pp. 49-52. Gideon White's manuscripts, which comprise the bulk of this article's evidence on Shelburne, can now be accessed on the Nova Scotia Archives and Record Management's website: http://www.gov.ns.ca/nsarm/virtual/white/. The author thanks the Social Sciences and Humanities Research Council of Canada for its financial support as well as the staff of the Shelburne County Archives and Genealogical Society for their assistance.

2. Mitchell to Admiralty, 19 July 1805, The National Archives of the United Kingdom [TNA], London, Admiralty Correspondence, ADM 1 / 496, North American Station, p. 81.

3. On Newfoundland, see Keith Mercer, 'The Murder of Lieutenant Lawry: A Case Study of British Naval Impressment in Newfoundland, 1794', *Newfoundland and Labrador Studies*, 21:2 (2006), pp. 255-89.

4. *The Nova-Scotia Royal Gazette*, 30 May 1805.

5. Keith Mercer, 'Sailors and Citizens: Press Gangs and Naval-CivilianRelations in Nova Scotia, 1756-1815', *Journal of the Royal Nova Scotia Historical Society*, 10 (2007), pp. 97-101.

6. Muster of HMS *Leander*, TNA, ADM 36 / 16,379.

7. Wentworth to Mitchell, 6-8 May 1805, Nova Scotia Archives and Records Management [NSARM], Halifax, RG 1, Governor Wentworth's Nova Scotia Letter Books, vol. 54, pp. 12-14; Executive Council Minutes, 16-18 May 1805, NSARM, RG 1, vol. 191, pp. 152-6.

8. Musters of HMS *Cambrian*, TNA, ADM 36 / 16,687-8.

9. Executive Council Minutes, 23 November 1805, NSARM, RG 1, vol. 191, pp. 161-62.

10. John Talbot Order Books, 14-24 July 1813, Library and Archives Canada, Ottawa, Microfilm Reel A-1632, no page numbers.

11. Berkeley to Admiralty, 15 August 1806, TNA, ADM 1 / 496, pp. 411-12.

12. Muster of HM Schooner *Whiting*, TNA, ADM 36 / 16,591; Pay Book of HM Schooner *Whiting*, TNA, ADM 35 / 2532; Muster of HMS *Cleopatra*, TNA, ADM 36 / 16,912.

13. Muster of HM Schooner *Whiting*, TNA, ADM 36 / 16,591; Pay Book of HM *Schooner Whiting*, TNA, ADM 35 / 2532; David Lyon, *The Sailing Navy List: All the Ships of the Royal Navy – Built, Purchased and Captured – 1688-1860* (London: Conway Maritime Press, 1993), pp. 160-61; *Steel's Navy Lists* (London, 1805-13); Frederick P. Schmitt (with H.G. Middleton), 'A Listing of Naval Ships Built in Bermuda', *Bermuda Historical Quarterly*, 18:2 (1961), pp. 49-56; William James, *A Full and Correct Account of the Chief Naval Occurrences of the Late War between Great Britain and the United States of America* (London: T. Egerton, 1817), p. 79.

14. Muster of HM Schooner *Whiting*, TNA, ADM 36 / 16,591; Pay Book of HM Schooner *Whiting*, TNA, ADM 35 / 2532; *The Commissioned Sea Officers of the Royal Navy, 1660-1815*, edited by David Syrett and R.L. DiNardo (Aldershot: Scolar Press for the Navy Records Society, 1994), p. 339; Steel's Navy Lists (London, 1805-13); Orkney to Admiralty, 10 April 1806, TNA, ADM 1 / 3057, Lieutenants Letters, 'O', 1801-7 (enclosure: John P. Beresford, acting commodore at Bermuda, to Orkney, 7 March 1806), no page numbers. Orkney received his Admiralty commission as a first lieutenant on 1 May 1804.

15 *The Diary of Simeon Perkins, 1804-1812*, edited by Charles Bruce Fergusson (Toronto: Champlain Society, 1978), v, 16 May 1805, 27 June 1805, p. 113 and p. 122.

16 *Diary of Simeon Perkins*, v, 29 June-4 July 1805, pp. 123-24.

17 Perkins to Crofton Uniacke, 17 May 1806, in *Diary of Simeon Perkins*, v, p. 476. Smith was a Black caulker with a house and family in Liverpool. At the time of Perkins's request for his discharge in 1806, he was serving in the Cleopatra and had been sent into Halifax on a prize vessel. The *Whiting's* records do not cite the specific places where Smith and the other men were pressed in southern Nova Scotia in the summer of 1805. Muster of HM Schooner *Whiting*, TNA, ADM 36 / 16,591.

18 *Diary of Simeon Perkins*, v, 5-10 July 1805, pp. 124-26.

19 *Diary of Simeon Perkins*, v, 6 August 1805, 28 September 1805, p. 132 and p. 146; Perkins and Snow Parker to Richard John Uniacke, in *Diary of Simeon Perkins*, v, pp. 473-74. Mitchell ordered the discharge of sixteen-year-old George Prince from the *Cleopatra* on 9 August; this was likely Prince Snow, who had been entered with an incorrect name. Muster of HM Schooner *Whiting*, TNA, ADM 36 / 16,591. Orkney pressed another man at Cape Negro, a native of Port Riviere to the east of Liverpool.

20 Orkney's Notice, 10 July 1805, NSARM, MG 1, vol. 954, Gideon White Family Papers, no. 818. This notice and the following records in this case are all enclosed in Draft of Letter to Chief Justice [Sampson Salter] Blowers, [1 August] 1805, NSARM, MG 1, vol. 954, White Papers, no. 826. In addition to being posted on NSARM's website (see no. 1), the White Papers are described in Margaret Ells, *A Calendar of the White Collection of Manuscripts in the Public Archives of Nova Scotia* (Halifax: Nova Scotia Public Archives, 1940).

21 Evidence from Special Sessions, 22 July 1805, NSARM, MG 1, vol. 954, White Papers, no. 819; Shelburne County Sessions Court Records, NSARM, RG 34 / 321, Box O, Officers and Officials, 1805, File 3; Muster of HM Schooner *Whiting*, TNA, ADM 36 / 16,591.

22 Evidence from Special Sessions, 22 July 1805, NSARM, MG 1, vol. 954, White Papers, no. 819. According to folklore, Philip Goodick, the son of a Hessian soldier who went to Shelburne after the American Revolution and settled at Sandy Point, was pressed into the Navy and stayed there for many years. He was likely a relative, perhaps even a son, of Andrew Goodick. Marion Robertson, *The Chestnut Pipe: Folklore of Shelburne County* (Halifax: Nimbus, 1991), p. 197.

23 Evidence from Special Sessions, 22 July 1805, NSARM, MG 1, vol. 954, White Papers, no. 819; Papers on the Conduct of the *Whiting's* Officers, [1 August] 1805, NSARM, MG 1, vol. 954, White Papers, no. 822; Shelburne County Sessions Court Records, NSARM, RG 34 / 321, Box G, Grand Jury, 1805-10, File 6. More data on the victims and witnesses can be found in the Shelburne Records, NSARM, MG 4, vol. 141.

24 Evidence from Special Sessions, 22 July 1805, NSARM, MG 1, vol. 954, White Papers, no. 819; Papers on the Conduct of the *Whiting's* Officers, [1 August] 1805, NSARM, MG 1, vol. 954, White Papers, no. 822.

25 Pay Book of HM Schooner *Whiting*, TNA, ADM 35 / 2532; Deposition of Charles Bower, 29 July 1805, NSARM, MG 1, vol. 954, White Papers, no. 820; Deposition of Anna Echlin, [1 August] 1805, NSARM, MG 1, vol. 954, White Papers, no. 823.

26 Muster of HM Schooner *Whiting*, TNA, ADM 36 / 16,591; Evidence from Special Sessions, 22 July 1805, NSARM, MG 1, vol. 954, White Papers, no. 819.

27 Deposition of Charity Fell, 1 August 1805, NSARM, MG 1, vol. 954, White Papers, no. 821; Muster of HM Schooner *Whiting*, TNA, ADM 36 / 16,591.

28 Papers on the Conduct of the *Whiting's* Officers, [1 August] 1805, NSARM, MG 1, vol. 954, White Papers, no. 822; Muster of HM Schooner *Whiting*, TNA, ADM 36 / 16,591. Unfortunately, none of the *Whiting's* log books have survived for this period; however, the

places at which sailors deserted in late July and early August 1805 demonstrate that the schooner was cruising in southwestern Nova Scotia, especially in the Barrington, Cape Sable, and Yarmouth areas. No records have survived that describe the *Whiting's* recruitment efforts in those places.

[29] Draft of Letter from Unnamed Citizens of Shelburne to Blowers, [1 August] 1805, NSARM, MG 1, vol. 954, White Papers, no. 824; Draft of Letter to Chief Justice Blowers, [1 August] 1805, NSARM, MG 1, vol. 954, White Papers, no. 826. These documents vary slightly. The other Shelburne magistrates involved in the special sessions were Stephen Skinner, Jacob Van Buskirk, and James Dore.

[30] Draft of Letter from Unnamed Citizens of Shelburne to Blowers, [1 August] 1805, NSARM, MG 1, vol. 954, White Papers, no. 824; Draft of Gideon White's Observations on John Hames's Letter, [1 August] 1805, NSARM, MG 1, vol. 954, White Papers, no. 825. It is unclear who Hames sent the letter to; rather than the special sessions, he likely contacted Blowers or Wentworth directly or perhaps the attorney general.

[31] Wentworth to Hames, 18 August 1806, NSARM, RG 1, vol. 54, Wentworth Letter Books, p. 113. Hames served as a magistrate until May 1809, when he moved to New Brunswick. He presided over general and special sessions with the same magistrates who wanted him punished for his role in the *Whiting* affair in 1805. He even sat in the general sessions in July 1805, when that affair took place. Hames served on the Shelburne fire brigade at the same time. He was involved in two altercations in 1808 that ended up in the Shelburne Sessions. In March, Hames and a yeoman named Owen Roberts filed competing claims of assault and battery. Hames stated that Roberts, a 'straggling vagabond', threatened to 'murder and kill' him in the open street. Roberts stated that it was Hames who, with force and arms, beat Roberts even though he was 'acting peacefully'. There is no record of a resolution in this case. Then in October, Hames deposed to Gideon White that he was 'evil treated' by Michael Gordon, the barrack master and assistant commissary for the Army at Shelburne. Hames stated that he was in Mary Buchanan's house (she was a tavern keeper) when Gordon came in and assaulted him without provocation. Gordon threatened Hames, abused him with the most 'unhandsome language', and challenged the magistrate to a boxing match. Gordon kept telling Hames that he was going to beat him until Buchanan asked Gordon to leave. The charges against Gordon were dropped when he paid a £100 fine. T. Watson Smith, 'A History of Shelburne County' (unpublished essay from 1871, copy at NSARM), p. 102; Shelburne County Sessions Court Records, NSARM, RG 34 / 321, Box P, Proceedings, 1805-14, Files 15-21; Court of General Sessions, Shelburne County, NSARM, RG 60, Court Cases, 1805-8, Files 76-81. For his part, Hollows, the master's mate, was promoted by Vice-Admiral Mitchell into HM Sloop *Bermuda* in February 1806. Pay Book of HM Schooner *Whiting*, TNA, ADM 35 / 2532.

[32] Blowers's papers have not survived.

[33] This narrative is discussed in Keith Mercer, 'North Atlantic Press Gangs: Impressment and Naval-Civilian Relations in Nova Scotia and Newfoundland, 1749-1815' (Dalhousie University, Ph.D. Thesis, 2008), chapter 3.

[34] Nicholas Rogers, *The Press Gang: Naval Impressment and its Opponents in Georgian Britain* (London: Continuum, 2007); Denver Alexander Brunsman, 'The Evil Necessity: British Naval Impressment in the Eighteenth-Century Atlantic World' (Princeton University, Ph.D. Thesis, 2004).

[35] Keith Mercer, 'Northern Exposure: Resistance to Naval Impressment in the Canadian Atlantic Region, 1775-1815' (forthcoming).

The Black Book

Terry Coleman

In the second half of the eighteenth century and the beginning of the nineteenth, when Great Britain was becoming the paramount world power, that power was assured by the Royal Navy. The government of the British realm and Empire was loose, local, and corrupt. The organisation of the Navy was tight, world-wide, and with little more corruption than might reasonably have been expected. The direction of the Navy's vessels – and in 1805 there were 850 of them – was somehow exercised from London by seven Lords of the Admiralty, two secretaries, and eighteen clerks. These vessels – in home waters, in the East and West Indies, in the Mediterranean and the Baltic, in the Atlantic and the Pacific – daily recorded their positions, the weather, their courses and actions, in logs, letters, and other documents which eventually found their way home. The doings of the Navy were, then, recorded in great detail. Its 4,000 sea officers, thousands of miles away and months from their last orders, exercised immense discretion and power of life and death, but for all this they had to account, in the end, to the Admiralty in London. Millions of letters to and from admirals, captains, and lieutenants, and millions of surveys, logs, and reports of courts martial, accumulated and are still preserved in the National Archives at Kew.

Among these documents are the four volumes of the Black Book.[1] They are often referred to in passing by naval historians and by Patrick O'Brian in his Aubrey-Maturin novels, but their rich material has hardly been touched.

These Black Books are ledgers bound not in the Navy's usual brown calf but in black morocco. From 1759 onwards it was the duty of one clerk 'to enter the names of all officers under censure in a Black Book to be kept for that purpose and to inform the secretaries if any of them should be directed to be again employed, that the same may not be done by surprise'. First Lords of the Admiralty like Sandwich, Keppel, Howe, Spencer, and St Vincent did not like to be taken by surprise. Navy discipline could be draconic. It was the complaint of many sea officers that though an army officer's commission addressed him as 'dearly beloved' and 'trusty', and was signed by the king, a naval commission was signed by three Lords of the Admiralty and, after adjuring strict adherence to orders, contained what amounted to a threat: 'Hereof nor you nor any of you may fail as you will answer the contrary at your peril'.

In the Black Book, and in the reports of their courts martial, are the desperate stories of broken captains and commanders, disgraced lieutenants, and rejected midshipmen. In so large a service, there are surprisingly few of them. Some of the censured officers were petty peculators, dismissed for 'wronging men of their provisions'. A few were mad, like the lieutenant broken for 'endangering lives... firing several loaded pistols'. A few were driven by wrong-headed passion or rage. One was a son of the Duke of Grafton, which made him a direct descendant of Charles II, the first duke having been that king's natural son by Barbara Villiers. A few were afraid. A few were black-hearted scoundrels, well rid of. Others were just dreadfully unlucky, decent men overwhelmed by mischance heaped on mischance. A few had been unjustly or maliciously accused. For most it was the end, but some, though written down in the Black Book, revived their fortunes, and at least three became admirals. Here are a few of their cases.

Wrongdoing, Disgrace, and Some Scoundrels

In December 1807 Commander the Hon. Warwick Lake of the sloop *Recruit*, irritated that one of his seamen, Robert Jeffery, a boy of seventeen, had stolen beer from a cask, marooned him at dusk on an uninhabited rock called Sombrero in the Caribbean, 100 miles north of St Kitts, allowing him to take no food, water, or clothes.[2] He was barefoot. None of the ship's officers protested. The men of the boat's crew that put him ashore whipped round to give him a hat, a pair of shoes, a knife, and a handkerchief to wave to attract a rescuer. Next morning the rock was still in sight but the ship did not put back. Jeffery's clothes were sold to his shipmates.

Back in Barbados the admiral, learning of this from seamen's gossip, sent Lake back a month later to search for the man. Only a pair of trousers was found. The admiral should have court martialled Lake but the commander was the son of a hero, a general who had distinguished himself with Wellington in India and been rewarded with a viscountcy and a pension of £2,000 for three lives. The admiral took the easy way out and sent Lake home on sick leave. By then his older brother had died in battle in Portugal, also a hero, and his regiment was planning a monument to him in Westminster Abbey. So Lake was twice recommended, as the son and brother of heroes, and the Admiralty, knowing nothing about the marooning, promoted him to

Robert Jeffery marooned on Sombrero Rock, contemporary engraving. Courtesy the author.

post captain and gave him command of a frigate. That would have been that if a disgraced purser with many grudges had not written directly to the First Lord of the Admiralty, incidentally mentioning the Sombrero incident and calling Lake a titled murderer. This could not be ignored. At a court martial in 1810 Lake's old crew gave evidence against him and he was discredited, disgraced, broken, and dismissed the service.

The fate of Jeffery the seaman became a national scandal. In the Commons the prime minister condemned Lake but said there could be no trial for murder without a body. The government sent a schooner to search the West Indian islands for any traces of Jeffery, and advertised in American newspapers. Rumours abounded – that Jeffery was dead, having first tried to eat his own flesh, or that he was alive and had been sighted on both sides of the Atlantic. Lake fled the country. Later that year Jeffery did turn up in Marblehead, Massachusetts, where he had become known as the Emperor of Sombrero. After nine days on the rock, with no food, and water only once when it rained, he had been rescued starving by an American vessel. The Royal Navy brought him home from Halifax. He was quietly discharged, persuaded not to exhibit himself, accepted the Lake family's hush money, declared himself willing to shake the captain's hand, and was reunited with his widowed mother in Cornwall where he took up his old trade of blacksmith.

In 1836, on the death of another brother, Warwick Lake became third Viscount Lake and succeeded to the £2,000 pension his father had earned a quarter of a century before. He died in Grosvenor Square in 1848 when, as the *Gentleman's Magazine* put it, 'all his honours became extinct'.

The Hon. Warwick Lake was worthless. Captain James Norman was not, and though he was not eternally disgraced as Lake was, he lost a reputation and felt it deeply, besides which he was poor.[3] In 1796 he was in his sixties, old for the command of the *Medusa* frigate, and on the thankless mission of escorting a convoy of 110 merchantmen to Jamaica. So large a convoy, with its slow sailers and fast sailers and bloody-minded ships' masters indifferent to naval signals, was impossible to keep together, and in the face of an attack a single frigate could anyway do little. But it was the Atlantic weather that scattered the convoy and destroyed Norman. At the end of the passage only twenty-five ships remained in sight, and by the time the rest drifted in, sixteen had been picked off by the French. The rich merchants of the West Indies and the City of London, always willing to celebrate showy victories with gold medals for captains and jewelled swords for admirals, fell upon Norman with writs and affidavits. The court martial was a necessary show to placate them. He pleaded that he had been so long in the service, more than thirty years before he was made captain. As another piece of necessary show he was entered in the Black Book, but the court did not find that he should rendered incapable of serving again, which was the usual formula if he was not to be absolutely dismissed the service, but pronounced instead that he should stay on half pay for the rest of his life. He would not starve, but the sentence meant he would he never have another ship.

Madness and Cowardice

Then there are the cases that show the endless strain and distracting madness that afflicted men who had been too long at sea. Captain George Luke of the *Terror* was so deranged that he went down on his knees crying on the quarterdeck, watched by his amazed men.[4] As if this were an earlier Caine Mutiny, Lieutenant Seth Skill arrested him, took command, and confined the captain to his cabin, but he too was mad and tied his superior officer down with an obsessionally intricate net of nautical knots, which he detailed to the court. The captain never went to sea again. The lieutenant was dismissed the service.

Admiral John Byng had been famously shot on his quarter deck for losing Minorca in 1757 – shot, as Voltaire put it, 'pour encourager les autres'. The only comparable case in the French revolutionary wars was after the Battle of Camperdown in October 1797, in which the Dutch fleet after a terrible brawl was utterly destroyed – an annihilation comparable to the French at the Nile.

Afterwards Captain John Williamson of the *Agincourt* (64) was charged that 'through cowardice, negligence, or disaffection he kept back and did not come into the fight'.[5] He was the only captain so charged in the whole of the long wars. He protested that he was charged with no particular or specific act but was called upon to account for every course he had steered and every sail he had set. 'For the charge merely states the nature of my offence, while my life, reputation, and honour are staked on the result'. The evidence referred to a chaos of signals, to engage the enemy more closely, to break the line, and so on, which he had not obeyed. Williamson pleaded that his foremast had been 'dangerously wounded,' but the evidence that he had kept his distance was plain. In a bloody battle in which one man in ten of the English fleet was killed or wounded the *Agincourt* had suffered no casualties, and received only ten shots.

Williamson was reduced to calling witnesses to state, as evidence of his loyalty to the king, that in the battle 'he stampt and swore and appeared to be in a very great passion,' and that in a mutiny some months before he had threatened he would not bother to seek out the ringleaders but would instantly shoot the man next to him. And there was also this – not of course given in evidence but known to every member of the court – that Williamson, as a lieutenant on Captain Cook's last expedition, was reputed to have failed to go to his assistance when he was hacked to pieces on Tahiti.

The court found the charges of cowardice and disaffection not proved, only the negligence. This was exactly same verdict as had been brought in against Byng. Byng was shot, but he had lost Minorca. Camperdown on the other hand was a glorious victory. Williamson was put at the bottom of the post captains' list and rendered incapable of ever serving again. Nelson, writing to a member of the court who was a friend, said this was lenient. For himself, if a man didn't take his chance of being shot by his enemies he should be certain of being shot by his friends.[6] It was academic. The degraded Williamson died the next year.

Legend would make Captain William Bligh a certainty for the Black Book, and he is there, but not for the *Bounty* mutiny. He was court martialled for the loss of that ship, as any officer automatically was for the loss of any vessel, but was acquitted of all blame. Bligh was really an outstanding sea officer. At the age of twenty he was chosen as navigator by Captain Cook on his last voyage of discovery. He played a brave part in two fleet engagements, and was commended by Nelson at Copenhagen as 'my second'. Any man distinguished by both Cook and Nelson is extraordinary. History has conspired against him. He was less of a flogger than most captains, loved his wife, and was gentle to women. But he was a perfectionist who could not tolerate mere competence in his officers, and he was an endless nagger with an inventive tongue.

In 1805 he was court martialled for grossly insulting his first lieutenant on the quarterdeck and for 'generally tyrannical, oppressive, and unofficerlike conduct'.[7] It emerged that he frequently called his officers and men blackguards, lubbers, Jesuits, and vagrants, and his gunner 'a damned long pelt of a bitch'. Bligh admitted that he was given to such 'ebullition of the mind', together with 'a great deal of action' with his hands. 'As if to knock a person down,' agreed a boatswain, who said that Bligh had torn his shirt and shaken him, but he believed the words no sooner escaped the captain than his passion ended. He would as soon sail with him as with anyone.

The charges were found to be proved, and Bligh was admonished to be more circumspect in his language in future. As he left the court he promptly denounced the officers who had spoken against him as the worst of serpents. He was entered in the Black Book. Two weeks later he was offered the governorship of New South Wales, which required the utmost tact. At Sydney he suffered another mutiny, at the hands of a venal rum-running militia, was deposed, then restored, and died a vice admiral.

A sea officer would not expect to find himself in the Black Book just for letting a prisoner escape at Spithead, but that is what happened to Commander Robert Philpot of the

CAP.ᵗ BLIGH.

Captain William Bligh (1754 –1817).
Courtesy Warwick Leadlay Gallery.

Prompte sloop.[8] He pleaded that he kept the man in irons from dusk to dawn, and that he could only have escaped dressed as a woman. The concern was because the man, who had been brought from the West Indies, was believed to be from the crew of the *Hermione* frigate. They had mutinied in an infinitely more atrocious fashion than the *Bounty's* men; had murdered and mutilated their captain and officers, and in a final act of treachery handed the ship over to the Spaniards.

Philpot was reprimanded and written down in the Black Book. There is of course no mention there of Richard Parker, who led the Nore mutiny of 1797, when twelve ships of the line and ten other vessels were seized from their officers, flew the red flag of revolution and would, if the French had known, have constituted a real danger to the country. Parker's court martial was conducted with decent ceremony and a weird courtesy. He insisted he had treated captains and admirals with respect during his time as chief delegate. Members of the court agreed he had, and several times counselled him not to ask witnesses questions which could elicit answers that incriminated him. Then they hanged him and, after some debate whether he should be tarred and gibbeted, handed over the body to his wife. At the time he was no kind of officer, only a supernumerary, and when he was dead there was no point in putting him in the Back Book as warning against future employment. He had never, as has sometimes been written, been acting lieutenant, though he had four years earlier been a master's mate, and had been broken for insubordination.[9] A few mates do appear in the Black Books, but at the time his offence probably seemed too trivial to include.

The *Hermione* mutiny touched Captain Sir Edward Hamilton too. Courts martial frequently ordered floggings of 100 or 300 lashes. A captain could legally order a dozen, and a blind eye was often turned to four dozen. But let him molest a man otherwise and he was in trouble. Hamilton was chronically dissatisfied with his gunner, an important warrant officer of his ship, and one day tied him up in the rigging as an example, and left him there. It was not at sea but at Portsmouth, but it was freezing cold and the man, who was not young, fainted after an hour and had to be brought down. Hamilton was court martialled.[10] He volunteered to the court that he had been in a violent passion and that since he received a violent wound in the head, his judgment could at times no longer curb his irritation. He said in mitigation that he had been at sea since he was eight, that he had served the whole of the French wars, and that he had seen much service ashore and at sea. He did not particularise this service.

It was a case that was by no means certain to have come to a court martial anyway. But it had, and Hamilton had done what he was charged with. The

Captain Sir Edward Hamilton (1772 – 1851).
Courtesy Warwick Leadlay Gallery.

court could have admonished him, or reprimanded him, or, more severely, dismissed him his ship. That would leave him on half pay and looking, perhaps with difficulty, for another command. But the court did more than that. It cashiered him, dismissed him the service altogether.

This was amazing. One of the actions he did not 'particularise' was his recovery from a Spanish Caribbean port of the mutinied and surrendered *Hermione*. The whole of the Navy's West Indian fleets had been searching for that ship to recover her and the Navy's honour. Hamilton found her in harbour, boarded her at night from small boats, fought a bloody hand-to-hand action, and brought her away. It was one of the most brilliant, brave, and symbolic actions of the whole war. It was during the boarding that his head was stove in with a musket butt and he sustained other wounds to the body. The king had knighted him, the City of London had given him a gold medal, and he had modestly declined a pension offered by the First Lord of the Admiralty. The court must have known all this, and it still cashiered him.

Either the First Lord or George III himself, who took a personal and minute interest in the Navy, saw the injustice of this. A few months later Hamilton was restored to his rank by Order in Council, by royal prerogative. He was given command of a royal yacht, a post of honour and profit. He was made a baronet. Wounds notwithstanding, he lived another fifty years, well into his eighties. But he never commanded another ship of war.

Interest and Interference

What was known as 'interest' could undoubtedly make a sea officer's career. Interest was knowing the right people who could put in a word or, better still, instruct a clerk to make out a commission. Interest was undoubtedly possessed by a son of the Duke of Grafton who ended up in the Black Book. Lord William Fitzroy, the duke's fifth son, had risen from midshipman to lieutenant to commander to post captain in three years, becoming post at twenty-two. Collingwood was twenty-nine before he achieved that rank, and the great Hood thirty-one. Very good men without interest never rose to post captain at all. Good men often never rose past lieutenant. But when we are thinking of the Black Book the question is not so much to do with promotion: it is how far interest could rescue a sea officer once he had fallen. In 1811 Fitzroy was court martialled for tyranny and clapping his ship's master in irons. He was dismissed the service and rendered incapable of ever again serving as an officer.[11] But his father was not only a duke and a knight of the Garter; he had also been prime minister in the 1760s. His son was reinstated in a few months and, though he never had another command, rose by inevitable steps to be Admiral of the White. He was saved by interest. The likes of Captain Norman of the straying Jamaica convoy had no chance. And nor did one officer who had the strong support of Nelson himself.

This was William Layman, commander of the sloop *Raven*, which ran aground in 1805 when the officer of the watch, who was drunk, mistook the lights of Cadiz for those of a fleet.[12] After the court martial sentenced Layman to be placed at the bottom of the list of commanders, Nelson himself wrote to the First Lord of the Admiralty saying Layman's services were a national loss and that if he (Nelson) had been censured every time he ran his ship into danger he would long ago have been out of the service. This helped not at all. The court martial minutes, when they reached the Admiralty, were quite exceptionally endorsed so as to make the sentence even more severe, and Layman was written down as not a fit person to be entrusted with one of His Majesty's ships. Admittedly the *Raven* was the second vessel Layman had run aground, and Nelson at the time was no favourite with the Lords of the Admiralty, whom he characterised to Emma Hamilton as a 'set of beasts'. For years Layman wrote long letters to the Admiralty suggesting ingenious improvements to hulls and riggings, and asking for any employment. But he never was employed again, and, as Sir Harris Nicolas puts it, he 'terminated his existence in the year 1826'.[13]

The *Iris* frigate was not a happy ship. On passage to Rio in 1814, in the south Atlantic under a vertical sun, Captain Hood Christian, who liked a dry ship, caulked down the scuttles and hatches and half suffocated his officers in the gunroom.[14] They beat the scuttles open and were all of five of them court martialled for breach of discipline. One unwise and verbose lieutenant, letting drop that he was a relation of the great Collingwood, asked the court to consider how he and his colleagues might have contributed to the dazzling glory of the Navy and to Britain's pinnacle of greatness amidst the present wreck of nations. He went on to relate that he had been at Trafalgar and brought down from the rigging the French soldier who had shot Nelson, an action that has somehow escaped the attention of historians. All this did not help him. He and the four other lieutenants were severely reprimanded.

Research Possibilities in Reprimand and Reprisal

But their captain should have been more prudent, since the accused officers in their turn then demanded a court martial of him. A reprimanded lieutenant told the court the *Iris* had been sailing in company with a merchantman carrying female convicts to Botany Bay and that just out of Madeira the captain asked if some of them couldn't be brought on board. The reply was that this could probably be managed, since the master of the merchantman was an old navy lieutenant who had sailed with the captain's father. Now the frigate captain, Hood Christian, was the son of an admiral, Sir Hugh

Christian, and moreover took his first name from Samuel Hood, who was a friend of his father's. So the young Hood Christian was well connected, and great things had been foreseen for him. As a midshipman had been on the royal yacht when she brought the Prince of Wales's new bride from Cuxhaven to England in 1795. Now, off Madeira in 1814, he wanted a woman, and there were female convicts to be had. His purser warned him that the bringing over would be done in the face of 300 men of his crew. 'Surely,' said the captain, 'no one could be such a damned rascal as to tell my wife?' He sent a cutter, which capsized and was lost, the men barely escaping drowning. At a second attempt three women were brought across. Two were sent to the officers in the gunroom and one to the captain. He thought her too old and sent a note to his officers saying: 'Do the decent thing and send up the young one'. They took no notice, and Captain Christian had to make do with the one he had. He complained she stank so damnably he had to pour a bottle of honey water over her, but kept her for two nights nonetheless.

He was somehow acquitted of the loss of the cutter and only severely reprimanded for the women. His wife Harriet learned of it from the newspapers. He continued to serve off the coast of Spain, became commodore at the Cape of Good Hope, and rose to rear admiral. It was an eccentric world. Procuring women on the high seas and endangering your men in order to do so was survivable. To break one's word was not. Edmund Temple was a midshipman on the *Narcisssus* frigate who was captured in a mad, gallant raid on the French coast at Hyeres.[15] He was imprisoned at Verdun. For breaking his parole by escaping, and incidentally for 'leaving behind debts to the amount of above £4,000 sterling,' he was court martialled and written down as 'never to be allowed to enter His Majesty's service again'.

So here, in the Black Books, is not only a richness of naval anecdotes but also an insight into a society where the patronage of the great could achieve almost anything, and where a man could sometimes get away with dark villainy, but not with breaking his parole.

---

[1] The Black Books of officers censured are at ADM 12/27B (1759-1794), 12/27C (1794-1807), and 12/27D (1807-15). The title Black Book appears on the spine of 12/27D. According to the usage of the time, 'officer' is taken to mean not only commissioned officer, but warrant officers like the master and surgeon and standing officers like the gunner and boatswain. In this article I have limited myself to sea officers and midshipmen. An alphabetical index of commissioned officers only, from 1741 to 1815, appears in 12/27E. Some early cases, from 1741, are mentioned in 12/27B, but seem to have been copied in when the book was started in 1759. Individual entries are brief, sometimes only three or four lines, but each gives the

date of the court martial (hereafter CM), which can then be traced by its date in ADM 1. A few CM reports are purely formal, giving only the charge and the decision. Most give summaries, sometimes at length, of each witness's evidence. A few appear to have been taken down in shorthand and to be more or less verbatim. Not all those men who appeared in the Black Book had been court martialled. Some, like one lieutenant who simply absconded from his ship in a foreign port, were entered after their admiral, or their ship's captain, wrote to the Admiralty secretary.

[2] CM 5 February 1810.

[3] CM 9 February 1796.

[4] CM 12-16 March 1795.

[5] CM 4 Dec 1797-1 January 1798.

[6] Nelson to Capt Albemarle Bertie, a member of the court, 4 Jan 1798. See Sir Nicholas Harris Nicolas, *Dispatches and Letters of Lord Nelson* (London: H. Colburn, 1846), iii, p. 1.

[7] CM 25 February 1805.

[8] CM 21 May 1801.

[9] CM 12 December 1793.

[10] CM 22 January 1802.

[11] CM 7 March 1811.

[12] CM 9 March 1805.

[13] Sir Nicholas Harris Nicolas, vi, p. 348 n.

[14] CM 28 October 1814.15 ADM 12/27D, p. 41.

Reasons for Going North: John Franklin, Nelson and Post-War Promotion

Andrew Lambert

While best known for the tragic, cannibal conclusions of his final mission to the high Arctic, perhaps the defining event of British Arctic exploration, Captain Sir John Franklin (1786-1847) began his naval career under Nelson and served at sea with distinction long before he headed north. To explain the disastrous end of his last expedition, a tale endlessly retold for moral improvement, morbid curiosity or the spread of geographical knowledge, Franklin is cast in many roles. For some he was a 'pathetic blunderer' and 'bungler' who lead his men, like some latter-day Grand Old Duke of York to their icy doom.[1] Others focus on his

Bronze bust of Franklin by Andrea Carlo Lucchesi, 1898, in the collections of the National Portrait Gallery.

age and his physical condition – he was 59, and in modern terms morbidly obese – to argue that he was the wrong man for the job. Even his apologists are content to leave him as the archetypal 'heroic explorer', a brave but simple soul, a type beloved by the Victorians. The truth, as ever, is very different. He remains an elusive subject, Traill's 1896 *Life of Sir John Franklin* was the first serious biography, but like many of those that have followed it was an explanation of a bronze statue in Waterloo Place to commemorate the so-called discovery of the North West Passage, rather than of the warm, humane man that book and bronze affected to portray.[2] Any attempt to understand that man needs to ask why he went to the Arctic, not once, or twice, but four times between 1818 and 1845.

Born on 15 April 1786 in the Lincolnshire village of Spilsby, John was the fifth son and ninth child of Willingham Franklin, local merchant and banker. Evidently the family had connections; by the time John reached school age his elder brothers had launched impressive careers. Willingham would become Chief Justice at Madras, while James entered the East India Company service as a military engineer, taking a prominent part in the survey of India. Rather than follow the eastward trend, John was determined to join the Royal Navy, against significant parental opposition. There is no evidence why he chose a naval career, a desire to travel, to escape from the bottom of the family heap, or just the exuberance of youth. He did have a local role model in Matthew Flinders, a relative by marriage and a close friend of his elder brothers Thomas and Willingham.[3] Critically he had the credentials and connections to enter the Navy as a candidate for commissioned rank. In the autumn of 1800 Franklin joined the Royal Navy on board the 64-gun battleship HMS *Polyphemus*.

At War and On Survey

He joined a navy at war, desperately stretched by the demands of a global conflict with France and Spain. While Franklin was coming to terms with his new life, living in the evil-smelling, airless bowels of the ship, working on the deck and climbing the rigging, Britain faced an existential threat. The neutral powers of Northern Europe, infuriated by Britain's aggressive use of naval power against France, especially the use of force to stop their highly profitable abuse of neutral rights to trade through the blockade, demanded a change of policy on pain of war. In late 1800 Paul I, the mad Tsar of Russia, dragooned Sweden, Denmark and Prussia into a coalition to demand concessions by the threat of force. If Britain backed down she would lose the war with France, if she rejected the Tsar's demands she faced four new enemies. The response was predictable: by March 1801 a powerful fleet had assembled, with Lord Nelson as second in command. When Nelson chose twelve ships to attack the Danish defence line of hulks and batteries guarding Copenhagen against a mortar bombardment he included the shallow draft *Polyphemus* among them.

On 2 April, a fortnight short of his fifteenth birthday, John Franklin found himself at the terrifying heart of a vicious naval battle. The two fleets fought to the finish. The Danes could not move; they had neither masts nor sails; the British were equally immobile, held in place by the iron will of their Admiral. Many men died that day, smashed to pulp by heavy iron shot or cut to ribbons by jagged oak splinters. After hours of stunning, cacophonous cannonade the Danes accepted an armistice, and Nelson persuaded them to leave the Coalition. Copenhagen was a savage baptism of fire, bringing Franklin face to face with the grim reality of his profession at a tender age. He was fortunate not to be among *Polyphemus's* thirty casualties.

Polyphemus returned to Britain just in time for Franklin to take up a midshipman's berth on Flinder's ship, HMS *Investigator*. They sailed that July to chart the coast of a continent Flinders would christen Australia. Family connections secured him the post, and Flinders, *in loco parentis*, would report back to Lincolnshire on the progress of his young protégée. There was good reason to report. Franklin had joined the remarkable dynasty of oceanic navigators that began with James Cook. Cook trained Bligh on his final, fatal voyage, while Bligh trained Matthew Flinders on his second, successful breadfruit voyage to Tahiti. Flinders would teach Franklin the business of navigation on the first circumnavigation of Australia.

Before they left England Flinders told Franklin's brother:

> *He is a very fine youth and there is every probability of his doing credit to the Investigator and to himself … after a few months he will be sufficiently of an astronomer to be my right hand man in that way. His attention to his duty has gained him the esteem of the first lieutenant who scarcely knows how to talk enough in his praise.*[4]

Captain Matthew Flinders (1774 –1814)
Courtesy Warwick Leadlay Gallery.

This voyage was the key to Franklin's character, ambitions and abilities. He left Britain a stunned schoolboy, and returned a proven seaman, raised in the school of Cook. Matthew Flinders was a living link with heroic voyages that had fired the imagination of the western world. Sir Joseph Banks, Cook's scientific companion, selected Flinders to combine the coastal survey of the entire continent with a large scientific programme. As commanding officer Flinders was responsible for the education of his midshipmen. He provided rich opportunities for practical and theoretical study, a forcing house of seamanship and science. Franklin was an enthusiastic student.[5] Only a blockhead would have missed the chance to master Flinders' curriculum, and Franklin was no blockhead. He profited from the fact that his Captain needed competent deck officers, surveyors and scientific observers when he reached Australia.

Flinders would use the voyage to develop his understanding of compass variation, a major issue for a seaman in distant, southerly latitudes. Magnetic science would be the key to Franklin's career, for at the very time he and Flinders were navigating the Australian coast the Prussian polymath Alexander von Humboldt was taking magnetic readings on the equator at Cajamarca in the Peruvian Andes. Franklin recorded compass deviation, astronomical observations and maintained the critical battery of chronometers used to determine longitude. Flinders communicated an enthusiasm for navigation, and Franklin learnt; 'everything that we can show him'.[6] Four years service on a smart frigate might have made Franklin a skilled ship handler under sail, and an able battle tactician, but this unimpressive, leaky merchant ship offered so much more, not least the suggestive original name of *Xenophon*. Franklin mastered the key elements of navigation and charting. Patience and thoroughness made him a trustworthy observer, and he had opportunities to demonstrate judgement and leadership.

The voyage was a typical mixture of long sea passages of almost interminable boredom, interspersed with periods of frenetic activity ashore and in the surveying boats. Whatever Flinders did Franklin was close by, and along with his naval lessons came a master-class in leadership. By 1804 Franklin was an adept student of navigation, astronomy and the other observational sciences that featured on the voyage. He picked up Flinders' obsession with the navigational problems caused by the deviation of the ship's magnetic compass. Flinders demonstrated that ship's own ironwork was a major cause of deviation and Banks published his findings in the Royal Society Journal *Philosophical Transactions* in 1805.

On the Australian coast Franklin also buckled down to the study of French, a decision prompted by the unusual experience of meeting a French warship during the brief Peace of Amiens. He found it difficult to converse with the French in Latin! Franklin also worked his way through Flinders' library, a fine cross-section of contemporary naval, exploring, cultural and scientific material. Above all, he profited from the example of his Captain.

Shipwrecked on the Barrier Reef, Flinders demonstrated how to lead men in adversity, calmly building camp and salvaging supplies before sailing an open boat back to Sydney for help. Anxious to bring his cartographic work before the Admiralty, Flinders took the first ship home after rescuing his men. There was little space on board, so he had to leave most of his officers and men behind. Franklin was fortunate to be among them. By now Britain and France were once more at war, and when he landed on Mauritius Flinders was arrested by General Decaen, the angry, punctilious French Governor, and detained for the better part of a decade without good cause.

However, Franklin was far from safe. He took a ship from Sydney to Canton for a passage home on an East India ship. French warships were at large in the Indian Ocean, they were looking for prizes and there were none richer than an East India Convoy. Fortunately Convoy Commodore George Dance was no fool, knowing his ships could neither run nor hide he prepared for trouble. His fleet of 18 lumbering merchant Argosies was intercepted in the Banda Strait by five powerful French warships, but Dance was ready. He drilled his big merchant ships to masquerade as battleships, and gave them a suitable coat of paint. The deception was almost credible, at a distance. The East Indiamen were big two decked vessels, but any naval officer worth his salt would see through the disguise at fighting range: they were too narrow in the beam, too lightly manned, and armed with pop guns. Undeterred by such obvious flaws in his scheme Dance drilled the convoy to behave like a battle squadron, his naval passengers providing signals expertise. As soon as he sighted the French Dance took the initiative, sailing towards Admiral Linois and conducting a series of smartly executed naval manoeuvres that bluffed the Frenchman into retreating. While Linois became the laughing stock of the French Navy Franklin, Dance's signal officer during the battle, earned a commendation for his 'zeal and alacrity'. Evidently he had read the naval tactical and signalling material in Flinders' library with some attention.

Trafalgar and New Orleans

The day after returning to Britain Franklin was appointed to HMS *Bellerophon*, the famous old 74, already the hero of the 'Glorious First of June' and the Nile. After a spell of blockade duty off Brest *Bellerophon* was detached to Cadiz, and on 21 October 1805 earned the ultimate battle honour in Lord Collingwood's division. Once again Franklin was the signals officer, but this time the quarterdeck lived up to its nickname 'the slaughter pen'.

Forty-seven men stood there that day, only seven, including Franklin, avoided death or injury. Many, like Nelson on *Victory*, were hit by musketry and canister from the enemy ships. Not until the last French gun fell silent, the marksmen shot by *Bellerophon's* marines, was Franklin safe. Captain John Cooke had not been so fortunate: his death placed First Lieutenant William Pryce Cumby in command, securing instant promotion to Captain.[7] Cumby and Franklin would be lifelong friends, meeting to commemorate the famous day under the old ship's flag into the 1830s. However, Trafalgar left Franklin stunned and deafened. His hearing never fully recovered, and although impaired hearing was not unusual for a career naval officer it proved to be a serious handicap when he moved into Colonial Government.

With the shattered *Bellerophon* under repair Franklin moved to another 74, HMS *Bedford*. This time his luck ran out. For the next decade he could only inch his way up the promotion ladder, lacking well-placed patrons, or the chance to secure promotion by some signal act of personal bravery. Finally commissioned Lieutenant on 11 February 1808, he was aged 22: Nelson had been a Captain at 20, and so had many of Franklin's contemporaries. Cruising service off Rio de Janeiro and the River Scheldt provided little opportunity for distinction. With Flinders far away, unable to help himself it seemed Franklin was doomed to a slow career. To make matters worse brother Thomas managed to lose the family business, and most of the savings. Franklin scraped together what he could of his meagre pay to help out.

In April 1814 Franklin's career prospects took a turn for the worse: Napoleon abdicated, peace was restored and the Navy would be paid off. There were far more lieutenants than the Navy could hope to employ in peacetime, and he had little prospect of promotion. It seemed that his career was as good as over when the *Bedford* joined the Duke of Clarence's fleet to escort the victorious allied sovereigns to England. Then Flinders, his only naval patron, died on the eve of fame.[8] Desperate for promotion Franklin wrote to old *Investigator* shipmate Dr Robert Brown, now installed as librarian, amanuensis and confidante in Sir Joseph Banks' Soho Square office. Brown enquired if Franklin would be interested in a naval expedition, voyages of discovery might resume now that peace had returned. If so, Brown would be happy to recommend him.[9] Banks added Flinders relative to his list of scientific seamen. Franklin was too old and wise in the ways of officialdom to give an unqualified acceptance. He was interested, but left Brown in no doubt that he would expect promotion in return for years of service and possible loss of health – Flinders had died of renal failure. Having made his terms he stressed his anxiety to serve on the type of scientific mission that Banks had in mind.

For the moment Franklin was fortunate that Britain had other enemies. His luck changed when *Bedford* was ordered the West Indies in late 1814, joining the fleet off New Orleans. The British planned an amphibious operation to capture the city, despite the difficulties posed by impassable terrain, vile weather and even the enemy. Finally Franklin had an opportunity to stamp his character on proceedings amid the ruins of a desperate, ill-starred enterprise. The British planned to cut into the Mississippi river from the east, across Lake Borgne. The Lake was occupied by five American gunboats, and

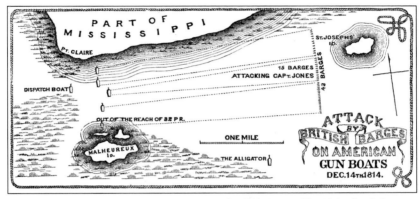

Plan of the British Attack on Lake Borgne, 14 December 1812. Courtesy Warwick Leadlay Gallery.

they had to be captured before the troops could be landed. In a daring attack fifty British boats sailed across the Lake to a point just beyond range of the American guns, about two miles. There they anchored, took lunch and rested for an hour. Suitably refreshed the boats rowed to attack the powerful American craft. All five American vessels were taken by boarding, at a cost of 17 dead and 78 wounded. Franklin commanded one of the *Bedford's* boats, leading by example: he was the first to board his chosen target, and was slightly wounded in the process.

Franklin spent the next nine weeks on detached service with the Army, helping to land and sustain the troops as they prepared to attack the city. This was dismal work, perpetually cold and wet. On the day of battle he led a party of seamen assisting General Thornton's troops to cross the river and attack a key American battery on the left bank, flanking General Andrew Jackson's main American defence line. Thornton's men, the sailors well to the front, stormed the American position under heavy fire. The operation had been entirely successful, all that remained was to turn the battery to enfilade

Jackson's trenches on the left bank, and let the sailors loose on the canon. Instead they were recalled. General Sir Edward Pakenham had not waited to learn the result of Thornton's operation: instead he launched a hopeless frontal assault on Jackson's well prepared entrenchments. Pakenham and many of his men were killed in a one sided exchange, leaving the Navy, once again, to evacuate a demoralised army. Finally, Franklin had made a name for himself, General Lambert mentioned him in dispatches, and recommended him for promotion. However the battle had been lost, and with that went Franklin's chance of becoming a Commander.

Returning to Britain the *Bedford* paid off on 5 July and two days later Franklin was appointed First Lieutenant of HMS *Forth*, Captain Sir William Bolton, serving during Napoleon's 'Hundred Days' and the second Bourbon restoration. Sir William was only a few years older than Franklin, but Nelson's nephew had been promoted quickly. If Franklin was going to make a career he had to catch up such sons of fortune by his own endeavours. His wartime career had not been without honour or merit, but promotion had been painfully slow. Flinders' imprisonment had been costly; his death could have been a disaster. After reading Flinders' narrative Franklin regretted the book was too dry for the general reader. It would establish Flinders' 'character as a good navigator' but he was disappointed not to be mentioned more favourably.[10] His own narratives would be more highly coloured, and he caught the popular audience.

Although stingy with praise Flinders left Franklin his telescope, that he might see his way ahead, an interest in magnetism, and the patronage of Sir Joseph Banks. That Banks, Flinders and Franklin were born not five miles apart in central Lincolnshire emphasised the personal nature of patronage at the turn of the nineteenth century. Banks made it possible for Franklin to begin his second career, in the ice. Flinders taught Franklin another vital lesson, his temper cost him six years detention on Mauritius. Franklin would be the very model of calm dignity. Flinders' name was made by a great voyage, and a great narrative, Franklin followed the model and reaped the rewards.

A Tragic Hero

While the prospect of promotion may have seemed distant when Franklin paid off in September 1815, he had been thinking about his career options. The First Lord of the Admiralty confirmed, in writing, that the only hope of promotion lay in service abroad. Once ashore he paid his respects to Flinders' widow, visited his family at Spilsby and called on Sir Joseph at nearby Revesby Abbey. Banks recommended studies 'that would better prepare me for the service of any other expedition which might offer.' Never one to miss a hint Franklin applied himself to mastering marine surveying, 'as a source of amusement and improvement during the time of my being unemployed, and even when employed I shall hope to have opportunities of practising, what I now learn by theory.'[11] The quality of those studies would soon be evident on the Arctic chart.

Sir John Franklin and his officers, engravings based upon the daguerreotype portraits of 1845, Gleason's Pictorial Drawing-Room Companion, 1851. Courtesy Huw Lewis-Jones.

Franklin was lucky not to be selected for the first post-war scientific exploring mission. James Tuckey's 1816 Congo expedition made some progress up river, but tropical diseases killed Tuckey and most of crew. Instead the Arctic became Franklin's theatre. In 1817 he was appointed to command the Lincolnshire built merchant ship *Trent* on a voyage towards the North Pole, which Banks and the Royal Society had secured to follow up observations made by Whitby whaling skipper and scientist William Scoresby.[12] By heading north these ships would demonstrate British territorial claims, by charting and naming the coast, while the leading scientists of the day entrusted the officers with a number of experiments, the most important of which dealt with magnetic phenomena and other navigational issues. Although slightly overawed by the eminence of his new friends Franklin found himself comfortable in the company of learned men, and leading social figures. His natural dignity and profound faith provided a strong reservoir of stability in what would be a challenging, dangerous and troublesome public life.[13] He might not have an illustrious pedigree, or the status of the Fellow of the Royal Society, but he had been round the world, made observations, and above all he had fought the King's enemies. He was somebody, and above all if this venture paid off he could expect to be promoted. Nor were those hopes disappointed. As he headed north he wrote to Banks, to ensure he would not be forgotten whenever a scientific expedition was projected.[14] Those letters established him as a member of the expeditionary branch of the Royal Navy, they emphasised his willingness to serve scientific agendas, and his attention to detail.

Within five years Franklin had marched across the Canadian Arctic, eating his boots and other unsavoury delicacies along the way, secured promotion to Post Captain, become a Fellow of the Royal Society and entered the social elite. He would go on to command a frigate, earn a knighthood from Nelson's old friend William IV, govern a colony and be entrusted with the most important scientific expedition of the age. Going north transformed Franklin's career, and it made many more careers, not least among those who went to search for him.

In their anxiety to obscure the failure of expedition, and horrific evidence of large scale cannibalism, Franklin's widow, his friends and the establishment created the myth that he had 'discovered' the North West Passage and died in completing his mission, and that such a barren achievement entitled him to be the second naval officer accorded a public statue in central London. Lady Franklin wanted to put him in Trafalgar Square, but he ended up in Waterloo Place, half between the Athenaeum, a club he helped to found, and the Royal Society, of which he had been a Fellow. Little wonder his name and reputation were shredded by revisionists who mistook the bronze effigy for the man. John Franklin was a scientific seaman, a superb navigator, and a combat veteran with a fine fighting record; his approach to post-war promotion reveals a steely inner resolve, and a sophisticated approach to playing the system. He checked the options, used his opportunities and tapped into the best source of patronage. Far from the bumbling duffer of revisionist accounts he was shrewd and calculating, traits he would display throughout a post-war career littered with prize appointments, preferment and plaudits. There were opportunities to earn promotion after 1815, but only for those who knew where to look, and how to earn it.

[1] Roland Huntford, *Scott and Amundsen: The Race to the Pole* (London: Hodder and Stoughton, 1979), p. 10 and p. 22.

[2] Henry Duff Traill, *The Life of Sir John Franklin* (London: John Murray, 1896).

[3] Miriam Estensen, *The Life of Matthew Flinders* (Sydney: Allen and Unwin, 2002).

[4] Flinders to Thomas Franklin 7 July 1801: Royal Geographical Society MS: Franklin Papers SJF.

[5] Estensen, p. 90 and p. 142. Jean Fornasiero, Peter Monteath and John West-Sooby, *Encountering Terra Australis: The Australian Voyages of Nicolas Baudin and Matthew Flinders* (Kent Town: Wakefield Press, 2004), p. 192 and p. 289.

[6] Estensen, p. 211 and p. 216.

[7] David Cordingly, *Billy Ruffian: The Bellerophon and the Downfall of Napoleon* (London: Bloomsbury, 2003).

[8] Franklin to Dr. Robert Brown 18 August 1814 and 28 August 1814: Scott Polar Research Institute (hereafter SPRI) Franklin MS 248/296/1 & 3.

[9] Brown to Franklin 25 August 1814: SPRI MS 248/296/2.

[10] Franklin to Brown 9 June 1815: SPRI MS 248/296/5.

[11] Franklin to Brown 5 March 1816: SPRI MS 248/295/4.

[12] Banks to Scoresby 18 February 1818: *The Banks Letters: A Calendar of the Manuscript Correspondence of Sir Joseph Banks etc*, edited by Warren Royal Dawson (London: British Museum, 1958), p. 740.

[13] Franklin to Isabella Cracroft (his sister) 6 April 1818: SPRI MS 248/298/7.

[14] Franklin to Captain Henry Kater, Royal Engineers, leader of the Royal Society geodetic project 9 May 1818: Wellcome Institute MS 7486/84. Franklin to Banks 7 May 1818: SPRI MS 962/11, original MS from McCord Museum McGill University Montreal.

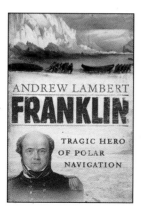

Editors' Note: Andrew Lambert's *Franklin: Tragic Hero of Polar Navigation* was published by Faber & Faber in 2009.

Lieutenant Henry T.D. Le Vesconte, daguerreotype by Richard Beard, London, 1845. The original is in the collections of the Scott Polar Research Institute, Cambridge. A second set, made at the same time is now presumed lost. For a long while it was supposed to be in the collections of the National Maritime Museum, or the Derbyshire Record Office, Matlock, but they have only print reproductions. This image, after a photograph by Martin Hartley, has been flipped horizontally in order to be viewed correctly.

'Nelsons of Discovery':
Notes on the Franklin Monument in Greenwich

Huw Lewis-Jones

We are of opinion that the Erebus and Terror should be moored hence-forth on either side of Victory, floating monuments of what the Nelsons of Discovery can dare and do at the call of their country in the service of the world.[1]

In 1845, Sir John Franklin and his crews bade their farewells as their ships *Erebus* and *Terror* slipped down the Thames, heading out on their scientific voyage into the Arctic and the unknown. They were last seen late that summer, moored to an iceberg high in Lancaster Bay.[2] They were never seen again. Over more than a decade of anguish, some thirty expeditions were sent out in search of the party. Traces of the missing expedition's first winter camp on Beechey Island were found in 1850 but its route in the years following remained unclear. In 1854, Dr John Rae brought back clues to their demise, with relics and Inuit stories that the expedition had perished somewhere to the west of the Back River. In 1859, 150 years ago this year, the Irish explorer Leopold McClintock returned to London bearing terrible news. With recovered artefacts, he finally confirmed that Franklin and all his men had perished. The nation mourned their loss – it was one of the greatest tragedies in the history of naval exploration.

In the Old Royal Naval College, Greenwich, there is a Monument to Sir John Franklin and those brave men who died alongside him. Designed by Royal Academician Richard Westmacott, the Monument was erected by Order of Parliament in the Painted Hall in 1858. Following building work, it was moved to the Chapel in 1938. A skeleton recovered by American explorer Charles Francis Hall was identified by family members as Lieutenant Henry Le Vesconte of HMS *Erebus*. His bones were returned for entombment in the Monument in 1873, the only remains that ever made it home to England.

After years of neglect, this Monument has been restored and relocated. This research note will detail this work and give additional information about some of the contemporary responses to memorialising Franklin's achievement. Conservation work began in May this year and has taken over five months to complete. The Monument now has pride of place in the Chapel vestibule, at the main entrance and fully accessible to public view. The impressive memorial comprises an inscription tablet with a list of the officers of the lost expedition, a pediment with wreaths of oak and olive, flanked by the figures of a naval officer and a desolate sailor. In the background - the upper yards of two departing vessels and, high above the crush of towering icebergs, the Pole Star.

'The End of an Epic'

One of the first men to see Admiral Nelson's famous signal at Trafalgar was likely the young signal officer on board the *Bellerophon*, John Franklin. In 1844, he would likewise respond to the Admiralty's call for another Arctic expedition with the words, ' … the highest object of my desire is faithfully to perform my duty'. In doing so, he was destined to become the most famous explorer of the nineteenth century, heralded in verse, eulogised in the newspapers, romanticised upon grand canvases, and memorialised in stone. Writing for *The Quarterly Review* in 1847, Francis Egerton, Lord Ellesmere, extolled Franklin's virtues:

> *Few greater pleasures, indeed, are ours than when, from our literary signal-post, we can make the number of one of those gallant vessels, returning 'rough with many a scar' of bloodless conflict with the floe and iceberg, and with its log one continuous record of danger and difficulty vanquished by courage and intelligence, and of triumphs unpurchased by other human suffering than the voluntary endurance of the wise and brave in pursuit of noble ends. Well pleased have we lingered so long within the confines of that Arctic Circle which had been penetrated by so many expeditions, and with interest which accumulates by the hour do we watch for the return of those two vessels which are, perhaps, even now working their southward course through Behring's Straits into the Pacific. Should the happiness be yet allowed us of witnessing that return, we are of opinion that the Erebus and Terror should be moored hence-forth on either side of Victory, floating monuments of what the Nelsons of Discovery can dare and do at the call of their country in the service of the world.*[3]

This buoyant optimism was soon replaced by the spectre of tragedy, horror, cannibalism and butchery. The honest truth of the Franklin disaster would not make for pleasant reading. Like his hero Nelson, his reputation would attract a close scrutiny, with elements of his successes picked over, in what

Sir Francis Leopold McClintock, and a view of the his steam-yacht Fox, photographed by Lieutenant John Cheyne in 1859. The dual images were available to the public as 'stereoscopic slides' in 1860. Courtesy Private Collection.

seems like an endless historical post-mortem. In an ongoing cycle of books, reviews, commentary and debate, Franklin has been as much maligned as adored ever since he left London that summer of 1845.

Those hopes that sent Franklin's voyage north, and longed for his safe return, were dashed with Leopold McClintock's arrival from King William Island, aboard the steam-yacht Fox. Anchored off the Isle of Wight on 21 September 1859, he wrote a lengthy report to the Admiralty. He went ashore at Portsmouth and took the train to London carrying with him his papers, the record found at Point Victory, and two cases filled with recovered objects belonging to members of the lost expedition. He wanted to call first upon Franklin's widow, Lady Jane, but she was in the south of France. The next day, on 22 September, he presented himself at the Admiralty. Within two hours information was sent direct to the Editor of *The Times*, and a leading article broke the news the following morning.[4] Within a few days the weeklies picked up the story and within the week news had spread across the world. The floodgates of publicity had been opened.

Upon arrival in London, McClintock was photographed by Lieutenant Cheyne, a shipmate from an earlier search expedition, appearing in a bold pose beside some of the relics, then on display in the museum of the United Service Institution. Many of relics were also later displayed in the Painted Hall, where the large Monument in Franklin's memory had been installed late in 1858, in advance of McClintock's homecoming.[5] The relics collected by Rae had also been shown in the Painted Hall in 1854.[6] Cheyne sold guinea-priced sets of these stereoviews direct from his London home to an eager public.[7] Having left shrouded in uncertainty and scepticism, the McClintock voyage was now afforded a hero's welcome, for finally putting an end to speculation about the fate of the missing explorers.

The Franklin saga found its way into homes on both sides of the Atlantic, and into the hearts of the public who had followed the search expeditions in the newspapers, in illustrated lectures, and in the books they bought. It had assumed such proportions of national disaster, that *Sharpe's London Magazine* tearfully declared the news, 'The End of an Epic'.[8] Voices from all sorts of periodical journals added to the clamour of commentary, within a vibrant print culture. 'The ephemeral at a penny and the portly quarterly up to six shillings all alike joined in the general exultation', as one hack put it. The reading public for the disaster now swelled to include 'millions of sympathizing souls', according to *The Illustrated London News* and editors scrambled to profit from the sensation. *Once a Week* imagined Franklin's final moments: '... then the shout of victory, which cheered the last hour of Nelson and of Wolfe, rang not the less heartily round the bed of the gallant Franklin, and lit up that kind eye with its last gleam of triumph. Like them, his last thought must have been of his country's glory'.[9] 'At last the mystery of FRANKLIN'S fate is solved', reported *The Times*:

> *... we know the very day of his death ... Alas! There can be no longer those sad wailings from an imaginary Tintagel to persuade the credulous that an Arthur still lives ... The dauntless soul dies out amid frost and snow; the spirit is never quenched though the body may perish ... We retire now from the contest with honour, if with grief, and we leave the name of FRANKLIN engraved on the furthest pillars which the energy of mankind has dared to erect as the landmark of its research in the dull and lifeless region that guards the axis of the world.*[10]

Yet, Arctic heroics insisted on staying in fashion. John Murray released McClintock's narrative of the expedition, *The Voyage of the Fox in the Arctic Seas*, in late December. The first edition – of 10,000 copies, a considerable printing – sold out within a month.[11] The volume was published in lavish octavo priced at sixteen shillings. It was expensive, a luxury item, but demand was high. Mudie's Circulating Library took 3,000 copies. The book was both a best-seller and a 'most-borrowed', even surpassing Dickens's latest novel. Work began on a second edition immediately and it appeared in March 1860. By way of comparison, Darwin's *The Origin of Species*, also published by Murray that winter, had by the same time sold about 5,000 copies. Darwin's fame would soon eclipse all, of course, but for the moment there seemed to be no end to the public interest in the Franklin drama. The evolution of his posthumous reputation, however, was just beginning.

The mystery and tragedy surrounding Franklin's voyage stirred balladeers and novelists to their own expressions of loss and elegy. Many turned to poetry as an outlet for their grief, whilst others responded to public interest in an effort to sell their work. Poems can be found in many of the periodicals and newspapers throughout this period, from Dickens's journal *Household Words* to *The Illustrated London News*.[12] Such was the public interest when McClintock returned, that one finds evidence of local polar poetry contests held in schools and village halls. Newspapers carry these poetic memorials – no real surprise, they are mostly rather bad. 'Sleep! Martyrs of discovery, sleep!', wrote Nicholas Michell in the *New Monthly*:

> *Your winding-sheets the Polar snows;*
> *What though the cold winds o'er ye sweep,*
> *And on your graves no flowret blows,*
> *Your memories long shall flourish fair,*
> *Your story to the world proclaim*
> *What dauntless British hearts can dare;*
> *Sleep! Lost ones, sleep! Embalmed in fame.*[13]

Several large institutions also held contests for the best poetic tribute. On 8 February 1860, for example, a national announcement in the *Guardian* declared: 'The Vice-Chancellor of Oxford has received from "a non-resident member of the University much attached to her interests" the sum of £50, for a prize to be awarded to the writer of the best English poem on "The Life, the Character and the Death of the heroic seaman Sir John Franklin, which special reference to the time, place, and discovery of his death'. The poem was to be in rhymed verse to be recited during the meeting of the British Association for the Advancement of Science, which was having its peripatetic annual gathering in Oxford that year. The contest was won by a Canadian undergraduate, Owen Alexander Vidal, for his *A Poem Upon the Life and Character of Sir John Franklin*. Far better was a poem that did not win, Algernon Swinburne's *The Death of Sir John Franklin* – his first

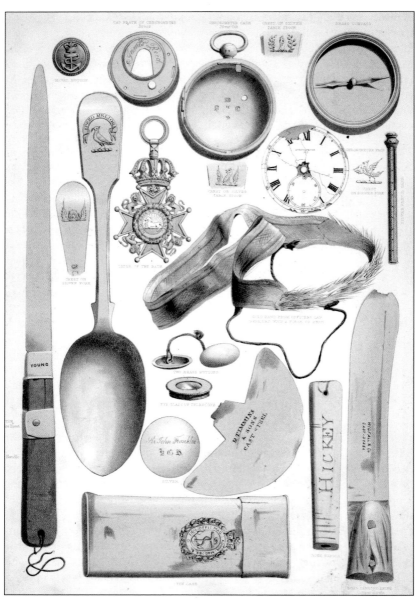

'Franklin Relics Brought by Dr Rae', from W. W. May's *A Series of Fourteen Sketches Made During the Voyage up Wellington Channel in Search of Sir John Franklin*, plate XIV, chromo-lithograph by Day, London, 1855. Courtesy Huw Lewis-Jones.

original poem and his first directly inspired by the sea, a theme for which he would later become well-known:

> This is the end. There is no nobler word
> In the large writing and scored marge of time
> Than such endurance is ...
>
> So long the record of these men shall stand,
> Because they chose not life but rather death,
> Each side being weighed with a most equal hand,
> Because the gift they had of English breath
> They did give back to England for her sake
> Like those dead seamen of Elizabeth
> And those who wrought with Nelson and with Blake
> To do great England service their lives long --
> High honour shall they have; their deeds shall make
>
> Their spoken names sound sweeter than all song ...
> These chose the best; therefore their name shall be
> Part of all noble things that shall be done,
> Part of the royal record of the sea.[14]

At the same time, Lady Franklin was doing her very best to script this 'record' and preserve her husband's enduring reputation.[15] A key component of McClintock's homecoming, for example, had been his assertion, urged by Lady Franklin, that the Northwest Passage had been 'discovered'. On 14 November 1859, before a huge meeting of RGS members, McClintock read a memoir of his *Fox* voyage that helped to construct this idea of Franklin's lasting achievement. Although McClure 'was worthily rewarded for making a North-West Passage', RGS President Sir Roderick Murchison would agree that 'Franklin was the man who had made *the* North-West Passage'.[16] In her dogged insistence that her husband be immortalized in this way, Lady Franklin turned failure into triumph by creating a legend. She quickly moved to set his legacy in stone.

In 1861 a statue was erected in Hobart, for which the Tasmanian Legislature voted one thousand pounds; later that year another statue, executed under Lady Franklin's supervision, was placed in the market place at Spilsby, the Lincolnshire town in which he was born.[17] Its pedestal bears the inscription that Franklin was 'Discoverer' of the Passage. Lady Franklin, it seems, had been unhappy with the first memorial ordered by the Admiralty in July 1855 at the Royal Naval Hospital in Greenwich. It was intended to honour the fallen, to provide closure: a chance for the Navy to reflect but also to *move on* from the tragedy. Westmacott's Monument to Franklin was duly approved, but Jane was dissatisfied that the official search would not continue. In 1858 in Greenwich, Westmacott carved the memory of Rear Admiral Franklin into stone, only for the returning hero McClintock, the following year, to demote him to captain by discovering his death had occurred before his promotion. The marble slab has forever been inaccurate, just one of many half-truths about the tragedy borne forward by the passage of time.

On 15 November 1866, in the heart of London and just a short walk from Nelson in Trafalgar Square, an eight-foot bronze statue was unveiled in

Sir John Franklin, tinted lithographic portrait, engraved by McFarlane and Erskine, Edinburgh, 1877. Courtesy Huw Lewis-Jones.

Waterloo Place before the First Lord of the Admiralty. Lady Franklin watched on approvingly from the upper windows of her husband's old club, the Athenaeum. The ceremony was widely covered in the papers. *The Spectator*, for example, gave its tribute: 'In the Arctic Seas Sir John Franklin's name is that of the first martyr, at Trafalgar – Nelson's. Franklin will always be remembered for his victory over the elements, and not over men'.[18] Franklin was memorialised in a heroic pose, 'addressing his officers and crew, and telling them that the North-West Passage had at last been discovered'.[19]

Yet, however deeply felt the mid-century fascination with Franklin's tale, press attentions soon moved to other stages, with public interest attracted to new heroes and exciting new types of colonial warfare. After such terrible cost – both human and financial – the Government would take great persuasion to look again to the North. The official search effort had cost over £600,000, and it is estimated the total amount spent by 1860 was nearly £2 million. In 1865, Sherard Osborn attempted to open a new campaign by reading a paper at the RGS calling for a renewal of Arctic endeavour. This time, however, the North Pole would be the prize. Echoing the arguments of that great expedition patron, the late Second Secretary of the Admiralty, Sir John Barrow, Osborn declared: 'The Navy needs some action to wake it up from the sloth of routine, and save it from the canker of prolonged peace. Arctic exploration is more wholesome for it, in a moral as well as a sanitary point of view, than any more Ashantee or Japanese wars'.[20] A heroic return to the fray was necessary, not least, to suppress the lingering truths, doubts and fears, about the cannibalistic demise of the Franklin party – those 'hobgoblin tales of the fate of the survivors', he later wrote.[21] It was time to go back, he declared, time to start anew. That RGS meeting, on 23 January, was one of the most crowded ever assembled. 'We are no more prepared to turn our backs upon the Arctic Regions because Sir John Franklin died off King William Island', he continued, 'than to do so to an enemy's fleet because Nelson fell at Trafalgar'.[22] The audience, with RGS Gold Medallist Jane Franklin among them, offered cheers in support. Whilst the promise of a return to the Arctic was met with approval here, the project was soon forestalled. The Arctic was no longer the best place for the formation of an empire's heroes. Exploration in central Africa, naval engagement in southeast Asia, and the suppression of a mutinous Indian sub-continent all provided a new crop of dutiful champions ready to die in the name of empire.

On 31 July 1875, shortly after Lady Franklin's death, a memorial was unveiled in Westminster Abbey, which further enshrined Franklin's claim as discoverer of the Northwest Passage. A bust by Noble in white Carrara marble sits beneath a canopy of 'rich gothic foliage' by Sir George Gilbert Scott. An inscription details Franklin's achievement, accompanied by a bas-relief of a ship beset in mountainous ice. The epitaph is by Tennyson, his nephew by marriage, and it elegantly captures his posthumous apotheosis:

> *Not here: the white North has thy bones; and thou,*
> *Heroic sailor-soul*
> *Art passing on thine happier voyage now,*
> *Toward no earthly pole.*[23]

Lady Franklin had campaigned vigorously to protect her husband's legacy by developing a series of official fictions that would endure, as if etched in stone. Though many approved of her proprietary zeal, an equal number thought the whole debate an unnecessary one; the Passage itself long revealed to be 'utterly worthless'. The Franklin expedition was a disaster – perhaps the most consummate tragedy of the nineteenth century – and he had neither 'discovered', nor completed, a Northwest Passage. Nevertheless his image as naval hero, an explorer without equal, would be passed swiftly on to the next generation.

The fiftieth anniversary of the departure of the Franklin expedition in 1895 presented an opportunity to celebrate past glories. The Royal Naval Exhibition of 1891 – with its impressive 'Franklin Gallery', stuffed full with portraiture, relics, and polar memories – had already set the stage, investing the tragedy with the qualities of a national epic. Franklin as sailor hero had found his martyrdom in a heady mix of science, piety and naval achievement.[24] The Royal Scottish Geographical Society commemorated the anniversary with a symposium and exhibition in Edinburgh.[25] The RGS organised a gala meeting and a dinner attended by a host of Arctic veterans. Two steamers were chartered on 19 May to take members of the public, including more than three hundred RGS Fellows, downstream to Greenwich to view the Franklin relics and the Painted Hall, stocked with 'so many portraits of England's naval heroes'.[26] Commandant Le Clerc, representing the Paris Geographical Society, placed a wreath on the obelisk erected there to Lieutenant Bellot. Clements Markham, now President of the RGS, justified the occasion:

> *A commemoration, such as that which we now celebrate, serves more than one useful purpose. It recalls the memory of brave men who did their duty well and nobly in their generation. It revives and freshens our knowledge of their work, and of what we owe to them for the examples they have set us, and for the credit their labours have secured for our country. It enforces on our minds the lessons to be derived from the past, in our efforts to work for the present and for the future. Above all, the renewal of an interest in former achievements has a tendency to incite among our younger associates a feeling of admiration, which is a direct incentive to emulation in the same glorious field of geographical research.[27]*

Markham engineered the commemorations, reconstructing an image of Franklin's achievements, both as a promotional exercise for the RGS and as way to vivify his polar ambitions. 'We look back then ... at those two brave ships moving down the river just half a century ago, as the starting-point whence to trace a continuous stream of high-souled effort, and of magnificent results, down to this present day, when we strive to make an Antarctic Expedition the chief and the most practical outcome of our Franklin Commemoration tonight'.[28] Before directing his audience to adjourn to a side-hall, which had been set up to contain an exhibition of Arctic relics and naval portraiture, the veteran explorer McClintock rose to offer the toast, describing the 'gallantry' of Franklin's 'heroic band of Christian men'. 'In laying down their lives at the call of duty, our countrymen bequeathed to us a rich gift', he declared, 'one more beacon light to guide our sons to deeds of heroism in the future. These examples of unflinching courage, devotion to duty, and endurance of hardship, are as life-blood to naval enterprise'.[29]

By the end of the nineteenth century, Franklin's very obvious failure had been reconstructed into a satisfying victory: not only he had 'forged the last link' to complete a Northwest Passage, but, more importantly, he had met death in the manner of a Christian hero. As a counterpoint to the worst excesses of the 'new imperialism' of the 1890s, with its aggressive triumphalism, many returned to the understated qualities of the Franklin story. Whilst new national heroes would in the future emerge in the Antarctic rather than in the North, this did not greatly erode the Arctic's appeal, which recent historians suggest to have been on the wane.[30] It was precisely because of renewed polar interest and the threat of new nations taking part in the 'race for the South', that the historical achievements of the Navy in the Arctic burned more brightly. Polar exploration and the Navy made ideal partners, Markham would conclude, encouraging 'that spirit of maritime enterprise which has ever distinguished the English people'.[31]

The first major biographical treatment of the 'Heroic Sailor-Soul' came in 1896 with the publication of Henry Traill's *The Life of Sir John Franklin*. It provided the details of Franklin's life that would form the basis for many subsequent accounts.[32] This was a late-Victorian Franklin, however; a figure born at the 1891 exhibition, a publicity image for the Navy undergoing a crisis of confidence, a monument shorn of his humanity and tenderness – redoubtable but not real. Richard Cyriax built on Traill's narrative to produce a classic account, first published in 1939, making excellent use of primary sources, Parliamentary papers and other surviving records, and it still stands as an accurate narrative of Franklin's life and career.[33] Whilst there was a trickle of new information, most notably the publishing of some private correspondence, and new insights into Franklin's career in Tasmania as a colonial administrator, most accounts stuck to the tragedy, and provided increasingly facile adventure narratives.[34]

A fine narrative by Roderic Owen, published in 1978, revisited Franklin's life in a well-illustrated iconography and added new details to Cyriax's account, yet offered little to explain his imaginative legacy.[35] Richard Davis, a Canadian academic, recognised the continuing irony of Franklin's posthumous reputation: 'The man who charted nearly 3,000 km of the coastline of North America is best remembered as the leader of an expedition that cost the British Admiralty two ships and the lives of 129 men and that made no direct contribution to the geographical unfolding of the Canadian Arctic'.[36] In 1986, the bicentenary of Franklin's birth, a commemorative service was held in the Chapel of the Royal Naval College. Franklin's biographer Owen gave an Address and Rear Admiral Sir Edmund Irving KBE CB – a former Hydrographer of the Navy, and a descendant of Lieutenant Irving of HMS *Terror* – read a Lesson in tribute to the men who fell alongside Franklin.

Clearly, explorers mean many things to many people. Attitudes range considerably over time, to be re-made and re-imagined by those who look again at the historical record, moving selectively through its cultural detritus. Even today Franklin is still chiefly remembered for his failure, a man cast into pantomime villainy; transformed into sound-bite in popular histories as a 'bumbling fool', a 'symbol of British doughtiness', a 'gallant loser' bound by naval hubris. He was a ripe target for this uneven modern critique, perhaps, elevated as he was by a host of Victorian admirers, but an endless and reductive anti-hagiography is injurious to the historical record. Nuance and balance is a must when scrutinising the heroes of our past. Not least, most of these polemics forgot some of the main reasons for British Arctic exploration during this period: as an operational training ground for naval men in their ships and motivated often as scientific enterprises, not a mere dash for a Passage, or for the Pole, although often described in this way by enthusiastic lobbyists. Franklin was a man of his time, excellent, limited, ambitious, innocent of our standards.

In 1984, the body of John Torrington, a seaman on the Franklin expedition, was exhumed from his grave on Beechey Island before the world's media, and the startling image of his frozen corpse was beamed across the globe.[37] The grizzly details of the Franklin story – a dramatic narrative of botulism,

man-hauling, cannibalism, and hardihood in the harsh northern landscape –
continue to capture public imaginations. There have been beautiful poetic
tributes; popular songs; a great number of 'disaster' novels and other less-
successful fictional re-creations; innumerable Internet sites; and some
engaging television documentaries.[38] One recent feature, *The Lost
Expedition*, revelled in the rumours of cannibalism and suffering to advertise
its programme. Andrew Lambert, Laughton Professor of Naval History at
King's College London, provided some well-needed rigour to the account.[39]
More satisfying, of course, was his elegant biography of Franklin, published
earlier this year.[40] He recognised that popular authors, journalists and
novelists have done wonders to reinvigorate general interest in Arctic
exploration history, but warned that there is real risk in sound-bite and
simplification. British explorers have suffered for too long under this re-
interpretative gaze. As Lambert noted, '… behind every bronze hero is a
human being, an urgent, flawed life in pursuit of some fragment of
immortality. We should listen, not judge, because our ancestors were human,
and in seeing their humanity we might recall our own before the lights go out
for ever'.[41]

In 2009, a special memorial service, once again in the Chapel in Greenwich,
rightly refocused attention back toward Franklin's scientific and
geographical achievements, whilst also celebrating the efforts of the many
brave men who went in search of him.[42] The service of thanksgiving was
attended by descendants of the explorers and also saw the re-dedication of
the restored and re-sited Monument there.[43] Though it may be fairly said that
the expedition was the worst disaster in the history of British naval
exploration, with the loss of two vessels and their crews, conserving the
Monument offered a suitable moment to reflect upon their sacrifice and,
more importantly, a chance to acknowledge British contributions to the
discovery and exploration of the Canadian Arctic, an area now the focus of
considerable geopolitical attention – over trade routes, access to resource
riches and other sovereignty issues.

The project to conserve the Monument also neatly coincided with current
efforts to find the remains of the ships of Franklin's expedition, a series of
surveys that is being led by Robert Grenier, Chief Underwater Archaeologist,
Parks Canada. Grenier gave a special speech in the Painted Hall after the
memorial service. It was a wonderful evening, and an appropriate location,
being the site where the Franklin relics were previously displayed to the
public and a place where toasts and tributes to the lost naval explorers were
frequently offered, no doubt over a glass or two, in the years after

Architectural elevation of the Franklin Monument, drawn by Kings Land Surveyors Limited in 2008.
Courtesy Greenwich Foundation.

McClintock's return. Fittingly, at our memorial service in 2009, H.E. James R. Wright, Canadian High Commissioner, read these enigmatic lines:

> *… cryptic marks, latitudes,*
> *signatures, journals,*
> *diaries of despair,*
> *official reports*
> *Nobody needs to read.*
> *I've seen the real journals*
> *You left us, you Franklin, you Crozier.*
> *I've seen the skulls of your men*
> *in the snow, their sterile bones*
> *Arranged around cairns like*
> *compasses,*
> *Marking out all the latitudes*
> *and longitudes*
> *Of men.*
>
> *Now the great passage is open,*
> *The one you dreamed of, Franklin,*
> *And great white ships plough through it*
> *Over and over again,*
> *Packed with cargo and carefree men.*
> *It is as though no one had to prove it*
> *Because the passage was always there.*
> *Or … is it that the way was invented,*
> *Franklin?*
>
> *that you cracked the passage open*
> *With the forces of sheer certainty?*
> *– or is it that you cannot know,*
> *Can never know,*
> *Where the passage lies*
> *Between conjecture and reality … ?* [44]

Grenier is due to resume his search for the shipwrecks in 2010. One hopes that this latest expedition will reveal some significant new insights into the factors that led to the deaths of the men of *Erebus* and *Terror*, though it is equally possible that nothing new will be discovered. It is clear that the crews faced impenetrable pack ice, dwindling supplies and near-certain starvation. Though it may prove impossible to unravel all the secrets of the demise of the expedition, the Franklin tragedy remains one of the most enigmatic mysteries of polar history.

Conservation Notes

The skilled team at Richard Rogers Conservation undertook the work on the Monument under the direction of Giles Quarme and Associates, and latterly Martin Ashley Architects, during the summer of 2009. The Monument was found to be in good condition and stable, with little evidence of any movement between the different pieces of marble. A number of old cracks, especially on the top panels, were noted as possible areas of risk whilst lifting. The entire marble surface was moderately covered with a layer of dirt and dust. There were also many paint splashes, which had occurred during the re-decoration of the niche in which it had sat since 1938. It was removed from the Painted Hall, just before the conversion of the Hall in 1939 to the Officers' Mess, as a staircase needed to be reconstructed.

All the elements of the Monument required detaching from the wall and adjoining marble sections. The process of cutting away the plaster grouting between the sections was initiated starting from the top of the Monument and working down. The traditional method of securing this sort of statuary would have been to secure to the back wall using metal 'cramps'. These would have been plastered into a drill hole on the top edge of the section and then bonded into a corresponding hole in the supporting wall. It was soon discovered that these methods were not always adhered to. The top three arched sections were loosened and it was revealed that they had no mechanical fixing at all. They were held in place by plaster alone.

The top edges of the next layer of marble elements were then revealed and securing cramps could be seen, but unfortunately these were set in concrete. It soon became evident that although metal cramps had been used to secure the sections, the uneven cavity behind the sections had been back filled using a combination of bricks and a pour of wet cement. This made it incredibly difficult to remove each section as the cement was very hard and had bonded the marble to the wall. A painstaking process of carefully chipping out the cement using hand tools was required until the marble became detached from the wall. When each section was free, it was lifted using nylon slings attached to a block and tackle and then transferred to ground level.

The Monument was composed of forty separate sections: the heaviest being the two figures, weighing roughly 500kgs each; and the largest, the 2.3m long 'Iceberg panel'. Each element required moving to the other end of the building. The route had to avoid going through the Chapel itself, which was to remain open for the duration of the works. Relocation of all the marble elements was completed in a series of phases. Firstly, all sections were detached from the existing location and transferred to ground level. They were then moved from the lower stairwell and lifted down to the outside courtyard, using a scaffold system. Third phase of movement, saw all sections lifted up to colonnade level and into the Chapel vestibule. Finally, a second scaffold was erected to lift all forty sections into place on the new plenum wall.

The design of the Monument meant that there would be a supporting core. The front inscription panel was inspected and a hairline crack was discovered. Before this could be safely removed it was decided that the panel required strengthening to reduce the risk of crack opening up any further. A sheet of 'Hexlite' - aluminium honeycomb core, between a fibreglass skin - was cut to size and bonded on the back face of the panel. After the inscription panel was carefully removed, a bricked up hidden cavity in the core was revealed. Careful removal of these bricks revealed a wooden casket, which research suggested would contain human remains. This box was removed in accordance with environmental health guidelines and taken away for analysis.

While the Monument was dismantled a process of cleaning was implemented. The build up of surface dirt and dust was removed using a 50:50 mix of white spirit and water with a few drops of non-ionic detergent. There were also a small number of disfiguring stains, which were removed using a steam cleaner. All paint splashes were also carefully removed using a scalpel blade. The south niche in the Chapel vestibule was chosen as the new location for the Monument. Due to the existing window, a freestanding plenum wall was designed and built. A brickwork core was then built to the exact specification of the original. The existing niche also had a carved stone skirting which needed to be replicated around the front of the Monument. A scaffold was erected and the elements were lifted in reverse order, starting with the figures. The figures were raised to the correct height using a layer of 28mm concrete tiles, to also allow for the bevelled slips at the front of the Monument. All sections were correctly levelled and a layer of wet plaster was used as a bedding layer. The central inscription panel required lifting from the core so a platform of concrete blocks was created as a stable mount.

Many of the sections were not self-supporting or required footings to project from the plenum wall. When this was the case, 15mm stainless steel studding was bonded into the wall where required. Where the marble sections required retaining against the wall, the traditional method of cramps was used – stainless steel, instead of brass – plastered into the marble cramp holes. Because the plenum wall was made of lightweight concrete blocks it was decided to bond the cramps into the pre-drilled holes using a polyester resin 'chem-bolt'. When all sections were in place grouting commenced with a gypsum plaster. The whole was cleaned, in preparation for the Monument's rededication ceremony on 29 October 2009. The full inscription reads:

TO THE MEMORY OF
REAR ADMIRAL SIR JOHN FRANKLIN KT., K.C.H.
AND OF THE UNDERMENTIONED OFFICERS
OF HER MAJESTY'S DISCOVERY SHIPS

EREBUS   AND   TERROR

EREBUS	TERROR
CAPT. JAMES FITZJAMES.	CAPT. FRANS. RAWDON MOIRA CROZIER.
COMMR. GRAHAM GORE.	COMMR. EDWARD LITTLE.
LIEUT. HENRY T.D. LE VESCONTE.	LIEUT. GEORGE HENRY HODGSON.
LIEUT. JAMES WALTER FAIRHOLME.	LIEUT. JOHN IRVING.
LIEUT. ROBERT ORME SARGENT.	LIEUT. FREDK. JOHN HORNBY.
LIEUT. CHARLES F. DES VOEUX.	LIEUT. ROBERT THOMAS.
LIEUT. EDWARD COUCH.	MR. JOHN SMART PEDDIE, SURGEON.
MR. CHARLES H. OSMER, PAYMASTER.	MR. ALEXR. MCDONALD, ASST. SURGEON.
MR. STEPHEN S. STANLEY, SURGEON.	MR.THOS. BLANKY, CIVILIAN, ICE MASTER.
MR. HARRY D.S. GOODSIR, ACTG. ASST. SURG.	MR. GILLIES ALEXR. MCBEAN, 2ND MASTER.
MR. JAMES REID, CIVILIAN, ICE MASTER.	MR. EDWIN JAMES HOWARD HELPMAN (CLERK IN CHARGE)
MR. HENRY F. COLLINS, 2ND MASTER.	
MR. THOS. TERRY, BOATSWAIN.	MR. JOHN LANE, BOATSWAIN.
MR. JOHN WEEKES, CARPENTER.	MR. THOS. HONEY, CARPENTER.

ALSO IN MEMORY OF
THE SEVERAL PETTY OFFICERS, SEAMEN AND ROYAL
MARINES WHO SAILED FROM ENGLAND IN THE SHIPS ABOVE
NAMED; AND WHO, WITH THEIR RESPECTIVE OFFICERS, LOST
THEIR LIVES IN THE SERVICE OF THEIR COUNTRY WHILE
EMPLOYED ON A VOYAGE TO THE ARCTIC SEAS, IN SEARCH
OF A NORTH WEST PASSAGE.
A.D.1845 – 1854

BENEATH LIE THE REMAINS OF ONE OF FRANKLIN'S
COMPANIONS WHO PERISHED IN THE ARCTIC REGIONS
1848
DISCOVERED AND BROUGHT AWAY FROM
KING WILLIAM'S LAND BY CAPTAIN HALL
THE UNITED STATES ARCTIC EXPLORER
1869

'These Bones': Identifying Lieutenant Le Vesconte

Henry Thomas Dundas Le Vesconte was born in 1813 in Netherton, Devon, first son of Commander Henry Le Vesconte, RN and Sarah Wills.[45] His father Henry had an interesting naval career.[46] He had joined the Navy on the *Cambridge* as one of Admiral Graves' retinue in 1790. As Lieutenant on Jamaica he saw action at the Battle of Copenhagen and later received a commendation from Nelson for the capture of six gun vessels on shore at St Valery. He was present at Trafalgar as Lieutenant of the 36-gun frigate *Naiad* under Captain Thomas Dundas; with the small fifth-rate playing an important role in relaying signals before the battle and in towing dismasted British ships to safety afterwards.[47] Henry Le Vesconte, the son, entered the Navy as a first-class volunteer on board *Herald* on 19 May 1829, joined *Britannia* on 22 November 1831, and was made Midshipman on 15 March 1832. He was transferred to the 40-gun frigate *Endymion* in December 1834 and served on her until 1836 under Captain Sir Samuel Roberts. He won his lieutenancy by 'repeated acts of conspicuous gallantry', as Mate on the sixth-rate *Calliope* during the Opium War. He later served on the sloop *Hyacinth* in the East Indies and as Fitzjames's first-lieutenant on *Clio* off the coast of Africa in cruises to suppress the slave trade.[48] Le Vesconte was appointed to the Channel Squadron later in 1844, serving aboard *Superb*. On 4 March 1845 he was made Second Lieutenant to the *Erebus*, as she was fitting out for the polar expedition at Woolwich Dockyard.

Little is known of Le Vesconte's activity on this expedition. We know he sat for his portrait with the photographer Richard Beard, as did a number of other officers, as the ship lay alongside. This was the first, and the last photograph, to be taken of him. It is reproduced at the head of this article.[49] He sent a number of letters and sketches home, as *Erebus* headed north into Baffin Bay late in 1845. But after that, as with the expedition as a whole, few exact details survive. At the Whalefish Islands, we know he spent some time surveying ashore with his friend Fitzjames, dodging mosquitoes. Franklin, Fitzjames records, was 'much pleased with him'. It is possible he endured the third winter and was alive into 1848.[50] The circumstances of his death are not known. He is remembered with two points of land in the Arctic, namely 'Le Vesconte Point' on the south-west coast of Baillie-Hamilton Island, and another, of similar name, on the west coast of King William Island.

Le Vesconte's remains were discovered by Captain Charles Francis Hall, at 'Point Hall' near Pfeffer River, during his second Arctic expedition. His search for possible survivors had spent its first winter near the Wager River and the following four at Repulse Bay, from where many journeys were made, including one to King William Island in the Spring of 1869, where the major part of the relics brought back by McClintock had been found. Hall returned to the United States in September 1869, and the news of his discoveries was soon relayed to London.[51] The skeleton came into the possession of Mr Brevoort, of Brooklyn, one of Hall's patrons, who eventually consigned it to Rear Admiral Edward Inglefield, the Arctic veteran, then Naval Attaché at Washington. Inglefield wrote to his friend Admiral George Henry Richards, then Hydrographer of the Navy, who in turn wrote to Lady Jane on 29 April 1872:

> *He has had a complete skeleton presented to him, which was found by Hall on King William's Land, of an officer – the remains of a silk undervest were on it – and one of the teeth stuffed with gold – all the other perfect. Aged between 35 and 40. My advice will be to put it in a box and bury it – for it could not be certainly identified – and would be no use to anyone – probably, if the skeleton was married – his widow has taken another skeleton before this.*[52]

Inglefield brought the remains to England a few months later and left them in Richards' care. Whose bones they were, however, were still in doubt. He wrote again by the end of June:

> *It is in the box Hall brought it home in and is said to be very perfect. I only looked at the head, which is a very remarkable one, all the teeth perfect but one stuffed with gold ... I should think there would be little difficulty in identifying it – indeed there cannot be more than four or five to choose from, the age cannot be much over 30. As soon as he arrived here the intelligence spread abroad and in one hour my room was taken possession of, so I sealed up the box and sent it straight away to Huxley, who promises to set it up and give an opinion.*[53]

A month later and they were still no closer to identifying the remains. Richards had yet to hear back from the venerable Professor Thomas Huxley - a former naval surgeon, famously 'Darwin's Bulldog', then Secretary to the Royal Society and the world's leading comparative anatomist. Richards wrote to Sophy Cracroft, Lady Jane's niece, in July: '... nor have I heard anything from Professor Huxley about the skellington – I wrote to him yesterday and asked what he had done'. By August, finally some news. Huxley had found time to examine the bones and relatives had been consulted. Richards then wrote to Lady Jane: 'I have little doubt that it is Le

THIS BOX CONTAINS HUMAN BONES, CONJECTURED TO HAVE
BEEN THE SKELETON OF THE BODY OF LIEUᵗ HENRYᵀᴰ LE VESCONTE
OF H M SHIP EREBUS, WHO PERISHED WITH MANY OTHERS, ABOUT THE
YEAR 1848, IN THE EXPEDITION TO THE ARCTIC REGIONS COMMANDED
BY SIR JOHN FRANKLIN. THE BONES WERE FOUND BY CAPᵀ HALL, THE
AMERICAN EXPLORER, IN KING WILLIAM'S LAND; AND TAKEN BY
HIM TO NEW YORK IN 1869, WHENCE THEY WERE BROUGHT TO
ENGLAND BY ADMIRAL INGLEFIELD. THEY WERE DEPOSITED HERE
BY ORDER OF THE LORDS OF THE ADMIRALTY IN 1873.

*These Bones were placed
in this Coffin
by the hands of Admiral Richards
Hydrographer of the
Admiralty
on the 30ᵗʰ of January A.D 1873
Geo Henry Richards*

Top of the wooden burial casket, and a small note found within it, photographed during conservation work on the Monument in 2009. Courtesy Greenwich Foundation and English Heritage.

Vesconte'.[54] Despite the positive identification, the 'skellington' was interred under the floor of the vestibule of the Painted Hall in 1873, by order of the Lord's Commissioners of the Admiralty, described simply as 'One of Franklin's companions'. When the Monument was moved in 1938, the items were 'reverently removed to the Chapel and there reinterred'. A hidden recess was made at the foot of the Monument, fronted by marble, where the bones remained undisturbed until conservation work took place in the summer of 2009.

The Greenwich Foundation – working closely with Richard Rogers Conservation, and assisted by the author – entrusted examination of the skeleton to English Heritage. The casket itself is comprised of three boxes.

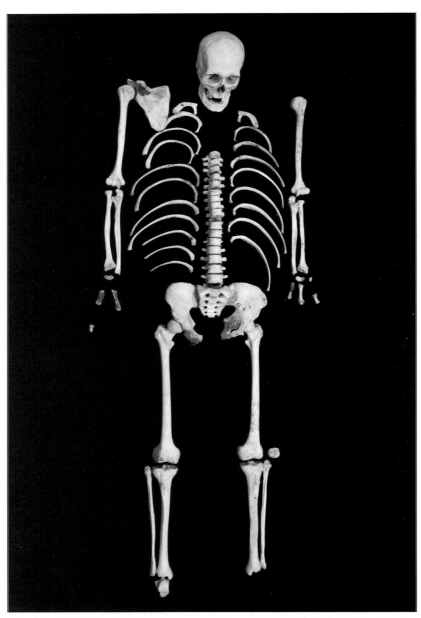

The skeleton of Lieutenant Henry T.D. Le Vesconte, photographed during conservation work, and shortly afterwards re-interred within the Monument. Courtesy Greenwich Foundation and English Heritage.

An outer box, made of wood (likely teak) measures 94cm x 23cm x 33cm. Upon its screwed down-lid the following text is inscribed:

> THIS BOX CONTAINS HUMAN BONES, CONJECTURED TO HAVE BEEN THE SKELETON OF THE BODY OF LIEUT HENRY TD LE VESCONTE OF HM SHIP EREBUS, WHO PERISHED WITH MANY OTHERS, ABOUT THE YEAR 1848, IN THE EXPEDITION TO THE ARCTIC REGIONS COMMANDED BY SIR JOHN FRANKLIN. THE BONES WERE FOUND BY CAPT HALL, THE AMERICAN EXPLORER, IN KING WILLIAM'S LAND; AND TAKEN BY HIM TO NEW YORK IN 1869, WHENCE THEY WERE BROUGHT TO ENGLAND BY ADMIRAL INGLEFIELD. THEY WERE DEPOSITED HERE BY ORDER OF THE LORDS OF THE ADMIRALTY IN 1873.

Inside this casket was a sealed lead casing, measuring 89cm x 20cm x 29cm. Carefully peeled back, the lead casing was revealed to contain a second wooden box, measuring 88 cm x 19cm (the third dimension is not known as the lead was only partially removed). Within the casket, excluding the skeletal remains, were as follows:

– An offering cross, 23.6cm in length, made of three layers of card onto which flowers had been stitched.

– A large, complete map entitled 'Discoveries in the Arctic Sea up to MDCCCLIX' bearing the legend 'London, Published according to the Act of Parliament at the Hydrographic Office of the Admiralty Jan 20th 1855, additions to 1860'. Due to its fragile nature the map was not fully unfolded; it shows the area in which the Erebus and Terror were then presumed lost.

– A section of map, bearing the title 'Louisiade Archipelago' and illustrating the Calvados Chain in Papua New Guinea. This map measures approximately 90cm x 35cm and has clearly been cut from a much larger map.

– A small white envelope measuring 21.5cm x 10.5cm, pre-printed with the words 'On Her Majesties Service' across the top and 'Hydrographic Department Admiralty' across the bottom in the left hand corner. Hand written on the envelope is 'Three teeth-one ... stopped with Gold', with the initials SHR. The envelope contained a folded 30cm x 20.5cm sheet of plain blue writing paper, which had been sealed with red wax, although the seal had pulled apart some time previous. Hand written on the paper was 'Teeth of upper jaw; right side; ... incisor; canine and m bicuspid', and inside were three teeth.

– A white invitation card, 9.7cm x 13.9cm, which has a pre-printed invitation on the front reading; 'The President and Council of the Royal Society request the honour of the company of Admiral Richards (handwritten name inserted) at Burlington House of Saturday, April 27th at 9 o'clock'. Not transferable: This card to be produced'. A handwritten note on the back of this reads: 'These Bones were placed in this Coffin by the hands of Admiral Richards, Hydrographer of the Admiralty on the 30th of January A.D. 1873' and is signed by Geo. Henry Richards.

– A parcel comprising a large sheet of white paper which has 'remains of blanket' hand-written on the top left, along with an unknown signature, tied with a pink ribbon. The parcel contains a quantity of material that is predominantly green in colour although areas of yellow and purple pigments can be seen. The material was not been unfolded to prevent damage so it is not possible to say whether the colour changes represent discolouration of the material or a pattern. It is possible that more than one type of fabric is included in the package as two distinct weaves can been observed: one very coarse and the other much finer. The coarse woven material is consistent with material found adhering to the skeletal remains. The complete parcel weighed 391g. The skeletal remains were wrapped in white linen.

An image of 'these bones' is presented here for the first time, to satisfy curiosity and in the hope that they need never be disturbed again. Shortly after this photograph was taken, the remains were returned to their lead-lined casket and respectfully reinterred in the Monument, now proudly re-sited at the entrance of the Chapel. With the Monument conserved for future generations, far from the terrible polar snows, may Le Vesconte and his companions rest in peace.

> *To thee, brave Franklin, and thy gallant crew,*
> *Are England's praise and England's sorrow due;*
> *Who braved at Duty's call the Arctic wave,*
> *And led by Science, found the untimely grave.*[55]

---

[1] Francis Egerton, 'Sir James Ross's Voyage to the Antarctic Regions', *The Quarterly Review*, 81 (1847), pp. 166-87 (pp. 166-67).

[2] The Franklin Expedition left England in 1845 under the command of Sir John Franklin (1786-1847), to discover and chart the remaining sections of a navigable North-West Passage, and to conduct a wide-ranging magnetic survey. Sir John was an experienced explorer who had served on previous Arctic expeditions. He sailed from the Thames in the two ships HMS *Erebus* and HMS *Terror*, with a crew of 24 officers and 110 men. 5 were invalided home from Greenland, making the party a total of 129 men. The expedition was last seen on 26 July 1845 by the crew of two whaling ships, the *Prince of Wales* and the *Enterprise*, moored to an iceberg in Lancaster Sound near the western edge of Baffin Bay. After two years, and no word from the explorers, Sir John's wife Lady Jane urged the Admiralty and the Government to mount a search effort to rescue the missing men.

[3] Francis Egerton, 'Sir James Ross's Voyage to the Antarctic Regions', *The Quarterly Review*, 81 (1847), pp. 166-67.

[4] The return of the expedition was celebrated in the press. Among many others, see 'Fate of Sir John Franklin's Expedition', *The Times*, 23 September 1859, p. 7; 'Fate of Sir John Franklin's Expedition: Proceedings of the Yacht Fox', *The Illustrated London News*, 1 October 1859, pp. 327-29, including a facsimile of the paper found in the cairn on Point Victory; 'Captain McClintock and the Franklin Expedition', *The Times*, 15 November 1859, p. 7; 'The Voyage of the Fox', *The Times*, 30 December 1859, p. 8. McClintock's reputation as an explorer, long in abeyance despite his immense popularity in the nineteenth century, has been revived by a recent biography. See David Murphy, *The Arctic Fox: Francis Leopold McClintock, Discoverer of the Fate of Franklin* (Cork: The Collins Press, 2004).

[5] See 'Monument to Sir John Franklin', *The Illustrated London News*, 8 January 1859, p. 35.

[6] The majority of Rae's finds were handed over to the Admiralty by the Hudson Bay Company. They were then given to Greenwich Hospital for display in the Painted Hall in 1854. The McClintock material was displayed initially at the Royal United Services Museum in Whitehall. The collection was later moved to the Royal Naval Museum, Greenwich and material from the Hall and Schwatka expeditions was added. The relics were transferred to the National Maritime Museum when this opened in 1937. Other material has been added since this date, mainly from the Royal United Services Museum after it closed in 1963.

[7] John P. Cheyne, *Descriptive Catalogue of Fourteen Stereoscopic Slides of the Relics of Sir John Franklin's Expedition, Photographed and Published by Lieut. Cheyne, R.N., at the United Service, Whitehall* (London: United Service, [1860]).

[8] See Joven, 'The End of an Epic', *Sharpe's London Magazine*, 15 (1859), pp. 242-46.

[9] See Osborn, 'The Last Voyage of Sir John Franklin', *Once a Week*, 20 October 1859, p. 366.

[10] 'Editorial', *The Times*, 23 September 1859, p. 6.

[11] Advertisement in the *Saturday Review*, 31 December 1860.

[12] It would be fascinating to trace the passage of the Franklin story in poetry, though there is no space here. The 1850's saw a number of works in verse, including George H. Boker's *A Ballad of Sir John Franklin* (1850), Chandos Hoskyns Abrahall's *Arctic Enterprise, A Poem* (1856), James Parsons' *Reflections on the Mysterious Fate of Sir John Franklin* (1857), and Joseph Addison Turner's *The Discovery of Sir John Franklin* (1858). McClintock's return inspired new enthusiasm, such as Walter White's *Erebus and Terror* (1859). Richard Doddridge Blackmore, who would later gain fame as the author of his novel Lorna Doone published his poem *The Fate of Franklin* in 1860.

[13] Nicholas Michell, 'The Franklin Monument', *New Monthly Magazine*, 177 (1859), p. 317.

[14] See Algernon Charles Swinburne, *Poems*, 6 vols (London: Chatto and Windus, 1904). The 'Death of Sir John Franklin' was written in 1860. The student Swinburne prefaced his poem with lines from Shakespeare's Pericles:
'The unfriendly elements
Forgot thee utterly ---
Where, for a monument upon thy bones,
And e'er-remaining lamps, the belching whale
And humming water must o'erwhelm thy corpse ;
Lying with simple shells.' [III.I].

[15] See 'Lady Franklin', *The Times*, 19 July 1875, p. 5; Frances J. Woodward, *Portrait of Jane: A Life of Lady Franklin* (London: Hodder and Stoughton, 1951). For a colourful, though at times misleading, recent account of *Lady Franklin's role in constructing her husband's achievements*, see Ken McGoogan, *Lady Franklin's Revenge: A True Story of Ambition, Obsession and the Remaking of Arctic History* (Toronto: HarperCollins, 2005).

[16] See 'Captain McClintock and the Franklin Expedition', *The Times*, 15 November 1859, p. 7.

[17] On the Spilsby statue – cast in bronze by Mr. Bacon, costing nearly seven hundred pounds, and inaugurated by Sir John Richardson on 26 November 1861 – see 'The Late Sir John Franklin', *The Times*, 30 August 1860, p. 5; 'The Franklin Memorial at Spilsby', *The Times*, 28 November 1861, p. 8.

[18] 'Sir John Franklin', *The Spectator*, 17 November 1866, p. 1271.

[19] 'Monument of Sir John Franklin', *The Illustrated London News*, 22 September 1866, p. 279; 'Statue to Sir John Franklin', *The Times*, 16 November 1866, p. 10. The 'national monument', executed by Mathew Noble, was erected by order of W.E. Cowper , with funds voted for it by Parliament. It had been supported in the House of Commons by Sir Francis Baring and by a Mr Coningham, the brother-in-law of the late Captain James Fitzjames. A bas-relief on the front of the pedestal represents Franklin's funeral, surrounded 'by the sorrowing officers and crew of the two ships'. In the panel at the back of the pedestal, which can now only be viewed from the garden of the Athenaeum and the Travellers' Club, is an embossed bronze chart of the Arctic showing the position of the ships and their crews at the time of Franklin's death.

[20] Sherard Osborn, 'On the Exploration of the North Polar Region', *Proceedings of the Royal Geographical Society*, 9 (1865), 42-71 (p. 52).

[21] Osborn to Roderick Murchison, 14 October 1867. BM Add. 46,217, f. 314. See also Andrew Lambert, *Franklin: Tragic Hero of Polar Navigation* (London: Faber and Faber, 2009), p. 297.

[22] 'The Franklin Commemoration', *Geographical Journal*, 6:1 (1895), pp. 31-44 (p. 41).

[23] See 'Sir John Franklin', *The Times*, 31 July 1875, p. 12; 'Sir John Franklin', *The Times*, 2 August 1875, p. 9; 'The Church', *The Illustrated London News*, 7 August 1875, p. 143. Tennyson's epitaph would long be cherished as a lament to fallen polar-heroes. Many early reports of the Scott disaster of 1912, for example, adapted his verse by changing 'North' to 'South'. See, for example, 'Victory and Death', *The Pall Mall Gazette*, 12 February 1913, p. 7.

[24] For more on the Royal Naval Exhibition, see Huw Lewis-Jones, 'Displaying Nelson: Navalism and 'The Exhibition' of 1891', *The International Journal of Maritime History*, 17:1 (2005), pp. 29-67; Huw Lewis-Jones, 'Heroism Displayed': Revisiting the Franklin Gallery at the Royal Naval Exhibition, 1891', *Polar Record*, 41 (2005), pp. 185-203.

[25] 'Franklin Commemoration in Edinburgh', *The Times*, 5 June 1895, p. 11.

[26] 'The Franklin Commemoration', *The Times*, 21 May 1895, p. 10.

[27] 'The Franklin Commemoration', *Geographical Journal*, 6:1 (1895), p. 33.

[28] Ibid., p. 42. See also John Murray, 'The Renewal of Antarctic Exploration', *Geographical Journal*, 3 (1894), pp. 1-42; 'Projects for Antarctic Exploration', *Nature*, 54 (1896), pp. 29-31.

[29] 'The Franklin Commemoration', *Geographical Journal*, 6:1 (1895), 31-44 (p. 43).

[30] See F. Guillemard, 'Franklin and the Arctic', *Blackwood's Edinburgh Magazine*, 161 (1897), pp. 238-56.

[31] Clements R. Markham, 'The Need for an Antarctic Expedition', *The Nineteenth Century*, 38 (1895), pp. 706-12.

[32] Henry D. Traill, *The Life of Sir John Franklin* (London: John Murray, 1896). Among many other accounts see Augustus Henry Beesly, *Sir John Franklin* (London: M. Ward & Co, 1894), part of the 'Heroes of History' series; Ernest Charles Buley, *Into the Polar Seas: The Story of Sir John Franklin* (London: Sunday School Union, 1909); and J. Kennedy MacLean, *Heroes of the Farthest North and Farthest South* (London: W. & R. Chambers, 1913).

[33] Richard J. Cyriax, *Sir John Franklin's Last Arctic Expedition* (London: Methuen & Co, 1939). Cyriax's original narrative is highly sought after by polar collectors, since the stocks are reputed to have been bombed during the Second World War. A facsimile reprint was republished in 1997, the one hundred and fiftieth anniversary year of Franklin's death on 11 June 1847.

34 See for example, *Some Private Correspondence of Sir John and Lady Jane Franklin, Tasmania, 1837-1845*, edited by George Mackaness (Sydney: D.S. Ford, 1947); Kathleen Fitzpatrick, *Sir John Franklin in Tasmania: 1837-1843* (Melbourne: Melbourne University Press, 1949). Historical narratives in the traditional mould include James Elgin Wetherell, *Three Centuries of Canadian Story: From John Cabot to John Franklin* (Toronto: Musson Book Co., 1928); Noel Wright, *Quest for Franklin* (London: Heinemann, 1959); Leslie H. Neatby, The Search for Franklin (London: Barker, 1970).

35 Roderic Owen, *The Fate of Franklin* (London: Hutchinson & Co, 1978).

36 Richard C. Davis, 'John Franklin (1786-1847)', *Arctic*, 38:4 (1985), pp. 338-39.

37 See John Geiger and Owen Beattie, *Dead Silence: The Greatest Mystery in Arctic Discovery* (London: Bloomsbury, 1993); Owen Beattie and John Geiger, *Frozen in Time: The Fate of the Franklin Expedition* (London: Bloomsbury, 1987).

38 For the work of novelists using the Franklin story, see Nancy Cato, *North-west by South* (London: Heinemann, 1965); Sten Nadolny, *The Discovery of Slowness*, trans. by Ralph Freedman (London: Viking, 1987); Rudy Wiebe, *A Discovery of Strangers* (Toronto: Alfred A. Knopf, 1994); Sheila Nickerson, *Disappearance: A Map* (New York: Doubleday, 1996); Andrea Barrett, *Voyage of the Narwhal* (New York: Norton, 1998); John Wilson, *North With Franklin: The Lost Journals of James Fitzjames* (Allston: Fitzhenry and Whiteside, 2000); Robert Edric, *The Broken Lands: A Novel of Arctic Disaster* (New York: St Martin's Press, 2002), among others.

39 *The Lost Expedition* aired in the United Kingdom on Channel Five during November 2005 in the six-part *Revealed* documentary series; a series which attempted 'to shed some light on the biggest mysteries in the past two millennia'. Other subjects included *Hannibal of the Alps*, the archaeology of Roman Britain seen through *Boudica's Treasures*, *The Da Vinci Code Myth*, a history of the 'love business' in *Secrets of the Dating Agency*, and a study of wartime criminality entitled *Bad Boys of the Blitz*. Andrew Lambert - Laughton Professor of Naval History at King's College London and popular Nelson biographer - cast Franklin's heroism in terms of his leadership qualities and his humanity.

40 Andrew Lambert, *Franklin: Tragic Hero of Polar Navigation* (London: Faber and Faber, 2009).

41 Ibid., p. 351.

42 The 'Service of Thanksgiving' on 29 October 2009, and the gala reception that followed it in the Painted Hall, was directed by Dr Huw Lewis-Jones and Kari Herbert, of Polarworld with assistance from the Greenwich Foundation and Canada House. It was attended by over 300 invited guests, with members of the polar community – historians, scientists, explorers, and enthusiasts – joining descendants of the men who served in the Arctic in the nineteenth century, to offer a tribute to their achievements. The families of Sir John Franklin, Captain Francis Crozier, Sir Leopold McClintock, Sir John Ross, Sir James Clark Ross and Commander Cheyne were represented, in addition to relatives of Captain Robert Falcon Scott, Sir Ernest Shackleton, Sir Wally Herbert, and Sir Vivian Fuchs, among many others.

43 For the Monument's listing on the superb Maritime Memorials database, see: http://www.nmm.ac.uk/memorials/Memorial.cfm?Search=franklin&MemorialID=M2370

44 Such is fashion, after the effusions of the 1860s, Franklin soon faded as a subject of poetry. He re-emerged in 1965, nevertheless, in *Erebus and Terror*, a verse drama originally written for CBC radio by award-winning Canadian poet Gwendolyn MacEwen. Her text finally appeared in print in a magazine in 1974. It was later published in *Afterworlds* (Toronto: McClelland and Stewart, 1987). MacEwen described beautiful images of the 'cold holiness of snow', through which wandering explorers dropped, one by one, amidst the 'crushed, complex geography of men'. The most notable recent poetic treatment of Franklin has been David Solway's verse cycle *Franklin's Passage* (2003), which was awarded the 36th annual Grand Prix du Livre by the City of Monteral; a first for an Anglophone writer.

⁴⁵ Henry was christened on 15 July 1813 in Combeinteignhead, Devon. He would have three sisters, Rose, Charlotte and Anna, and three younger brothers, Philip, Charles and James.

⁴⁶ Henry's father, also Henry Le Vesconte, was the son of Philip Le Vesconte, a naval veteran who lost a leg in the action off the Dogger Bank in 1781. He served as a warrant officer and purser on various vessels, the last being the *Royal William*, on the books of which he was borne until his death on 25 May 1807. Henry Le Vesconte had three bothers all of whom served in the Navy. James Le Vesconte, a Lieutenant in the Royal Marines, was wounded at Trafalgar in the *Royal Sovereign*. Philip Le Vesconte saw service as Midshipman of *Saturn* in an action with the French in 1795, and was wounded at Copenhagen when Lieutenant of the *Monarch*. He was later wrecked off Brest in 1804 and was in captivity in France until 1810. George Le Vesconte, the youngest son, was Midshipman of the *Druid* in 1807, but left the service shortly after his father's death.

⁴⁷ Too small to take part in the battle itself, *Naiad* lay to windward of the action. She towed the 74-gun *Belleisle* to Gibraltar after the storm. *Naiad* served in other actions and was finally paid off in 1826. She later acted as a depot ship in Chile and Peru. Broken up in 1898, *Naiad* was the longest survivor of any of the ships at Trafalgar save *Victory* herself. Henry Le Vesconte, father, retired from the Navy in 1828 and the family then emigrated to Upper Canada. He received a grant of 1,000 acres of Crown Land in the Trent River Valley, Seymour Township, for his service in the Napoleonic Wars. He died on 7 July 1850 in Belleville, Ontario, unaware of his son's demise in the far north a few years before.

⁴⁸ 'The Franklin Commemoration', *Geographical Journal*, 6:1 (1895), p. 37. See also *The Mariner's Mirror*, 18 (1932), pp. 321-22. Among the Franklin relics in the collections of the NMM are silver table forks and spoons bearing his name on the shanks. See AAA3273-5, AAA2474 and AAA2488. The Société Jersiaise has a silver fork bearing his name and an etching of his, showing *Erebus* and *Terror* at Boat Creek, Whale Island, on 12 July 1845.

⁴⁹ The unique daguerreotype images were later copied by Beard for reproduction in the newspapers. See, for example, *The Illustrated London News*, 13 September 1851, p. 329.

⁵⁰ See Richard J. Cyriax, *Sir John Franklin's Last Arctic Expedition* (London: Methuen & Co, 1939); J. E. Nourse, *Narrative of the Second Arctic Expedition Made by Charles F. Hall* (Washington: G.P.O., 1879), p. 401, p. 409, and p. 418.

⁵¹ See 'Letter from Captain Hall to Mr Grinnell', *The New York Herald*, 30 September 1869; 'America', *The Illustrated London News*, 2 October 1869, p. 319. 'Dr Hall, the Arctic explorer, arrived at New Bedford last Sunday, from Repulse Bay, after an absence of five years. He had discovered the skeletons of several of Sir John Franklin's party at King William's Land, and brings numerous relics of the Franklin expedition'.

⁵² Quoted in Roderic Owen, *The Fate of Franklin* (London: Hutchinson & Co, 1978), p. 421.

⁵³ Ibid., p. 421.

⁵⁴ See also *United Service Gazette*, 30 November 1872; Ann Savours, 'Franklin Memorial', *The Mariner's Mirror*, 72 (1986), pp. 480-81. The skeleton of Lieutenant John Irving also made its way to Great Britain. Lieutenant Schwatka of the United States Army built a cairn over his grave at Point Victory, removed the bones and took them to America. He then sent them to Irving's relations in Scotland, carried across the Atlantic on SS *Circassia*, as special cargo at the invitation of the Anchor Line. They were interred with full naval honours at Dean Cemetery, Edinburgh on 7 January 1881. For a record of this memorial, see http://www.nmm.ac.uk/memorials/Memorial.cfm?Banner=4&MemorialID=M552

⁵⁵ Spencer Smith, 'The Deserted Boat', in *Repton School Prize Poems* (Derby: W. Bemrose, 1860), pp. 11-12.

'The Brave, Rough, English Admiral…': Sir Cloudesley Shovell and his Monument by Grinling Gibbons in Westminster Abbey, 1708

Justin Reay

In 1883 James Cooke FSA read a paper to a meeting of the Society of Antiquaries at Burlington House. His title was: 'The Ship-wreck of Sir Cloudesley Shovell on the Scilly Islands in 1707'. His paper dealt largely with the legends that had grown up around the loss of the *Association* and three other Royal Navy warships in a terrible tragedy off the Isles of Scilly, in which Admiral Shovell died. In my current paper, expanded from my own lecture to the Society of Antiquaries in November 2007, I will give a brief background to that great naval officer's career and to the shipwreck itself, and also consider the three legends Cooke reported. This paper also describes something very different arising from the tragedy: the great monument to Cloudesley Shovell raised in Westminster Abbey in 1708.

The monument to Admiral Sir Cloudesley Shovell, South Quire Aisle, Westminster Abbey, by Grinling Gibbons, erected 1708, engraving by Dowling from John Dart's History of Westminster Abbey, London 1723. Courtesy of the Dean and Chapter of Westminster Abbey.

In October 2007 the three-hundredth anniversary of the deaths of Sir Cloudesley Shovell and the 2,000 other men who died with him in the shipwreck, was commemorated at a service organised by The 1805 Club and the Britannia Naval Research Association in Westminster Abbey. We stood in the South Quire Aisle and, after a eulogy and a simple service concluded by a Sergeant Bugler of Royal Marines playing *Last Post* and *Reveille*, the representatives of the Royal Navy, other navies, Trinity House and naval history groups laid wreaths at the foot of the immense memorial to Shovell, commissioned by Queen Anne from the great carver, Grinling Gibbons.

By the beginning of the Eighteenth century Gibbons was the country's leading carver. His talent lay in his incomparable working of limewood, where his complex *disegno* of flowers, fruit and lace could be realised, and where his delicate hand could, in the words of Horace Walpole: 'bring to wood the light and airy looseness of flowers', making foliage appear as if it would move with the slightest breeze, as in life. Gibbons was the nation's favourite carver, so it was natural that the sovereign would turn to him to memorialise the nation's favourite admiral in the nation's pantheon to its greatest heroes. But to be honest, he was not very good at sculpting stone. Joseph Addison, the Under Secretary of State, abhorred Gibbons' quirky and elaborate memorial to his friend. Writing in *The Spectator* he compared it unfavourably with the masculine, restrained tombs of the great Dutch naval heroes such as Cornelis Tromp and Michel de Ruyter, and complained that it did not do justice to Shovell, whom he called 'that plain gallant Man'.[1]

Background and Career

Although far from being of humble birth, as is often stated, and aided somewhat by having kinsmen in the Navy, Cloudesley Shovell rose above his social station by his own efforts and abilities, to become one of the most highly regarded and successful naval officers this country has ever seen. His many honours and titles – among them Rear Admiral of England; Commander in Chief of the Fleet; a member of the Lord High Admiral's Council; Governor of the Hospital for Sick and Wounded Seamen at Greenwich; a Comptroller of the Navy Board, and an Elder Brother of Trinity House – attest to a life of action and of service to the Navy and to his country above that even of Horatio Nelson.

But, more important than these glittering prizes, Shovell was admired by his peers, respected by the enemies he fought, and loved by the men under his command. Queen Mary wrote to her consort William III, that Cloudesley Shovell was the best officer of the age. Jodocus Crull, writing in 1711, described Shovell as a person of uncommon courage, and praises his 'Temperance, Humanity, and Affability in Conversation'.[2] Professor

Nicholas Rodger, in his seminal history of the Royal Navy at this period, says of Shovell that he: 'was perhaps the only truly popular English admiral of the age, beloved by officers and men, respected by politicians of all parties.'[3] So how did this paragon earn such a wonderful reputation?

Cloudesley Shovell was born about 1650 in the hamlet of Cockthorpe, on the coast of Norfolk. His family were originally Netherlandish immigrants working in the dyeing and weaving trades; his great grand-father became Sheriff of Norwich, then England's third city, and his father was a cloth merchant and a land-owner whose will confirms that he held the social rank of 'gentleman'.[4] Cloudesley's striking first name was a matronymic, given to honour his mother's family, who were gentleman farmers. The Cloudesleys and the Shovells were related to the Myngs family of the neighbouring village of Salthouse, and it was Admiral Sir Christopher Myngs who first took Cloudesley Shovell to sea at the age of eleven, as an officer's servant aboard the frigate *Centurion*.

Captain Cloudesley Shovell c.1680, oil on copper, anon. Courtesy Guildhall Museum, Rochester.

A junior officer on the ship was John Narbrough, another Cockthorpe man who took Cloudesley under his wing and, in that lovely term of the time, became his 'sea-daddy', teaching him what he knew of seamanship, of navigation, of commanding men in the harsh world of a sailing warship, and of leading them in action. Indeed, this was an era of much action, as England began its rise to become the world's greatest sea power. By the age of 14 Cloudesley had seen battle in the Second Anglo-Dutch War and legend has it that, at the battle of Lowestoft he swam between the warships through shot and shell, bearing vital dispatches between his teeth.

After their mentor's death from wounds received during the Four Days Fight in 1666 John Narbrough was promoted and Cloudesley became his personal servant. When Narbrough gained his first command, Shovell went with him as a midshipman, and before he was 20 they had sailed half way around the world. Under the influence of Samuel Pepys, by this time the Secretary to the Board of Admiralty, the Royal Navy from the 1670s became led by men qualified by experience and expertise, no matter what their family background or connections. Pepys early noted Shovell's ability, and in 1673 signed Shovell's Commission from the King.

As a junior Lieutenant in Narbrough's Mediterranean fleet, Shovell was given an unusual assignment, conducting peace negotiations with the Dey of Algiers, whose state-sponsored corsairs wreaked havoc amongst European merchant ships in the Mediterranean and engaged in piracy and white slaving as far as the Cornish coast and the tideway of the Thames. Shovell's diplomacy, aided by his renowned pleasant disposition, was allied with a quick tactical brain, and when the negotiations failed due to the Dey's intransigence, Shovell proposed a daring attack against the Barbary corsairs in their own port. Narbrough gave him command of the squadron's boat flotilla for this attack and its success – which temporarily halted the activities of the Algerine pirates – made Shovell a national hero in Britain. Pepys must have taken smug pleasure in writing of him: '… Lieutenant Shovell with whose management his Majesty and my Lords [of the Admiralty] are most particularly satisfied.'[5]

In 1677 he gained his first command, and spent several years in the Mediterranean fighting the well-armed corsairs, earning the approbation of his commander-in-chief, Admiral Arthur Herbert, who said: 'Captain Shovell showed all the prudence and all the valour that becomes a brave and experienced Commander and is indeed a man to be admired'.

At this period a Royal Navy ship's captain could earn extra money by carrying cash or valuable cargo on behalf of British merchants across hostile waters – a so-called 'good voyage'. It was also common for enterprising sea officers to earn a great deal of money by capturing vessels which were then sold by the Admiralty Court. Shovell was very good at taking well-armed opponents which fetched a good price, and in the 1680s earnings from 'good voyages' and his prize-money from Algerine pirate galleys, and from captured French and Spanish warships taken into the British service, made him very rich. Over a fifteen-year period from the end of the 1670s, Shovell invested in land in Norfolk, bought a large country estate at Crayford in Kent, and a town house in the most fashionable quarter of Westminster.

During the Glorious Revolution of 1688 which saw the Stuart dynasty replaced by William of Orange and his wife Mary, Shovell – a staunch Whig and anti-Papist – was a senior officer in the fleet which deliberately delayed leaving port to attack William's fleet, until the so-called 'Protestant wind' allowed the new monarchs to land unopposed at Torbay. After the battle of Bantry Bay in 1689, at which he defeated a large French fleet supporting James II's invasion force, Shovell was knighted by William III. At the battle of Barfleur in 1692, Shovell led his squadron to weather the French line, scattering the enemy fleet, many of which took shelter at the port of St Vaast – La Hogue where they were embayed. Admiral George Rooke's squadron was able to destroy the enemy's warships and troop transports there under the eyes of James who was waiting for them ashore with his invasion troops, but Shovell's ship did not take part in this second and decisive action which his tactics had enabled, as he had been severely wounded in the thigh by a splinter after a round-shot had hit the ship's bulwark close by him.

Recovered from his wounds, Shovel was appointed one of the three Joint Admirals of the Fleet, with Henry Killigrew and Ralph Delaval; this was an unfortunate triumvirate of three very capable seamen and commanders who were bitterly opposed politically. On their watch occurred the taking by the French of the Smyrna convoy (Battle of Lagos, 1693), an infamous action which was one of the very few blots on Shovell's record, as the main English fleet under the triumvirate had turned back to the Channel too early, leaving an Anglo-Dutch squadron commanded by Rooke to guard one of the richest and most important trade convoys ever to sail for the Mediterranean. With a charge of treason hanging over him, Shovell was ordered to account for the loss to Parliament, where he displayed his usual scrupulously honourable character by defending his Tory colleagues in a clear account of the affair; they were all acquitted, but there was a suspicion that someone at the Admiralty had given intelligence to the French leading to their successful ambush of the convoy.[6]

In 1691 Shovell had married Elizabeth, the widow of Sir John Narbrough, who had died three years before. Shovell had two daughters with Elizabeth, and adopted her sons John and James, who went to sea with him as gentlemen volunteers after they were matriculated into Christ Church College, Oxford in 1703.[7] From 1695 until his death, Shovell was the Member of Parliament for Rochester, and spent some of his personal wealth on new civic buildings in the city and in 'beautifying' the Main Chamber of the Guildhall.

With the new century and the War of the Spanish Succession, Shovell was back in the Mediterranean. In the summer of 1703 he captured Barcelona on behalf of the Hapsburg King of Spain, supporting British and Austrian soldiers on shore in alliance with the Catalan junta.[8] Returning home early in November, Shovell sailed into the Great Storm in the English Channel, a hurricane which cost the lives of nearly 6,000 men in the naval and merchant fleets. Being blown close to the Goodwin Sands which had already claimed several ships with the loss of all hands, Shovell's decisive thinking and excellent seamanship saved his ship and the lives of his men. In 1704 he commanded the allied Dutch and British fleets in the battle of Malaga, and he played the key role in the strategically important capture of Gibraltar as a permanent naval base, again commanding troops ashore and conducting the naval bombardment.

Disaster off the Isles of Scilly

By 1707 Shovell was Britain's leading admiral at sea, highly successful in action, apparently loved by all who knew him and the darling of the public. From a base in allied Portugal, he commanded the Anglo-Dutch fleet on a long campaign in the eastern Atlantic and across the western Mediterranean, where for the first time British ships kept the sea over the winter and spring, culminating in the summer in the siege of Toulon where Shovell's naval and amphibious support ensured a partial, if temporary success.

The political decision to attack Toulon was taken late in the summer, and it was autumn by the time the British ships could return home, carrying many British soldiers on board in addition to their own ships' companies. The fleet headed north-west from the Strait of Gibraltar and on the evening of the 22 October was in the mouth of the English Channel. It is clear that most of the officers of the 21 ships in the fleet thought they were many miles south-west of their actual position.

Analysis of the surviving ships' logs by Commander May of the Institute of Navigation in 1960, indicates that the main cause of this mistake was simply poor mathematics by the navigating officers, when determining their position by Dead Reckoning from their last landfall, Cape Spartel.[9] This caused a fatal error in their estimate of their latitude, as well as their longitude. Usually a vessel unsure of its position would run down a line of latitude until it until it reached a familiar seamark on land, but this was too dangerous in the mouth of the Channel, where the northerly and southerly lines of latitude of clear water between the Isles of Scilly and the Race of Alderney run close together.

Normal practice for a sailing ship making a landfall was to heave to in the hours of darkness, but the weather was deteriorating and they thought they had enough sea-room for a safe passage up Channel to Plymouth. At six o'clock Shovell ordered his ships to wear onto what they thought was the correct course north-east by north, and as night fell the fleet sailed into the gathering gloom. They were 70 miles north of their estimated position and standing into danger.

Myths and Legends Surrounding the Shipwreck

In his paper given to the Society of Antiquaries in 1883, Dr Cooke repeated three legends which had grown up around the shipwreck and the death of Cloudesley Shovell, and which still have currency today. The first concerns the so-called conference of captains and sailing masters on the afternoon of the 22 October, at which they discussed their likely position, and several sailing masters disagreed with the majority view that they were off Ushant, one saying they were within three hours' sail of the Isles of Scilly.

No such conference is recorded in any of the 44 surviving Captains', Masters' or Lieutenants' Logs, as it certainly would have been. It is likely that this story arose from sailors recalling swinging out the boats from their ships when hove-to to take abyssal soundings that afternoon, which was recorded in the logs. However, the Master of the *Panther* did state in his log, which is still extant, that he thought they were close to the northern opening of the Channel, and it is interesting that the *Panther* was the southern-most ship in the fleet when the disaster occurred and one of the few which did not need to take avoiding action.

The second legend has it that a young seaman warned Shovell that they were too close to the Scillies, and was hung from the yard-arm for mutiny. This is an absurd myth. It is quite likely that some sailors thought they were closer to the Isles of Scilly than to the Breton coast – an experienced sailor can often detect changes in the lie of the sea which indicate a familiar landfall. It is also possible that lower-deck men might have communicated this intuitive feeling to their divisional officers, and that this came to the ears of the Admiral. However, the story of a hanging on the *Association* is nonsense.

First is the obvious fact that no-one in the ship survived the shipwreck, so we have no basis for the story at all. Secondly, such extreme punishment for insubordination of this kind would have been completely against Cloudesley Shovell's character. Lastly, Shovell was a stickler for following the Admiralty's orders, even against his own judgment, after two early incidents in which he did not do so and which were the only two black marks in his professional career, earning the enmity of Samuel Pepys. Executing a man could not be done without the guilty verdict of a court martial presided over by the three senior officers of the port, station or fleet in which an alleged offence took place, and at the time two of those officers were on other ships battling a storm. This then is just a vicious rumour, which started on the Scillies and has been repeated ever since, even in a recent international best-seller on the search for the solution to the 'Longitude problem', to the detriment of Shovell's reputation.

The third legend may have a basis in fact. When Shovell was washed ashore on the island of St Mary's after the sinking, it is said that a fisherwoman found him still alive, and smothered him having cut off one of his fingers for a large emerald ring. This story began many years later when the local rector on St Mary's is said to have reported the woman's death-bed confession, itself unlikely, and was given the ring which he sent to one of Shovell's friends. Against this gruesome myth it can be said that Shovell was an obese man in late middle age, and it is doubtful that he could have lived in those seas at that time of year for more than 30 minutes or so. No-one else from his ship, most of them young and fit, survived. When Shovell's body was first seen by the island's more reputable citizens, some ten hours after the sinking, it was intact – with only a small scratch above an eyebrow – although there were the residual indentations of rings on two of his fingers and most of his outer clothes had been stolen. The ring itself – a large oval emerald surrounded by diamonds on a gold mounting – certainly did exist, and records show that it was in the Marsham family related to Shovell's daughter Anne at the end of the eighteenth century but has since disappeared.

Whatever the truth of these legends, it is today possible to piece together what happened to the fleet on the fateful night of 22 October, from analysis of the surviving ships' logs and eye-witness accounts.

The Shipwreck and its Aftermath

Within an hour of setting sail from their soundings, the storm was all about the ships of the fleet, high seas, streaming fog and rain impeding their vision. All the ships shortened sail but it was too late. At about 7.30pm the leading vessel, Shovell's flagship the 90-gun *Association*, ran hard onto the Outer Ledge of the Gilstone Rocks, the southern-most reef of the Isles of Scilly.

As his crew fought desperately to save the *Association*, Shovell tried to warn the other ships by firing a gun, but they were on a lee shore, the winds and high seas

The Gilstone Rock, with the Gilstone Outer Ledge beyond, taken from the MV Sea King, 22 October 2007. Photograph by Alan Jones, Shipwrecks UK.

pushing them towards the jagged granite reefs. Although most were able to wear, turning through the wind onto a safe course, five other ships also struck the rocks of the Gilstone Ledges, the Bishop and Clerks and the terrifyingly-named Tearing Ledge. One, by dint of consummate seamanship and good luck, was beached in shallow water with no loss of life. Another, the *St George*, also had a lucky escape. Her commander reported that she was caught on the Outer Ledge alongside the *Association*, but that she was swept free by the same wave which smashed the flagship's stern counter. Within minutes the *Association* slipped beneath the raging sea into a deep gully between the Gilstone Rocks, where she lies today. Three other ships sank with her, the *Eagle*, the *Romney* and the *Firebrand*. 23 men survived from the *Firebrand*, one from the *Romney*, but nearly 2,000 of their comrades died that night.

The next morning the sea was full of broken timbers, torn canvas and dead bodies. Cloudesley Shovell's body was washed ashore in Porth Hellick cove on St Mary's, seven miles from the Gilstone, with those of his step-sons, John and James Narbrough, the son of Bishop Trelawney, the son of Admiral Aylmer, and Shovell's nephew, Captain Edward Loades, the commander of the *Association*. Shovell's body was stripped of its fine clothes and precious rings by Scillonians quick to scavenge – to paraphrase an old wreckers' prayer – what God had brought their way, and was later buried a few yards from the beach, a spot marked today by a granite pillar.

By order of Queen Anne, Shovell's body was exhumed and taken to Falmouth, where it was embalmed before being conveyed to London, the entire route lined with shocked and silent onlookers. In London it lay in state at his town house in Soho Square until, on 22 December 1707, his body was taken in a cortege of over 100 coaches along Pall Mall and down Whitehall to Westminster Abbey, where it was interred under the South Quire Aisle.

The Monument at Westminster Abbey

Early in 1708 Grinling Gibbons started work on the *disegno* for Shovell's memorial at Westminster Abbey. It would take his sculptors six months to make and cost £322 and 10 shillings (equivalent to about £650,000 today), the account paid by Queen Anne personally.[10] The Monument is very large, being twenty feet high and ten feet wide, projecting two and a half feet into the aisle of the South Quire. Gibbons conceived the Monument as a classical figure lying as in life, upon a sarcophagus between a pair of coupled columns interspersed with drops of laurel and oak leaves. The capitals are in the Corinthian order supporting pediments on which cherubs hold armorial shields. One shows Shovell's heraldic achievement, granted in 1692 – gules, a chevron ermine, in chief two crescents argent, in base a fleur-de-lis or. The other shows Shovell's arms conjoined with those of his wife's family.

Deeply-cut drapery is drawn up as a baldachino, supporting a Saracenic helmet commemorating his actions against the Barbary corsairs, its plume covered by a deep chaplet of laurel leaves surmounted by Shovell's heraldic crest, a gilded naval crown out of which rises a demi-lion rampant gules displaying a flag with an anchor sable. The sarcophagus and the columns rest upon a wide base carrying three large panels. The centre panel shows a scene in high relief of the *Association* and the other warships foundering on the rocks of the Scillies, and the outer panels display high-relief carvings of anchors, trumpets of fame, naval ensigns and naval weapons.

The realisation of the figure is unsatisfactory. Grinling Gibbons – Master Sculptor to the Crown since 1684 – was not an accomplished sculptor in bronze or stone. His atelier had produced many excellent statues in each material, but after Arnold Quellin had left their partnership, Gibbons' interpretation of figures in metal or stone became clumsy, attempting classical elegance but achieving something less. With his marble memorial to Sir Cloudesley Shovell this wonderful carver in wood – perhaps the best ever to sharpen a chisel – fails to convey the heroic nobility of his subject.

Shovel is shown lying on a cushioned banqueting couch. He is dressed as a Roman general, an Imperial toga wrapping his ample body like a night-gown, but opening at the torso to reveal anthropomorphic body armour, its six-pack of abdominal muscles incongruous on this fat ox of a sailor. We could, just, accept this as lionising a great sea-captain with an allusion to the heroes of antiquity, were it not that the effect is ruined by the full Stuart periwig, which flows in tight curls in two floppy swathes to Shovell's shoulders like some great Cocker Spaniel. The pose is awkward, the attempt at classical *contraposto* lapsing into an uncomfortable slouch, the angle of Shovell's supporting left arm implying an impatience to be off rather than elegant relaxation. The face, podgy and unlined, more Nero than Caesar, however does have something of Shovell's famous geniality.

I greatly admire Gibbons' work, and I am convinced that he carved the delightful over-mantel of celestial navigation instruments, flowers, fish, weapons and cherubs in the Board Room at the Old Admiralty Office on Whitehall. The quality of *disegno* and execution of that unique piece are outstanding.[11] If Gibbons had only added a similar jaunty nautical flavour to his immense memorial to Shovell, we could forgive his less than excellent design. One looks in vain at the panels on Shovell's monument for the maritime decoration which Joseph Addison thought so appropriate to the subject, the 'rostral Crowns, naval Ornaments, with beautiful Festoons of Seaweed, Shells and Coral'.[12]

Such elements enliven the (sadly much weathered) panels of Gibbons' equestrian statue of Charles II, now at Windsor Castle, and make the monument by William Kent and Peter Scheemakers to Admiral Monck at the Abbey dignified and stately, and they are joyously entwined with floral garlands, cherubs, fish and strings of pearls which make Gibbons' carvings at New River Head House so rich in maritime references. While it may have been too ironic to include navigation instruments on this particular tomb, it suffers as much from this lack of appropriate maritime allusion as from its unimaginative *disegno* and poor figurative sculpting.

The memorial inscription on a tablet behind Shovell's head – perhaps written by a Court official with no feeling for naval action – is largely a list of Shovell's honours and a dismal recounting of the tragedy which struck him down, rather than the inspiring recitation of his valour and martial successes and his great services to the nation which one expects on monuments to heroes. It compares badly with this eulogy to Shovell written in 1708 by Abel Boyer:

This was ... one of the greatest sea commanders of our age, or, indeed, as ever this island produced; of undaunted courage and resolution, of wonderful presence of mind in the hottest engagements, and of consummate skill and experience; but more that all this, he was a just, frank, generous, honest, good man. He was artificer of his own good fortune, and his personal merit alone, from the lowest, rais'd himself to almost the highest station in the Navy of Great Britain.[13]

Few who knew Cloudesley Shovell, as a man or as a sea-officer, would have disagreed with that. With Shovell's tomb at Westminster Abbey, Grinling Gibbons produced a Monument of giant proportions, memorable and imposing, but which in the quirky realisation of its subject and its relatively poor execution, falls far short of what we might wish for the man it memorialises, one of Britain's greatest heroes, that 'brave, rough, English admiral', Sir Cloudesley Shovell.

---

[1] Joseph Addison, *The Spectator*, 30 March 1711.

[2] Jodocus Crull, *The Antiquities of St Peters: or, The Abbey Church of Westminster* (London: John Morphew, 1711), p. 110.

[3] N.A.M. Rodger, *The Command of the Ocean: A Naval History of Britain, 1649-1815* (London: Allen Lane, 2004).

[4] Simon Harris, *Admiral Sir Cloudesley Shovell: Stuart Admiral* (Staplehurst: Spellmount, 2001), p. 7.

[5] Tanner, Pepys MSS vol IV 179, Bodleian Library.

[6] John Campbell, *Lives of the Admirals, and Other Eminent British Seamen* (London: T. Waller, 1750), ii, pp. 375-76.

[7] See *Alumni Oxonienses: The Members of the University of Oxford, 1500-1714* (London: Parker, 1891).

[8] Speech by Queen Anne to the Houses of Parliament, August 1703, quoted in Harris, *Admiral Sir Cloudesley Shovell*, p. 63.

[9] Commander W.E. May, *Institute of Navigation Journal* (1960), p. 352 et seq.

[10] *Inflation: The Value of the Pound, 1750-2005*, House of Commons Library Research Paper 06/09, 2006, p. 20 et seq.

[11] For a description of the Admiralty Board Room carvings, see the author's paper 'Nelson at the Admiralty: In the footsteps of the Hero in the Royal Navy's Headquarters in London', *The Trafalgar Chronicle*, 16 (2006), pp. 24-42, and a more detailed exposition in his forthcoming book *The Great Ship Ashore: The Admiralty in London*.

[12] Joseph Addison, *The Spectator*, 30 March 1711.

[13] Abel Boyer, *The History of the Reign of Queen Anne, Digested into Annals: Year the Sixth* (London: Margaret Coggan, 1708).

Why Didn't John Bull Volunteer?

Tamara L. Hunt and Scott Hughes Myerly

John Bull and the Alarmist, caricature by James Gillray, published 1 September 1803.
Courtesy Warwick Leadlay Gallery.

'After 1792 John Bull served in cartoons as a soldier and sailor against Napoleon,' Peter Mellini and Roy T. Matthews claimed in a 1987 article on the figure of John Bull.[1] But analysis of English caricatures shows that in the era of Britain's longest modern war, out of some 4,400 known caricatures, John Bull was depicted as a soldier only about a dozen times, and in virtually every case as a volunteer, not a member of the regular army.[2] Since he appeared in approximately one out of every ten graphic satires published between 1793 and 1815,[3] it is most striking that caricaturists did not depict him as a regular, especially considering the sensational impact on the public when news of great land victories reached England – victories won by the regular army.

But it wasn't that John Bull backed down from a fight; he was often depicted as pugnaciously defending his country and defying his enemies, but he did so as a civilian, and only rarely as a volunteer. Although one might easily assume that this could be explained by the long-standing English dislike of standing armies,[4] this does not adequately cover the situation. With several very real invasion scares, and an ongoing twenty-year conflict against a highly successful French army, the British army was vital in defending the state, and its soldiers were often celebrated and epitomized with overwhelming public zeal as the embodiment of heroism, glory and valour.[5] Yet an analysis of caricatures suggests that the attributes associated with John Bull made his character incompatible with soldiering.

By the 1790s, the character of John Bull had come to be well-established. In his first appearance in 1712, he symbolized the nation, but over the course of the century he came to personify the common people.[6] Honest, simple, loyal, somewhat credulous, and attached to his beef and ale, John Bull was content when left alone to enjoy his homely pleasures, but could be roused to action if provoked. Thus, he came to have a somewhat different allegorical connotation than other national symbols, such as Britannia or the British lion; while he might represent the country's interests as a whole, more often he was used to denote the characteristics or opinions of the English people. This made him a versatile figure, as he could represent Everyman who could be praised for his virtues, but also criticized for his shortcomings and urged to rectify them.

Of Freedom, Beef and Ale

One of John Bull's faults was his credulity, and as the French Revolution became more radical, artists turned to emphasizing the superiority of existing English conditions to the reforms proposed or enacted by the French. Caricaturists and writers often deplored efforts to stifle public debate on political issues, even when the fear was greatest that the common people would be seduced by demagogues espousing French revolutionary ideology. Many emphasized that John Bull's liberty-loving, independent character required persuasion, not force, to resist the blandishments of would-be reformers. As one London newspaper reminded its readers in August 1792, 'Treat John Bull but gently, and much may be done with him.'[7] Several months earlier, the same newspaper had assured its readers that 'John Bull has too much good sense' to listen to 'mad Democrates [sic]' who wanted to 'pollute the sacred fabric' of the Constitution. Another paper expressed the hope that 'John Bull will not be fool enough to attempt to be better than well' by listening to the reformers, while in November, a news report noted with satisfaction that John Bull was refusing to rise in revolt, despite the instigation of radical reformers, because 'John Bull enjoys liberty and grows prosperous in trade as long as he continues honest; and he knows too much of self-interest to revolt against that Government under which he has flourished.'[8]

These themes appeared in caricature frequently. James Gillray's *French Liberty. British Slavery* (21 December 1792) contrasted a recognizable John-Bull type figure – a rotund citizen eating beef and drinking ale who nevertheless complains of slavery that stemmed from ruinous taxes – with a thin, ragged Frenchman seated in a sparsely-furnished garret eating raw onions and praising the blessings of liberty that have brought him to this state. *Reform Advised, Reform Begun, Reform Complete* (8 January 1793) takes a similar theme. In the first frame, a stout John Bull sits beside a loaded table, holding a foaming tankard and exclaiming that his bounty is the result of 'the blessed effects of a good Constitution'. Thin, ragged Frenchmen cajole John Bull with promises that he will be even better if he undertakes reform. In the second frame, reform has begun, and a much thinner John Bull has lost his leg,

Reform Advised, Reform Begun, Reform Complete, caricature after Thomas Rowlandson, published 8 January 1793. Courtesy the authors.

while in place of beef and pudding, he has only a frog to eat; French *sans-culottes* now threaten rather than entice as they urge him towards even more reform. In the final frame, *sans-culottes* trample a ragged John Bull, telling him that he is lucky they let him live.

The theme that French ideology threatens John Bull's well-being was prominent in the early years of the war, reflecting the fear that the poor and middling sort would be seduced into French-style rebellion. But French armies also threatened the British state, and the ideological and military dangers were combined in James Gillray's *Sans-Culottes Feeding Europe with the Bread of Liberty* (12 January 1793). Published just weeks before war was declared, this print shows thin, ragged *sans-culotte* soldiers forcing citizens of Holland, Savoy, Germany, Prussia and Italy to swallow 'liberty' in the form of bread impaled on bayonets. Meanwhile Charles James Fox and Richard Brinsley Sheridan, English opposition politicians who had loudly praised the French Revolution, are shown dressed as *sans-culottes* who are forcing the same bread on John Bull.

John Bull's Progress, caricature by James Gillray, published 3 June 1793.
Courtesy Warwick Leádlay Gallery.

Despite these fears of a French threat that was both ideological and military, once war was declared early in 1793, caricaturists James Gillray and Isaac Cruikshank suggested that John Bull would experience a similar disaster if he enlisted in the army. Two of the few satires published throughout the coming generation of conflict that depict him as a regular soldier were published during the disastrous 1793 campaign in Flanders, and both show that John Bull was better off as a civilian. Gillray's satire, *John Bull's Progress* (3 June 1793), is a four part design. In the first scene, John Bull is a stout, happy countryman. In the second panel, he has enlisted and is proudly marching off to war, leaving a weeping wife and children behind him. The third shows his destitute, dispossessed family vainly asking for assistance from the Treasury. In the final panel, he returns home as a gaunt, maimed veteran who has lost an eye and a leg, only to find his family starving in a wretched hovel. Isaac Cruikshank took a similar approach in *He would be a soldier, or the History of John Bull's Warlike Expedition* (1 July 1793). In this satire, John Bull, a young farmer, enlists in the army; after training, and life in camp and in battle, he returns home 'Loaded with honors of War' as a one-eyed, one-legged beggar followed by his destitute wife and children.

'Damn fear, drink on, be jolly, boys!'

As these satires suggest, despite the rhetoric of honor and glory promoted by military recruiters, the condition of the ordinary soldier was a bad lot.[9] In both of these prints, John Bull returns home to his family while still a young man solely because his injuries made him physically unable to serve; otherwise, the term of service for young men who 'took the king's shilling' was twenty-one years. Since many did not survive that long, this often meant that the term of service was for life. Soldiers' low pay was further reduced by deductions for clothing and food (only after 1806 did the army stop charging soldiers for bread), accommodation was often miserable, and victimization by their own officers was not uncommon.[10] Superiors had the power to impose harsh discipline at will; as one Napoleonic war veteran recalled:

> *If a man, when accused by superiors of something of which he was not guilty, ventured to speak in his own defense, he was called a lawyer, and desired to give no reply. If he said that he thought it was hard ... the answer was 'D-n you sir, you have no right to think ... do what you are ordered, sir, right or wrong.'* [11]

This observation that soldiers blindly followed orders was echoed in satire published in the autumn of 1793, as unusually bad weather made conditions for the army increasingly dire. *The Wet Party or the Bogs of Flanders* (7 December 1793) by Isaac Cruikshank, shows British soldiers half submerged in the Flemish mud, while verses beneath the print declare: 'Why Soldiers Why / Should we be Melancholy, boy; / Why, Soldiers, why? / Whose business is to die / What sighing fie! / Damn fear, drink on, be jolly, boys! / 'Tis he, you or I -- / cold hot wet & dry; / We're allways [sic] bound to follow, boys, annd [sic] scorn to fly!' Coupled with the bravado (men 'whose business is to die' nevertheless 'scorn to fly!') is the reminder that soldiers are 'bound to follow' whatever the conditions or orders.

This demand of unquestioning, unthinking obedience was at variance with the character of John Bull as it had developed by the 1790s. *Rule Britannia*, with its assertion 'Britons never shall be slaves' was highly popular,[12] and served as a reminder that Englishmen would not bow to foreign or domestic tyranny, yet the notion of soldiers as 'slaves in red coats' was one of the era's clichés.[13] This staunch adherence to British independence may well be one of the reasons why John Bull was not depicted as a soldier as the war continued. He might have been simple, honest and loyal, and he might be victimized by his superiors, but he was never servile.

During the 1790s, John Bull tended to be used mainly in satires on domestic affairs,[14] and prints published during invasion scares suggest that John Bull was not suited to military discipline, even going so far as to imply that civilians rather than volunteers should defend the country. *French Invasion or Brighton in a Bustle* (1 March 1794), and *England Invaded, or Frenchmen Naturalized* (16 March 1798) both show civilians helping to fend off invading French soldiers, while satires on the volunteers, such as *Essex-Calve-lry for Internal Defense* (12 May 1794), depict the volunteers as awkward and incapable of dealing with the French invaders; in this print, the volunteers, mounted on calves, flee from lean and ragged French sans-culottes.

Given these attitudes, the public was delighted when peace appeared imminent in 1801. Thomas Rowlandson used the occasion to once again make the point that John Bull flourished as a civilian, not a soldier. *John Bull in the Year 1800! John Bull in the Year 1801!* (12 October 1801), contrasts the sorry state of volunteer John Bull in 1800 with the peace and plenty he will enjoy as a civilian when the wars ended. While the print emphasizes the expected fall in prices, it also shows his relief at being released from volunteer duty, as he plays 'The Soldier Tired of Wars Alarms' on his fiddle.

But the peace proved only temporary, and war broke out again in 1803 with the renewed threat of French invasion. Dozens of invasion prints were published, many featuring John Bull defending his island home. Significantly, some of the handful of prints that showed him as a volunteer emphasize his disheveled dress. *Gillray's Buonapartè, 48 Hours after Landing! Vide John Bulls Home Stroke, Armed en Masse* (26 July 1803) shows John Bull dressed in a volunteer's uniform, but with unkempt hair and a checkered neckcloth, carrying Napoleon's head on a pitchfork. His sloppy appearance, which was so much at variance with the uniformity and order insisted upon in the military to maintain discipline, further emphasizes both his independence and resistance to martial servitude.

Nevertheless, some prints suggest that the attitude towards volunteers had changed somewhat; several artists now portrayed John Bull as an efficient and fierce (albeit obese) volunteer. G. M. Woodward favorably contrasted John Bull, a well-fed volunteer, facing a cowering, emaciated tattered Frenchman in *Facing the Enemy* (c. July – August 1803). An unknown artist created *John Bull Arming* (c. July – August 1803), depicting John Bull at home, dressed in his volunteer's uniform, preparing to fight off 'Master Bonny' (i.e. Bonaparte).

Defying Napoleon

These prints and others that feature John Bull show that the caricaturists now took a different approach to the conflict against Napoleon's forces. In the 1790s, John Bull had been largely used for domestic caricature, but in 1803 he became the chief opponent of Napoleon, superseding George III, Britannia and British politicians. Dozens of prints appeared during the wars that depicted him defending his country, and many of these appeared in 1803, when invasion threatened. *A Stoppage to a Stride Over the Globe* (c. July 1803) is unusual in that it reversed the relative sizes of John Bull and Napoleon; a huge Napoleon straddles the globe, while tiny John Bull waves his sword and swears to defend his island.

Another element that fostered the comparison between John Bull and Napoleon was the perceived difference in their characters. James Gillray in particular portrayed Napoleon as the personification of deceit and malevolence. In *John Bull offering Little Boney Fair Play* (2 August 1803), John Bull, wearing the striped trousers of an English sailor, stands unarmed

Oh who is it dares intorupt me in my Progress

why tis I little Johnny Bull Protecting a little yet I clan my hand on and I — n me if you come any Farther thats all

A STOPPAGE to a STRIDE over the GLOBE

A Stoppage to a Stride Over the Globe, caricature by P[iercy] Roberts, published c. July 1803. Courtesy the authors.

in the middle of the English Channel, defiantly calling on Napoleon to try to make good on his threat to invade England. In contrast to John Bull's jaunty gallantry in calling for a fair fight, a scrawny Napoleon cowers behind his fortress walls. A slightly later print, *The Ballance [sic] of Power or the Issue of the Contest* (c. October 1803), used the traditional device of a scale to show a comparison between John Bull and Napoleon. The latter proves heavier than his British foe because he is weighted down with 'Shame, Disgrace, Obliquy [sic], Cruelty, Murder, Rapine, Plunder, Albivion [sic] Hypocricy,' and has the assistance of hellish figures. Around townsman John Bull's head are inscribed his many virtues, including 'Integrity, Honour, Justice, Valour, Commerce, Firmness, Trade, Heroism, Virtue.' Thus, although Napoleon outweighs John Bull, it is due only to his evil traits and the assistance of the Devil.

Throughout the remainder of the war, John Bull – as a civilian – continued to defy Napoleon and cheer on his own forces. He celebrated British victories in the Peninsula but only once was depicted as a regular, in George Cruikshank's *The Battle of Vittoria* (7 July 1813). A handsome grenadier, John Bull personifies the heroic British soldier as contrasted with his ragged and emaciated French foes, but this was a unique image. Much more common were prints that showed a civilian John Bull reacting to victories by British troops, such as in *Extraordinary News* (September 1808), where John and his wife celebrate French General Junot's defeat by drinking the health of 'our noble commanders in Portugal.' In William Heath's *The Flushing Phantasmagoria – or – Kings Conjurors Amuseing [sic] John Bull* (September 1809), countryman John Bull is delighted at the naval victory at Flushing, which Prime Minister Spencer Perceval shows him through a telescope.

Yet even with the dramatic victory at Waterloo, arguably the most spectacular, exciting and celebrated event of the entire nineteenth century,[15] caricatures depict John Bull as a civilian, not a soldier. George Cruikshank's *John Bull, in Alarm; or, Boney's Escape, and a Second Deliverance of Europe* (c. April 1815) shows Napoleon kicking Louis XVIII from his throne, and John Bull, a townsman, promising to restore him 'as fast as he kicks you down.' A two-part design by Cruikshank published after Napoleon's surrender, *Buonaparte on the 17th of June – Buonaparte on the 17th of July – 1815* (August 1815) shows a civilian John Bull dismissing Napoleon's threats in June, and accepting his abject surrender after Waterloo.

A Civilian Solider

So why was John Bull not a soldier? Although he grumbled about the expense of the wars and mistrusted a peace-time military which could be – and was – used to oppress civilians in times of domestic upheaval, by the end of the wars British soldiers were viewed as heroes, and John Bull cheered their victories. Such was the enthusiasm, one Scotsman noted in 1803 that: 'we were all soldiers, one way or another.'[16]

Yet despite such military enthusiasms, caricatures suggest that during the long conflicts with France

Buonaparte on the 17th of July – 1815, caricature by George Cruikshank, published by S. Knight, August 1815. Courtesy the authors.

John Bull's love of his rights and independence ran much deeper than his temporary zeal for the intoxicating vision of martial valor. He could be militant when roused, but he was not suited for the servitude of military discipline. He was loyal, but independent, which made unquestioned obedience to a superior incompatible with his character and his rights as a free-born Englishman. The greatest irony of all is that although Britons liked to see martial show and parade about in 'second-hand uniforms,'[17]

John Bull's true identity was incompatible with the army's royal 'livery' of the military uniform with its many appealing, eye-catching emblems of glory, the Englishman's sacred duty of defending the realm, and identification with and loyalty to the British state and crown; after all, these visual tokens were also signs of subservience to a rigid, hierarchical system of governance. In order to persuade John Bull that he had a constitution worth preserving without adopting the reforms proposed by French Revolutionaries and their English admirers, and the militarism that emerged with Napoleon, writers and artists thus emphasized his distinctive, independent, civilian character. When danger threatened, he was willing and able to repel the tyrannical forces of revolutionary France, but it was in his character as a free civilian, not a soldier.

---

[1] Peter Mellini and Roy T. Matthews, 'John Bull's Family Arises', *History Today*, May (1987), p. 22.

[2] John Bull as Jack Tar was somewhat more popular, appearing in several dozen caricatures; this essay, however, will focus on John Bull and the army.

[3] Based on the M. Dorothy George's *Catalogue of Political and Personal Satires Preserved in the Department of Prints and Drawings in the British Museum* (London: Trustees of the British Museum, 1942-1949), there were approximately 4,400 caricatures published between 1 January 1793 and 31 December 1815, and John Bull appeared in some 450.

[4] See Scott Hughes Myerly, *British Military Spectacle: From the Napoleonic Wars through the Crimea* (Cambridge, MA: Harvard University Press, 1996), p. 10 and passim.

[5] According to one account, an estimated 200,000 enthusiastic people turned out at a grand review in 1811 at Wimbledon Common. Louis Simond, *An American in Regency England: The Journal of a Tour in 1810-1811*, edited by Christopher Hibbert (London: The History Book Club, 1968), p. 146.

[6] He first appeared in literature in a series of pamphlets attributed to John Arbuthnot, collected under the title *Law is a Bottomless Pit; Exemplify'd in the Case of the Lord Strutt, John Bull, Nicholas Frog and Lewis Baboon* (London: John Morphew, 1712). The collected pamphlets went through several editions, and were republished in 1727 in an edited version as *The Law is a Bottomless Pitt; or the History of John Bull*. This work was extremely popular, and references to its imagery continued into the second half of the century. For example, the *London Gazetteer and New Daily Advertiser* (September 5, 1766) carried a mock advertisement for a new book, *Reliquae Polesworthianae*, or, *The Sequel of the true and delightful History of John Bull*, a satire on the current political situation. Interestingly enough,

John Bull appears to represent George III, who was 'fool enough' to employ 'Roaring Will' (i.e., William Pitt the elder), who became Prime Minister again in 1766. In 1769, the reviewer of a pamphlet, *The Present State of the Nation*, made use of the figures of John Bull and Louis Baboon (representing France) in his criticism of the pamphlet. *The Gentleman's Magazine*, May (1769), p. 255. Caricaturists, however, were relatively slow to pick up on this imagery; see Tamara L. Hunt, *Defining John Bull: Political Caricature and National Identity in Late Georgian England* (Aldershot, Hampshire: Ashgate, 2003), especially chapter 4, 'Britannia, John Bull and National Identity'.

7 *The Times*, 19 August 1792.

8 *The Times*, 9 April 1792; *St. James's Chronicle*, 2 June 1792; *The Times*, 17 November 1792.

9 Caricaturist James Gillray visited the army in Flanders during the early part of the campaign in 1793 and thus had a first-hand look at the conditions soldiers experienced in the field. George, Catalogue of Political and Personal Satires, vii, p. 245.

10 Myerly, *British Military Spectacle*, pp. 3-4.

11 [Joseph Donaldson], *Recollections of an An Eventful Life, Chiefly Passed in the Army* (Glasgow, 1824), p. 85.

12 Advertisements in the 1790s indicate that in times of crisis, theatre audiences expected *Rule Britannia* and *God Save the King* to be included as part of the evening's entertainment; see, for example, the notice of a concert by Mr. Stabilini in Edinbugh, *The Edinburgh Advertiser*, 29 January 1793, or notices for upcoming performances at London theatres, e.g., *The Times*, 3 July 1794 or *The Times*, 24 March 1797. The song was also used in a celebratory context; for example, in 1794 when news of Lord Howe's naval victory on 'the Glorious First of June' reached London during a performance at the Opera, the band interrupted the performance and immediately 'struck up the national song of *Rule Britannia*'. *European Magazine and London Review*, June 1794, p. 485. For those who wanted to enjoy *Rule Britannia* at home, enterprising music publishers provided sheet music for piano; see the advertisement of music publisher John Watlin of Edinburgh, *The Edinburgh Advertiser*, 29 March 1793.

13 In this era, slaves were literally bought by the state to raise new regiments. Myerly, *British Military Spectacle*, p. 54.

14 Despite France's threat to invade Britain, the war tended to be unpopular. It increased the public's financial burden, and during the 1790s scarcity and real want were prominent. John Bull rarely appeared in prints dealing with actual military conflict and was most frequently utilized to criticize the government. For example, when William Pitt's ministry suspended habeas corpus (1794) and introduced the 'Convention Bill' (1795) that tightened control over public meetings, caricaturists reacted with satires such as *The Modern Hercules or a Finishing Blow for John Bull* (17 November 1795). John Bull, bent double under a heavy burden of taxes, subsidies, pensions, and debt, reacts with horror as Pitt swings a club at him labeled 'Convention Bill'.

15 As one officer who fought at Waterloo wrote in 1838, 'I shall not be far wrong in asserting that there exists not in the United Kingdom, man, woman or child, who has not either seen pictures or panoramas or Waterloo, heard songs on Waterloo, read books on Waterloo, talked for weeks about Waterloo, and [a] full two-thirds of the adult population could not rest until they journeyed forth to have a look at Waterloo'. Harry Austin, *Guards Hussars and Infantry. Adventures of Harry Austin* (London, 1838), iii, p. 311.

16 Henry Cockburn, *Memorials of His Time*, edited by Karl F. C. Miller (London: University of Chicago Press, 1974), pp. 180-81.

17 Myerly, *British Military Spectacle*, p. 149.

Rule Britannia:
The Development of an Icon, 1770-1820

Jennifer Bodie

The following selection of prints illustrates the visual development of Britannia in caricature from 1770 to 1820, examining her origins in satire and through what means she has become the ageless warrior-goddess recognizable today. Britannia appears in many guises, and in her status as a woman we see reflected certain gender issues that affected how she was portrayed at the pens of her male satirical illustrators. She was not seen as suited to the same subjects as John Bull, and in the 1770's and 1780's came to be associated with a distinct set of subjects, in particular those relating to the Constitution. Britannia's relationships with other figures like America and Hibernia emphasized her nature as a symbol for English liberties that remained separate from class loyalties, however over time she deferred her popularity in caricature to her male complement, John Bull. As war in the nineteenth century dominated national concerns, she lost much of her political association and became something of a simplified character intended to instil patriotism: the dignity and fighting spirit of a nation personified in female form, elegant and powerful.

The images showcased here range from magazine illustrations to well-known prints by Gillray. They are all drawn from the extensive collection of satirical prints in the British Museum and are catalogued in Dorothy George's *Collection of Political and Personal Satires*. This series is by no means exhaustive; rather it provides an overview of Britannia's development in political prints comparable to similar studies of John Bull.

1. This print, originally published anonymously in Holland, is the first known appearance of Britannia in satire. This English copy was published in London in 1673 and formed an illustration to Stubbes's 'A Justification of the Present War against the United Netherlands'. Britannia, without her shield and spear, has slipped from her globe and is trampled by the triumphant Dutch Maid as a Dutchman chops the tails from a number of English dogs. The image was one of several anti-English prints published in Holland around this time regarding the commercial enmity between the English and the Dutch. [British Museum Number: 1852,0424.73]

2. *Britannia Intoxicated, or The Great Ones in a Bagnio* (1772): In her early appearances, satirists engaged Britannia in the action of the image, most frequently as the victim and dressed in women's clothes of the day. In this etching, she is clad like a common wench and sits intoxicated amongst her indiscreet

Britania intoxicated, or the Great ones in a Bagnio.

ministers. Her shield and spear are trampled underneath her, a motif repeated throughout the eighteenth century to illustrate her loss of power. Published in the *Oxford Magazine*, 1 June 1772, the explanatory text asks: 'Who are the greatest drunkards? – Those at the helm – Who set the most glaring examples of adultery, fornication...' [British Museum Number: 1868,0808.10009. BM Satire 4954]

The Blood & Vitals from her Wounds he drew,
And Fed the Hounds that help'd him to pursue.

Dryden.

3. *The Operation* (1773): The image of Britannia physically abused by her ministers is repeated throughout this decade. Presenting Britannia as a vulnerable woman assaulted by her protectors exposed ministerial corruption as attacks on the body politic. Early prints of Britannia, which generally displayed Radical tendencies, exploit her femininity and evoke the need to protect her from the corruption of those who should defend her. Here, a minister stands above her with a dagger raised to strike. Two others hold basins to catch the gushing blood, while Lord Talbot sits in the foreground drinking from a bowl of blood. In the background, a lawyer hands a bowl to Bute, seated at right in a high-backed chair. Lord Bute, a Scot, was especially vilified in prints of the period due to his close relationship with George III, and in other similar prints of Britannia is frequently the 'foreign' orchestrator of the violence. Beneath the design is engraved, 'The Blood & Vitals from her Wounds he drew,\ And Fed the Hounds that help'd him to pursue. Dryden'. [British Museum Number: 1868,0808.10049. BM Satire 5127]

4. *The Convention Makers* (1771): The association between Britannia and the Constitution is established early in the 1770's. Here she serves two roles; when the Constitution is attacked, Britannia is the contemporary woman embodying the Constitution without the pomp and circumstance of her armour (note the broken bowl in *Britannia Intoxicated*), yet when she takes an active role to defend it, she dons the weapons of a warrior. This satire on the convention between Spain and Britain on the Falkland Islands, signed on 22 January 1771, illustrates Britannia and Justice charging in with shield and spear to protect Magna Carta and National Honour, while stumbling ministers flee to the left. [British Museum Number: 1868.0808.9941. BM Satire 4849]

The Convention Makers.

5. *The Able Doctor, or America Swallowing the Bitter Draught* (1774): Contemporary intellectuals such as Edmund Burke traced the republican tradition in Britain back to antiquity and viewed the government's taxation policy towards the British in America as a repression of English liberties. The

The able Doctor, or America Swallowing the Bitter Draught.

thirteen colonies constituted an important part of the British Empire as an extension of England, with the same rights, culture, language and religion as their countrymen at home. Britannia's stance towards her 'children' in America demonstrates the sympathies felt by the English towards their compatriots before the war. In this print, Britannia turns away in shame as Lord North forces tea down America's throat, while France, Spain and Lord Bute look on in glee. This print was published in response to the Boston Port Bill, one of the 'five intolerable acts' following the Boston Tea Party. [British Museum Number: 1855,0609.1926. BM Satire 5226]

6. *The Parricide, A Sketch of Modern Patriotism* (1776): As hostilities in the American colonies increased, the 'mother/daughter' relationship between Britannia and America was turned on its head in satires on the subject. America, supported by a wild Indian, lunges with a dagger and tomahawk at Britannia who is held down by Bute and others, as a harnessed British lion attempts to defend her. Dominating the foreground is Britannia's shield and broken spear, with an image of a pelican pecking its breast to symbolize the sacrificial loss of the colonies. [British Museum Number: 1868,0808.10075. BM Satire 5334]

Engrav'd for the Westminster Magazine.

AD 1776

The Parricide.
A Sketch of Modern Patriotism.

7. *A New Administration, or The State Quacks Administring* [sic] (1783): This print is one of many on the Coalition of Fox and Lord North. Britannia kneels on top of her cracked shield as Fox lifts up her dress and North holds

A New ADMINISTRATION, or — The State Quacks ADMINISTRING.

a large syringe. In the 1780s, Britannia's links to the Constitution become secondary to commentary on the political landscape and the means in which her femininity could be exploited. As a woman, Britannia's sexual vulnerability was her greatest weakness as a female political icon. This kind of physical subservience implied she had no power of her own, and while such prints did contain a certain perverse humour, North's 'administration' was equally shameful to the country as to the woman about to suffer it. [British Museum Number: 1867,0309.763. BM Satire 6201]

8. *Liberty and Fame introducing Female Patriotism to Britania* [sic] (1784): The furore caused in the 1784 Westminster Elections by the Duchess of Devonshire redirected the extent of Britannia's symbolism and the forms Britannia assumed in subsequent decades. Georgiana Cavendish, Duchess of Devonshire, faced considerable public criticism for her personal methods of canvassing and her image as a 'woman of the people', which was likened to prostitution. Foxite prints attempted to justify the Duchess by associating her with Britannia as a female patriot. This print by Thomas Rowlandson shows Britannia and her lion enthroned, presenting a laurel garland to the Duchess who is led by the characters of Liberty and Fame. Under the title is a quote from Shakespeare's *The Tempest*, 'She smiles- infused with a fortitude from Heaven'. [British Museum Number: 1868,0808.5320. BM Satire 6599]

Liberty and Fame introducing Female Patriotism to Britania
She SMILES —
INFUSED WITH A FORTITUDE FROM HEAVEN." VIDE Shakespears Tempest.
25ᵗ MAY 1784

9. *The Funeral of Trade* (1785): Immediately following Pitt's election, Britannia is seen to celebrate the young hero, however by 1795 she falls victim to his tax burdens and Irish resolutions. In contrast to her relationship with America, references to Hibernia as a 'sister' illustrate the relationship with Ireland as it was popularly perceived; the two figures are like partners, yet the way Britannia suffers at Hibernia's economic gains implies that Britannia should have been first among equals. This print combines criticism of Pitt's Shop Tax and Irish Propositions. Two ministers prepare to throw the coffin of British trade into a 'Pit', as Britannia sits in rags with a broken shield and spear while Hibernia whips the burdened British lion behind her. [British Museum Number: 1868,0808.5436. BM Satire 6798]

10. *The Contrast* (1793): With revolutionary war raging in nearby France from 1792, satirists found ways to reconnect Britannia overtly to the Constitution, particularly when it concerned issues of democracy and arbitrary power. In France, the figure of Liberty came to represent the revolution, appearing in painting, statuary, and on the official seal in a similar way that Britannia appeared on the currency and in nationalistic statuary. The two female figures were contrasted in satire to emphasize the difference between 'British liberty' and 'French slavery' for propaganda and ironical ends. This print, disseminated by the anti-radical campaign in London, shows two roundels, with 'French Liberty' on

the right as a fury laying waste to the scene, and Britannia, labelled 'British Liberty', seated in serenity holding Magna Carta and the scales of justice with a demure British lion at her feet. The print had appeared in two sizes and at varying prices, indicating the attempt to issue it as a widespread piece of propaganda. [British Museum Number: 1861,1012.47. BM Satire 8149] **See Colour Plates.**

11. *Britannia between Scylla and Charybdis* (1793): Francophobia and the fear of arbitrary government at the end of the eighteenth century provided ample material for satirists like Gillray to engage Britannia with 'Jacobin' ministers. *Britannia between Scylla and Charybdis* shows Fox, Sheridan and Priestley as sharks chasing Britannia, a pretty and buxom damsel, in the boat of the 'Constitution'. Pitt, here shown as Britannia's last hope, attempts to steer the raft between the 'Rock of Democracy' posted with a Jacobin cap, and the 'Whirlpool of Arbitrary Power'. [British Museum Number: 1851,0901.649. BM Satire 8320] **See Colour Plates.**

12. *The Genius of France Triumphant...*(1795): The Jacobin threat continued as a theme during the early years of the French Revolution. The fear demonstrated in the prints of the period had strong connections to the persistent threat of the 'Norman yoke' that had long overshadowed England, and the notion that if revolutionary ideals spread to the British Isles, chaos would reign and Norman influence would be reestablished. In *The genius of France triumphant...*

Britannia is cast to the ground with Fox, Sheridan and Stanhope who are dressed as *sans-culottes*. The group presents Magna Carta and the Crown as gifts to a French revolutionary. This print was issued in response to attempts by the Opposition to make peace with France, and illustrates how such attempts were destructive to British pride and made a grovelling whore of its national icon. [British Museum Number: 1868,0808.6409 BM Satire 8614] **See Colour Plates.**

13. *The Nursery, with Britannia Reposing in Peace* (1802): By the beginning of the nineteenth century, images of Britannia depicted her as a mere pawn in the political struggle with France. Gillray represents her three times in the first few years of the century as an oversized, complacent child or wench coddled by her ministers. The images attacked the defeatist strategies of the government. Addington, Hawkesbury and Fox, dressed in the colours of the tricolour, rock a sleeping Britannia beside a bowl of 'French pap'. [British Museum Number: 1851,0901.1099. BM Satire 9895] **See Colour Plates.**

14. *Physical Aid, or Britannia Recover'd from a Trance!* (1803): Gillray's vitriolic prints make clear not only the way the external threat to British politics brought the Constitution and all its unspoken elements back to public attention, but also the symbolic changes Britannia had undergone since a decade earlier. The visual change was a gradual development from the mid 1780's when politically active women, particularly the Duchess of Devonshire, proved themselves influential throughout the electorate. Retaining Britannia as an outspoken character was not only too representative of women in politics, but also denoted revolutionary or radical tendencies that conservatives, who gradually appropriated her image from the 1790s, were keen to erase. Britannia sits dishevelled at the feet of Addington, Hawkesbury and Sheridan, who look over a cliff at an advancing navy of tiny French ships. Addington holds a tonic of gunpowder to her nose as she cries a line parodied from Hamlet, 'Doctors and Ministers of [dis] grace defend me!' [British Museum Number: 1851,0901.1111. BM Satire 9972] **See Colour Plates.**

15. *Britannia in Tribulation* (1807): In the only known print from this period with Britannia and John Bull interacting, Britannia as a Roman warrior-goddess kneels before John Bull to plead for advice at the desertion of her allies. He advises her, 'What are you to do- why stick to me, your old and faithfull ally John Bull, who will never desert you while he has a timber to support him'. John Bull's unpretentious dress and connections with English symbols of prosperity such as beer and roast beef in satire made him the emblem of the English free man, one trait Britannia could never embody. The lines between the two are drawn, and visually the image creates a national agenda- to support Britannia's glorious history and liberties that can only survive with the aid of her faithful people. [British Museum Number: 1868,0808.7588. BM Satire 10757] **See Colour Plates.**

16. *Britannia Repremanding a Naughty Boy!* (1803): From 1803, Britannia took on the martial form that has remained static to the present day. Her feminine qualities were deemphasized in favour of an androgynous stock-image, like a statue come to life. A popular image that was repeated time and again for the remaining years of the war with Napoleon was the juxtaposition of the 'Little Corsican' and Britannia as correcting matron. There are only subtle, if hardly any, references to the English Constitution that had been so central to Britannia's associations in the 1770's and 1780's; she represents rather a character of the resilience to the foreign threat. Britannia stands on one side of the Channel towering over Napoleon with a birch, saying 'Stay where you are you troublesome little Urchin,\ If you once cross the Dyke you'll get a good birchin!' [British Museum Number: 1868,0808.7110. BM Satire 9987] **See Colour Plates.**

17. *Britannia Correcting an Unruly Boy!* (1803): Prints depicting Britannia and Napoleon bore no political message and it is clear from the simplicity of design and language that they were generally aimed at the lower print market. These images brought the political situation to a popular level, without actually engaging politics. In her Roman armour and large shield, Britannia had been distilled into two-dimensional character, aloof from any consequential meaning yet engaging with the figure of the enemy like a matron with a schoolboy. By portraying the battle against Napoleon in 1803 as sport, it deflected public opinion away from peace and provided fresh imagery to a conflict that had been begun some ten years previously. [British Museum Number: 1868,0808.7136. BM Satire 10012] **See Colour Plates.**

18. *Britannia weighing the Fate of Europe, or, John Bull too heavy for Buonaparte* (1803): Britannia makes a fool of Napoleon as she balances him on a scale with the stout and heavier John Bull. Although she dominates the image, she is a passive figure. John Bull carries the humour with his no-nonsense speech and typical resilience, saying to a miniscule Napoleon, 'A Conceited little Boaster – to pretend to be weigh'd against me – does he think I eat Beef and pudding for nothing'. [British Museum Number: 1985,0119.377. BM Satire (Undesribed)] **See Colour Plates.**

19. *Death or Liberty!...* (1819): From 1815 to 1820, Britannia appears in very few satires. *Death or Liberty!...*, produced in 1819 by George Cruikshank, shows the spectre of Death assaulting Britannia against the rock of religion as she defends herself with the flaming sword of The Laws. This late print represents an entire shift of Britannia's association with the Constitution from the radical perception of the 1770's, which called for free speech, ministerial reform and tax alleviation, to the conservative desire for maintenance of the *status quo* that associated reform with sedition and revolution. [British Museum Number: 1868,0808.8469. BM Satire 13279]

Britannia's image became popular once more in the nineteenth century with Leech and Tenniel's frequent use of her image in the *Punch* cartoons. After Victoria's accession to the throne, Britannia became a moral symbol for the virtues of the Victorian Empire, representing the period's ideals and close, at times identical, associations with Queen Victoria. Thus an image that in 1770 had been used to link national pride and liberties with the British people, and had shied away from too strong overtures to her female power, had expanded to encompass the spirit of an entire Empire, becoming the embodiment of a virtuous Victorian woman.

Britannia has become the quintessential British emblem, surpassing even her old friend, John Bull, in popularity. At the heart of Britannia's origins is the glorious Constitution that still resonates in the hearts of those that call themselves 'British'. Today, for citizens of the British Isles, there remains a certain fondness for the Roman warrior goddess who continues to connect the history Britain to ideals of liberty, freedom and national pride.

DEATH or LIBERTY! or Britannia & the Virtues of the Constitution in danger of Violation from the great Political Libertine, Radical Reform!

THE CONTRAST 1793

BRITISH LIBERTY   FRENCH LIBERTY

RELIGION, MORALITY,	ATHEISM, PERJURY
LOYALTY, OBEDIENCE to the LAWS,	REBELION, TREASON, ANARCHY, MURDER
INDEPENDANCE, PERSONAL SECURITY	EQUALITY, MADNESS, CRUELTY, INJUSTICE,
JUSTICE, INHERITANCᴱ, PROTECTION of	TREACHERY, INGRATITUDE, IDLENESS,
PROPERTY INDUSTRY, NATIONAL PROSPERITY	FAMINE, NATIONAL & PRIVATE RUIN,
HAPPINESS.	MISERY.

WHICH IS BEST?

T. Rowlandson fecit.   Price 3ˢ Plain, Coloured 6ˢ

SHARKS; Dogs of Scylla.

BRITANNIA between SCYLLA & CHARYBDIS.

or — The Vessel of the Constitution steered clear of the Rock of Democracy, and the Whirlpool of Arbitrary Power.

140

The Genius of France Triumphant. _ or _ BRITANNIA petitioning for PEACE. _ Vide The Proposals of Opposition. _
To the Patriotic Advocates for Peace, this Seemly sight is dedicated.

The NURSERY; _ with Britannia reposing in PEACE.

141

Physical Aid, — or — Britannia recover'd from a Trance; — also the Patriotic Courage of Sherry Andrew, & a peep thro' the Fog.

BRITANNIA in tribulation for the loss of her ALLIES or JOHN BULLS advice. Aug. 1807

142

Britannia reprimanding a *Naughty Boy!*

143

BRITANNIA Correcting an Unruly Boy.

144

A Conceited little Boaster – to pretend to be weigh'd against me – does he think I eat Beef and pudding for nothing.

Pub.d Dec.r 1803, by W. Holland, N.o 11 Cockspur Street London.

BRITANNIA weighing the FATE of EUROPE;
or
JOHN BULL too heavy for BUONAPARTE.

Editors' Extra: *Britannia, an installation by the artist Banksy (c.1974- present). Shown at his exhibition Banksy versus Bristol Museum, June to August 2009, Britannia reveals a post-modern image of the Roman goddess. How art the mighty fallen! Whilst she remains depicted in her traditional pose, the artist makes use of her trident to pun with the CCTV and anti-clamber spikes of the modern inner city experience. Likewise, the Union flag is shown draped upside down; for hundreds of years inverted flags have been commonly used at sea as the signal of distress. Courtesy Michael Mouse.*

The spiritual form of Nelson guiding Leviathan by William Blake (1757-1827), c. 1805-9. Tempera on canvas. Courtesy Tate Britain, London.

'Too Sublime for our Comprehension': William Blake's *Nelson*, Reconsidered

Huw Lewis-Jones

The times require that every one should speak out boldly;
England expects that every man should do his duty,
in Arts, as well as in Arms, or in the Senate.[1]

Two centuries ago, in May 1809, William Blake held his only one-man exhibition. London's art lovers were urged to come and admire his 'Poetical and Historical Inventions'. However, the solo show could not have been more disastrous; hardly anyone visited, no works appear to have been sold, commissions slowed in the months that followed and Blake sank deeper into obscurity. A single review that survives mocked the paintings as blotted, blurred and very badly drawn, whilst branding the artist 'an unfortunate lunatic'.[2] In the *Descriptive Catalogue* written to accompany the exhibition – rejected by the same critic as a farrago of nonsense and vanity – Blake borrowed some famous words in service of his artistic agenda, declaring 'England expects that every man should do his duty, in Arts, as well as in Arms'.[3] In appropriating Nelson's admonition about doing one's duty, Blake hoped to raise a clear signal to his audience. Perhaps not so clear, if truth be told, as this call-to-arms was muted by the cacophony of his other bizarre ramblings. But this was familiar territory for Blake, pressing his perennial case for recognition *and support* of a distinctive native English art. This was an art whose vitality, he hoped, if given appropriate encouragement might make 'England like Italy, respected by respectable men of other countries on account of Art'.[4]

The works he put on show in 1809 were extravagant, although not altogether successful, compositions that paid homage to the masterly ideas of Raphael, his pupil Giulio Romano and the great Michelangelo. Some were delicate, touching watercolours whilst others were small panels, buttered thickly with dense layers of gesso, gold leaf and tempera in a range of gaudy pigments, in imitation of the Fresco miniatures of antiquity. Sensuous, modern oil paints, Blake claimed, were the immoral 'destroyer of colour … a fetter to genius, and a dungeon to art'.[5] This exhibition was, clearly, Blake's overt response to more fashionable oil paintings by Titian, the 'fleshy corruption' of Rubens and 'licentious, slovenly' Rembrandt.[6] These were works, one learns from his *Catalogue*, to be rejected if painters were ever again to equal the skills of Raphael, Albrecht Dürer and other Renaissance savants who reached for the artistic empyrean. The whole exhibition, he thought, would be an uplifting paradise of painting: a revival perhaps, the cue to a homegrown cultural rebirth. The demise of art in Britain, he surmised, was not down to a scarcity of artists of sufficient vitality – he offered himself as proof of that – but instead that the right artists were being ignored. For Blake, it was as if taste itself had fallen by the wayside. It was nothing short of a civic duty – a moral duty too, perhaps even an intellectual one, so he claimed – for the public to help the band of impoverished English artists. But it wasn't so much the 'public' to whom his appeal was directed, rather to the Government and a group of wealthy art buyers to exercise their patriotism through patronage. Thus went his commentary, Blake expects that every man will do his duty – and buy one of his paintings. That was the plan, at least.

Blake's works now stand as clear testimony to the idea that all art – indeed all writing too – is inherently complicated and often political, no matter how simple or esoteric its subject matter may appear to be, whether to the eyes of the artist's contemporaries or to our own.[7] Though neglected in his lifetime, justice has long been done to Blake's enigmatic output. A writer of lyrics unsurpassed in the English language, an expressive draughtsman, printmaker and inventor of design, he is now hailed by many as a profound mystic philosopher, an attractive antirationalist proclaimed by modern-day authors and rock musicians alike.[8] Freedom of thought, freedom of speech, the right to roam, the right even to go without clothes – Blake represents them all. He was art's wild radical, the admirable idealist, and the original free spirit.

Blake and Slavery

In 2007, we had two exhibitions in Britain devoted to the theme of slavery and oppression in Blake's art and writing, dually significant as they coincided with the two hundred and fiftieth anniversary of his birth and the bicentenary of the abolition of the British Transatlantic slave trade.[9] Then in 2009 the small gallery at Tate Britain, 'Room 8', was re-hung in bicentennial honour of Blake's first, and only, solo exhibition.[10] Ten of the original sixteen paintings were shown. Of the remaining six, five are lost and one is in an American collection. Blake may have been a perplexing eccentric, but even those who can't summon one of his enduring images to mind – bows of burning gold, chariots of fire, satanic mills – know that Blake, in life as in art, was a master of the unorthodox. At a time when a growing Empire was sustained by the profits of slavery he created some of the most piercing images of shackled souls and torturous injustice in the history of British art. He railed against cruelty, false authority, the tyranny of imposition and the loss of personal freedoms. Thus, it follows, Blake became the exemplary abolitionist artist. But is it this simple? And, not least, what compelled Blake to create such a remarkable work about Nelson?

The timely exhibition at Tate Britain in 2007 drew attention to the circle of progressive writers and artists associated with the publisher Joseph Johnson in the 1790s and 1800s, and to the atmosphere of public debate that gave impetus to the abolition movement, and which may have helped shape Blake's thoughts. Through his work as an engraver, Blake came into contact with some of the leading intellectual dissidents of the day; the philosopher Richard Price; Mary Wollstonecraft, an early feminist; and Thomas Paine, American revolutionary, among many others. In fact, we know Blake aspired in his art to be like Paine, who 'could overthrow all the armies of Europe with a small pamphlet'.[11] However, rather than rising as the prophet of a creative, popular movement that would bring down the 'dark Satanic Mills' of emergent capitalism, liberating the benighted masses by building in their place the community of a new Jerusalem, Blake had little influence in his own time or for a long while afterwards. Yet, in a well-chosen selection of poetry and prints in this Tate exhibition we were able to gain an entry to his manifold protests against the enslavement of Man's mind and body; that radical defiance which now inspires a new generation of artists, writers, and political dissenters.

Blake was, for example, repulsed by the first-hand account of plantation life in Surinam by the adventurer and mercenary John Gabriel Stedman, and his engravings for Stedman's *Narrative* presented a shocking gallery of execution and grotesque torture. The horrors of the middle-passage and the plantations were also brought forward in other visual materials by Blake's contemporaries. Little-known anti-slavery prints after paintings by George Morland and vivid caricatures, such as Gillray's *Barbarities in the West Indies* (1791), drew upon an incident, reported by Wilberforce, of a slave thrown into a vat of boiling sugar. Yet this was a sour joke – one senses that Gillray abets the casual prejudices of his late-century audience. One could consider *The Little Black Boy*, one of the plates from the series of illuminated poems *Songs of Innocence* (1789), written, illustrated, coloured, and printed by Blake. Traditionally celebrated for its anti-slavery message, the poem reiterates the notion that a black body might contain a white soul capable of Christian redemption, but it is possible too that Blake intended it as an critique of the assumption of black servility towards those with white skin. Though it precedes by some years Blake's exposure to the horrors of slavery in his work for Stedman's *Narrative*, it was likely prompted by the climate of public discourse surrounding the growing campaign against the trade. Yet many centuries on, this poem's ambiguities still challenge us: Blake simultaneously 'humanises the black slave, yet invites us to look at torture as erotic fantasy'. He is deliberately misleading.

Blake understood bondage not merely as a physical condition, but also a mental state. Throughout his work he continued to ask questions of the slavery of intellectual repression, the perils of having limited perception, of intolerance, the cruelness of society, the folly of mercenary pursuits, the corruption of childhood innocence by greed, even the bonds wrought by marriage. One recalls the frontispiece to *Visions of the Daughters of Albion* – so complicated an image, yet one that has become shorthand for Blake's critique of the multiple sufferings of slavery. The three protagonists appeared in many other plates on display in both exhibitions, and they each represent different forms of enslavement: on the left is Bromion, the possessive and brutal husband, the slave owner, chained to Oothoon who seeks her liberty; on the right is Theotormon, her ineffectual lover whose manacles are 'mind-forg'd'. Tied in knots by impotence, he must bear his agony alone.

Mental slavery was Blake's major concern – the way in which the mind can be imposed on by others, but also the ways in which one's own mind, as he believed it, could enslave itself by false belief,

Frontispiece to Visions of the Daughters of Albion by William Blake, c. 1795. Hand-coloured relief etching, ink on paper. Courtesy Tate Britain, London.

151

excessive materialism, the suffocating rationalism of a Locke or a Newton, or the constraints of conventional religion. Many of Blake's most dramatic and complex images show a confrontation between the forces of repression and those seeking the freedom that they lack. One turns to the marvelous series of etchings from *Jerusalem*, whose themes now grimly resonate in our modern times: we see 'Skofeld' in chains – war personified as an anti-heroic state of enslavement – and we behold 'Albion', the nation embodied, toiling in despair, self-enclosed in a mental prison: 'Each Man is in His Spectre's power / Until the arrival Of that hour, / When his Humanity awake / And cast his Spectre Into the Lake.'

'Modern Heroes'

Yet, the undeniable gem of the exhibition in 2007 at Tate Britain, and its follow up recreation show in 2009, was *The spiritual form of Nelson guiding Leviathan, in whose wreathings are infolded the Nations of the Earth*. It is certainly the most intriguing depiction of the 'Hero of Trafalgar' – one of the few works Blake exhibited at the family home, and it deserves further analysis here.[12] The picture is a 'species' of tempera laid over a white gesso on canvas, and belongs to the varied class of turbid, earthy, swamp-like productions, some on wood, some on copper and some on canvas, which Blake thought to be called 'frescoes'. Their clear colours were to be unmuddied by oil and excessive shading, but their brightness has not fared well over time. It is unsigned and undated, but obviously cannot have been painted later than 1809, the year of the exhibition, and should probably be placed a number of years earlier.

Gaudy, ironic and consciously ambiguous, Blake's *Nelson* has nonetheless been celebrated for its sublime and elevated ambition; he appears in full glory, the troubled, yet liberated, Albion, a nation triumphant. The British Everyman has found redemption in victory. Yet this is surely an unadulterated, demonic parody: a triumph instead of the mock-heroic. Though Blake declared his desire to apply a 'grandeur' to 'Modern Heroes', in his self-published *Catalogue*, we remember, in private, he also wrote of 'contemptible Idiots who have been call'd Great Men of late Years', vehemently adding: 'I wonder who can say Speak no ill of the dead when it is asserted in the Bible that the name of the Wicked shall Rot'.

In Blake's writhing critique the Hero directs the sea serpent Leviathan – an appropriate symbol of the 'War by Sea' but also, perhaps, one suggesting the reach of a tyrannical state – in whose jaws Christ himself is devoured, whilst he also tears the hair of France in female form.[13] Within the coils are agonized figures, presumably representing the naval enemies of Britain. The flesh is of a golden tone, flames are laced with red, the scales of Leviathan are green, the background a bluer green, with the whole enhanced with a golden, if a little subdued, clarity. Amongst seething waves, at Nelson's feet lies a black African figure with hidden face and manacled wrists. The exhausted slave is presumably safe after rescue from the ghastly sea-borne trade, but is this really the shore of freedom? The heroic Antichrist Nelson offers no protection. He is about to be embraced, and so struck down, by a ring of flame-tipped lightning. We know that 1807 and the abolition of the slave trade certainly did not mean the abolition of slavery, nor the gift of equality for former slaves within Britain. The slave continues to be a victim of an Empire growing more powerful through the throes of conquest.

Sketch for The spiritual form of Nelson guiding Leviathan, c. 1805-9. Courtesy British Museum.

The painting, along with its companion *The spiritual form of Pitt guiding Behemoth*, were originally intended as modelli for gigantic canvases to go in public places, to show the acts of Nelson and Pitt in the light of Biblical history as a reminder of the vanity of worldly power. These were to be 'epic' compositions, abstractions rather than direct historical narratives – according to Fuseli, 'Epic paintings ... to impress one general idea, one great quality of nature, some great maxim', a heroic endeavour, a powerful presence. In the midst of this second picture, 'riding upon the whirlwind', is the angelic form of the young Prime Minister, calm and inexorable, clothed in a robe of greenish grey lined with gold, guiding the neck of the beast in one hand, and with his left 'directing the storm of war'.[14] Blake's peculiar explanation of these works, is worth quoting at length:

> *The two pictures of Nelson and Pitt are compositions of a mythological cast, similar to those Apotheoses of Persian, Hindoo, and Egyptian Antiquity, which are still preserved on rude monuments, being copies from some stupendous originals now lost or perhaps buried till some happier age. The Artist having been taken in vision into the ancient republics, monarchies, and patriarchates of Asia, has seen those wonderful originals called in the Sacred Scriptures the Cherubim, which were sculptured and painted on walls of Temples, Towers, Cities, Palaces, and erected in the highly cultivated states of Egypt, Moab, Edom, Aram, among the Rivers of Paradise, being originals from which the Greeks and Hetrurians copied Hercules, Farnese, Venus of Medicis, Apollo Belvidere, and all the grand works of ancient art. They were executed in a very superior style to those justly admired copies, being with their accompaniments terrific and grand in the highest degree. The Artist has endeavoured to emulate the grandeur of those seen in his vision, and to apply it to modern Heroes, on a smaller scale ...*

> *... Those wonderful originals seen in my visions, were some of them one hundred feet in height; some were painted as pictures, and some carved as basso relievos, and some as groupes of statues, all containing mythological and recondite meaning, where more is meant than meets the eye. The Artist wishes it were now the fashion to make such monuments, and then he should not doubt of having a national commission to execute these two Pictures on a scale that is suitable to the grandeur of the nation, who is the parent of his heroes, in high finished fresco, where the colours would be as pure and as permanent as precious stones though the figures were one hundred feet in height.[15]*

Blake's ambition was to make this exhibition a launch pad for vast public pictorial schemes, to recover the original spiritual power of art, and he expected his *Nelson* to achieve this. One can be sure that Blake would have been in part inspired (if only to contradiction, rather than emulation), by John Flaxman's monument in St Paul's, commissioned by Parliament in 1807 though not fully completed until 1818. Blake met the sculptor in 1782 having been admitted to the Royal Academy as an engraver; they grew to be friends and Flaxman would later become his patron. He was certainly also inspired by Benjamin West's stunning *Apotheosis of Nelson*, which was exhibited at his house in 1806. Blake had indeed, in his advertisement for his exhibition, called the *Nelson* and its companion *Pitt*, the 'grand Apotheosis of NELSON and PITT'.[16] The first owner of the *Nelson* was Blake's almost solitary patron 'Mr Muster-master' Butts – Thomas Butts of Fitzroy Square – whose representatives sold it at Foster's auction rooms in 1853 for £1 2s. In 1876, when it was shown again in public, at the Blake exhibition of the Burlington Fine Arts Club, it belonged to Mr T.W. Jackson, a fellow and tutor of Worcester College, Oxford. In 1914, shortly after his death, it was sold to the Tate Gallery.[17]

It had become obvious to the more successful artists and entrepreneurs that there was money to be made in a Britain enriched by imperial wars and international trade. Wealthy aristocrats, landowners and the new industrial rich, were stirred by patriotism and by the social challenge of investing in culture in some way. Art exhibitions had become a regular feature of the social calendar in London since the 1760s, enabling artists to directly engage this emerging cultural 'public', whilst also serving their own commercial needs.[18] From the austere annual Royal Academy exhibition, the gentlemanly British Institution, to small one-man displays mounted in an artist's studio, art was being looked at, and talked about, more than ever before. Blake's friend Henry Fuseli, for example, had spent the best part of a decade preparing his solo show, the 'Milton Gallery', to display his interpretations of the epic poetry of John Milton in a succession of enormous canvases, but this had flopped badly when it opened in 1799. In contrast, the leading portrait and landscape painter Thomas Gainsborough, held successful annual shows in his own house and in 1804 Turner had opened a gallery of his own pictures at his studio in Harley Street. Blake's exhibition of 1809 was not, then, in many respects that unusual as an event – just that his paintings were too unusual, too challenging, too outlandish perhaps, for those he hoped might buy them. And given the overcrowded nature of the art market by this time, with many hundred, perhaps thousands, of artists competing for a limited number of private commissions, other painters would try a whole range of 'tricks' to get attention (nothing has really changed in this respect). Painting portraits of notable figures, or infamous celebrities, was one favourite route. Some created garish, shocking pictures in a bid for notoriety, with elaborate frames and extravagant dressing. Even as early as 1772, Joshua Reynolds was concerned that 'our Exhibitions, while they produce such admirable effects by nourishing emulation and calling out genius, have also a mischievous tendency, by seducing the Painter to an ambition of pleasing indiscriminately the mixed multitude of people who resort to them'.[19]

'A Farrago of Nonsense'?

The scene of *Nelson's* first foray, Number 28 Broad Street, Golden Square, was an ordinary London town house and shop. Blake was born there in 1757, the third of seven children. He spent much of his childhood here and his father sold stockings and underwear from the premises. By 1809 Blake's older brother James was running the hosiery business. Blake's one-man show opened in mid-May 1809 and was scheduled to close on 29 September, however the pictures seem to have been there well into 1810, gathering dust, moth and cobwebs. Its ambitious, some may say absurd, scope was summed

Numbers 27 and 28, Broad Street, Golden Square, London, c. 1910. Number 28, where Blake's 1809 exhibition was held, is the house on the left. The artist was also born here. The original building, on the corner of Broad Street (now Broadwick Street) and Marshall Street, was demolished in 1965. Courtesy the author.

up in the title of Blake's brochure: *A Descriptive Catalogue of Pictures, Poetical and Historical Inventions, Painted by William Blake, in Water Colours, Being the Ancient Method of Fresco Painting Restored: and Drawings, For Public Inspection, and for Sale by Private Contract.*[20] The catalogue itself was advertised in a printed note that Blake sent to friends and associates. In this he proposed, more fully, that the exhibition represented 'The grand Style of Art restored; in FRESCO, or Water-colour Painting, and England protected from the too just imputation of being the Seat and Protectoress of bad (that is blotting and blurring) Art'. Blake's exhibition, it was claimed, presented 'real Art', as left by Raphael, Romano, and the other great artists of the past.

Despite these grand claims, the upstairs space where the exhibition was actually held was a cramped living area and the lighting may have been poor. The strangeness of Blake's pictures would have been all the more alarming in these conditions, and an odd bunch they were: *Satan calling up his Legions, Sir Jeffery Chaucer and the nine and twenty Pilgrims*, and experimental pictures such as *The Goats* and *The spiritual Preceptor* which now don't survive. Also lost, *The Ancient Britons* was Blake's largest painting, commissioned by the Welsh antiquarian William Owen Pughe, and was reported to have been ten by fourteen feet. It featured three war-weary, life-size figures, the only men to survive the last battle of King Arthur, stumbling through the picture naked but 'nourished by the spirits of forests and floods', with Druid Temples and a setting sun far in the distance. A confusion of allegory and imagination, the mind boggles at what this histrionic picture may have looked like.

Sadly, only a handful of people left any record of visiting the exhibition, and it is a surprise anyone went at all, considering the eye-watering admission fee of two shillings and sixpence. His friend George Cumberland noted it consisted of 'part vanity, part madness – part very good sense'.[21] The journalist Henry Crabb Robinson saw the exhibition on 23 April and took Charles Lamb and his sister there on 11 June. That there were visitors to the show as late as the summer of 1810 indicates not that the exhibition had been a triumph, but rather, perhaps, 'that it had been such a flop – painfully so, for Blake and his friends – that he had not the heart to take it down'.[22] The fullest report was also the most critical. Robert Hunt, writing in the radical newspaper *The Examiner*, was brutal:

> ... [T]he poor man fancies himself a great master, and has painted a few wretched pictures, some of which are unintelligible allegory, others an attempt at sober character by caricature representation, and the whole 'blotted and blurred' and very badly drawn. These he calls an Exhibition, of which he has published a Catalogue, or rather a farrago of nonsense, unintelligibleness, and egregious vanity, the wild effusions of a distempered brain.[23]

Warming to his theme, he concluded that Blake was 'an unfortunate lunatic'. When Blake died in 1827, his reputation stood much where Hunt had left it, which is to say pretty much in tatters.[24]

During his lifetime, Blake never made the 'breakthrough' of securing a public reputation as a creative artist. He secured neither fame nor fortune. He never won the large public commission that he had so wanted, particularly for his *Nelson*. His hopes for the restoration of the 'grand

Style' were also fruitless. His exhibition had taught him a bitter lesson – whilst he assumed the 'public' would respond warmly to the technical integrity and originality of his work, in truth the body of middle-class men and women who attended exhibitions, read reviews, and hung tasteful pictures on their walls, really did not understand his art and certainly had little interest in buying it. After the 1809 exhibition Blake contributed to a public show only once more, when in 1812 he offered works to a display for the 'Associated Painters in Water Colours'. This show included the *Pitt* and *Nelson*, the painting of Chaucer's pilgrims, and detached examples from an original illuminated poem that was destined to become so famous, 'Jerusalem the Emanation of the Giant Albion'.[25] The *Chaucer* was commended for its accuracy, but Thomas Stothard's oil version, now well known, was preferred, whilst the *Nelson* and *Pitt* were reckoned, diplomatically, as 'too sublime for our comprehension'.[26]

In all then, Blake's valiant attempts at conceiving of, and energizing, a public for art had fallen flat – his 'agenda-setting' exhibition faded into obscurity. Yet, in the 200 years since the first show prompted such bile from its only reviewer, the 'unfortunate lunatic' has entered the canon as a national treasure, a visionary on a par with Turner or Milton. Today, Blake is often considered one of the greatest of British artists. The reception of the 1809 exhibition is an 'object lesson in the fickleness of art history', a simple reminder perhaps of how dramatically reputations can change over time. Nelson too has met with varying critiques over more than 200 years of immortality, adoration and scrutiny.

As always, Blake's art defies easy interpretation and divides opinion. The *Nelson* painting was restored in 1906, but was damaged severely when the Thames flooded the lower ground floor of the Tate Gallery in 1928. It seemed, for a moment, even nature was venting its fury at this challenging piece. Only about half of Blake's original paint now remains. For one critic, writing in 2009, pictures such as this *Nelson* 'are badly painted, their drawing naïve, their composition wonky'.[27] To some extent this might be true, but then their point was to be, in various ways, non-conformist; and that they certainly are. Blake produced images that challenge the viewer through their paradoxes and it is often hard to penetrate the many layers of his ideas. This is the frustrating joy of Blake's craft. His talent was matched by a fierce imagination, but perhaps his greatest gift was his willingness to dissent from orthodox opinion and to pursue his own beliefs. It is impossible not to admire this aspect of his genius.

[1] *A Descriptive Catalogue of Pictures, Poetical and Historical Inventions, Painted by William Blake, in Water Colours, Being the Ancient Method of Fresco Painting Restored: and Drawings, For Public Inspection, and for Sale by Private Contract* (London: Printed by D.N. Shury for J. Blake, 1809). See *The Complete Poetry and Prose of William Blake*, revised edition, edited by David V. Erdman (Berkeley: University of California Press, 1982), p. 549; and G.E. Bentley, *Blake Books: Annotated Catalogues of William Blake's Writings, etc* (Oxford: Oxford University Press, 1977).

[2] See Robert Hunt, *The Examiner*, 17 March 1809. The fullest account of the exhibition may be found in G.E. Bentley, *Blake Records: Documents (1714-1841), Concerning the Life of William Blake (1757-1827) and His Family: Incorporating 'Blake Records' (1969), 'Blake Records Supplement' (1988) and Extensive Discoveries Since 1988* (New Haven: Yale University Press, 2004), pp. 281-95. See also the limited account by Troy Patenaude, 'The Glory of a Nation: Recovering William Blake's 1809 Exhibition', *The British Art Journal*, 4:1 (2003), pp. 52-63.

[3] See *The Complete Poetry and Prose of William Blake*, revised edition, edited by David V. Erdman (Berkeley: University of California Press, 1982), p. 549.

[4] Ibid., p. 549. Blake was discussing his drawing *The Angels hovering over the Body of Jesus in the Sepulchre*, which he hoped would be made into an enlarged fresco to ornament church altars. For an image, see Martin Butlin, *The Paintings and Drawings of William Blake* (New Haven: Yale University Press, 1981), cat no. 500.

[5] William Blake, *Seen in My Visions: A Descriptive Catalogue of Pictures*, edited by Martin Myrone (London: Tate, 2009), p. 47.

[6] The Flemish master of history paintings and portraits, Peter Paul Rubens (1577-1640) was admired for his dynamic compositions but his rich evocation of flesh often meant we was treated with caution by theorists. For Fuseli, in particular, he represented the total corruption of art by fleshy desires: 'His male forms, generally the brawny pulp of a slaughterman; his females, hillocks of roses in overwhelmed muscles, grotesque attitudes, and distorted joints, are swept along in a gulph of colours, as herbage, trees and shrubs are whirled, tossed, and absorbed by innundation' – Gisela Bungarten, *J.H. Füsslis 'Lectures on Painting': Das Modell der Antike und die Moderne Nachahmung* (Berlin: Gebr, Mann, 2005), i, p. 234. Dutch painter and printmaker Rembrandt van Rijn (1606-69), was also highly regarded for his naturalism, yet the overly rich and descriptive nature of his works was derided in equal measure by those committed to the ideals of the Grand Style. 'No part of Rembrandt's excellence', declared the Irish artist James Barry, 'is derived from the loads of colour which he has employed, or from the obtrusive, licentious, slovenly conduct of his pencil, or his *trowel*, which he is said to have used' – *The Works of James Barry, Esq. Historical Painter*, edited by Edward Fryer (London, 1809),i, p. 550. James Barry (1741-1806) who had died notoriously unkempt and neglected, was an exemplary figure for Blake: as the artist who, in dedicating himself to the cause of high art and by pursuing his highly individual aims, was forced into martyrdom. See William L. Pessly, *James Barry: The Artist as Hero* (London: Tate, 1983).

[7] See Stephen C. Behrendt, 'Blake's Bible of Hell: Prophecy as Political Program', in *Blake, Politics, and History*, edited by Jackie DiSalvo, G.A. Rosso, and Christopher Z. Hobson (London: Garland, 1998), pp. 37-52.

[8] The literature on Blake's intriguing artistic career is voluminous, and his multifarious sources of inspiration still defy easy interpretation. For a selection of this secondary work, see Mark Schorer, *William Blake: The Politics of Vision* (New York: Holt, 1946); George Wingfield Digby, *Symbol and Image in William Blake* (Oxford: Clarendon Press, 1957); David V. Erdman, *Blake, Prophet Against Empire: A Poet's Interpretation of the History of His Own Times* (Princeton:

Princeton University Press, 1969); Jacob Bronowski, *William Blake and the Age of Revolution* (London: Routledge and Paul, 1972); *The Complete Portraiture of William and Catherine Blake*, edited by Geoffrey Keynes (Jura: Trianon Press for the William Blake Trust, 1977); David Bindman, *Blake as an Artist* (Oxford: Oxford University Press, 1977); Peter Ackroyd, *Blake* (London: Vintage, 1998); Jason Whittaker, *William Blake and the Myths of Britain* (Basingstoke: Macmillan, 1999); and *William Blake: The Painter at Work*, edited by Joyce H. Townsend (London: Tate, 2003), among many others.

⁹ '1807: Blake, Slavery and the Radical Mind', was at Tate Britain, London from 30 April through to 21 October 2007. 'Mind-Forg'd Manacles: William Blake and Slavery', was held at Ferens Art Gallery, Hull, 7 April to 20 May 2007, at the Burrell Collection, Glasgow from 3 November to 6 January 2008, and finally at the Whitworth Art Gallery, Manchester from 26 January to 6 April 2008. A small catalogue, accompanying the show and written by its curator David Bindman, was published by the Hayward Gallery and the British Museum in 2007.

¹⁰ Entitled 'Blake 1809', the unique recreation was devised by curator Martin Myrone. It was on display until 4 October 2009. Myrone, explained: 'If [the show] had been more successful we might well be less interested in Blake now. The fact that he struggled and was mis-understood in his lifetime added an allure and an idiosyncrasy that we have come to expect of our artists'. For a listing of the works and additional information, see also http://www.tate.org.uk/servlet/CollectionDisplays?venueid=1&roomid=5649.

¹¹ *The Complete Poetry and Prose of William Blake*, revised edition, edited by David V. Erdman (Berkeley: University of California Press, 1982), p. 671.

¹² *The spiritual form of Nelson guiding Leviathan* by William Blake (1757-1827), c. 1805-9. Tempera on canvas, 76 x 62 cm. Now in the collections of Tate Britain, London, the painting was purchased in 1914 shortly after being displayed there in a new exhibition of Blake's work. See The National Gallery of British Art, *Catalogue of an Exhibition of Works by William Blake* (London: HMSO, 1913), and Martin Butlin, *The Paintings and Drawings of William Blake* (New Haven: Yale University Press, 1981), cat no. 649.

¹³ The entwining serpent became a familiar motif – see, for example, *Lucifer and the Pope in Hell*, c.1794-96, the 1795 print *Elohim Creating Adam*, the watercolour Satan Spying on Adam and Eve, c. 1807, and in two versions for his 1806 illustration *Vision of the Last Judgement*. In *Nelson*, the snake enfolds all the figures except its guide, Nelson. For Leviathan and Behemoth as symbolizing the forces of the sea and land subject to man, see Job XL, 6 to XLI, 34.

¹⁴ *The spiritual form of Pitt guiding Behemoth* by William Blake (1757-1827), signed 1805. Tempera heightened with gold on canvas, 74 x 63 cm. Originally in the collection of Samuel Palmer, it was bought for £100 in 1882 and sold to the National Gallery. It was transferred in 1931 to the Tate. In the catalogue of Blake's exhibition the title continues: ' … he is that Angel who, pleased to perform the Almighty's orders, rides on the whirlwind, directing the storms of war: He is ordering the Reaper to reap the Vine of the Earth, and the Plowman to plow up the Cities and Towers'.

¹⁵ William Blake, *Seen in My Visions: A Descriptive Catalogue of Pictures*, edited by Martin Myrone (London: Tate, 2009), pp. 45-47.

¹⁶ See Martin Butlin, *The Paintings and Drawings of William Blake* (New Haven: Yale University Press, 1981), cat no. 649 and 651, and commentary pp. 472-73. Another tempera *The spiritual form of Napoleon* is now lost.

¹⁷ The picture was exhibited three times during the nineteenth century: at Blake's exhibition in 1809; at the 'Associated Painters in Water Colours' show of 1812; and 'B.F.A.C.' in 1876. It was shown at Messrs. Carfax's in 1906. When it was exhibited that year it was in a terrible state of preservation: the pigment was much discoloured and the design was disfigured by

streaks and patches of white gesso, where the pigment had come away. In order to prevent further deterioration, the owner Mr Jackson was persuaded, 'not without difficulty', to entrust it to Mr W.S. Littlejohn, 'the first restorer who has ever succeeded in preserving Blake's work without ruining it ... Mr Littlejohn, with amazing skill and patience, brought the pigments back to their original state, and fixed them permanently to the gesso, and Mr W. Graham Robertson cautiously tinted the exposed gesso to protect it from any longer distracting the eye. This preservative process was highly successful, though it is due to Mr Jackson to say that long and appreciative possession of the picture in its decay had so mellowed it to his eyes that he was never quite reconciled to it after it had been restored, even though it was then much nearer the state in which it had left Blake's hand'. See 'William Blake's Nelson', *The Burlington Magazine*, 142:26 (1915), pp. 138-40.

[18] On this subject see David H. Solkin, *Painting for Money: The Visual Arts and the Public Sphere in Eighteenth-Century England* (New Haven: Yale University Press, 1993); and Morris Eaves, *The Counter-Arts Conspiracy: Art and Industry in the Age of Blake* (Ithaca: Cornell University Press, 1993).

[19] *Sir Joshua Reynolds: Discourses on Art*, edited by Robert Wark (New Haven: Yale University Press, 1975), p. 90.

[20] There are several existing facsimiles of the intriguing *Descriptive Catalogue*. An edition published by Woodstock Books includes a short introduction by Jonathan Wordsworth (Oxford, 1990; revised edition Otley and Washington, 2001). For the most recent edition, see William Blake, *Seen in My Visions: A Descriptive Catalogue of Pictures*, edited by Martin Myrone (London: Tate, 2009).

[21] G.E. Bentley, p. 287.

[22] William Blake, *Seen in My Visions: A Descriptive Catalogue of Pictures*, edited by Martin Myrone (London: Tate, 2009), p. 10.

[23] *The Examiner*, 17 March 1809. See G.E. Bentley, p. 282.

[24] See 'Misunderstood Master', *The Independent on Sunday*, 19 April 2009, p. 25 and *Independent on Sunday*, 26 April 2009, pp. 60-61. 'By the turn of the 20th century, Blake the Flake had been replaced by Blake the Troubled Genius. In the introduction to his 1927 study of the artist, the pacifist Max Plowman could confidently write that "the day seems not far distant when ... apologies will be unnecessary and ... Blake will be no longer regarded as a narcotic for numbskulls". Instead, he has been claimed in turn by Surrealists, hippies, Allen Ginsberg, Marxists, Bob Dylan, university undergraduates and anyone else for whom madness might usefully be construed as an act of political rebellion'.

[25] See Robert N. Essick, 'Blake's Exhibition of 1812', *Blake: An Illustrated Quarterly*, 27 (1993), pp. 36-42.

[26] See G.E. Bentley, p. 314.

[27] See Charles Darwent, 'Blake the Flake unwrapped', *The Independent on Sunday*, 26 April 2009, pp. 60-61. He continued: 'I'll own up here to finding Blake a great poet but a tiresome artist, the eccentricity of his drawn vision (or visions), oddly unconvincing. It is now almost impossible to see him other than through the historical spectacles of Yeats and Rossetti, Ginsberg and Dylan'. See also Brian Sewell, 'Blake the Bleak', *Evening Standard*, 24 April 2009, pp. 35-36.

The Making of a Hero:
Captain Cook's Last Voyage

Glyn Williams

In the annals of British maritime history Captain Cook remains a towering figure, one of that small group of seaman who needs no first name to confirm his identification. Drake, probably, and Nelson, certainly, are others, but there can be no doubting the instant recognition accorded to plain 'Captain Cook'. His fame was based on three extraordinary voyages that transformed Europe's sketchy knowledge of the Pacific. Sailing thousands of miles across a largely uncharted ocean he mapped lands from New Zealand in the south to Alaska in the north. It is not too much to say that he redrew the map of the world. Added to this, the observations made by Cook and his shipboard companions played an important role in the development of anthropology, astronomy, oceanography and much else. In the realm of natural history, the voyages were among the great collecting expeditions of all time, and the specimens and drawings brought back were overwhelming in their profusion. And not least of Cook's achievements was that he lost virtually no crewmembers to scurvy, that age-old scourge of long voyages.

All this, and more, we take for granted, and we assume that this was the contemporary reputation of Cook; but I shall argue here that his achievements were slow to gain recognition, and that only after his death – and in part because of the circumstances of his death – did he become the famous, the incomparable, 'Captain Cook'.

We begin with the first voyage, as the expedition of the *Endeavour* in 1768-71 is often called. This perhaps overlooks the fact that Cook had been at sea for twenty years by then, a dozen of them in the navy, and that he had carried out surveying work of the highest quality along the coasts of Newfoundland. That experience played at least a part in explaining the Admiralty's appointment of Cook to the ex-collier *Endeavour* in April 1768 for a voyage to the Pacific. In origin the projected expedition was not one of exploration, for its main task was to convey a group of natural philosophers (scientists, as they would later be called) to Tahiti where they were to make astronomical observation associated with the transit of Venus. Not only was Cook well qualified to help with these observations, but his years in the Whitby coal trade had made him familiar with the type of vessel chosen. Moreover his newly-awarded junior rank of lieutenant seemed appropriate to the command of a former collier (of his immediate predecessors in the Pacific John Byron had commanded line-of-battle ships, and Samuel Wallis was a captain of eight years standing). By the time that the rumours from Wallis's crew of the possible sighting of a continental land-mass south of Tahiti added a second objective to the *Endeavour's* voyage, it was too late to change either the vessel or its commander. For some of the newspapers that carried the first reports of the forthcoming voyage he did not even have a name – 'a Lieutenant in the Navy' had to serve – and there was more interest in the 'Gentlemen of Fortune' on board: the astronomer Charles Green; the Swedish naturalist, Dr Solander, from the British Museum; and the young Joseph Banks, already a Fellow of the Royal Society.[1]

The same priorities held when the *Endeavour* returned in the summer of 1771 after a voyage that had charted the twin islands of New Zealand and located the hitherto unknown east coast of Australia. In the newspapers it was usually described as the voyage of Mr Banks and Dr Solander. Banks was presented to King George III on 5 August, Cook only eleven days later (when, it is true, he was promoted captain). *The London Evening Post's* wording of the occasion referred to Captain Cook, 'who sailed round the Globe with Messrs. Solander, Banks etc.' – almost as if he were a passenger and they the navigators. *The Public Advertiser* took things a step further when it noted that 'Very great expectations are formed from the discoveries of Dr Solander and Mr Banks, and tis expected that the territories of Great Britain will be widely extended in consequence of these discoveries.'[2] And to cap it all, interest in the popular press in the expedition's explorations was far outweighed by Banks' amorous exploits in Tahiti.

Captain James Cook. Engraving (1784) after the painting by Nathaniel Dance. Courtesy Huw Lewis-Jones.

As these reports indicated, a further Pacific voyage was under consideration, but again the public prints had no doubt whose voyage it was to be. 'Mr Banks is to have two ships from Government to pursue his discoveries in the South Seas' as one newspaper saw it, or as another explained, 'The celebrated Mr Banks will shortly make another voyage to St. George's Island [Tahiti] in the South Seas, and it is said that the Government will allow him three ships, with men, arms and provisions.'[3] Banks himself seemed to believe that the next voyage would be his. As the *Resolution* (another Whitby collier) was being prepared for the voyage Cook wrote in his journal that there 'was scarcely a day past on which she was not crowded with strangers who came on board for no other purpose but to see the ship in which Mr Banks was to sail round the world.' In all, Banks planned to be accompanied by a retinue of fifteen – artists, naturalists, secretaries and musicians – and it was the extra accommodation for these that made the Resolution so top-heavy that her first lieutenant, Charles Clerke, expostulated: 'By God, I'll go to sea in a grog-tub if required, but must say I think her by far the most unsafe ship I ever saw or heard of.' The Admiralty ordered the changes to be undone, a disgruntled Banks 'swore and stamp'd upon the Warfe, like a Mad Man, and instantly order'd his servants and all his things out of the Ship', and the voyage became Cook's in name as well as in reality.[4]

Cook's second Pacific voyage from 1772 to 1775 is regarded as one of the greatest, most perfect, of all seaborne voyages of discovery. But it is worth remarking that there was no great enthusiasm among the crews allocated to the *Resolution* and *Endeavour* for participating in what was to become an epoch-making venture. More than half the complement of the *Resolution* (58 out of 112 officers and men), and almost half that of the *Adventure* (37 out of 81) deserted before sailing.[5] It was while Cook was away on his second voyage that the official account of his first voyage was published, together with those of Byron and Wallis. The editor, Dr John Hawkesworth, merged Cook's journal with that of Banks, and gave preference to the botanist's lively effort rather than the more technical, workaday prose of Lieutenant Cook. The resultant three-volume publication was advertised as being compiled from the journals of the several commanders (none was named), and from the papers of Banks and Solander. The emphasis was clear.

The second voyage would surely be different in terms of personal publicity, for this time Cook was deliberately writing a journal that would, with a few tweaks here and there, be suitable for publication. Nor was there any Joseph Banks on board to rival Captain Cook (as he now was) in public interest, for the naturalist's replacements, the learned but crabby Johann Reinhold Forster and his son George, had none of Banks's swashbuckling charisma. Yet the outlines even of this magnificent voyage were blurred for a time. Cook's report to the Admiralty when he reached the Cape of Good hope in March 1775 on his way home covered only the final year of the voyage since he assumed that when Captain Tobias Furneaux of the *Adventure* reached England in July 1774 he would have reported on the explorations carried out before the two ships lost company with each other off New Zealand in October 1773. Inexplicably, Furneaux seems to have said little about these – his letter to the Admiralty from the Cape took up most space describing the grisly episode in which a boat's crew from the Adventure was killed and eaten by Maori at Grass Cove, New Zealand.[6] When Furneaux arrived home he seems to have made no further report on the voyage other than handing in his journal. Both he and the newspapers of the day were most interested in the story of the massacre and in the arrival in England of the Society Islander, Omai (Mai).

It was left to an unnamed lieutenant of the *Resolution* to alert the public at home that Cook's second voyage had been a remarkable one. His letter from the Cape appeared in the London press at the end of June 1775. It made much of the fact that the crew had been 'amazingly healthful', losing not a single man to scurvy, and that in the search for the southern continent the *Resolution* had sailed through islands of ice after crossing the Antarctic Circle.[7] Cook himself was back in late July, and within two weeks was presented to the King and promoted post-captain. In naval and scientific circles in London Cook's reputation was high, and in the winter of 1775-6 he was elected Fellow of the Royal Society. His nomination papers, signed by no fewer than 25 Fellows (an unusually high number), described him as 'a gentleman skilfull in astronomy, & the successful conductor of two important voyages for the discovery of unknown countries, by which geography and natural history have been greatly advantaged and improved.'[8]

Another sign of public recognition for Cook came when he was painted by Nathaniel Dance (at Banks's arrangement), although it should be noted that Omai had been painted not only by Dance but by Joshua Reynolds, the leading portrait painter of the day. As yet there was no publication of Cook's journal, although he and his editor, Dr John Douglas, were busy working on it. Instead, readers had to rely on a short unauthorised account of the voyage written by gunner's mate John Marra. This was damned with faint praise by Cook's biographer, J.C.Beaglehole – 'the book is by no means useless … it yields some grains of new information'[9] – but it obtained popular circulation in the pages of the *Gentleman's Magazine*, the monthly periodical edited by David Henry. He also seems to have been the editor of Marra's book, and published four long extracts from it in the winter of 1775-76. They revealed for the first time to the general reading public the nature of Cook's achievement, and so Marra and Henry between them perhaps deserve more credit than they are generally given.

Cook's own account was not published until May 1777, nine months after he left England on his third voyage, this time to the North Pacific to search for a northwest passage. Only with this publication was the true greatness of the second voyage revealed, from the descriptions of the long sweeps of the unknown southern ocean to the journal's final sentence – 'Having been absent from England three years and eighteen days, in which time I lost only four men, and only one of them by sickness.' In the published account Cook included a description of the methods he had used to combat scurvy, another version of which was printed in the Philosophical Transactions of the Royal Society. Cook had left England before this was read to the Society on 30 November 1776, on which occasion he was presented, in absentia, with the Society's Copley Medal by the President, Sir John Pringle.[10] In his oration Pringle declared:

> *If Rome decreed the Civic Crown to him who saves the life of a single citizen, what wreaths are due to the men who...perpetuates in your Transactions the means by which Britain may now, on the most distant voyages, preserve members of her intrepid sons, her Mariners.*

A summary of his remarks, and of Cook's account of his methods of preserving shipboard health, was printed in the widely-read pages of the *Gentleman's Magazine*. This concluded:

> *As a navigator Captain Cook undoubtedly ranks as the first of this of this or any age or nation. Not a gun, it appears, was ever wantonly or unnecessarily fired by his order, and his attention to the health of his own mariners was so singularly successful that he lost only one man by sickness. How meritorious must that person appear, who hath not only discovered but surveyed vast tracts of new coasts, who hath dispelled the illusion of terra australis incognita, fixed the bounds of the habitable earth as well as those of the navigable ocean in the southern hemisphere.*[11]

It seemed altogether appropriate then that when Josiah Wedgewood issued his medallions of 'Illustrious Moderns' in 1777, the fifty or so 'Statesmen and Commanders' in the series included Captain Cook.

The two-volume official account of Cook's second voyage, illustrated by William Hodges' luminous views of the Pacific islands and their inhabitants, therefore fell on fertile ground when it was published in May 1777. There was

A Wedgwood medallion (1779), simply inscribed 'Capt.Cook'. Courtesy The British Museum.

a second edition later in the year, and a third in 1779. The account was to take on a sad significance when the first reports of Cook's death at Kealakekua Bay, Hawai'i in February 1779 reached England in early 1780, for obituarists turned to its pages for information to remind readers of what they had lost. *The Morning Chronicle* of 14 January 1780 set the tone when it lamented that Cook's 'murder' was 'not only a national loss, but a misfortune in which all Europe must feel itself deeply interested.' A few days later the same newspaper printed a eulogy in which the figure of the hero was more firmly drawn. He was of humble origins, a navigator whose technical skills were matched by his humanity, whose care for his crew was shown in his attention to their health, and – crucially – in the end sacrificed himself in his concern for their safety.[12]

Cook's death was especially felt in the learned circles of the Royal Society, whose members had elected him a Fellow only four years earlier. At meetings in late January 1780, chaired by Sir Joseph Banks (as he now was), the Council agreed to raise a subscription among members for a commemorative medal in 'memory of so valuable and eminent a man'. The designer was Lewis Pingo, chief engraver to the Royal Mint, but for reasons that are not clear, the medal, struck in gold (19), silver (291), and bronze (574) was not issued until the summer of 1784.[13]

In October 1780 the *Resolution* and *Discovery* arrived back in the Thames, and within weeks preparations began to publish an authorised account of the voyage, edited once again by Dr John Douglas. Because of production delays, mostly concerned with the engravings, the account took almost four years to see the light of day. Meanwhile, despite Admiralty attempts at prohibition, unofficial narratives were published by members of the crew. The first and most important of these, published in May 1781, was based on the journal of

The Death of Captain Cook, engraving c. 1784 after John Webber. Courtesy Warwick Leadlay Gallery.

John Rickman, second lieutenant of the *Discovery*. Extracts were published in the periodicals, and for a year it was the only book-length account of Cook's last voyage.[14] Rickman's Cook was a more violent figure than the humane commander of the first two voyages. His furious retaliatory burning of huts and canoes on Moorea in the Society Islands in October 1777 after the theft of two goats left the island 'a scene of desolation', while in an improbable scene not mentioned in any other account he cruelly submitted two young hostages to a mock execution. More puzzling still was Rickman's description of Cook's initial reception at Kealakekua Bay when, surrounded by prostrate islanders, he was led to a shrine and, apparently, worshipped as their god Lono. It would be hard to imagine anything more repellent to readers in a Britain coming increasingly under the influence of evangelical groups than the thought of the country's foremost explorer accepting a status as a heathen god.

All in all, the unofficial accounts hinted that not all was well on Cook's third voyage. They introduced an element of doubt – no more – into Cook's growing reputation, and made the delay in publishing the official account the more frustrating. In June 1784 it at last appeared, a sumptuous affair that dwarfed previous voyage narratives: three quarto volumes, 1,617 pages, ninety-seven plates, and an atlas. The work was an instant success, and was followed by reprints of the quarto edition, cheaper and pirated editions, and generous extracts in all the leading periodicals. For the crucial events during the stay in Hawaii, there was no record by Cook. His log, unaccountably, stopped midway down the page on the day of the ships' arrival at Kealakekua Bay, more than three weeks before his death. So it was left to Douglas, using for the most part the journal of Lieutenant James King, to describe what had happened. On the Lono issue King was cautious and noncommittal: 'Captain Cook generally went by this name among the natives of Owhyhee [Hawai'i] but we could never hear its precise meaning'.[15]

As far as Cook's death was concerned, King found that collecting evidence was not a straightforward business, for 'the accounts that were given now begin to differ'.[16] Witnesses differed on the fundamental question of whether Cook's death came about because of his aggressive behaviour in attempting to take the high chief, Kalani'opu'u, hostage in an effort to regain a stolen cutter; or whether it was the consequence of what midshipman John Watts called his captain's 'ill-timed restraint' in using first, only small-shot on his attackers, and then ordering the boat crews to stop firing. To put the question at its simplest – did Cook die because of his anger or because of his humanity? The authorised account had no doubt. It made much of the fact that Cook at the water's edge had his back to his assailants as he gestured to the boat crews lying off the beach to stop firing. 'It is not improbable that his humanity proved fatal to him', it concluded.

The publication of Douglas's official account of Cook's third voyage set the seal on the explorer's fame. Until Beaglehole's scholarly edition of the manuscript journals of the voyage published in 1967 it remained the indispensable account, the deep quarry from which generations of readers and writers took their materials as they struggled to understand the events of the voyage. Only with the 1967 edition did it become clear that Douglas had made numerous changes to Cook's text – as he admitted, 'I took more Liberties than I had done with the Acct of the second Voyage'.[17] Throughout the 1784 edition he altered the syntax of Cook's journal to stress the role of the first-person narrator, the commanding officer who was forever ordering, directing, mastering. Douglas's Cook was heroic and just, stern but compassionate. As he surveyed, charted, took possession he was the representative of the monarch, the flag-bearer of a patriotic endeavour that few queried. For the weeks in Hawai'i, when he no longer had Cook's journal to draw upon, Douglas was highly selective in his use of information from other journals. The disappearance of Cook's own record allowed Douglas and his advisers at the Admiralty to portray the story of the stay in

The 'king' of Hawai'i in his great double-hulled canoe bringing gifts to Captain Cook on the Resolution.
Engraving after John Webber. Courtesy Warwick Leadlay Gallery

Hawaii as they wished. Lieutenant King's journal formed the basis for the authorised account, but Douglas in consultation with Banks and the Lords of the Admiralty decided how it should appear. Douglas's edition offered more than an apologia for a voyage with some awkward moments. It played a major part in establishing Cook as a hero.

The interpretation of Cook's death advanced in the authorised account was given a dramatic visual dimension in the depiction of the scene by John Webber, the expedition's official artist. Webber produced two paintings of the death scene soon after his return to England. As far as we know, Webber was not in either of the boats near the beach that morning. The paintings show a crowded and chaotic scene, with Cook gesturing to the boats to stop firing as he is about to be struck down. Only a privileged few would see the paintings, but engravings based on the paintings were published in London and enjoyed widespread circulation. The title of one impression ran: 'The Death of Captain Cook … by the murdering Dagger of a Barbarian at Carakakoa … He having there become a victim to his own humanity.' Webber's Cook stands tall and upright, musket in hand, making a choice between war and peace at the cost of his own life, a moving tribute to a hero about to die. Predictably, both because of its creator and because of its interpretation, Webber's picture became the standard version of the death of Cook. And the magnificent engravings from Webber in the authorised account also conveyed the message of Cook as a man of peace. Webber, or perhaps Douglas, was careful to select for inclusion scenes of greetings, ceremonies and exchanges. Stone-throwing, jeering crowds, musket and cannon fire, were little in evidence.

In Britain the time was right for a less conventional hero than the military supermen of the past. The War of American Independence had dragged to a close, but the colonies had been lost, the Navy was rent by political quarrels, and growing doubts were being expressed about British activities in India. The concept of a hero devoted to the arts of peace rather than war had considerable appeal, and was reflected in the literary responses to Cook's life and death where the contrast was drawn between Cook and the rapacious discoverers of a earlier era. As William Cowper expressed it in his poem, 'Charity', perhaps rather extravagantly:

> *While Cook is loved for savage lives he saved,*
> *See Cortez odious for a world enslaved.*

This stage in the process of elevating Cook the saintly hero concluded with the publication in 1788 of Andrew Kippis's deferential and admiring *Life of Captain James Cook*, that included a selection of tributes, elegies and poems written in the explorer's honour. At least forty-eight editions have been traced up to the early twentieth century, and during that time it remained – if only by default – the essential biography of Cook. As Bernard Smith has put it, Cook was 'a new kind of hero for a new time'.[18]

This interpretation, however, has its limitations, for the time was not so new that it was not able within twenty years of Cook's death to produce a more warlike hero whose fame was to eclipse the explorer's. During the long wars against France, while in the Pacific explorers, traders and missionaries followed in the wake of Cook, at home his light dimmed before the bright glow of Nelson's battle honours. There could be no greater contrast than that between the national mourning and the ceremonial funeral procession to St Paul's that followed Nelson's death, and the reluctance by government, national or local, to set up a monument to commemorate Cook. Kippis made the best of a bad job when having regretted that there was no monument to Cook in Westminster Abbey he reassured his readers that the explorer's fame 'stands upon a wider base … The name of Cook will be held in honour, and received with applause, so long as the records of human events shall continue.'[19]

Members of the same service, Nelson and Cook had little in common except the respect of their superiors and the affection of their crews. In terms of

A figure of Britannia adorning an obelisk to Cook; behind is the spar of a ship, and below a nude corpse lying over a globe with two putti; in the foreground a sarcophagus with a bas-relief with the scene of Cook's death. 1781 Etching and aquatint. Courtesy The British Museum.

temperament, personal morality, and professional achievement, the two seamen represented different strains of national endeavour. The gulf was not unbridgeable, for some saw British naval power as the key to opening the Pacific, and Cook and Nelson as different sides of the same coin. When Captain John Erskine, the first Senior Officer of the Royal Navy's Australian Division, sailed for the Pacific in 1840 he had only two portraits in his cabin, one of Nelson, and one of Cook.[20]

[1] *St James Chronicle*, 16-18 June 1768; *Lloyd's Evening Post*, 14-16 June 1768; *Public Advertiser*, 20 June 1768.

[2] *London Evening Post*, 16 August 1771; *Public Advertiser*, 21 August 1771.

[3] *Public Advertiser*, 29 August 1771; *Westminster Journal*, 31 August 1771.

[4] James Cook, *The Voyage of the Resolution and Adventure 1772-1775*, edited by J.C. Beaglehole (Cambridge: Cambridge University Press for the Hakluyt Society, 1969), p. xxviii and p. xxx.

[5] Ibid., pp. 872-73.

[6] Furneaux's report of 5 April 1774 is in TNA: Adm 1/1789.

[7] *Lloyd's Evening Post*, 30 June-3 July 1775.

[8] Andrew S. Cook, 'James Cook and the Royal Society', in *Captain Cook: Explorations and Reassessments*, edited by Glyndwr Williams (Woodbridge: The Boydell Press, 2004), p. 38.

[9] Beaglehole, *Voyage of Resolution and Adventure*, p. cliv.

[10] Pringle's address was printed in James Cook, *A Voyage towards the South Pole, and Round the World* (London: W. Strahan and T. Cadell, 1777), pp. 369-96.

[11] *Gentleman's Magazine*, xlvii (1777), p. 179 and p. 493.

[12] *Morning Chronicle*, 22 January 1780.

[13] For the most recent research on the medal see Cliff Thornton, 'The Royal Society's Captain Cook Medal', in *Cook's Log*, 31 (2008), nos. 3 and 4; 32 (2009), no. 2.

[14] [John Rickman], *Journal of Captain Cook's last Voyage to the Pacific Ocean* (London: E. Newbery, 1781).

[15] James Cook and James King, *A Voyage to the Pacific Ocean, by the Command of his Majesty, for making Discoveries in the Northern Hemisphere* (London: W. and A. Strahan, 1784), iii, p. 5 n.

[16] James Cook, *The Voyage of the Resolution and Discovery 1776-1780*, edited by J.C. Beaglehole (Cambridge: Cambridge University Press for the Hakluyt Society, 1967), i, p. 556.

[17] Ibid., i, p.cxcix.

[18] Bernard Smith, 'Cook's Posthumous Reputation', in *Captain James Cook and His Times*, edited by Robin Fisher and Hugh Johnston (Vancouver: Douglas and McIntyre, 1979), p. 168.

[19] Andrew Kippis, *The Life of Captain James Cook* (London: G. Nicol and G. G. J. and J. Robinson, 1788), ii, p. 316.

[20] Jane Samson, *Imperial Benevolence: Making British Authority in the Pacific Islands* (Honolulu: University of Hawai'i Press, 1989), p. 17.

'The Idle Apprentice Sent to Sea': Sailors and Urban Youth Culture in the Eighteenth Century[1]

Roland Pietsch

This article explores the status the eighteenth-century deep-sea sailor had in youth culture on land, and in how far the sailor took up the role of a subculture hero. Furthermore, the article argues that the sailors' culture itself can be seen as a youth subculture: Eighteenth-century deep-sea sailing crews were not only remarkably young, their behaviour on shore often resembled more what society was used to from urban youths than from adults. The sailor's particular working conditions, and the fact that seafaring attracted rebellious youths, may have promoted a tendency to hang on to youth-typical behaviour into a higher age than pre-industrial society was used to.

The Real Jim Hawkins?

Jim Hawkins, ship's boy in Robert Louis Stevenson's *Treasure Island*, is a character that most readers of *The Trafalgar Chronicle* surely fondly remember. Ever since *Treasure Island* was first published as a book in 1883, Jim's adventures have captured the imagination of generations of young readers, through the book itself and countless radio, stage, television and cinema adaptations. The adventures of a boy encountering all those colourful eighteenth-century sailor characters hit a universal nerve among young readers, crossing national boundaries and even the hardened ideological borders of the twentieth century: in the case of my own childhood in West-Berlin, I grew up with a West-German television adaptation of *Treasure Island*, accompanied by the actual book and a record produced in Communist East Germany, gifts from the auntie from the other side of the wall. Yet, while the ship's boy, thanks to Stevenson, has become an international celebrity in juvenile fiction, historians have so far grossly neglected him.

For me, this negligence was incentive enough to spend years of research trying to find out more about the real-life Jim Hawkins, focussing on boys

Treasure Island (1934), MGM, with Jackie Cooper as Jim Hawkins and Wallace Beery as John Silver. Courtesy David Long.

William Hogarth, Industry and Idleness 1747, plate 1, 'The Fellow Prentices at Their Looms'. Courtesy Warwick Leadlay Gallery.

who joined the eighteenth-century Royal Navy as captains' and officers' servants. One question that affords a bit of speculation is what were the motivations that drove those real-life Jim Hawkinses to sea? Did some of them have similar romantic notions as Jim? What status did the sailor have in eighteenth-century youth culture on land, and in how far was the sailor an object of fascination to the real-life Jim Hawkinses and attracted them to enlist in the Royal Navy? Historians usually have a different and rather sober answer to the question of what drove boys into the eighteenth-century Navy: seafaring, they say, has largely been a hereditary trade; most youngsters went to sea simply because that was how their fathers or communities earned their living. However, a comprehensive study proving this assumption is still missing. And when investigating the social backgrounds of eighteenth-century ships' boys in the wartime Royal Navy, I was very surprised to find that the boys with non-seafaring fathers and from inland towns often made up the majority on board.

So what led all these boys from a non-seafaring background to the Royal Navy? There seem to be two different archetypes: one is indeed a bit of a Jim Hawkins, and the other one is more of a Tom Idle, the anti-hero in William Hogarth's (1697-1764) morale tale *Industry and Idleness* of 1747. At exactly the period in history where Stevenson placed the adventures of his fictional boy sailor Jim Hawkins, London's most popular artist and social commentator, Hogarth, had created a rather different stereotype of a juvenile sailor: The *Idle Apprentice* Tom, whose laziness and unruliness had convinced the adults around him that sending the boy to sea was the only way out. So one archetype has his head full of romantic notions and dreams of fortunes at sea, and the other one is an urban juvenile hooligan that appears to have been dumped into the sea. I have encountered both in the historical sources on numerous occasions. Yet my personal feeling is that many boys could actually be Tom Idle and Jim Hawkins in one person. What dragged them to sea was what being a sailor stood for, the sailors' culture and the sailor's status in youth culture on land. Of course, these two archetypes also share another characteristic: both boys had lost their father, a very common experience for children in the eighteenth century,[2] which is a reminder that while this article will investigate the attraction of the sailors' culture, we should never forget that the boys often also had poverty driving them to sea.

There is also no doubt that some boys were not just pushed into the Navy by poverty but by people. The Royal Navy itself though was primarily after proper seamen; inexperienced unwilling young boys made no interesting prey for the press gang. The pressure for boys to enlist came from the other end, from authorities on land: Parish overseers, magistrates, churchwardens, dissatisfied apprenticeship masters, and frustrated parents all tried to dump boys in Royal Navy, in line with the common stereotype illustrated by Hogarth's *Idle Apprentice*, that for boys who had failed to settle in any trade the last resort was the sea. Furthermore, eighteenth-century poor laws, apprenticeship laws, and laws against vagabonds and rogues, all ignored the personal liberty of the children of the poor and gave local authorities the power to force them into the sea service.[3] However, my research left me with the impression that all this only worked if the boy and the Navy were willing to cooperate. Despite Navy Regulations to the contrary, captains did not hesitate to discharge an annoying boy at the nearest British port rather than going through the ordeal of turning him into a sailor. If a boy like Tom Idle would have been utterly opposed to the Navy, then he would have been quickly back on land.

Hogarth does actually not tell us explicitly if Tom Idle had agreed to being sent to sea. *Industry and Idleness* was a moral tale for apprentices illustrating the lives of the two fellow weaver apprentices Francis Goodchild and Thomas Idle, and the rise of the former and simultaneous decline of the latter. After Tom enraged his apprenticeship master with his laziness and shunned Sunday service to enjoy a bit of gambling, plate five of the series depicts the idle apprentice Tom eventually being 'turned away and sent to sea'. The boatmen delivering Tom to his ship are grinning devilishly: one of them, possibly also just a boy, is showing Tom the cat-o-nine-tails as a taste for the discipline on board. The other boatman points to the waiting ship and to a hanged pirate or thief, displayed as a warning on Cuckold's Point in Rotherhithe. Tom's mother, dressed as a widow, is weeping for her son. The engraving's message seems to be that with no father, master or any other authority being able to control Tom, sending the troublesome youth away to the sea was regarded as the only way out. Meanwhile, Tom himself still looks rather defiant. He responds to the boatman that is pointing to the hanged at Cuckold's Point by showing him the horns, the symbol of cuckoldry, while carelessly dropping his old weaver's apprenticeship indenture into the river.

The Idle Apprentice

Tom is representative of many eighteenth-century youths who failed to settle in any trade on land, for whom the out-dated poor relief and apprenticeship system could not find suitable employment. It would certainly be wrong to stereotype all the Navy's teenage recruits as troublemakers like Tom, yet there were thousands of youths, who went to sea being influenced by similar economic, social and cultural pressures as Tom. The potential problems an apprentice like Tom faced are well researched. Apprenticeship court cases featured regular complaints about masters who had no work in which to employ the apprentice and who misused the apprentice over many years as cheap labour without providing any training. Masters could financially fine, but also physically punish their apprentices: the boatman was certainly not the first to threaten Tom Idle with a beating. On the first plate of *Industry and Idleness*, when Tom's apprenticeship master catches Tom asleep at work, while Francis Goodchild is diligently working his loom, the master already carries a cane in his hand. And so too does the sadistically grinning beadle or churchwarden who catches Tom gambling outside the church. Tom was used to corporal punishment, so while Hogarth's polite audience perceived the boatman's threat as a worrying taste of shipboard-life's brutality, it made much less of an impression on Tom. Apprenticeship masters could even get their apprentices sent to a house of correction for a week, some even went for a month.[4] Being whipped and put to hard labour were often part of these establishments.

Weaving, Tom Idle's trade, was swamped with apprentices from poorer backgrounds, who commonly received no pay and, if there were placed by the parish, had by law to remain in this unpaid servitude till they reached the age of twenty-four,[5] with uncertain employment prospects afterwards. In most trades the youth would be able to fulfil all the tasks of his work long before his apprenticeship was over, which was a reward for the master for training the boy. The apprentice, however, grew impatient in the meantime, longing to work, live, and earn money on his own. Of course misbehaviour of one side always provoked the other side to act equally: Hogarth's idle apprentice Tom was indeed a familiar eighteenth-century stereotype; the youths were mocked in popular theatre plays such as *The Apprentice*, 'a satire on those young mechanicks, who neglect the business of their trade to attend to the diversions of the stage'.[6] It was not just idleness that apprentices were commonly accused of, but also proneness to drinking, partying, gambling and other riotous behaviour – all rather sailor-like stereotypes. Eighteenth-century guidebooks laying out rules of good behaviour, which in reverse read like a catalogue of frequent misdemeanours among apprentices, show a sometimes amusing resemblance to the antics of today's youth. If we acknowledge that a youth comparable to modern youth existed in the eighteenth century,[7] then we may also suspect that the extensively observed mental turbulences

William Hogarth, Industry and Idleness 1747, plate 3, 'The Idle Apprentice at Play in the Churchyard, during Divine Service'. Courtesy Warwick Leadlay Gallery.

of today's teenager – such as anxiety, search for identity and thrills, questioning of authority – could have been present in the mind of his eighteenth-century peer.

Apprentices faced a multitude of rules of behaviour imposed on them by apprenticeship indentures and company guidelines, which could include forbidding the visit of bowling alleys, dances, tennis courts, or even to wear the hair long, or to wear clothes other than those provided by their masters. These rules were restrictive, but they were also very frequently broken by eighteenth-century youths eager to have their share of enjoyment. Tom Idle's misdemeanours were gambling during the hours of church service and laziness at work, which got him sent to sea. Notably, Hogarth's series does not show that his idle apprentice Tom had committed any serious crime until then. *Industry and Idleness* was mass-produced and sold inexpensively, and it was primarily aimed at masters, who would hang the prints as educational tales on the walls of their apprentices' workplaces. Yet Hogarth-expert Ronald Paulson has suggested that the one with whom most apprentices sympathised was not the industrious Francis Goodchild, but instead Tom Idle, because they would have perceived Tom as a victim rather than

William Hogarth, Industry and Idleness 1747, plate 5, 'The Idle Apprentice Turned Away and Sent to Sea'. Courtesy Warwick Leadlay Gallery.

a wrongdoer.[8] To the apprentices, Tom Idle was a 'subculture hero', perhaps comparable to all those stylised rebels that populate the music and movies of twentieth-century youth culture.

The two apprentices represent the two extremes between which any apprentice would have found himself eternally torn, with rebellious Tom doing what he likes and diligent Francis doing what is expected of him. Remarkably, Hogarth gave Tom Idle, and not Francis, a face resembling his own, suggesting that even he himself must have felt drawn between these two extremes as an apprentice.[9] Hogarth probably deliberately chose Tom Idle to be a weaver's apprentice because weaving was one of the worst-paid crafts and had the worst prospects.[10] Being bound to such a trade, possibly to the age of twenty-four, mostly unpaid, with perhaps a fourteen-hour day, could have hardly been motivating for any youth. The age of twenty-four appears light-years away to a teenager. It is no surprise that restless youths like Tom would have longed for some diversion from such a bleak work-life, and that they would dream of escaping from this endlessly dull routine altogether, perhaps to an imagined life at sea promising more adventure and quicker financial rewards with less drudgery.

'Wild, Hairbrained Sailors'

The best examples for the eighteenth-century Royal Navy's attractiveness to youths are all the runaways who enlisted without the consent of their apprenticeship masters or parents. Young Robinson Crusoe threatened to do just that at the start of Defoe's novel, and there were many eighteenth-century boys like the cooper's apprentice John Nicol or Robert Hay, who claimed in their sailing memoirs that reading *Robinson Crusoe* had made them weary of their work and eager to run away to sea.[11] The latter, Robert Hay from Paisley, had often regretted that his own life did not provide him with such adventures as Crusoe's. Robert's parents struggled to make a living, and from an early age he had to contribute to the family's income by working in a cotton factory – at the loom, just like Tom Idle did. Robert longed for a more active life and understandably perceived his work-life as very confined. Hence his efforts at the loom were modest, his idleness earning him the occasional beating from the master. Robert eventually ran away to sea as a thirteen-year old in 1803. Although many historians have warned us not to overestimate the romance of the sea as a motive for seafarers, I would argue that if we explore the alternative employment opportunities available particularly to boys from poorer backgrounds, then we get an understanding how the lure of the imaginary sailor's life could work so effectively on the boys.

The sea lured with her myths of adventure but also financial gains. In many boys' eyes, the sea still appeared like a world in which a daring young man, even if he came from humble origins, could get rich without having to work a lifetime for it, and if not that then at least gloriously die trying. Even youngsters that made more realistic calculations would have realised that as servants in the Navy they could bank on being rated as fully paid seamen around the age of eighteen, which meant it would take them a much shorter time than in any land-based or maritime apprenticeship to become a wage earner. And in comparison to the bleak economic prospects of some trades on land to which particularly parish-supported boys were apprenticed, seafaring promised at least in times of war better employment opportunities.[12] As a good example, we can take a number of parish-supported boys sent to the Navy by MP Charles Gray from Colchester that I came across in documents of the London Marine Society in the 1750s: for these boys being sent far away from their home-town for an apprenticeship was anyway a likely scenario. Commonly, such parish boys would have been apprenticed to a weaver or similar, bound until the age of twenty-four, misused as cheap labour, and with meagre employment opportunities afterwards, or placed in a maritime apprenticeship, being given no pay at all, not even any clothing before their service was finished.[13] To such pauper boys the Royal Navy, offering a free set of clothing and bedding from the Marine Society, a yearly allowance of around forty shillings, the prospect of becoming a wage earner around the age of eighteen, and the possibility of earning prize money must have looked very attractive, that is to those who ignored the occupational hazards of naval service.

Considering that the Navy offered a quicker route to independence than any apprenticeship, it would also be no contradiction if boys with a history of troubles with authority, like Tom Idle, volunteered for the Navy. One feature that the Navy and deep-sea sailing definitely offered, unlike what a Colchester parish boy had to expect as a weaver's or waterman's apprentice, was what the modern youth would call 'action'. When analysing the attraction that deep-sea sailing could exert on young people, it is important to take the viewpoint of an eighteenth-century boy stuck in an arduous job as a servant or apprentice, and not from the viewpoint of an educated contemporary like Samuel Johnson, who called the lure of the sea a perversion of the imagination.[14] Eighteenth-century popular culture was full of tales of seafaring adventures. Theatres, for examples, featured numerous plays with nautical themes. Then there was the public image of the sailors themselves, the behaviour that 'Jolly Jack Tar' displayed when on land. Press and popular art jumped on the sailors' excesses like today's tabloid press jumps on the escapades of touring rock musicians or travelling football fans. Regardless of whether this image was an accurate representation of the majority of sailors, to many restless youths the drinking, singing, raucously partying and womanising sailor in the taverns was probably a better advertisement for the sea service than the Royal Navy could ever come up with.

Surely, the sober mind, and boys that had grown up with seafaring fathers, knew the sailor's other side: the hardship and the dangers at sea. Yet among the boys that joined the Navy in a conflict like the Seven Years War these boys were actually the minority. A 'land-boy' like William Spavens, who first went to sea in 1754, only remembered how he looked at the sailors with envy and never considered any of the perils and hardships they were exposed to: 'I thought sailors must be happy men to have such opportunities of visiting foreign countries.'[15] While sailor turned author John Nicol even recollected that his 'youthful mind could not separate the life of a sailor from dangers and storms, and I looked upon them as an interesting part of the adventures I panted after.'[16] The great economist Adam Smith remarked in his *Wealth of Nations* (1776) that 'the dangers and hairbreadth escapes of a life of adventures, instead of disheartening young people, seem frequently to recommend a trade to them.'[17] The boys with no family connection to seafarers only knew the sailor ashore, who, dressed in his fancy shore-going clothes, enjoyed the time in between the voyages with the aid of his recently earned pay, boasting about his exploits. They only knew the sailor that was raucously celebrating his release from many months of confinement. The colourful stories of his seafaring cousins were the first thing that attracted Samuel Leech to the Navy, which he joined as a twelve-year old in 1810. It was their action-packed tales, but also other encounters with men that Sam identified as sailors, such as on his journey in a stage coach when a sailor among the passengers entertained them:

> We had another source of relief in the antics of a wild, hairbrained sailor. From spinning yarns, which looked amazingly like new inventions, he would take to dancing on the roof of the coach; at the foot of a hill he would leap off, and then spring up again with the agility of a monkey, to the no small amusement of the passengers. The more I saw of this reckless, thoughtless tar, the more enamored I became with the idea of a sea life.[18]

Samuel Leech was to be shocked by the reality of naval life. Then again, he had never experienced the drudgery in which other boys had been employed before they went to sea. After thirty often horrible years at sea in the early nineteenth-century Navy, Leech looked back very critically at the jolly tars that once enticed him to become a sailor: he wondered whether their entire joyous act was not simply adopted to distract themselves from the tough reality of life in the Navy.19 Leech also felt that in this self-deception the sailor was even encouraged by the Navy, who found the jolly, merry-making, don't-care sort of seamen easier to handle.

> Bold Jack, the sailor, here I come;
> Pray how d'ye like my nib,
> My trowsers wide, my trampers rum,
> My nab, and flowing jib?
> I sails the seas from end to end
> And leads a joyous life;
> in ev'ry mess I finds a friend,
> In ev'ry port a wife.[20]

So sang Charles Dibdin (1745-1814), travelling entertainer and composer of many popular songs celebrating the sailor's supposedly wild life and fashion.

Dibdin's songs were performed everywhere, sold in every music shop, and reprinted in newspapers. Dibdin boasted that his songs produced more recruits for the Royal Navy than all the press gangs that swept through the streets of London. During the war against Napoleon, Dibdin and other performers were even paid by the government to write songs celebrating the sailor's life and thus to excite the young male audience to enlist. Dibdin dressed and acted like a sailor, but he had never been a sailor himself. Twentieth-century philosophers of popular culture, such as those of the renowned Frankfurt School, who view the modern music industry as nothing but an exploitation of its young and naive consumers, could be tempted to have a go at Dibdin for being the pre-industrial harbinger of modern-day rock and rap music stars with their manufactured personal history aimed at gaining credibility with their young audiences. But then again Dibdin at least did not hide the fact that he was just acting.

The Sailor's World as a Youth Subculture

Dibdin is just one element of many that make it worth spending a little more time analysing eighteenth-century sailors from a modern youth-cultural angle. This can aid our understanding of what attracted the real-life Jim Hawkins to deep-sea sailing, and additionally this youth-behavioural approach can also deliver an interpretation of the sailors' culture itself. Deep-sea sailing in the eighteenth century was a profession for young men, and for men who kept elements of 'youthfulness'. It is true that the hardships and dangers at sea rushed the ship's boy from being a child into meeting the physical and psychological demands of a grown man, yet in many other ways the sailor's culture fostered a youthfulness that lasted into a much higher age than society on land was accustomed to. Contemporaries frequently described seamen as being particularly boyish and immature. The Navy's crews were indeed very young, most averaging around the age of twenty-five and often younger. And many deep-sea sailors settled down in later years of their life with shore-based occupations or working in the coastal trade and on the rivers.

Various work-related factors might have promoted the sailors' youthfulness and extended it into a higher age: marriage, for example, one of the key moments in the transition from youth to adulthood in Western Europe, was difficult to achieve for a deep-sea sailor. Setting up his own permanent home, another key moment in the move from youth to adulthood in Western Europe, was equally difficult. Generally, saving any money or investing it in anything lasting was complicated, as the sailor needed a trustworthy place to deposit it, and as there was occasionally the threat of the press gang taking him with no chance to settle his affairs. Furthermore, similar to apprentices, sailors sometimes were forced to work, and corporal punishment was common to discipline them. And like youths they were housed and fed, living like students in a large and close male-only community. Sailors hardly owned any means of production; and employers and workplaces could be changed at the end of each voyage or by running away. All these work-related factors perhaps created a more unsettled, a much more youth-like workforce than pre-industrial European society was accustomed to.

The sailors' youthfulness was supplemented by a general feeling of otherness among frequent deep-sea sailors. Like most contemporaries, the famous naval surgeon Thomas Trotter reckoned that all the sailor's 'peculiarities are the offspring of a sea-life, from the little communication it affords with the common manners of society'.[21] However, considering that even frequent deep-sea sailors still spent large parts of the year in the harbour, or employed in trades near the coast and even on land, the sailors' behaviour should not be seen as solely the natural result of their work environment. It must have also been a conscious attempt to distinguish themselves from society on land. The best sailor's clothes were after all reserved for the shore leave. Cultural historians like Isaac Land, Cheryl Fury and Peter Burke have therefore proposed to view the sailors' culture not as a specific maritime culture, but rather as a subculture, in the words of Burke: a culture that was 'partly autonomous rather than wholly autonomous, distinct yet not completely severed from the rest of popular culture.'[22] In line with Land, I think we can go further and draw parallels to those subculture models used by sociologists to describe youth cultures in modern Britain. If we count such groups as subcultures which show a conspicuous, intentional distinction from society's norms in dress, hairstyle, jewellery (later also tattoos), language, music, behaviour, religious believes, and plenty more provocative and hedonistic elements, then the behaviour of many sailors could fit well into such a model. Endless further parallels can be drawn, such as the non-conformity with society being accompanied by conformity within the group, the 'tribal' gathering for rituals and entertainment around the mainmast, the understatement or glorification of danger and death, and the acts of bravado and deliberate ignoring of safety precautions. The sailor's life was full of such follies that adults with a family depending on them were unlikely to commit.

Songs and music, books and plays, but also the fact that sailors were in constant contact with sailors from other regions provided the 'mass-media' for this eighteenth-century subculture. During the long voyages there was enough idle time for story-telling, a time when the older shipmates could pass down the myths and characters of their sea-stories to the next generation. There was enough time to exchange wisdoms and sayings, and music and dances from all over the world. The Navy vessel was at times a melting pot of cultures from all over the globe. There were people performing all sorts of poetry, songs, and anything from spontaneous comic acts to dances and proper theatre plays. Many men brought musical instruments to sea; on board Robert Hay's ship there was 'black Bob', a fiddler who was almost constantly in demand to provide music for those longing to dance, and when there were more dancers than within the sound of Bob's fiddle, then the Admiral's band was ordered up in support of Bob.[23] What to the captain might have been a sensible exercise for the men's spirits and legs, sounds to us today like a possibly wonderful mixing of European and African music and dance. Dancing within the constraints of a limited space and without female partners was, by the way, one of the things that needed to be cultivated. Music was of course not just used for recreation, but also for work, when foremen and crew communicated and encouraged each other with 'calling-and-answering' songs. Here too sailors were willing to be inspired by other cultures. Robert Hay described in detail how in the local rowing crews at the coast of Madras steersman and rowers communicated via song: the steersman singing a stanza, and then pausing every eight to ten words when all the rest of the crew joined their voices in a short chorus that to Robert sounded like 'ey-yaw'. Any time we switch on our popular music radio stations today, we are still hearing the same elements.

Sailors had kept many youthful desires, but unlike younger boys they possessed physical and sexual maturity, and unlike apprentices they had the ready money, to fulfil all these desires. The sailor-subculture was made up of a multitude of components of style, language and behaviour. Many of the elements show that sailors were very aware of their audience on land: when, for example, towards the end of the century the fashion on land had shifted to darker colours, and to a reduction in decoration, the bright colours with gold and silver ornaments in which the sailor paraded through the streets, the striped trousers, hats, ribbons and decorations, were all worn to be noticed. And Jolly Jack walked with a swagger, as his contemporaries on land always noted, a swagger that was said to be the result of the sailor being used to walking on a rocking deck. Yet is it really that difficult to get used to a steady surface? No. In reality, the sailor was, at least partly, putting on a show, just like the almost choreographed walk with which some groups of youths walk along our high streets today.

Wapping, 1807, etching by Thomas Rowlandson. Courtesy Warwick Leadlay Gallery.

Cultural historians and sociologists sometimes argue that youth culture only emerged with the arrival of the 'teenage consumer' in the mid-twentieth century, when the young received a hitherto never experienced buying power and the markets were flooded with affordable mass-produced fashion. Yet sailors were artists in creating and altering their own clothes, in a way that would have impressed any modern youth. Eighteenth-century sailor slogans such as 'a Rolling Stone never gathers Moss', or the praise of a 'Short life and Merry life', are also something that even today is expected from anyone wanting to qualify as a youth-cultural icon. Many other sailor maxims are unquotable, as seamen were generally acknowledged to be champions in swearing – again something attractive to young men for its anti-authoritarian tone. And so too is the excessive use of slang among sailors, and of (international) sign language and rituals – language and communication that excludes and impresses outsiders. The sailor's language was as mysterious to the rest of society on land as the slang of modern youths is to their parents.

The list of elements in the sailors' culture which were attractive to teenage boys, and which can be found even in today's youth cultures, could be continued for much longer, from the sailors' heavy drinking culture to the boisterous promiscuity. It appears hard to summarise the common denominator of all such youth cultures and subcultures. Perhaps they are about creating a separate colourful dream-world, away from the dire realities of life; a parallel universe with its myths, iconic characters, saints and martyrs, with its music, language, codes and fashions, and with dreams of quick fortunes, adventures, and all with restricted access, with entry having to be earned by dressing and acting like a member. Of course, this subculture model has limits, and one has to be very careful not to fall victim of the iconisation of seafarers in later epochs of youth culture. While some eighteenth-century sailors would have fitted perfectly into it, for the masses of them, particularly those working most of the time in coastal shipping or fishing, it may go a little far. However, it is important to remember that this model is also about the public's perception and the land-boys' imaginations, which encourages them to enlist in the Royal Navy, more than about the reality at sea. Furthermore, even the subculture models applied to modern youths emphasise that the core of a subculture is made up of only a few, while the majority of youths remain somewhere in the middle between conformity to society and sympathy with the subculture, just as most eighteenth-century boys remained somewhere in the middle between Tom Idle and Francis Goodchild.

---

[1] The findings and interpretations in this article were presented in a paper with the same title at the British Maritime History Seminar (National Maritime Museum and Institute of Historical Research), on 10 March 2009.

[2] Possibly around a third of eighteenth-century children lost their fathers before they grew out of their teens, among the sons of sailors the percentage might have been as high as fifty percent.

[3] See the following acts regulating apprenticeships: 2 and 3 Anne, c. 6, s. vi and xvi (1703), and 4 and 5 Anne, c. 6, 19 (1705), building on the older acts 39 Elizabeth, c. 4 (1597-1598); and 11 and 12 William III, c. 18 (1700). See also E.G. Thomas, 'The Old Poor Law and Maritime Apprenticeship', *Mariner's Mirror*, 63 (1977), pp. 151-63, and Cheryl A Fury, 'Training and Education in the Elizabethan Maritime Community, 1585-1603', *Mariner's Mirror*, 85 (1999), pp. 147-60.

[4] See Jonas Hanway, *Observations on the Causes of the Dissoluteness which Reigns Among the Lower Classes of the People* (London, 1772), p. 23.

[5] In 1767, the long apprenticeship of parish boys was reduced to the age of twenty-one by one of the so-called 'Hanway Acts', named after Marine-Society founder Jonas Hanway (see the act 7 George III, c. 39, s. xiv [1767]).

[6] Advertisement for *The Apprentice* in the *London Magazine*, January 1756, pp. 3-5.

[7] Some historians have argued that the concept of youth, as we know it today, is a product of the late eighteenth century and did not exist in pre-industrial Europe – see for example Philippe Ariès, *Centuries of Childhood* (Paris, 1960; London: Pimlico, 1996); John R. Gillis, *Youth and History* (London, 1974, London: Academic Press, 1981); or Ilana Krausman Ben-Amos, *Adolescence and Youth in Early Modern England* (New Haven and London: Yale University Press, 1994), pp. 183-205. For an overview of how other historians followed the theory of youth being a product of the last two centuries see Roger Thompson, 'Adolescent Culture in Colonial Massachusetts', *Journal of Family History*, 9 (1984), pp. 127-29. For case studies that suggest that adolescence/youth was not only present in the eighteenth century, but also in previous centuries see for example S.R. Smith, 'The London Apprentices as Seventeenth Century Adolescents', *Past and Present*, 61 (1973), pp. 149-61; N.Z. Davis, 'The Reasons of Misrule: Youth Groups and Charivaris in Sixteenth-Century France', *Past and Present,* 50 (1971), pp. 41-75; or A. Yarbrough, 'Apprentices as Adolescents in Sixteenth-Century Bristol', *Journal of Social History*, 13 (1979), pp. 67-82.

[8] See Ronald Paulson, *Popular and Polite Art in the Age of Hogarth and Fielding* (Notre Dame/London: University of Notre Dame Press, 1979), pp. 16-17, 22-23; and Paulson, *Emblem and Expression: Meaning in English Art of the Eighteenth Century* (London: Thames and Hudson, 1975), pp. 72-73.

⁹ Hogarth had something else in common with Tom: he too had grown up without a father.

¹⁰ Unless the apprentice had family connections to a master, or married the master's daughter, as Francis Goodchild does later in the series.

¹¹ See John Nicol (Gordon Grant), *The Life and Adventures of John Nicol, Mariner* (1822, London: Cassell and Co, 1937), and *Landsman Hay: The Memoirs of Robert Hay, 1789-1847*, edited by M.D. Hay (London: Rupert Hart Davis, 1953).

¹² On top, naval service was afterwards rewarded with the liberty to take up any trade they desired in any town they wanted (as regulated by the following acts: 12 Charles II, c. 16 [1660]; 12 Anne, c. 14 [1712]; 3 George III, c. 8 [1762]). This perk cannot be overestimated, providing the ex-sailor with flexibility on the job market at a time when changing one's place of abode and trade were heavily restricted by settlement and apprenticeship laws, and by the privileges of the corporations.

¹³ See Ralph Davis, *The Rise of the English Shipping Industry in the Seventeenth and Eighteenth Centuries* (Newton Abbot, 1962, Newton Abbot: David and Charles, 1972), p. 119.

¹⁴ James Boswell, *The Life of Samuel Johnson* (London, 1791), quoted in Christopher Lloyd, *The British Seaman, 1200-1860* (London: Paladin, 1970), p. 209.

¹⁵ William Spavens, *The Narrative of William Spavens, a Chatham Pensioner* (Louth, 1796; London: Chatham Publishing, 1998), p. 1.

¹⁶ John Nicol (Gordon Grant), *The Life and Adventures of John Nicol, Mariner* (London, 1822, London: Cassell and Co, 1937), p. 37.

¹⁷ Adam Smith, *An Inquiry into the Nature and Causes of the Wealth of Nations* (London, 1776; Indiana: Liberty Fund, 1994), p. 127.

¹⁸ Samuel Leech, *A Voice from the Main Deck: Being a Record of the Thirty Years Adventures of Samuel Leech* (Boston, 1857, Annapolis: Naval Institute Press, 1999), p. 14.

¹⁹ Ibid., pp. 41-42.

²⁰ Charles Dibdin, *The Sea-Songs of Charles Dibdin* (London, 1852), p. 96.

²¹ Thomas Trotter, *Medicina Nautica: An Essay on the Diseases of Seamen* (London, 1797), p. 35.

²² Peter Burke, *Popular Culture in Early Modern Europe* (New York, 1978, Aldershot: Scolar Press, 1994), pp. 43-46. Cheryl A Fury, *Tides in the Affairs of Men: The Social History of Elizabethan Seamen, 1580-1603* (Westport: Greenwood Press, 2002), pp.86-93; Isaac Land, 'Domesticating the Maritime: Culture, Masculinity, and Empire in Britain, 1770-1820' (Unpublished PhD thesis, University of Michigan, 1999), pp. 225-48.

²³ See M.D. Hay, *Landsman Hay: The Memoirs of Robert Hay, 1789-1847* (London: Rupert Hart Davis, 1953), pp. 44, 72, 94, 108-109, 201.

Editors' Note: Roland Pietsch's *The Real Jim Hawkins*, the story of boys in the eighteenth-century Royal Navy, will be published by Seaforth Publishing in 2010.

Why did Captain Robert FitzRoy really take command of HMS *Beagle*?

James Taylor

HMS Beagle in Murray Narrows, Beagle Channel, watercolour, by Conrad Martens. Beagle was launched at Woolwich Dockyard in May 1820 as a small general-purpose warship. She was converted to a barque with three-masts and had a length of 90 feet and a breadth of 24ft 6ins. For her second voyage 74 souls were onboard. Courtesy English Heritage.

As is now well-known, the pioneering voyage of HMS *Beagle* (1831-36) enabled Charles Darwin to collect the evidence to support his celebrated and controversial publication *On The Origin of Species*, published in 1859. Though there has been much celebration this year to mark this great work's 150th anniversary, many aspects of the voyage itself continue to offer interesting new areas of research. Darwin was sailing on *Beagle's* second survey voyage and it has become synonymous with his name, although in recent years, for example, a small number of biographies have helped to redress the balance by focusing on the significant role of Robert FitzRoy (1805-65), the ship's commander. FitzRoy selected Darwin as his naturalist, messmate and gentleman companion. *Beagle's* captain was determined to create a visual record of the expedition and personally paid for two shipboard artists Augustus Earle and Conrad Martens. FitzRoy also painted, and he drew the only known portraits of the Fuegians enticed aboard *Beagle* during her first survey expedition to South America (1826-30). They were the real reason why *Beagle* was commissioned again.

Darwin's Captain

Captain Robert FitzRoy, wash-drawing, by Philip Gidley King (1817-1904). Courtesy State Library of New South Wales.

Robert FitzRoy was born in the year of Vice-Admiral Horatio Nelson's death. He was from aristocratic stock although untitled. He was directly descended from King Charles II's illegitimate son the Duke of Grafton by the King's mistress Barbara Palmer. His maternal uncle Lord Castlereagh had committed suicide and FitzRoy was conscious of a family history of depression and hence was eager to select a gentleman companion onboard the *Beagle* with whom he could confide without breaking naval protocol. His selection of Darwin turned out to be prudent planning as he did become depressed during the voyage and Darwin and loyal officers persuaded him not to relinquish his command.

FitzRoy was an outstanding cadet at the Royal Naval College, Portsmouth passing with 'full numbers'. He was a colourful and complex character and this was, in part, captured in a slight profile sketch by one of *Beagle's* midshipmen Philip Gidley King. This profile portrait reveals a gentleman with an aristocratic air, a determined man of lofty principles, although with a highly strung demeanour. You can sense the emotional restraint. He also had a hot temper and famously fell-out with Darwin on several occasions during the expedition. But Darwin also described him as his 'beau ideal' of a captain. They became friends during the voyage but this friendship faded after Darwin's writings on the origin of species became widely known. After the *Beagle* voyage FitzRoy became a fundamentalist Christian.

FitzRoy was born at Ampton Hall, Suffolk in England, and from the age of four he lived at Wakefield Lodge in Northamptonshire, the grand Palladian style family mansion. He was a remarkable seafarer and surveyor driven by devotion and duty to his country and became a Vice-Admiral. FitzRoy was the world's first full-time weather forecaster and invented the term 'weather forecast'. He is regarded as the founding father of the Met Office. His concern was for the safety of all sailors at sea. FitzRoy also contributed greatly to the work of the Royal National Lifeboat Institution. In February 2002 the sea area Finisterre was renamed FitzRoy in recognition of his services.

Beagle's first expedition into South America waters relates to British colonial expansion, investment and trade opportunities after the end of the Napoleonic Wars. Offensive warfare was replaced by exploration and survey expeditions and the British Hydrographic Office recommended specific places for naval ships to undertake survey work and oversee the production of Admiralty charts (maps of coasts and the sea). Existing charts of many parts of South America were known to be inaccurate and so a significant part of *Beagle's* brief was to produce up-to-date examples.

The Fuegians

Beagle's return to South America, and specifically Tierra del Fuego, links to a hasty action of FitzRoy after he took over the command of the *Beagle* during her first expedition in 1828 (the ship's first captain, Pringle Stokes had committed suicide – worn down and depressed by the arduous survey work). After one of *Beagle's* boats had been stolen by a group of Fuegians FitzRoy took several of them onboard initially as hostages and interpreters to assist him to retrieve the boat. It was never recovered and so he decided to take four of them back to England – the so named, York Minster, Jemmy Button, Boat Memory and Fuegia Basket. They would be educated at an infant school in Walthamstow, Essex, converted to Christianity, and then returned to Tierra del Fuego to help civilise their own people and be of practical assistance to visiting British seamen. That was the theory, but the reality turned out to be far from beneficial. They reverted to their native state and abandoned their purpose built settlement. York had robbed Jemmy of his possessions and fled with Fuegia.

On 28 February 1830 York Minster was acquired in Christmas Sound, where FitzRoy had selected as the place to build a replacement boat. Captain James

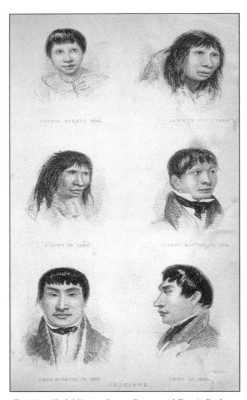

Fuegians: York Minster, Jemmy Button and Fuegia Basket,
engraving, after Robert FitzRoy from the Narrative (1839).
Courtesy Private Collection.

Cook had stopped here over the period on his second voyage of discovery (1772-1775) and hence the name. The outline of a nearby towering rock on Waterman Island had the appearance (in the opinion of Captain Cook) of York Minster and this inspired FitzRoy to call his first Fuegian after that historic ecclesiastical building. On the following day a child was taken aboard and the little girl of around eight years old was christened by the seamen Fuegia Basket alluding to the makeshift craft (a temporary replacement for the stolen boat) that sailed from Cape Desolation. Around a week later Boat Memory joined the other hostages. He derived his name after his apparent knowledge of what had happened to *Beagle's* boat. Finally on 11 May during another surveying trip the fourth Fuegian, Jemmy Button, was acquired and this time named after the 'large shining mother-of-pearl button' he was given to entice him onboard.

Charles Darwin provides good descriptions of the three Fuegians:

> [York Minster] … *a full-grown, short, thick, powerful man: his dis-*
> *position was reserved, taciturn, morose, and when excited violently*
> *passionate; his affections were very strong towards a few friends on*
> *board; his intellect good. Jemmy Button was a universal favourite, but*
> *likewise passionate; the expression of his face at once showed his nice*
> *disposition. He was merry and often laughed, and was remarkably*
> *sympathetic with anyone in pain: when the water was rough.*

Jemmy was short, thick, and fat, but vain of his personal appearance; he used to wear gloves, his hair was neatly cut, and he was distressed if his well polished shoes were dirtied. He was fond of admiring himself in a looking glass; and a merry-faced little Indian boy from the Rio Negro, whom we had for some months on board, soon perceived this, and used to mock him: Jemmy, who was always rather jealous of the attention paid to this little boy, did not at all like this, and used to say, with rather a contemptuous twist of his head, 'Too much skylark'.

Fuegia Basket was a nice, modest, reserved young girl, with a rather pleasing but sometimes sullen expression, and very quick in learning anything, especially languages. This she showed in picking up some Portuguese, and Spanish, when left on shore for only a short time at Rio de Janeiro and Monte Video, and in her knowledge of English. York Minster was very jealous of any attention paid to her; for it was clear he determined to marry her as soon as they were settled on shore.

After *Beagle's* return to England in 1830 the Fuegians were inoculated against smallpox at the Royal Hospital at Plymouth and Boat Memory had an adverse reaction and died. FitzRoy felt personally responsible for his death. But he now had three Fuegians to accommodate and educate in England. The Church Missionary Society came to his rescue and provided accommodation and education at an infant school ran by the Reverend William Wilson at Walthamstow in Essex. The education offered was rudimentary and included the 'plainer truths of Christianity', English lessons, 'the use of common tools, a slight acquaintance with husbandry, [and] gardening'.

In the late summer of 1830 FitzRoy and the Fuegians were summoned to the royal palace of St. James's for an audience with King William IV and Queen Adelaide. The Queen offered one of her own bonnets and a ring to Fuegia Basket. She and the young teenager Jemmy Button had responded well to their English education, but York Minster who was older, probably in his early twenties, was far from being a model pupil and was openly expressing his feelings for Fuegia Basket, however, the suggestion that they were caught near the infant school *in flagrante* is almost certainly spurious. That said, FitzRoy had initially planned to keep the Fuegians in Britain for two or three years and so something, or someone, changed his mind. He engaged influential friends and family members to canvas the Admiralty to persuade them to honour their initial promise to provide a ship to return the Fuegians.

It is doubtful the voyage would have happened without the support of Captain Francis Beaufort, the Admiralty Hydrographer, a kindred spirit who recognised the benefits of a further follow up expedition and it was he who largely drew up the Admiralty Instructions of the key places for stopovers, survey work and to make chronometric measurements. It was Beaufort, rather than Darwin, who recommended visiting the Galapagos. FitzRoy was finally appointed again to command the *Beagle* in the Summer of 1831.

Darwin succinctly summed up the Admiralty objectives of *Beagle's* second expedition:

> ... *to complete the survey of Patagonia and Tierra del Fuego (started on Beagle's first voyage 1826-1830) ... to survey the shores of Chile, Peru, and some of the islands of the Pacific; and to carry a chain of chronometrical measurements round the world.*

Stopovers in various countries around the world including many areas of South America, the Galapagos, Tahiti, New Zealand, Australia and South Africa were made to undertake survey work and complete the 'measurements', or in other words to accurately fix their longitudinal positions using the ship's chronometers. FitzRoy's success in completing this 'chain' was cited as one of his supporting sections for his election to Fellowship of the Royal Society in 1851.

FitzRoy invited Darwin to incorporate his journal into three main volumes with the rather ponderous title *Narrative of the Surveying Voyages of His Majesty's Ships Adventure and Beagle Between the Years 1826 and 1836: Describing Their Examination of the Southern Shores of South America, and the Beagle's Circumnavigation of the Globe*. They were published by Henry Colburn, London in 1839. FitzRoy compiled the first and wrote the second volumes. Darwin produced the third that was later published separately and is known today as *The Voyage of the Beagle*. It is still in print and ranks as one of the world's bestselling travel books.

FitzRoy's 'Painting Men'

The first two volumes of the *Narrative* are illustrated with black-and-white engravings after drawings and watercolours of the people and places produced by Earle and Martens. There are also illustrations after pictures by some of the naval officers and crew. They include portraits of the surviving Fuegians and a depiction of Woollya, near *Beagle* Channel, where the Fuegians were settled. Both were illustrations after original artwork created by FitzRoy.

Trainee naval officers were taught to draw and to use watercolour. These were useful skills for the practical purpose of making images of coastal profiles, headlands, landfalls among other points of interest to seafarers that often featured on Admiralty charts. Sometimes naval officers, and seamen too, produced their own pictures for personal interest and profit. As a cadet FitzRoy had been taught by the eminent marine painter John Christian Schetky (1778-1874), who was also Professor of Drawing at the Royal Naval College. Schetky provided sketches of naval ships for J.M.W. Turner's vast oil painting of the Battle of Trafalgar, 21 October 1805, now at the National Maritime Museum.

Robert FitzRoy's official survey artists were very different in character. This was reflected in how and what they painted. He was well aware of the promotional benefits to be derived by employing artists to create original artworks. *Beagle's* captain knew that pictorial material could be translated into printed formats for a variety of publications and prints. Artistic creations of the strange people, habits, rituals and customs, as well as the architecture, dwellings and views of exotic lands encountered during previous voyages of exploration had certainly been highly advantageous to their naval commanders, participants and patrons.

'Woollya', detail from an engraving by Landseer, after Robert FitzRoy from the Narrative (1839).
The Fuegians were settled at Woollya, in the south-east of Tierra del Fuego,
towards the end of January 1833. Courtesy Private Collection.

Pictorial material derived from earlier voyages had significantly raised the profiles of Sir Joseph Banks and Captain James Cook. Banks was the first gentleman-scientist to actively encourage draughtsmen to participate on voyages of exploration and survey expeditions. Banks, the gentleman scientist and patron became President of the Royal Society, while Cook was hailed as a seafaring hero for his remarkable seamanship and navigational achievements. Some of the pictures created during, and worked up after, their voyages were exhibited at the Royal Academy of Arts in London, incorporated into published journals and accounts and offered as individual prints for sale. These illustrations and artworks confirmed and underlined their achievements and helped to further raise their status.

FitzRoy had read these publications, seen the accompanying illustrations and admired some of the original artworks. In the first instance Banks had paid for the artists and illustrators, and this lead was followed by the British Admiralty for the second and third of Cook's voyages. FitzRoy followed their example and he personally paid for his 'painting men' to accompany him on his *Beagle* voyage. However, unlike the success enjoyed by Banks the eventual outcome for FitzRoy's artistic patronage would turnout to be very different. Illness and lack of space would determine *Beagle* sailed without an official artist for the last two years of the voyage. Although the amount of time spent by the painters formally employed on the *Beagle* was limited they produced some excellent work.

Earle and Martens were not professional ship portrait painters, or marine artists, who carefully and sometimes painstakingly described the vessels they were commissioned to portray. Earle had a gift for drawing people while Martens excelled at landscape painting. So historians have to be careful to balance what might at first glance appear to be a faithfully reproduction of the lines and appearance of the *Beagle* (a converted 10-gun brig), or for that matter any maritime vessel they drew or painted, with the reality that these artists incorporated into their work, varying degrees of artistic license. From time to time FitzRoy advised them to alter details to achieve nautical accuracy in their sketches, drawings and watercolours.

Augustus Earle (1793-1838) was a painter, panoramic artist, printmaker, writer, and poet of sorts. Of American parents he was born in London and exhibited drawings at the Royal Academy of Arts in his early teens. His artistic style is closely allied to the caricatures of the Cruikshank family. On 17 November 1831 Augustus Earle was recorded in the ship's Muster Tables as a 'Draughtsman' under the category of Supernumeraries for Victuals only.

Although Admiralty approved, he was paid from FitzRoy's own pocket an annual salary of £200. He was a veteran of earlier voyages of adventure, but became seriously ill during *Beagle's* residence at Montevideo in Uruguay, and towards the end of 1832 he had parted company from the *Beagle* expedition. Darwin described him as 'openly licentious' and his sexual activities may well have contributed to his premature death.

In late November of the following year his position had been taken up by Conrad Martens (1801-1878), who had heard of the vacancy while his ship called at Rio de Janeiro. Martens was born in London on 21 March 1801. His forebears included merchants and bankers from Hamburg. He was taught by the extravagantly named landscape watercolourist and popular art teacher Anthony Vandyke Copley Fielding. Martens' work is remarkably similar to his early teacher, and although he never loses his feeling for the picturesque due to his involvement with the *Beagle*, he

Self Portrait of Conrad Martens, 1834.
Courtesy State Library of New South Wales.

became increasingly focused on factual topography. He was also influenced by Turner and believed that there was 'no higher authority in landscape'.

In May 1833 Martens had sailed from England independently as a travel artist aboard HMS *Hyacinth*. On 4 October 1833 FitzRoy recorded his first meeting with Martens in an upbeat letter to Charles Darwin, who at that time was exploring the pampas near Buenos Aires. 'Mr Martens … a stone pounding artist who exclaims in his sleep 'think of me standing upon a pinnacle of the Andes, or sketching a Fuegian Glacier!!!' I am sure you will like him'. He further commented on his manners and intelligence and compared his skills to those of Earle: 'he is a gentlemanlike well informed man. His landscapes are really good (compared to London men), though perhaps in figures he cannot equal Earle'.

Martens was industrious and by far the larger number of his illustrations – twenty-nine (compared to seven by Earl) – featured in the official *Narrative*.

They included powerful portraits of Patagonians and Fuegian families, views of natives in the *Beagle* Channel, as well as a depiction of the *Beagle* ashore at the Rio Santa Cruz. Martens' original watercolours and drawings effectively captured the bleakness, desolation and wilderness of many of the places visited. However, the *Narrative* engravers, no doubt working under FitzRoy's instructions, often altered and enhanced the originals by bringing the subjects into closer focus, and enlivening the scenes with people, and sometimes animals.

Four of Martens' numbered sketchbooks compiled onboard the *Beagle* have survived. They reveal a methodical working process. Sketchbooks I and III are in the Cambridge University Library, England, and II and IV are in a private collection in Australia. Although numbered, the first sketchbook in terms of chronological order is in fact sketchbook III, which includes images relating to his passage on the *Hyacinth* from England to South America. The Cambridge University sketchbooks contain around a hundred images, mostly in graphite with a small number in colour.

It was with great regret that FitzRoy had to part company with Martens after being forced by the Admiralty to sell his schooner *Adventure*, the vessel he had acquired to assist his survey work. With everyone and everything (including many more of Darwin's specimens) now back onboard the *Beagle* there was insufficient living and working space. This time someone had to go. Writing to Captain Beaufort from Valparaiso on 26 September 1834 he was economical in his chosen words but the grammatical under-scoring reveals his frustration: 'My Schooner is sold. Our painting man Mr Martens is gone'. From Valparaiso on 5 November 1834 FitzRoy wrote a letter of reference for Martens to Captain Philip Parker King, the former Commander of the first *Beagle* expedition, who was then based in Sydney, Australia:

> *The bearer of this letter, Mr Conrad Martens, has parted from me, I am sorry to say, because there is no longer room for him on board the Beagle, nor money for him in his pocket. Had I more money, and more storage rooms, I should not think of ending my engagement with him. He has been nearly a year with us, and is much liked by my shipmates and myself. He is quiet, industrious, good fellow, and I wish him well. He thinks of visiting and perhaps settling at Sydney, therefore I write this letter by way of an introduction to you. Enclosed is a letter I received about him from Captain Blackwood of the Hyacinth. You will be able to judge of his abilities, by a glance at his works, far better than any words of mine. He has a host of views of Terrs De. [Tierra del Fuego] in his sketchbook. His profession is his maintenance.*

Martens duly made his way to Sydney and established himself there as a successful painter and art teacher. He is now acknowledged as one of the founding father's of colonial art in Australia. When the *Beagle* arrived in Sydney in 1836 Darwin visited Martens and purchased two of his watercolours. Writing to his sister Susan from Sydney, 28 January 1836, Darwin admitted he had been 'extravagant & bought two water-colour sketches, one of S. Cruz river & another in T. del Fuego, 3 guineas each, from Martens, who is an established artist at this place. I would not have bought them if I could have guessed how expensive my ride to Bathurst turned out'. The Tierra del Fuego watercolour is now known by a more expansive title, 'The *Beagle*, Murray Narrows, *Beagle* Channel'. This picture still hangs in Darwin's study at Down House in Kent.

But what became of the Fuegians? York Minster was killed in retaliation for a murder he had committed. Fuegia outlived him, probably dying of old age. Although the most devastating news FitzRoy received related to Jemmy Button's participation in another missionary project. Jemmy was implicated in the murder of several British seamen. In fact, it was later discovered that the evidence against Jemmy did not entirely stack up. Darwin's captain was a complex and sensitive soul who had a history of depression, what he called his 'blue devils', and this disaster affected him greatly.

FitzRoy had a spectacularly varied but largely unfulfilling career. Among his various appointments he had been MP for Durham and Governor of New Zealand. He was exhausted and over-sensitive to the criticism levelled at the accuracy of his weather-forecasts published in *The Times*. The Fuegians were the catalyst for *Beagle's* return to South America and the participation of Charles Darwin. They were also a factor in FitzRoy's premature death. Before breakfast on Sunday 30 April 1865 he locked the door to his dressing-room and with his razor slit his throat.

Editors' Note: Purchase a copy of *The Voyage of the Beagle* for only £15.00 including free UK p&p. Call 0870 787 1613 and quote reference CH1253. Alternatively, send a cheque – made payable to Anova Books – to Conway Mail Order, Anova Books, 10 Southcombe Street, London W14 0RA. Please quote reference CH1253.

Cochrane and the Battle of Basque Roads

David Cordingly

Plan of the fireship attack at Basque roads on the evening of 11 April 1809. Courtesy the author.

In April 1809 Lord Cochrane led a fireship attack on a French fleet in Basque Roads, the great estuary off La Rochelle on the west coast of France. The French warships were anchored behind a floating boom and were protected by the guns of the Isle d'Aix. The attack took place at night and the fireships were helped on their way by the flood tide and a fierce following wind. Leading the fireships were two 'explosion vessels', which were like floating bombs and were blown up with devastating effect when they reached the floating boom. The combined effect of the explosions and the rapidly approaching fireships caused panic among the crews of the anchored French ships. All except two cut their anchor cables and were swept aground on the mudbanks at the mouth of the River Charente. For several hours they were at the mercy of the guns of the British fleet that was anchored out in the estuary. Cochrane sent urgent messages to Lord Gambier, the British commander-in-chief, to send in his warships but Gambier delayed doing so for several hours. He was worried about the depth of water in the approach channel and concerned that his warships would go aground and be a sitting target for the guns on the Isle d'Aix. By the time Gambier did send in frigates and a bomb vessel, many of the French ships had floated off. In the ensuing action five of the French ships were destroyed, two of them having been set on fire by their French crews to prevent them falling into British hands.[1]

The fireship attack itself was a brilliant and daring action comparable with Drake's attack on Cadiz, or Nelson's attack on the anchored French fleet at Aboukir Bay, but in terms of results it was deeply disappointing, particularly for Cochrane. Many years later he was in Paris with Lord Brougham. They had paid a visit to the palace of the Tuileries and when Cochrane's name was mentioned a shudder went through the assembled company. Brougham told Cochrane that this ought to make up for his disappointment at Basque Roads. Cochrane answered that he would rather have had the ships.[2]

Following in the aftermath of Nelson's annihilation of the enemy ships at the Nile and Trafalgar it is perhaps not surprising that Basque Roads has been relegated to little more than a minor episode in the long war against Revolutionary and Napoleonic France. Its chief interest today lies not in the action itself but in the clash between the opposing and very different characters of Cochrane and Gambier. The clash led to the court martial of Gambier and sharply divided public opinion at the time. The poet Wordworth was on the side of Cochrane, 'that noble hero,' and believed that 'if the matter were investigated, heavy blame would be attached to Gambier for not having his ships where they could be brought up in time'.[3] But there were many who regarded Cochrane with suspicion. His friendship with William Cobbett and his activities as a radical MP had earned him enemies among the political establishment while his vociferous attacks on naval abuses and corruption had angered many senior admirals. When the court martial gave Gambier an honourable acquittal there was little sympathy for Cochrane. In the words of Admiral Bowen:

> *It will be a lesson to restless and inexperienced young officers not to hazard a mischievous opinion tending to weaken the respect and confidence due to able and tried officers – particularly to commanders-in-chief.*[4]

The whole episode marked the first step in the downfall of Cochrane. His subsequent involvement in the Stock Exchange scandal of 1814 was an opportunity for his enemies to get their own back. In a highly charged and politically motivated trial he was found guilty by association with the instigators of the plot and was sentenced to prison and a fine of £1,000. Within weeks he was struck off the Navy List, expelled from Parliament and stripped of the knighthood he had been awarded after Basque Roads. Blacklisted by the naval high command he was left with little option but to take his considerable talents overseas.

It is arguable that if Cochrane had not called into question Gambier's conduct, the Battle of Basque Roads would have been seen as a bold and successful action and not as a wasted opportunity. Its effect on French morale was certainly devastating. One French officer said that 'they had now no security from the English in their harbours, and they expected we should next go into Brest and take out their fleet whenever it suited our convenience'.[5] Napoleon was scathing about the panic-stricken reaction of the French crews and four of the French captains were put on trial. One captain was found guilty of abandoning his ship in the presence of the enemy and was condemned to death. He was shot on the deck of flagship *Ocean* on 9 September. Two other captains were sentenced to prison. Most important from the British point of view was the fact that the fireship action achieved its objective. British intelligence had learnt that it had been the intention of the French fleet gathered at Basque Roads to sail to the French island of Martinique and from there to launch an attack on the West India trade which was so vital a part of Britain's economy. The fireship action put an end to this ambition.

Revisiting the Attack

To mark the bicentenary of the Battle of Basque Roads a symposium was held at the Royal Naval Museum, Portsmouth, in April 2009.[6] The aim was to re-examine the circumstances of the fireship attack and to answer a number of questions. Was Cochrane justified in blaming Gambier for his failure to follow up on the fireship attack? If warships had been sent in earlier would the result have been very different? Was Gambier right to be cautious and did his decision to delay sending in his line of battle ships save British lives and the loss of several ships? The majority of the captains who were present at the action certainly supported Gambier when they gave evidence at his court martial, and Rear-Admiral Stopford, whose 80-gun flagship Caesar was aground on the shoals for some time, had no doubt that Gambier's caution was justified. As he told the court:

> In my opinion the dislodgement of the enemy's ships by fire-ships removed but a small part of the obstacles. With the wind as it then was (strong from the north-west), and the broadsides of the enemy's ships still commanding the approaches, we should have been so crippled in going into and in working out of the passage a little more than a mile in breadth, that I think I should not have risked the ships, had they been under my command.[7]

Gambier's activities as an evangelical Christian had earned him the nickname of 'Dismal Jimmy'. He campaigned against alcohol and bad language and irritated his fellow officers by issuing them with religious tracts that he expected them to read and distribute to their men. This made him an easy target for the newspapers and cartoonists of the day and has led to some of Cochrane's biographers treating him as a figure of ridicule. However, Gambier was no coward. He had seen combat during the American War, and had achieved heroic status during the Battle of the Glorious First of June when in command of the 74-gun ship *Defence*. He had sailed her into action under full sail, including her topgallant – the only British ship to do so. Surrounded by French ships the *Defence* was totally dismasted but continued to

'Dismal Jimmy' - Admiral Lord Gambier, 1813. Courtesy the author.

discharge her guns and refused to surrender. At the height of the action one of his lieutenants ran up to Gambier and said, 'Damn my eyes, Sir, but here is a whole mountain coming upon us: what shall we do?' Captain Gambier looked gravely at him and said in a solemn tone, 'How dare you, sir, at this awful moment, come to me with an oath in your mouth? Go down. Sir, and encourage your men to stand to their guns, like brave British seamen'.[8]

Praised by Lord Howe for his role in the battle, Gambier was awarded the King's gold medal, raised to flag rank and given a seat on the Admiralty Board. In 1807 he was commander-in-chief of a massive British fleet that bombarded Copenhagen into submission. In this controversial action he showed a ruthlessness that appeared at odds with his strongly held religious convictions. By contrast his work as a social reformer and his work on behalf of the welfare of ordinary seamen had earned him the name of the Sailors' Friend. At the time of Basque Roads he was aged fifty-three, and though he had spent much of his naval career in Whitehall, he had certainly seen more action than many senior admirals.

Thomas Cochrane was thirty-four in April 1809, and had been almost continuously in action ever since he had joined his uncle's frigate at the unusually advanced age of seventeen. The eldest son of an impoverished Scottish aristocrat, he had enjoyed a rapid rise from midshipman to lieutenant and had made his name as commander of the 14-gun brig sloop Speedy when he captured the Spanish xebec frigate *Gamo* against

*'Dismal Jimmy' – Admiral Lord Gambier,
1813. Courtesy the author.*

overwhelming odds in 1801. He had made a fortune in prize money while in command of the frigate *Pallas*, and had acquired a formidable reputation as a coastal raider in the Mediterranean while commanding the 38-gun frigate *Imperieuse*. The sheer audacity of some of his attacks on shipping and forts suggest that he had a gung-ho mentality and that his success owed more to luck than good judgement.

This was far from the case. He achieved his results through careful preparations, the rigorous training of his crew, and his mastery of shiphandling. Captain Jahleel Brenton, who had preceded Cochrane in the *Speedy*, and observed him in action on several occasions, wrote, 'he admired nothing more in Lord Cochrane than the care he took of the preservation of his people. Bold and adventurous as he was, no unnecessary exposure of life was ever permitted under his command. Every circumstance was anticipated, every provision for success was made'.[9] The thoroughness of his preparations was also noted by Edward Brenton, the naval historian and the brother of Jahleel. He observed of Cochrane that '[b]efore he fired a shot he reconnoitred in person, took soundings and bearings, passed whole nights in boats under the enemy's batteries, his lead line and spy glass incessantly at work'.[10]

Knowledge and Daring

If we follow the sequence of events at Basque Roads from the moment when Cochrane was first ordered to lead the attack, we can see how his knowledge of the area and his preparations paid off. In March 1809 Cochrane returned to Plymouth, exhausted after his prolonged defence of Fort Trinidad on the Mediterranean coast near Barcelona. On going ashore he found a despatch waiting for him from William Johnstone-Hope, the Second Lord of the Admiralty, which informed him:

> *There is an undertaking of great moment in agitation against Rochefort, and the Board thinks that your local knowledge and services might be of the utmost consequence, and, I believe, it is intended to send you there with all expedition.*[11]

Back in May 1806 Cochrane had carried out a detailed reconnaissance of Basque Roads and the French anchorage off the island of Aix. He had spent four hours within gunshot of the French fleet making a careful assessment of the landmarks, shoals and defences. When he sent his report back to Admiral Thornborough he had observed that the French ships could easily be burnt by fireships.

Johnstone-Hope's letter was followed by a telegraphic message from the Admiralty that summoned Cochrane to Whitehall. On his arrival in London he was invited to a private meeting with Lord Mulgrave, the First Lord of the Admiralty. Mulgrave took Cochrane into his confidence and told him that the Admiralty Board were determined to strike a blow before the French fleet had an opportunity to elude the British blockade at Basque Roads and attack British commerce in the West Indies. He asked Cochrane for his assessment of the likely success of a fireship attack and showed him a letter he had received from Gambier that expressed his abhorrence of fireships and pointed out that the use of them would be 'hazardous if not desperate'.[12] Cochrane agreed that fireships on their own would not be effective if the enemy had rowing boats standing by to tow them clear of the anchored warships. However, if the fireships were accompanied by explosion vessels, bomb vessels and rockets, and the attack was made with a fair wind and and flowing tide, he believed there would be no risk of failure.

Impressed by Cochrane's confidence and expertise Mulgrave asked him to put his proposals in writing so that he could show them to the Board of Admiralty. The minutes of the Board's meeting on 25 March duly recorded 'Orders to Lord Cochrane to proceed with the *Imperieuse* off Rochefort, and put himself under the command of Lord Gambier'.[13] To Mulgrave's surprise Cochrane was reluctant to take part in the attack himself. As a junior captain Cochrane rightly anticipated there would be resentment from senior naval officers out in Basque Roads if he was asked to lead the attack, and he also suspected that he was likely to be made a scapegoat if the planned attack went wrong. However, the Board would not entertain any refusal or delay and Cochrane was despatched to Plymouth to rejoin his ship. Ten days later the *Imperieuse* dropped anchor in Basque Roads and Cochrane went aboard the flagship Caledonia and reported to Lord Gambier, who received him with great courtesy. Gambier was in a difficult position. He had received orders from London 'to leave no means untried to destroy the enemy's squadron' and had been informed that he was being sent twelve transport vessels to be fitted out as fireships, as well as five bomb vessels, and a supply of Congreve rockets. In a detailed response to the Admiralty he explained his reservations about the proposed attack:

The enemy's ships are anchored in two lines, very near each other, in a direction due south from the Isle d'Aix … The most distant ships of their line are within point-blank shot of the works on the Isle d'Aix; such ships, therefore, as might attack the enemy would be exposed to be raked by red-hot shot, etc, from the island, and should the ships be disabled in their masts, they must remain within range of the enemy's fire until they are destroyed – there not being sufficient depth of water to allow them to move to the southward out of distance.[14]

Gambier's assessment of the dangers would prove to be wrong in all respects. The guns on Aix were ineffective and hardly damaged a single ship; they did not fire red-hot shot; and there was sufficient depth of water both in the approach channel and to the south of the Aix anchorage out of range of the guns.

As Cochrane had anticipated there was considerable resentment among senior officers in Gambier's fleet when they learnt that Cochrane was to lead the fireship attack. Rear Admiral Eliab Harvey, a veteran of Trafalgar, was outraged and came storming aboard the *Caledonia* and had a furious row with Gambier which resulted in him being sent home to face a court martial. Cochrane did not allow the attitude of Harvey or other officers to deflect him from his mission. Early the next morning, 4 April, he sailed the *Imperieuse* to within gunshot of the Isle d'Aix and got close enough to note that the gun batteries which Gambier so feared, appeared to be in ruins. The next morning he made a second reconnaissance trip to the island and deliberately fired a shot at the enemy batteries to gauge the response. When nothing happened he tacked the *Imperieuse* and fired an exploratory shot at the enemy fleet. This provoked a desultory response but the shot fell harmlessly short. He returned to the fleet and sent a report to Gambier:

I reported to the commander in chief the ruinous state of the Isle d'Aix, it having the inner fortifications completely blown up and destroyed, which I not only ascertained from the deck with perfect precision as to the side towards us, but also as to the opposite side from one of the tops of the ship.[15]

From a position high up in the fighting tops of his frigate Cochrane had counted thirteen mounted guns and some mortars. This was later confirmed by Captain Rodd of the *Indefatigable* and many others including William Richardson, the gunner on the *Caesar*, 80 guns, who wrote after the action, 'In passing the Aix batteries, where our French pilots said there were as many guns as days in the year, we could not find above thirteen guns that could be directed against us in passing, and these we thought so little of that we did not return their fire'.[16]

Having completed his reconnaissance Cochrane devoted the next few days to supervising the fitting out of four explosion vessels. These were old ships packed with large casks of gunpowder, and hundreds of shells and grenades. These highly explosive cargoes were to be ignited by fuses consisting of canvas hoses filled with prime powder, which led out through holes cut in the vessels' quarters. It was calculated that the fuses would burn for twelve to fifteen minutes 'so as to give the people alongside in the boat who set it on fire sufficient time to escape before she exploded'.[17] The twelve fireships were each fitted with Congreve rockets on frames made fast to their yard-arms.

By midday on 11 April the preparations for the attack were complete. Five or six volunteers had been selected to man each of the fireships and explosion vessels. Cochrane himself would lead the attack in an explosion vessel, accompanied by five members of the crew of the *Imperieuse*, including his younger brother Basil. Midshipman Marryat (the future author Captain Marryat) was one of the crew in the second explosion vessel. Conditions that evening were in many ways ideal for the attack. Low tide was at 8 pm which meant that for the next six hours it would be flooding in along the channel towards the anchored enemy fleet. The north-westerly wind was likewise favourable and was so strong that the French had withdrawn the rowing boats normally stationed by the boom to tow away fireships.

Entering the 'Gates of Hell'

At 8.30 pm on the evening of 11 April the attacking force cut their anchor cables and set sail. Marryat later recalled his terror as they set off:

> *It was a fearful moment; the wind freshened and whistled through our rigging. And the night was so dark that we could not see our bowsprit. We had only our foresail set; but with a strong flood-tide and a fair wind, with plenty of it, we passed between the advanced frigates like an arrow. It was like entering the gates of hell.*[18]

The attackers were guided towards their target by two brig sloops, the *Redpole* and the *Lyra*, which were were anchored on each side of the approach channel with distinctive lights in their rigging. The two explosion vessels blew up with terrifying force and the leading fireship, the *Mediator*, broke the boom, exposing the French fleet to the fireships following in her wake. Although some of the fireships were abandoned by their crews too early and never reached the enemy fleet, the combined effect of the explosions, the fireships,

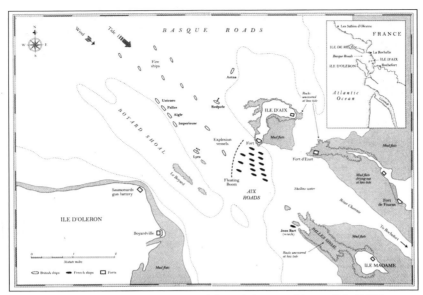

Plan showing British ships attacking grounded French ships around 4pm on 12 April 1809.
Courtesy the author.

and the Congreve rockets darting through the air, caused such alarm among the French crews that eleven of them cut their cables and were swept aground on the shoals at the entrance of the River Charente.

The next morning Cochrane, now back on board the *Imperieuse*, observed the vulnerable state of the grounded French ships and sent a series of signals back to Gambier's flagship, which were duly recorded in the *Caledonia's* log. At 5.48 am he sent his first signal: 'Half the fleet can destroy the enemy: seven on shore'. At 6.40 am, as dawn revealed more of the enemy ships, he sent the signal, 'Eleven on shore' At 7.40 am, 'Only two afloat'.[19] It was now approaching low water which was around 8.20 am and the French crews were throwing guns overboard to lighten their ships and laying out anchors ready to haul themselves off the mud. At 9.30 Cochrane sent a fourth signal, 'Enemy preparing to haul off'. Now was the ideal time for Gambier to send in frigates and three or four line of battle ships. They could sail in on the rising tide, destroy the enemy, most of whom were still aground, and sail out on the ebb tide. At 10.45 am Gambier did at last order his fleet to get under way but at 11.30 am the fleet anchored in 12 fathoms three miles from the Isle d'Aix to the exasperation of many of his officers, one of whom later wrote, 'I cannot describe the indignation expressed by all hands when the signal was made to anchor again'.[20]

The explosion ship Mediator breaking the boom at Basque Roads, 1809. Engraving by Robert Dodd. Courtesy the author.

Cochrane now realised that Gambier had no intention of risking his warships and so he decided to take matters into his own hands by making a lone attack on the enemy. At 1 pm he drifted the *Imperieuse* on the tide towards the grounded ships:

> *I did not venture to make sail, lest the movement might be seen from the flagship and a signal of recall should defeat my purpose…the object being to compel the commander-in-chief to send vessels to our assistance.*[21]

At around this time Gambier did send in the *Aetna* bomb vessel and three gun brigs. At 1.30 Cochrane signalled to Gambier, 'The enemy is superior to the chasing ship but inferior to the fleet'. And ten minutes later he sent a signal which he knew could not be ignored; 'The ship is in distress and requires to be assisted immediately'.[22] The *Imperieuse* was not in distress but as a 38-gun frigate she was heavily outgunned by the three French warships which she anchored opposite: the *Aquilon*, 74 guns, the *Calcutta*, 56 and the *Ville de Varsovie*, 80. Gambier did now send in ships to support the *Imperieuse*. At 2.40 pm the frigates *Emerald, Aigle* and *Unicorn* joined the *Imperieuse*, and at 3 pm the 74-gun ships *Valiant* and *Revenge* arrived on the scene. At 4.30 pm the 80-gun *Caesar* joined the attacking force.

The bombardment of the French ships continued throughout the night and most of the next day. The net result of the action was the destruction of five French warships. The French lost 200 men killed and 650 were taken prisoner.

The British losses were 10 killed and 37 wounded. Cochrane left the scene of the action reluctantly. He was recalled by Gambier and ordered to take the *Imperieuse* back to England carrying Sir Harry Neale with Gambier's despatches. When news of the battle reached London there was rejoicing on a scale not seen for many years. Bonfires were lit in the streets, public buildings were illuminated and a theatre in Westminster staged a dramatic re-enactment of the battle. There were promotions for the naval officers who had distinguished themselves in the attack and Cochrane, who was everywhere recognised as the hero of the action, was made a Knight of the Bath.

Recrimination and Re-Assessment

Rumours circulating that the victory was not as complete as it might have been, and Cochrane's decision to oppose Parliament's vote of thanks to Gambier, led inevitably to Gambier demanding a court martial to clear his name. The court martial took place on the hulk *Gladiator* in Portsmouth harbour on 26 July 1809. It was presided over by Admiral Sir Richard Curtis who was a friend of Gambier and sitting with him was Admiral William Young, a long-standing enemy of Cochrane, and five other admirals and four senior captains. The charge against Gambier was that on 12 April, 'the enemy's ships being then on shore, and the signal having been made that they

The Imperieuse attacking the grounded French ships at Basque Roads on 12 April 1809, engraving by Robert Dodd. Courtesy the author.

could be destroyed, did for a considerable time neglect or delay taking effectual measures for destroying them'.[23] The court cross-examined sixteen of the captains who had been with the fleet, and five of the ships' masters, and the signal lieutenant and signal mate of the *Caledonia*. A lot of time was devoted to discussing tidal depths, tidal streams, the wind and weather, and the strength of the French defences.

Cochrane was cross-examined at length and in an exceedingly hostile manner. He was not allowed to refer to his notes and when he produced a copy of the French chart, which he had used, this was ruled to be inadmissable. He was not allowed to question any witnesses and was excluded from the court when Gambier's defence was read out. The only charts used in evidence were those prepared by Mr Stokes, the master of Gambier's flagship, and by Edmund Fairfax, the master of the fleet. These showed the approach channel to be barely a mile wide and the depths to be considerably less than those shown on the French chart – or the soundings taken by some of the British ships. For instance Captain Seymour of the 74-gun *Revenge* found 5¼ fathoms (32 feet) at the dead of the spring-tide ebb (mean low water springs) in the Maumusson Passage which was out of reach of the guns of the Isle d'Aix and where there was room for five or six sail of the line.[24] The draft of a loaded 74-gun ship at the stern was about 22 feet.

Only four captains were prepared to question Gambier's actions, or lack of action. The testimony of Captain Broughton of the *Illustrious* was, however, fairly damning. He had been within gunshot of the fortifications on Aix and reckoned there were only 14 to 20 guns commanding the roadstead and no furnaces for heating red hot shot. He went on, adding 'I think it would have been more advantageous if the line-of-battle ships, frigates and smaller vessels had gone in at half flood, which I take to be about 11 o'clock'.[25] He added that his French chart showed a safe anchorage with 30 to 40 feet of water out of range of shot and shells in any direction. After hearing evidence and cross-examining witnesses for nine days the court delivered its verdict on 4 August. Gambier was honourably acquitted and the court concluded that his conduct 'was marked by zeal, judgement, and ability and an anxious attention to the welfare of His Majesty's service'.[26]

Whatever one's views of Cochrane and Gambier, it has to be said that the court martial failed to answer a number of pertinent questions. Why did Gambier fail to carry out a full reconnaissance of the channel and the fortifications on the Isle d'Aix as Cochrane did within a day of his arrival on the scene? Why was Gambier not able to get hold of a French chart of Basque Roads? Why did he position his blockading fleet so far from the fire-ship operation? Had he been closer he would have seen the vulnerability of the grounded French ships and been able to respond quickly to the unfolding situation. We shall never know whether sending in his warships earlier would have drastically changed the outcome but it is hard not to agree with Admiral Harvey who said at his own court martial, 'if Lord Nelson had been there he would not have anchored the Fleet in Basque Roads but have dashed at the enemy at once'.[27]

Gambier continued to carry out good work for sailors' causes and became the first president of the Church Missionary Society but his reputation as a naval commander never recovered from the doubts cast on his leadership at Basque Roads.[28] Cochrane went on to gain world-wide fame for his astonishing feats as commander of the patriot naval forces of Chile where he is regarded today as one of the saviours of the country from Spanish rule. He also played a key role in liberating Brazil from the Portuguese while in command of the Brazilian navy. Returning to England in 1825, he spent the rest of his life fighting to establish his innocence of the Stock Exchange fraud. He was eventually granted a pardon and restored to the rank of Rear Admiral in the Royal Navy. By the time of his death in 1860 he had become a Victorian hero and was buried with considerable pomp in Westminster Abbey. However, recent publications have revealed his darker side, in particular his obsession with money and his endless disputes and personal vendettas.[29] His *Autobiography of a Seaman* – a classic of naval literature, which provided inspiration for Patrick O'Brian, C.S.Forester and others – is now regarded as 'a mendacious work of self-justification to be used with extreme caution'.[30]

[1] The details of the action at Basque Roads described in this article are taken from the logs of the *Imperieuse, Caledonia, Aetna, Emerald, Beagle and Mediator;* W.B. Gurney, *Minutes of a Court Martial...on the trial of the Right Honourable James, Lord Gambier* (Portsmouth: Mattley, Harrison and Miller, 1809); William James, *The Naval History of Great Britain*, (London: Richard Bentley, 1878), vi, pp. 394-431; *Naval Chronicle*, 21 (1809), pp. 344-414; William Richardson, *A Mariner of England* (London: Smith, 1908), pp. 243-44; Captain Frederick Marryat, *Frank Mildmay* (London: George Routledge, 1865), pp. 132-37; Thomas Cochrane, *The Autobiography of a Seaman* (London: Richard Bentley, 1861); and various charts and documents in the Dundonald Papers in the National Archives of Scotland, especially GD233/71/35, GD233/78/35, GD233/81/82, GD233/81/84, GD233/83/93 and GD233/12183-7; and a detailed account in John Sugden, 'Lord Cochrane, Naval Commander, Radical, Inventor: A Study of his Early Career, 1775-1818' (University of Sheffield, unpublished PhD thesis, 1981).

[2] Brougham to Dundonald, 31 October 1860. Quoted by Dundonald and Bourne, *The Life of Thomas, Lord Cochrane* (London: Richard Bentley, 1869), ii, pp. 360-61.

[3] Wordsworth to Thomas de Quincey, 5 May 1809, in *The Letters of William and Dorothy Wordsworth: the Middle Years*, edited by Ernest de Selincourt (Oxford: Clarendon Press, 1937), i, p. 299.

4 Georgiana, Lady Chatterton, *Memorials, Personal and Historical of Admiral Lord Gambier* (LondonL Hurst and Blackett, 1861), ii, p. 334.

5 *Naval Chronicle*, 21 (1809), p. 407.

6 The conference, entitled 'Fireships Re-Ignited: Cochrane at the Basque Roads Action 1809', was held on 18 April 2009. The speakers were Dr Sam Willis, Dr David Cordingly, Richard Blake, Captain Mike Barritt and Dr John Sugden.

7 Quoted in C. Northcote Parkinson, *Britannia Rules: The Classic Age of Naval History, 1793-1815* (London: Weidenfeld and Nicolson, 1977), p. 151.

8 Quoted in Oliver Warner, *The Glorious First of June*, (London: Batsford, 1961), p. 80.

9 *Memoir of Vice-Admiral Sir Jahleel Brenton*, edited by Henry Raikes (London: Longman, 1855), p. 339.

10 Edward Brenton, *The Naval History of Great Britain* (London: Richard Bentley, 1837), ii, p. 125.

11 Hope to Cochrane, 21 March 1809, National Archives of Scotland: GD233/82/84

12 Gambier to Mulgrave, 11 March 1809, quoted in William James, *The Naval History of Great Britain*, (London: Richard Bentley, 1878), iv, p. 396.

13 Admiralty Board minutes, 15 March 1809. National Archives, Kew: ADM.3/167.

14 Gambier to Pole, 26 March 1809. William James, *Naval History*, iv, p. 398.

15 W.B. Gurney, *Minutes of a Court Martial*, p. 58.

16 William Richardson, *A Mariner of England*, p. 248.

17 Ibid., p. 244.

18 Frederick Marryat, *Frank Mildmay*, p. 133.

19 All Cochrane's signals are recorded under the heading 'Signals made 12th April 1809' in the *Caledonia's* log, National Archives, Kew: ADM.51/1981.

20 Gordon to the eleventh Earl of Dundonald, 12 April 1861. National Archives of Scotland: GD33/74/3-4.

21 Thomas Cochrane, *The Autobiography of a Seaman* (London: Richard Bentley, 1861). The edition cited is the Chatham Publishing edition of 2000 with an introduction by Richard Woodman.

22 Log of Caledonia. National Archives, Kew: ADM.51/1981.

23 W.B. Gurney, *Minutes of a Court Martial*, p. 2

24 William James, *Naval History*, iv, p. 416

25 W.B. Gurney, *Minutes of a Court Martial*, pp. 218-20.

26 Ibid., p. 231.

27 Court martial of Admiral Harvey, 22 May 1809. National Archives, Kew: ADM.1/5396.

28 See Richard Blake's entry on Admiral Lord Gambier in the *Oxford Dictionary of National Biography*.

29 David Cordingly, *Cochrane the Dauntless: The Life and Adventures of Thomas Cochrane* (London: Bloomsbury, 2007); Richard Dale, *Napoleon is Dead: Lord Cochrane and the Great Stock Exchange Scandal* (London: Sutton Publishing, 2006); Brian Vale, *The Audacious Admiral Cochrane: The True Life of a Naval Legend*, (London: Conway Maritime Press, 2004); Brian Vale, *Cochrane in the Pacific: Fortune and Freedom in Spanish America* (London: Taurus, 2008).

30 N.A.M. Rodger, *The Command of the Ocean: A Naval History of Britain, 1649-1815* (London: Penguin Books, 2004), p. 794.

'A Local Remedy to a Local Grievance': British Countermeasures against Spanish Privateering, 1822-23

Matthew McCarthy

Powering towards the Spanish colony of Puerto Rico in late December 1822 was a British naval squadron, guns bristling, brimming with men, and victualled and stored for the special service with which it was charged. In the two weeks preceding the departure of this force, a flurry of interest had been generated by the drawing together at Plymouth Sound of this substantial six-vessel squadron, consisting of the flagship HMS *Gloucester*, of 74 guns, *Phaeton*, 46, *Eden*, 26, *Valorous*, 26, the *Billette* sloop and the *Pioneer* schooner.[1] Onlookers included an anxious Spanish chargé d'affaires, who fearing British designs on the Spanish island of Cuba, made urgent enquiries to the British government as to the squadron's intentions.[2] One man who was well aware of the true purpose of the squadron's deployment was its commodore, Sir Edward Owen, who had received secret orders from the Admiralty earlier in the month. These instructions conferred upon him the authority to capture or destroy any armed vessel bearing the Spanish flag, issuing from or entering the ports and harbours of Puerto Rico, and to capture and detain merchant ships under the same flag in the same location.[3]

But Britain was not at war with Spain. Britain was officially at peace with the entire world and Spain was her ally. The deployment of Owen's squadron was no act of war; rather, in the words of the British Foreign Secretary, George Canning, it marked the application of 'a local remedy to a local grievance'.[4] The grievance to which Canning referred was an upsurge in captures of British vessels by Spanish privateers in the West Indies. These vessels were casualties of the war on trade accompanying the Latin American Wars of Independence, fought between Spain and her rebel colonies in the New World in the early nineteenth century. Despite Britain's neutrality in this conflict, her shipping suffered frequent interruptions and spoliations in the period 1815-1830, a problem that became most acute in the early 1820s after the Spanish governor of Puerto Cabello declared the whole coast of Colombia in a state of blockade. By virtue of this declaration, Spanish privateers took to the seas to make prize of all vessels found trading with the rebel Spanish American colonies, regardless of their nationality.

The trigger that compelled the British government to retaliate against this upsurge in Spanish prize-taking activity, the nature of the countermeasures adopted, and the outcomes of the British strategy are discussed in this article. Such an investigation reveals that Britain's 'local remedy' had far-reaching ramifications.

The Trigger

A letter to the Editor of *The Times* in July 1822 spoke of a case of 'very considerable importance' to Britain's burgeoning trade with the newly independent provinces of Spanish America.[5] 'A Spanish privateer', the letter continued, had 'made the experiment of capturing a British ship ... on the grounds of her being engaged in a trade interdicted by Spain'. That ship was the *Lord Collingwood*. Her seizure in the West Indies in late 1821 was the event that triggered the British government's response to the threat posed by Spanish privateers.

Loaded with jerk beef and in a rather leaky state, the *Lord Collingwood* had been labouring along the coast of Cuba on 18 September 1821.[6] Her master, Thomas Domaille, having heard 'very favourable news from Havana', had set his course for that port and anticipated a ready market for the sale of his cargo. What he never bargained for was the fact that nearby, and equally spurred on by the prospect of netting a tidy profit, was Don Juan Bautista Escurra, captain of the Spanish privateer *La Pancheta*. At eight o'clock that very morning, the two men came face to face and so began a process that would soon pit their respective governments at loggerheads. After overhauling and conducting a rigorous search of the *Lord Collingwood*, Domaille was taken on board the privateer and told to sign a declaration confirming his vessel as a prize. Domaille refused. Britain was an ally of Spain, he protested, to which Escurra allegedly uttered the stern warning to his stubborn captive – 'take care that my blood don't get warm'. Domaille signed the declaration. The *Lord Collingwood* was duly manned by a prize crew and carried into Aguadilla, Puerto Rico, where she dropped anchor on 20 September 1821.

Within two months, the prize court at Aguadilla had wound up its investigation into the legitimacy of the capture and passed its final judgement in the case: the *Lord Collingwood* was a 'good prize'.[7] The grounds upon which this determination was founded were multiple. Chief among them was the fact that the *Lord Collingwood* had loaded her cargo at Buenos Aires. As the former viceroyalty of the Rio de la Plata had formally declared itself independent from Spain in 1816, the judge considered the *Lord Collingwood* to be exporting the commodities of an enemy. Lending further weight to the sentence of condemnation was the fact that Domaille had been captured navigating in the seas of South America without special leave from the Spanish government. Moreover, the *Lord Collingwood* was deemed to have been holding an indirect course, being bound initially for St. Thomas before putting into Rio de Janeiro to repair a leak and clearing for a new destination – the port of Havana. The papers found on board the vessel gave the judge further reason to doubt the virtues of Domaille's voyage. There was no original crew list, no contract of freight, nor indeed anything other than some navigation papers for the Mediterranean from the year 1814. On these grounds, the judge ruled that the vessel and cargo were good and lawful prizes and condemned them to be delivered up, with all effects, to Captain Escurra and the owner of the *Pancheta*, Don Francisco Espelo.

The Response

News of the capture of the *Lord Collingwood* spread quickly. Reeling at their estimated loss of upwards of £6,000, the owners of the vessel and cargo, De Lisle & Co of London, penned a letter to the Admiralty representing their case and expressing their confidence that His Majesty's government would 'never suffer depredations on British property … to pass with impunity'.[8] This letter was forwarded to the man who would orchestrate the British government's response to this case of prize until his suicide in August 1822, the Foreign Secretary, Lord Castlereagh.

On learning of the sentence passed by the Puerto Rican prize court, Castlereagh slammed the grounds of condemnation as 'futile, subversive of justice and contrary to national law'.[9] He took particular issue with the claim that the *Lord Collingwood* had been illegally trading in the seas of South America without special leave from the Spanish government. This contravened an agreement made between Britain and Spain in 1819, which permitted British merchants to trade with those parts of Latin America no longer *de facto* under Spanish rule. Accordingly, the grounds of condemnation not only represented an injustice to the owners of the *Lord Collingwood*, but also threatened all British commercial interests in Latin

America. The case was thus catapulted into being one of national importance. The British representative in Madrid, Lionel Hervey, was ordered to make an 'unqualified and formal protest' against the sentence and to point out that nothing but the complete restitution of the vessel and reparation for the owners would satisfy the British government.[10]

Castlereagh also spotted the opportunity to use this protest as a vehicle to settle other outstanding grievances held by British subjects against the Spanish government. Since the Napoleonic Wars, British subjects had been experiencing losses at the hands of Spaniards, whether by having their property captured at sea or confiscated in Spanish ports and cities, by the imposition of excessive duties and tariffs, or by the failure of Spanish subjects to repay loans. This catalogue of grievances accumulated to such an extent that by 1819, the Spanish government was informed that Britain would resort to reprisals if these claims were not swiftly liquidated.[11] At the time, the Spanish government gave assurances that indemnification would be made to the British claimants, but in 1822 the injured parties were still waiting. Castlereagh saw the protest against the capture and condemnation of the *Lord Collingwood* as the ideal opportunity for all British claims on the Spanish government to be brought under review. In August 1822, Hervey delivered Castlereagh's demands to the Spanish government.[12]

Months passed without an answer, during which time the reins of the Foreign Office passed from Castlereagh to his successor, George Canning. The new Foreign Secretary quickly set about finding a remedy to the threat posed by Spanish privateers. Britain had been 'trifled with too long ... in matters so vitally important', he said, and Britain's new representative in Madrid, William à Court, was instructed to repeat demands for redress and reparation, only this time in a tone that would elicit an immediate and categorical answer.[13] Following the precedent set by his predecessor, Canning continued to use the example of the *Lord Collingwood* as a test case. He instructed à Court to acquire atonement specifically in the case of the *Lord Collingwood* as this would more directly test the disposition of the Spanish ministers.[14] Given that the case was recent in memory and had been the subject of repeated discussion, the Spanish ministers could not make the promises of investigation that had enabled them so often to elude British remonstrations.[15] But à Court was also directed not to abandon the quest for redress in the other 'numerous and flagrant instances of unjust capture and of commercial oppression'.[16]

After a meeting with the Spanish Secretary of State, Evaristo de San Miguel, William à Court reported to Canning on 20 November that San Miguel had promised to give a satisfactory answer in the case of the *Lord Collingwood* as soon as an opinion had been given by the Council of State – the body to which the question had been referred.[17] À Court was pessimistic about the prospect of this answer being satisfactory, identifying the Spanish constitution as the principal obstacle in the British government's pursuit of justice. He observed that Spanish ministers were crippled by such a fear of deviating from established norms and were so inclined to shift the onus from one side to another that the Spanish government was incapable of replying to the commonest questions.[18] À Court warned Canning that the British government may yet be driven to the necessity of reprisals.[19]

Canning concurred and had in fact already put the wheels of a contingency plan in motion. A Memorandum was presented to the Cabinet on 15 November 1822, in which Canning declared:

> *The cure for all the evils and dangers of the present state of things in the West Indian seas is to be found ... not in a perseverance in that system of forbearance and submission which we have hitherto observed towards Spain, but in a prompt and vigorous vindication of our rights by the means which Providence has placed in our power.*[20]

The providential means to which Canning referred was the Royal Navy, which he proposed utilising in order to apply what he described as 'a local remedy to a local grievance'.[21] The harbours of Cuba, Puerto Rico and Puerto Cabello, Canning insisted, should be made answerable for the injuries inflicted by ships and perpetrators finding shelter ashore.[22] His plan involved deploying a sizeable naval squadron to sail first to Puerto Rico and demand the restitution of the *Lord Collingwood* and any other British vessels 'taken and condemned under the like unjust pretences'.[23] Should the local authorities fail to give satisfaction, the squadron would then be authorised to detain every Puerto Rican merchant vessel fallen in with as a deposit for the indemnification of the injured British parties. Meanwhile, any Spanish armed vessel found cruising in those seas would be captured or destroyed. The squadron would then proceed to Puerto Cabello to remonstrate against the blockade declared by the commander of that port, and if finding British vessels detained on the grounds that they had been trading with the former Spanish colonies, the squadron would begin to detain Spanish shipping, just as it had done at Puerto Rico.

Such measures promised to meet the immediate concern of protecting British commerce, but Canning hoped to go one step further, suggesting to the Cabinet that the time had arrived for Britain to formalise its trade with Latin

America by extending official recognition to the former Spanish colonies.[24] Canning saw this as the ideal opportunity to offer recognition given that grounds now existed to render such a step justifiable towards Spain. He told the Cabinet that he would prepare a paper on the matter, which would be submitted for their perusal by the time the Duke of Wellington returned from the Congress of Verona, which had been underway since late October.[25]

Canning's proposals met with the approval of his Cabinet colleagues. Orders were drawn up in anticipation that the plan would be put into action and in early December, Edward Owen was directed to prepare HMS *Gloucester* for foreign service. But whether he would sail in pursuance of his orders or not, hinged upon the Spanish government's answer to the list of British demands. When William à Court received that answer on 5 December, he reflected that 'a more unsatisfactory document could hardly ever have been penned'.[26] It entirely evaded the demand for restitution and indemnification in the case of the *Lord Collingwood* and justified the condemnation on the very grounds that the British government required its disavowal. The Spanish government showed its intent to maintain the right of Spain to capture vessels in the South American seas and dismissed the 1819 agreement with Britain as a mere temporary arrangement. The other outstanding British claims were waived aside as it was considered an inappropriate time to discuss them. William à Court therefore informed the Spanish government of Britain's intention to take reprisals in the West Indies.[27]

San Miguel begged for more time and submitted a Memorandum to the Council of State, where the case was discussed for three consecutive days. The subsequent answer put an end to all hopes of an amicable settlement and all possibility of avoiding immediate reprisals. William à Court reported on 22 December how, in a 'haughty and offensive tone', the Spanish government stated itself to be the aggrieved party, avoided giving a decision in the case of the *Lord Collingwood* and absolved itself of responsibility in similar cases by referring claimants to the tribunals of the country, which had jurisdiction in such matters.[28] The only point that the Spanish government was willing to concede was that the blockade of Colombia, ordered by the governor of Puerto Cabello, should be discontinued. Days later, Owen's squadron left Plymouth to execute its orders.

The Outcomes

As William à Court sat penning a letter to the Foreign Office on Christmas Eve 1822, pondering 'eight fruitless years' of diplomatic negotiations regarding Spanish insults to British trade, he received an unexpected visit from Evaristo de

San Miguel.[29] The Spanish Secretary of State hastily excused himself for all the offensive parts of his answer to à Court's memorandum and thrust papers in front of the British minister that were to be taken immediately to the Cortes demanding full powers from that body to settle all differences between Britain and Spain.[30] This was enough to satisfy the British government. À Court abandoned his previous report and immediately began to relay the details of this turn of events to Canning. With an amicable agreement in prospect, the race was now on to intercept Owen's squadron before a blow had been struck in anger. In early January 1823, a frigate left Plymouth charged with the task of overtaking Owen's squadron at Barbados or Puerto Rico. Both governments anxiously awaited news from the West Indies and when it came, the news was good. With only a matter of hours to spare, the squadron had been found lying at Barbados, busily readying itself to depart for Puerto Rico the following morning.[31] On receipt of his new orders, Owen suspended his operations and placed himself under the command of Rear-Admiral Sir Charles Rowley on the Jamaica Station.

While this frantic chase had been unfolding across the Atlantic, the Cortes in Madrid had unanimously passed the resolutions outlined by San Miguel, satisfying once and for all the grievances of the British government. The Cortes confirmed that the blockade issued by the governor of Puerto Cabello was null and void.[32] It stopped short of repealing the restrictive colonial laws that prohibited foreigners from trading with Spanish America but it was conceded that British vessels should be permitted to trade with the provinces no longer *de facto* under Spanish rule for a period of ten months, in order to allow for the two governments to reach a final arrangement.[33]

The Spanish government accepted responsibility for having done Britain wrong by capturing her vessels and consented to appoint arbitrators to examine into the claims of British subjects.[34] In order to liquidate these claims, a sum of 40,000,000 *reales de vellón* (approx. £500,000) was placed at the disposal of the arbitrators, to be augmented or diminished as required. This Spanish promise was quickly converted into a formal agreement in March 1823 by the signing of an Anglo-Spanish treaty, which officially created a mixed commission to investigate the British claims.[35] It was publicised that claimants had a period of six months in which to submit supporting evidence of their claims and when that period had expired, a total of 331 claims had arrived at the office of the commission in London.[36] One of these claims belonged to De Lisle & Co, who sought a compensation package of just under £8,000 for the loss of the *Lord Collingwood* and her cargo of jerk beef.[37] But De Lisle & Co and the other British claimants would find themselves waiting for a number of years before they received any kind of pay-out from the Spanish government.

The work of the mixed commission was hampered by great difficulties. The French invasion of Spain in April 1823, and the subsequent act of the restored King Ferdinand VII to annul all decrees made by the outgoing constitutional regime, brought the commission's work to an abrupt halt. Though Ferdinand later permitted the commission to continue with its investigations, disagreements between the British and Spanish commissioners were commonplace. In October 1828, a second convention was entered into by the two governments in the hope of alleviating these difficulties.[38] This time, the British commissioners alone would have the power to adjudge and satisfy the legitimate claims of British subjects. The King of Spain promised to make good to His Britannic Majesty the sum of £900,000 in specie, as the amount of the whole of the English claims presented to and registered by the mixed commission established in 1823. Within twelve months, the 331 British claims had been brought under review and payments were made to those claimants whose cases were proved by the evidence submitted. To De Lisle & Co, the commissioners awarded the net amount of £4,745.10.4, having disallowed a sum of £2,958.7.8 due to a lack of satisfactory evidence and deducting four per cent from the amount awarded to cover the commission's operating costs.[39] Whereas the departure of Owen's squadron from England in late 1822 had brought an end to the British government's eight year search for satisfaction, De Lisle & Co and hundreds of other British claimants had been forced to wait almost another eight years before their grievances against the Spanish government had finally been settled.

The Wider Ramifications of a Local Remedy

In 1822-23, the British government responded to a local grievance – the capture of British vessels by Spanish privateers in the West Indies. But the response that this generated was far more than a local remedy. When formulating its policy with regard to Spanish privateering, the British government had to carefully consider the wider ramifications of its course of action. The desired outcomes of the policy were twofold – to protect British trade with Latin America, but to do so without jeopardising peace in Europe. The British government wanted to re-establish the right for British vessels to trade freely with Latin America but recognised that this had to be done without rupturing relations with the Spanish government.

These wider economic and political objectives were cornerstones of British foreign policy in this period and lay behind the British government's decision to remain neutral in the Wars of Independence from the very earliest stirrings of revolution in Latin America. Spanish goodwill was essential to British aims in Europe, firstly in defeating Napoleon, and after 1815, as a crucial component in the post-war collective security system.[40] The British government therefore abstained from recognising the rebel Latin American governments for a number of years. But despite courting Spanish goodwill, the British government stopped short of assisting the Spanish re-conquest of Latin America. Support for the Spanish counter-revolution would have halted Britain's burgeoning commercial intercourse with the newly independent Spanish American provinces.[41]

The capture and condemnation of the *Lord Collingwood* upset the balance that Britain had struck between these two competing interests and action had to be taken. The form and firmness of the response that this event triggered was determined by which of the British government's two wider objectives – maintaining European peace and trading with Latin America – was most pressing at a given moment. Since 1815, British policy towards the insults of Spanish predators had been characterised by forbearance. As Canning stated in November 1822, all notions of taking firmer measures in the past had been 'checked by the fear of shaking the peace of Europe to its foundations'.[42] But by the time of the capture of the *Lord Collingwood*, this threat was no longer perceived as being so immediate, while Britain's commercial interests in Latin America had grown considerably.[43] Protecting these economic interests therefore began to exert the stronger influence over British policy.

When Canning became Foreign Secretary and British trade with Latin America remained in peril, the time had arrived for the British government to take stronger action. In his memorandum to the Cabinet, Canning acknowledged that important discussions were due to take place at the Congress of Verona, but stated that 'no question relating to Continental Europe is more immediately and vitally important, than those which relate to America'.[44] 'Our commerce is exposed to daily depredations in the American seas', he warned, 'and the accustomed awe of our maritime preponderancy is daily diminishing in the eyes of other nations'.[45] Canning therefore made his proposal to deploy the Royal Navy to seize Spanish shipping in the West Indies and also to begin preparations for the British government's official recognition of the independence of certain Latin American states.

But before Canning's plans could be executed, mounting political concerns forced a reassessment of British countermeasures against Spanish privateering. When representatives of the so-called 'European Alliance' – Austria, Britain, France, Prussia, and Russia – met at the Congress of Verona in October-December 1822, Spanish affairs unexpectedly topped the agenda.

The Duke of Wellington quickly informed Canning that the other members of the great-power concert were seriously considering invading Spain in order to overthrow the constitutional regime and reinstall Ferdinand VII to power. Norihito Yamada has recently argued convincingly that Canning tried every possible means to prevent this war.[46] Canning feared another revolution in France, an invasion of Portugal through occupied Spain and the prospect of the other powers meddling in Spanish American affairs – all of which had the potential to drag Britain into war.[47] In this altered political context, Canning was forced to shelve his plans to recognise Latin American independence because such a move would have given off the impression that Britain approved the invasion of Spain and would have scuppered all possibility of Britain mediating between Spain and her potential enemies.[48]

Once again, the British government was forced to adopt countermeasures against Spanish privateering that would maintain the balance between its wider political and economic objectives. Canning's 'local remedy' promised the greatest chance of success. This plan would obtain redress for past grievances, as well as preventing future attacks on British commerce by lifting the blockade declared by the governor of Puerto Cabello. But crucially, by isolating this action from European affairs and using rhetoric that designated the policy as 'a local remedy to a local grievance' and nothing more, the British government could avoid rupturing relations with Spain and therefore keep the door open to preventing war in Europe by offering to mediate between Spain and the vulture-like European powers that were eagerly watching events from beyond the Spanish borders.

While the British government's countermeasures had been shaped by its wider foreign policy objectives, they also yielded results that furthered these wider political and economic interests. The deployment of Owen's squadron and the subsequent Spanish capitulation re-established Britain's right to trade with Latin America. Although the Cortes only went as far as to suspend the colonial laws for ten months, never again would Spanish armed vessels attempt to capture British merchantmen on the sole grounds that they were trading with the dissidents of Spanish America. By the mid-1820s, British consuls had been sent out to the major ports in Latin America and British trade was made official soon after when recognition was conferred upon several Latin American states.

Political outcomes of the 'local remedy' were also favourable to Britain. The creation of a mixed commission to investigate British claims removed the necessity of taking reprisals, relieving the threat that such a course of action posed to Anglo-Spanish relations. Despite the difficulties encountered by the mixed commission, such tensions were no longer felt between two governments; rather, they were problems exclusive to the British and Spanish commissioners. Just as the 'local remedy' had been before it, the commission was another device by which the two governments could isolate the issue of Britain's maritime losses from the much more pressing concerns of great-power politics. By early 1823, the burning issue was undoubtedly the looming threat of a French invasion of Spain. While the British government ultimately failed to prevent the invasion, its countermeasures against Spanish privateering were in no way to blame for the failure. As Yamada argues, Canning's inability to prevent war was mostly due to circumstances beyond his control.[49]

Britain's neutral position in the Latin American Wars of Independence has been compared to the act of walking a tightrope.[50] Given that the 'local remedy' managed to achieve its objectives without causing the British government to slip and fall from this tightrope, the strategy, from the point of view of the British government at least, should be considered as a highly effective means of countering the threat of Spanish privateering in the early 1820s. What is particularly striking about this success is the nature in which it was achieved. For eight years, the British government had applied diplomatic pressure on the Spanish government to little or no avail. But as soon as it was made known that Owen's squadron was powering its way towards Puerto Rico in late December 1822, the Spanish government instantly capitulated. If, as Canning claimed, the depredations of Spanish privateers in the West Indies had diminished the accustomed awe with which Britain's maritime superiority was viewed by other nations, in the blink of an eye, the Royal Navy had reversed that deficit without even having to strike a blow in anger. Perhaps this short-lived and time-forgotten naval action was one of the Royal Navy's most successful campaigns.

---

[1] Croker to Canning, 5 December 1822, The National Archives (TNA), FO 72/267.
[2] Canning to Chevalier de Colomb, 5 December 1822, TNA, FO 72/262.
[3] Croker to Canning, 5 December 1822, TNA, FO 72/267.
[4] Canning, Memorandum to the Cabinet, 15 November 1822, TNA, FO 72/266.
[5] *The Times*, 3 July 1822.
[6] Following paragraph based upon the protest of Thomas Domaille against the capture of the *Lord Collingwood*, 26 October 1821, TNA, FO 316/1, no. 7.
[7] Following paragraph based upon the Decree of Final Judgement, 22 December 1821, TNA, FO 316/1, no. 8.
[8] Barrow to Castlereagh, 3 January 1822, TNA, FO 72/263.
[9] Castlereagh to Hervey, 19 July 1822, TNA, FO 72/254.
[10] Ibid.
[11] Ibid.

12 Hervey to Castlereagh, 13 August 1822, TNA, FO 72/257.
13 Canning to À Court, 18 October 1822, TNA, FO 72/258.
14 Ibid.
15 Ibid.
16 Ibid.
17 À Court to Canning, 20 November 1822, TNA, FO 72/259.
18 Ibid.
19 Ibid.
20 Canning, Memorandum to the Cabinet, 15 November 1822, TNA, FO 72/266.
21 Ibid.
22 Ibid.
23 Ibid.
24 Ibid.
25 Ibid.
26 À Court to Canning, 13 December 1822, TNA, FO 72/259.
27 À Court to Canning, 22 December 1822, TNA, FO 72/259.
28 Ibid.
29 À Court to Canning, 24 December 1822, TNA, FO 72/259.
30 Ibid.
31 Barrow to Canning, 13 March 1823, TNA, FO 72/280.
32 À Court to Canning, 8 January 1823, TNA, FO 72/269.
33 Ibid.
34 Ibid.
35 TNA, FO 94/297.
36 TNA, FO 316/64.
37 TNA, FO 316/1.
38 TNA, FO 94/298.
39 TNA, FO 316/28.
40 D. A. G. Waddell, 'International Politics and Latin American Independence', in *The Cambridge History of Latin America*, edited by Leslie Bethell (Cambridge: Cambridge University Press, 1985), iii, p. 200.
41 Ibid., p. 200.
42 Canning, Memorandum to the Cabinet, 15 November 1822, TNA, FO 72/266.
43 Waddell, 'International Politics', in *Cambridge History of Latin America*, iii, p. 206.
44 Canning, Memorandum to the Cabinet, 15 November 1822, TNA, FO 72/266.
45 Ibid.
46 Norihito Yamada, 'George Canning and the Spanish Question, September 1822 to March 1823', *The Historical Journal*, 52:2 (2009), pp. 343-62.
47 Ibid., p. 352.
48 Ibid., pp. 353-54.
49 Ibid., p. 360.
50 Waddell, 'International Politics', in *Cambridge History of Latin America*, iii, p. 200.

'Intrepidity and Perseverance': Searching for HMS *Wager* in the Gulf of Pain

Chris Holt

In early 2006, the British adventurer John Blashford-Snell asked me whether I would lead an expedition to find a lost warship on a remote and uninhabited island in Patagonian Chile. The ship in question was HMS *Wager* – Anson's supply vessel made famous by a mutiny and the subsequent adventures of her crew in returning to England. It was an irresistible challenge, and, under the umbrella of the Scientific Exploration Society, a team of divers travelled to Wager Island in November 2006 to search for the ship's remains.[1] As far as I am aware, this was the first organised group to attempt to locate *Wager* since *Beagle* had visited the island with the intention of locating her wreck.

As a retired Army Officer, I stake no claim to being a naval historian, but a brief background to HMS *Wager* will place the expedition in context. Among the general public, and outside naval circles, the story of HMS *Wager* is not widely known. Patrick O'Brian's *The Unknown Shore* is probably the best-known dramatisation of the tale. But for the fourteen of us who spent a month away from home, it was this epic tale, with momentous feats of human endeavour that ensured we had ample motivation to maintain a sense of purpose.

Previously an East Indiaman, *Wager* was purchased in 1739 for conversion into a sixth-rate ship. After England had declared war on Spain on 19 October 1739, *Wager* was one of the seven ships that formed Commodore Anson's Squadron. While preparations for Anson's voyage were woefully inadequate, and the operation itself did not go to plan, the expedition would have a massive effect on the Royal Navy. Anson returned a hero to Spithead in HMS *Centurian* in 1744, and the official version of the expedition, articulated in *A Voyage around the World in the Years 1740-44*, would become a bestseller.[2] Its closing lines carry this conclusion:

> *Thus was this expedition finished, when it had lasted three years and nine months, after having, by its event, strongly evinced this important truth: That though prudence, intrepidity and perseverance united are not exempted from the blows of adverse fortune, yet in a long series*

of transactions they usually rise superior to its power, and in the end rarely fail of proving successful.

Wager was the stores vessel for the rest of the Squadron. She was carrying, among other goods, field guns, ammunition, part of a siege engine, a spare anchor for *Centurion* and 20 tonnes of merchandise to trade and win favour with the inhabitants of South America. She had a crew of 105, but there were also 142 marines and invalids onboard.

One member of the crew was the young John Byron, who as a midshipman was about to embark on his first naval escapade. Grandfather of the poet Byron, he later rose to the rank of Admiral and came to be known as 'foul weather Jack' on account of his connection with a number of unsuccessful outings. His narrative of the *Wager's* wrecking and subsequent mutiny is an inspiring account of a young British officer experiencing a true baptism of fire. Lord Byron is even said to have based the shipwreck scenes in *Don Juan* on 'my grandad's narrative'.[3]

By the time the squadron had reached Brazil, about a tenth of the ship's company were dead, including the ship's Captain, Dandy Kidd, who had died allegedly proclaiming with his last breath that the expedition would end in 'poverty, vermin, famine, death and destruction'. His death led to the appointment of David Cheap as Captain, whose leadership would ultimately be challenged.

Having rounded Cape Horn, and believing that they were west of land, Anson turned north, and it is from this point that

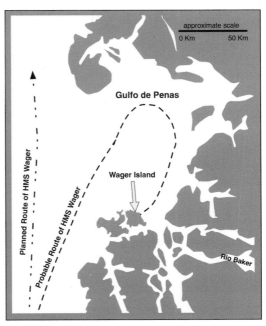

Chart of the Gulfo de Penas (Gulf of Pain) showing Wager Island, and the planned and probable routes of HMS Wager. Courtesy the author.

the Squadron began to disperse. *Wager* lost her mizzen mast, and on 25 April 1741, crippled by the missing mast and with only twenty crew fit enough to sail her, *Wager* lost sight of the Squadron for ever.

While they were heading north in an attempt to rejoin the Squadron, the ship's carpenter John Cummins believed he saw land to the west, and it soon became apparent that *Wager* had been pushed into a large gulf. While it is probable that the name relates to a mountain feature in the area, the direct translation of Gulfo de Penas is the *Gulf of Pain*, which would be a fitting description.

At some point during the turning of the ship in a vicious storm, Captain Cheap was injured and played no further part in the desperate attempt to steer *Wager* out of the gulf. In the early morning of 14 May 1741, HMS *Wager* first struck bottom. In the impact, the spare anchor broke loose and fell through the bottom of the ship. In the next hour or so, a handful of crew tried desperately to get the ship closer to land, but *Wager* was indeed lost. John Byron recalled:

> *Now we run in between an opening of the breakers, steering by the sheets and braces, when providently we struck fast between two great rocks; that to windward sheltering us in some measure from the violence of the sea.*

To attempt to summarise the drama of the immediate rescue of the crew, the mutiny and subsequent adventures is almost impossible. The key headlines are that eighty-one surviving men, led by the ship's gunner John Bulkeley, believed that their responsibility was ultimately to their souls and no longer to the Navy. They embarked on a 2,000-mile journey from which only thirty men survived. Bulkeley eventually returned to England to face a court marshall on New Year's Day, 1743. Cheap and Byron were among the seventeen officers and men who stayed on Wager Island with the intention of rejoining the Squadron. After encounters with Indians, unbearable conditions and a period of time at the pleasure of the Spanish, four men returned to England in the spring of 1746. From wreck to home, their journey had taken just under five years.

The Expedition: 'You Have to Start Somewhere'

The aim of the expedition in the autumn of 2006 was to locate the wreck site of HMS *Wager*, and to conduct a rudimentary survey of her remains in order to inform some subsequent professional archaeological research. In preparation for the expedition, I attended some courses run in Portsmouth by the Nautical Archaeological Society.[4] The team there took an interest in the project and introduced me to a number of stakeholders, including English Heritage. This was important to ensure that our aims were understood, and to reassure people that we were not embarking on a 'treasure-hunting' adventure.

From initial discussions with maritime archaeologists, including those at the Mary Rose Trust, it became clear that, as well as being of historical interest, *Wager* could potentially also be of archaeological relevance, because of her conversion to carry twenty-eight guns. A find of her hull section could be informative as to how this process might have been achieved.

There are five personal accounts from the *Wager* that are at times conflicting about specific geographical locations.[5] However, these publications were crucial for our team, as they represented the only factual pointers as to where *Wager* might have come to rest. There is almost no recent information relating to HMS *Wager*, and we had only a small body of evidence to guide us to *Wager's* location. The key elements of planning information were:

- an assumption that Wager Island had been named correctly as the island where Wager had come to rest;

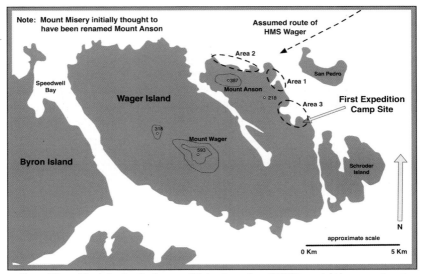

Chart of Wager Island showing the three possible locations where HMS Wager might have come to rest. Courtesy the author.

- multiple accounts of the ship ending up 'within a musket shot' or '100 yards' from shore;

- multiple accounts of the ship coming to rest between two giant islands or rocks;

- multiple descriptions of 'Mount Misery' being a high piece of ground at the northern end of the bay referred to as Cheap's Bay.

So in October 2006, having trawled through historical accounts, scanned satellite imagery and spoken to round-the-world yachtsmen and eminent historians, we concluded that there were three probable locations where the *Wager* might have come to rest.

With such flimsy information, it was necessary to remain flexible. The only certainty was that our plan would have to adapt to changing circumstances. In outline the plan was as follows:

- The team would consist of twelve divers from the Scientific Exploration Society and two divers from the Armada de Chile. The team would include a maritime archaeologist, a doctor and our camera lady, Lynwen Griffiths.[6]

- Once in Chile, we would travel to the remote village of Tortel, and then make a 120-kilometre boat journey to Isla Wager.

- We would camp on the beaches of the island and mount searches using small inflatable crafts.

- We would dive areas that were consistent with the accounts of the time, and, if something was located, conduct a simple survey to act as a starting point for a subsequent professional archaeological expedition.

- In the case of a medical emergency, we would rely first on assistance from the Armada de Chile and then on civilian emergency rescue organisations. We could expect to be at least twenty-four hours away from medical evacuation and, if the weather was bad (which we were expecting), this could be as long as five days.

Uncertain Beginnings

On the morning of 7 November, we arrived in the tiny village of Tortel to begin the journey up Rio Baker to the archipelago where Wager Island is located. Tortel is unlike anything I had ever seen before. Perched on the steep sides of a fjord, it has no roads and no cars. Wooden walkways link the houses and buildings, and, apart from walking, the main form of transport is a flotilla of small boats.

In addition to the practical interest in the *Wager* story, on the basis that it might bring tourists, the residents had a compelling fascination in what we were doing. Such a remote and insular community can trace its heritage in the area for generations. As in many isolated South American communities, it is possible to see the bloodlines of Spanish and indigenous Indian played out in the faces of the locals. The town mayor was in no doubt that descendants of people involved in some way in the *Wager* story would be living either in Tortel or nearby. *Wager* was an important part of their cultural heritage, and they were just as keen as we were finally to locate her resting place.

On 8 November, after some initial concerns about our transport out to the Island, our deliverance arrived in the form of the Armada de Chile patrol vessel *Puerto Natales*. The Armada de Chile not only provided us with transport and two exceptional divers; they also gave us safety cover, which was to prove deeply reassuring.

At 8 am on the morning of 9 November, as we were about to leave Tortel, I had a chance meeting with a local fisherman and diver by the name of Carlos Wager. His surname and his knowledge of the diving conditions in the area grabbed my attention. Standing by an old oil drum with a chart laid on top, he jabbed at the area of Wager Island with a grubby finger, and my interpreter started to translate:

> *There are a number of wrecks along this northern coast of Wager Island. I found a wreck here, British I am sure and a Man of War, very well preserved. She lies in about 12 metres of water only a hundred metres or so away from the shore. She is lying in between two giant white rocks.*

Could it be that this man had already found *Wager* and that all we had to do was survey the remains? As he looked in more detail at the chart, he picked out Penguin Island, lying about 10 miles south of Wager Island and identified a precise location for me. Thirty minutes before boarding our ship, there was now the possibility of a British wreck near Penguin Island in a location sounding very much like that described by Bulkely and Byron. Was it possible that Wager Island had been wrongly named?

Wager Island

From a comment in one of the accounts, we had accepted the assumption that Mount Misery had been renamed Mount Anson. No one had disagreed with this assumption during our research, so over time it had developed credibility, and we aimed to strike camp in its shadow on the eastern end of Wager Island. The remote nature of the island meant that imagery of the area is difficult, so it was therefore not surprising to find that, once we could see them, none of the bays immediately presented itself as a match for Cheap's Bay. With no ideal options and late in the day, we cross-decked our equipment using our small inflatables and established a camp on the east of the island in an area we called Driftwood Cove.

The first afternoon was a blur of activity. The highly competent team quickly established a relatively comfortable camp. We survived in fairly basic conditions for our time on the Island. Operating from a large tent and a lean-to shelter, we established the working and administrative areas required for fourteen people to live and operate in extremely challenging weather conditions. This included water purification, medical treatment, potential evacuation areas, cooking and washing facilities and, of course, relatively clean spaces to service and recharge diving equipment. In order to maintain daily structure, we kept to a routine of morning briefings, regular mealtimes, evening de-briefs and plenty of time for individuals to deal with their personal administrative needs. It is safe to say that for every minute spent working towards the expedition goal, there was an equal amount of time spent ensuring that conditions were safe, sustainable and enjoyable.

The team itself was a wonderfully mixed, multinational (two Americans, an Australian and two Chileans) and complementary group. The oldest team member was 64, the youngest 22, and diving experience ranged from competent novice to seasoned old-timers. There were five serving or retired members of the British Army in the group, and a serving American Army Officer, which probably led to a particular 'flavour' to the general conduct of business. This eclectic mix of primarily men, balanced with a strong female presence, meant that, despite some challenging moments, almost everything was conducted in a calm, measured and matter-of-fact way. The group dynamic, and therefore life on the island, was fantastic.

Over the next week we mounted extensive searches both in the water and over land to search for the remains of *Wager*. Diving conditions were pretty average, normally between 8 and 10 metres of depth and with a visibility of around 2 or 3 metres. The bottom was particularly silty in the less agitated areas. Over land the terrain was severe. The following excerpt from my journal describes a fairly average excursion.

> *Near the shore the vegetation is dense and unforgiving; it saps the energy and it snags on buckles and bootlaces; it takes frustratingly long to get through-the first 50 metres can take about 20 minutes. Beyond this rocks protrude through tight moss and tuft grass, and lichens grow on them in abundance.*

After a week of early starts, energy-sapping daily searches and no progress, we needed to take stock of our situation and our options. We had all reached similar conclusions about the island: first, that the area we were occupying did not lend itself naturally to the descriptions made by Bulkely and Byron, and, second, that the northern shore of the island was far more treacherous and leant itself to the wrecking of ships. These conclusions, combined with some background information we had relating to seismic activity in the area, led me to a decision point: we needed to look elsewhere.

The members of the team who had most keenly studied the accounts of *Wager's* wrecking before our departure looked again for the most probable location of Cheap's Bay, but this time only along the island's northern shore. We re-read the copies of accounts we had with us (rather than the books about the accounts) and came up with only three facts we felt were consistent and relevant:

- The crew believed that the ship was only feet from making clear water and missing the island before she struck.

- When Bulkeley first launched the converted *Speedwell*, he immediately turned away from the wind and across the 'inlet' to Speedwell Bay. (Frustratingly, we had all somehow neglected to see the relevance of this until this point.)

- From Mount Misery looking towards land (i.e. east), it was not possible to see whether they were on an island, because there were hills in the way.

All these points suggested that we needed to be on the north-western shore, immediately adjacent to Speedwell Bay. The diagram overleaf shows how these three 'facts' relate to each other. In retrospect, this deductive logic may appear simple, but it should be noted that the narratives can be read to support a number of theories about location.

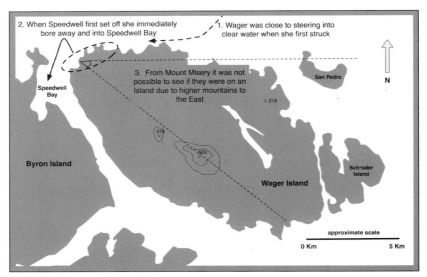

Chart of Wager Island illustrating the deductive reasoning behind finding the remains of HMS Wager.
Courtesy the author.

We also revisited the information that one of the team had bought with him relating to the earthquakes in the area. Between 1741 and 2006 there were ninety-four earthquakes recorded in the Gulfo de Penas. On 22 May 1960 the largest ever recorded earthquake, a 9.5 on the Richter Scale, hit the Chilean coast within miles of Wager Island. No accurate data exists as to how this earthquake may have affected the island.

Clearly, plate tectonics is a highly complex science, and we were ill-equipped to come up with anything genuinely meaningful, but we had some data on tectonic plate movement and converted this using rudimentary maths into vertical measurements; we felt that the quake could have created a rise in the seabed of up to 7 metres. Observations of the vegetation near the foreshore and comparisons of the historical charts with modern satellite imagery tended to support this.

The very real possibility dawned on us that not only could we be in the wrong spot, but that we were probably not on a diving expedition any more. The bay that presented itself most readily on the old chart in the north-western corner of the island no longer existed; all that was visible on the satellite photos was a large sandy beach and acres of forest. The diagram opposite shows how the charts of the time compare with current satellite imagery of the island.

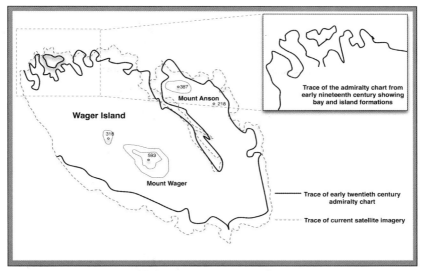

Chart of Wager Island showing how the coastline of the past compares with current satellite imagery. Courtesy the author.

If at First you Don't Succeed

So with a refreshed enthusiasm we loaded our equipment and the whole team onto a tiny fishing boat we had managed to charter, and those with a sense of mortality kept their dry suits on for the journey from the east to the north-west of Wager Island. Partway through the journey the boat's engineer disappeared into a smoke-filled space below my feet. The engineer was working in a tiny space with a rapidly rising water level. Two large truck batteries were floating in sea-water and, as they arced alarmingly against the side of the large metal fuel tank, the engineer relit his permanent cigarette … Miraculously we made it safely to the large sandy bay to the north-west of Wager Island and quickly set about searching the area.

One of the key tasks was to get a small team to the top of the 'mountain' that was 400 metres or so inland, as it was fast becoming the top candidate as a possible Mount Misery. After a couple of days of preliminary searches, a large team headed inland, half to carry equipment to the base of the mountain and half to climb its slopes. We travelled using our inflatables in what was now a vastly expanded river because of the violent rainfall we had experienced. Once the climbing team had set off, we tied up the boats, swam back to camp, and waited a call on the radio to replay the whole performance in reverse. When we met the climbing team back at the boats, they were excited about what they had seen and the potential correlation with the narrative accounts of Mount Misery.

The whole team was excited, and the journey back to camp seemed to take half the time and effort. Reaching camp, and before we discussed their findings in detail, there was one task left. Having nearly lost one of our small inflatable craft to the ferocious wind, we removed them from the water at the end of every day and tied them down firmly. As I was heaving on the bow of one of the boats, I heard a flurry of ripe language from the stern.

Chris Hunter, one of the serving members of the Armed Forces, had badly stubbed his toe on something in the riverbed. On his hands and knees, he worked away the sand around the offending item in order to remove it and prevent a second 'stubbing'.

It was an unusual moment, one of those where everyone goes quiet at the same time. As Chris fanned the sand, the outline of a significant worked timber became visible. More hands joined his, and within three or four minutes we had uncovered 1.5 metres of hull planking. We were 10 metres away from my tent, in the very spot where we had been washing our pots, pans, smalls and bodies for almost a week, and it was entirely possible that we had just stumbled over part of the wreck of HMS *Wager*. We toasted our success with a bottle of wine between fourteen and were all on top of the world.

The following morning, we laid a line of boulders and rocks upstream to prevent the area being backfilled with sediment flowing downstream. The wreckage was in a remarkably well-preserved condition under about 50 centimetres of water and 10 centimetres of sand. We had found four frames of a hull section with at least eight pieces of hull planking attached. Constructed completely of timber, the joints were made with treenails, or wooden fixing pins that could be clearly seen. More importantly, the size and shape of the timbers were consistent with *Wager's* construction

There were a number of interesting areas: three rectangular cut blocks that could either be repairs of a splitting timber or perhaps evidence of her conversion from an East Indiaman to a sixth-rate warship, some ceramics applied to one of the timber ends, perhaps as a waterproofing putty used when she was repaired in Brazil, and finally evidence of rough cutting and burning at the edges of some of the timber planks. We found only one artefact at the site, a musket ball discovered wedged between two of the frames.

Over the next two days, we made a complete survey of the timbers and took a series of photos using an underwater camera to create a 'photo mosaic' of the entire site. So, with three days remaining on the island, we had effectively completed what we had set out to do: find evidence of *Wager's* final resting place and make a survey that could be used for a follow-up expedition by an archaeological team.

Archaeologists and Indians

To our surprise and delight, we were joined at the site by a Chilean team of archaeologists, who were in the area recording indigenous Indian sites and searching for *Wager* remains.[7] The team, led by Chilean archaeologist Diego Carabias, explained the fate of the *Wager* after the crew had left the site. The Spanish in Chiloe had set out on a salvage mission in 1745 using local Indians as their workforce. The team had salvaged *Wager*, using a fairly robust cutting and burning approach. As well as high-value items, including the ship's forge, the Spanish recovered a number of cannon to Chiloe, where they can still be seen today.

It appears that the *Wager* salvage camp became a regular meeting place for the local Indian tribes and that the Jesuit priests identified it as a suitable location to convert Indians and encourage them to move to Chiloe. It is entirely possible that, as a direct result of the wrecking of HMS *Wager*, the traditional hunter-gatherer way of life of many local Indians was traded in for a Catholic and urban lifestyle.

Work has continued on the site for the last three years and significant progress has been made. Key findings of the research were presented by Diego Carabias at the Third International Congress on Underwater Archaeology in London in July 2008:

- An opinion has been formed after analysis that the section of wooden hull discovered in November 2006 is probably part of HMS *Wager*.

- A cluster of artefacts was found just south of the original find containing several lead musket balls, ceramic tiles and glassware associated with animal bones and charcoal.

- Along the river feature, multiple finds were made, including iron bolts, different parts of barrels and a sheave.

- There were significant articles relating to the Mapuche-Huilliche population of Central and Southern Chile found at the site. These include some cultural artefacts and the remains of a sewn wooden plank canoe found with iron nails used in construction; this is a unique find.

While the current view is that the remains found in November 2006 and several others found in March 2008 are part of *Wager*, the story remains complex and tightly interwoven with the fortunes of the local Indians. The site is continuing to release more secrets, and a new field research season is planned to start in March 2010.

Finding shipwrecks is a notoriously hit-and-miss affair, but in November 2006 we set out with the aim of finding HMS *Wager* and enabling a follow-up archaeological survey. Both of these aims were achieved. That HMS *Wager* continues to pose questions (there is now the possibility that a significant element of the vessel may actually be located on Byron Island) only serves to increase my affection for this complex and compelling story. The remote nature of Wager Island means that it will no doubt keep many of its secrets. The perverse opposite is that we have detailed accounts of remarkable acts of intrepidity and perseverance by members of the crew, but yet the story of HMS *Wager* has fallen out of the public psyche. I believe the next aim should be to rekindle interest in this wonderful story.

[1] The Scientific Exploration Society is a UK-based charity founded in 1969 by Colonel John Blashford-Snell OBE and his colleagues. As a non-profit-making organization, it initiates a worldwide programme of scientific expeditions, focusing on scientific, conservation, education and community-aid projects. For more information visit: www.ses-explore.org. In 2008, the 1805 Club presented a one-day conference 'Anson's Voyage Round the World of 1740-44 and its Aftermath', which touched upon the wreck of the *Wager* and consequent events. Among the illustrious speakers were Professor Richard Harding, Professor Glyn Williams, Rear Admiral Kit Layman, Surgeon Vice-Admiral Sir Godfrey Milton-Thompson, and Surgeon Vice Admiral Sir James Watt.

[2] *A Voyage around the World in the Years 1740-44. Compiled by Richard Walter, Chaplain to his Majesty's Ship the 'Centurion'* (London: Printed for the author by John and Paul Knapton, 1748).

[3] *The Cambridge History of English and American Literature in 18 Volumes* (1907–21), vix, 'The Victorian Age', part two.

[4] The Nautical Archaeological Society is a non-government organisation and registered UK charity that was formed to further interest in our underwater cultural heritage. See: www.nasportsmouth.org.uk

[5] There are five accounts I am aware of in publication that describe either the wrecking of HMS *Wager* or the subsequent events, they are:

1. *A Voyage to the South Seas, in the Years 1740-41: Containing, a Faithful Narrative of the Loss of his Majesty's Ship the Wager on a Desolate Island in the Latitude 47 South, longitude 81 : 40 West*, by John Bulkeley and John Cummins (published 1743).

2. *The Sequel to Bulkeley and Cummin's Voyage to the South-Seas, or, The Adventures of Capt. Cheap Late of His Majesty's Ship the Wager*, by Alexander Campbell (published 1747).

3. *An Affecting Narrative of the Unfortunate Voyage and Catastrophe of His Majesty's Ship Wager*, attributed to John Young (published 1751).

4. *A Narrative of the Dangers and Distresses which Befel Isaac Morris, and Seven More of the Crew, Belonging to the Wager Store-Ship which Attended Commodore Anson, in his voyage to the South Sea; containing an account of their Adventures, after they were Left on an Uninhabited Part of Patagonia, in South America; where they Remained 'till they were Seized by a Party of Indians, and Carried above a Thousand Miles into the Inland Country after which they were Carried to Buenos-Ayres*, by Isaac Morris (published 1752).

5. *The Narrative of the Honorable John Byron containing an Account of the Great Distresses Suffered by Himself and his Companions on the Coast of Patagonia, from the Year 1740, till their Arrival in England, 1746. With a description of St Jago De Chile, and the Manners and Customs of the Inhabitants. Also a Relation of the Loss of the Wager Man of War, one of Admiral Anson's Squadron*, by John Byron (published 1768).

There is also an unpublished sixth account in the form of a letter from Captain David Cheap in relation to the wrecking of the *Wager*. The letter is in the possession of Admiral Kit Layman, who has written a book (as yet unpublished) that draws together all six accounts.

6   Lynwen Griffiths produced a DVD of the expedition and is contactable through her website at www.bamboochicken.tv

7   The team, part funded by CONAF, was from Arka Chile Archaeological consultancy, www.arkachile.cl

The Navy on Silver:
Early Photographic Images of the Royal Navy

William J. Schultz

It is interesting to contemplate what famous figures of the past would have looked like before the eye of the camera. Before photography, what we have at best are the works of a talented intermediary, an artist, whose work is based on his ability to reproduce visual reality as he saw or interpreted it. Within a mere forty years after the death of Admiral Nelson, a number of men who served with him in the Battle of Trafalgar would have their image recorded with a daguerreotype portrait. This technical milestone was discovered in 1839 by the French inventor Louis Daguerre, and represents the first time in the history of mankind that a fixed and detailed image could be taken that was an exact duplication of nature. The daguerreotype was able to record historical events as they actually happened and therefore provides a direct window onto life in the Victorian world.

For a naval historian of this time period, we are rewarded with a good number of daguerreotype portraits of naval officers and sailors serving in the Royal Navy. It was a common practice for many mariners to have their image taken for family or loved ones before departing for long months or even years at sea. Many times the hazards of travel and the sea would make this image a final remembrance for family and friends. It is little wonder that many of the earliest daguerreotypists had a studio near a large port or naval base. A good example being the pioneer British photographer Richard Beard who captured the portraits of the officers of the ill-fated Franklin Expedition of 1845 shortly before their departure from London. These images were later engraved in newspapers on both sides of the Atlantic – the naval photographic portrait had begun its remarkable journey. This article will focus on identifying and interpreting some of the earliest images taken of members of the Royal Navy to give a better insight into the life of the Victorian mariner.

The Daguerreotype

Photography went through a number of different processes in its first fifty years, each method being popular for a comparatively short time before

Dageurrotype Apparatus c. 1850. Courtesy the author.

being replaced by a process that was cheaper or technically easier to produce. Though invented in 1839, the daguerreotype was not commercially viable until the start of the 1840s and lost its popularity by the end of the 1850s. To make a daguerreotype in these early years was a long and complicated process. A copper plate was electroplated with silver and then buffed to a mirror-like finish. The plate was then exposed to iodine fumes forming the photosensitive silver iodide on the plate's surface. It was then placed into a light-tight plate holder in the darkroom until it was ready to be loaded into the back of the camera. The cover was then pulled from the plate holder and the lens cap removed, exposing the plate to the light reflected off the subject.

During this process, two major obstacles had to be overcome. First was the need for optimal lighting at a time before electricity. This problem was partly solved by placing daguerreotype studios on the top floor of buildings under a skylight. Unfortunately, this was of no help on cloudy days or during winter months when there wasn't enough sunlight. The second problem was the long exposure time that could last for up to minutes and left the image a total blur if the subject moved. To prevent this, a photographer's stand was placed behind the patron with a head clamp to keep the subject still.

The daguerreotype is a reversed or negative image because it was the actual plated in back of the camera when the image was made. After the plate had been exposed, the photographer would fix the image in sodium thiosulfate and the present it to the sitter for their approval. Its incredible to realize that the very person depicted in the image had held this very image as long as 150 years ago. The daguerreotypes were then placed in small cases with glass covers to protect the plate from abrasions and the elements. The ambrotype makes its appearance in 1851 as a cheaper alternative to the daguerreotype and lasted into the 1860s. Here the silver plate was replaced by a glass plate which was coated with a tough, opaque, membranous material called collodion and was light sensitized. This too was replaced around 1856 by the melainotype or ferrotype. Commonly known as the tintype, a thin lightweight sheet iron plate replaced the ambrotype's fragile glass.

The Navy during Victoria's Reign

The British Empire of the mid-1800s literally circled the globe. The fact that England, a sea-bound island, relatively small in land mass and without an excessive population, could maintain its presence over such vast area was, in good measure, due to its naval superiority. The period of the daguerreotype, 1840 to 1855, fits squarely in the first half of Queen Victoria's reign of 1837 to 1901, and found the British Empire at its prime. It is during this time that Great Britain was engaged in many endeavors that took it far from its own shores. The industrial revolution was transforming its major cities, and the manufacture of goods and the search for raw materials was stepping in time with the opening of new and foreign markets. Britain had been at peace with its archrival France since the Battle of Waterloo, and its Navy, now unchallenged, ruled the seas.

It is during this period – often called by historians the *Pax Britannia* – that the country again expanded its horizons and renewed its attention toward polar exploration and the discovery of a navigable sea route through the 'Northwest Passage'. It was also a time of scientific observation and global discoveries with a renewed interest to 'unearth' past civilizations and to search the ends of the earth for 'lost' or unknown peoples. This was the heyday of scientific expeditions and natural history. Darwin's discoveries while on board HMS *Beagle* were to challenge the established view of the natural world and to spur on a debate that continues to this day. Throughout this time members of Her Majesty's land and sea forces not only played crucial roles in expanding and maintaining the colonial empire but also in key roles of exploration and discovery. It is our good fortune that the daguerreotype process was available at this time to visually document individuals so important to the Victorian world.

Studying British Naval Daguerreotypes: Dating the Image

The first step in studying a naval daguerreotype portrait is to determine as closely as possible the date and, if possible, where the image was taken. On rare occasion this information may be written within the daguerreotype case, or documented in family records. Lacking that, the style of the case, brass mat, platemarks, and photographer's name become key in dating the image (see my article 'Silver Shadows Before the Storm', *Daguerreian Society Annual*, 2002-03). British images were often placed in a 'flip-top' style of case (hinged along the top edge), and photographers' names were more commonly embossed on the exterior of the case than in American examples. Knowing the photographer's name greatly aids in determining when the image was taken. *A Faithful Likeness: The First Photographic Studios in the British Isles 1841 to 1855* by Bernard and Pauline Heathcote is an essential reference, for it gives the time period at which a photographer was in a particular location in Great Britain. Directories containing daguerreotypists in foreign-port cities with British naval stations are also invaluable in determining the date of an image.

If the daguerreotype is unsealed, a platemark or platemaker's cartouche can at times be found at one corner of the plate. As in America, a great number of daguerreotype plates were imported into Great Britain from France, though examples of British naval images on American-manufactured plates are known. This may reflect that not only may have American-manufactured plates been imported to the British Isles, but more likely, British naval officers and seamen could have had their image taken at numerous ports around the globe, including the British Possessions in North America (Canada) and South America, where American-manufactured plates were imported.

Studying British Naval Daguerreotypes: Identifying the Uniforms

In the case of naval uniforms it should be determined if they represent those of a steam packet mail service, the merchant navy, or those of a foreign navy.

British naval uniforms from this period could also represent members of the Royal Navy, Royal Navy Reserve (beginning in 1859), or Royal Coast Guard, which, apart from the buttons or belt plate, might be indistinguishable during this time. The East India Company also had its own navy with a distinctive uniform and the Trinity House officers wore a naval uniform as port pilots along with their other duties.

As with all military daguerreotypes, British naval daguerreotypes are best studied by visually correcting the image, flipping it horizontally using a computer program like Photoshop®. Correcting the image greatly facilitates the study of the many details in the wearer's uniform – military decorations, weapons, and accoutrements – which may also provide important clues to the sitter's identity. The critical reference in the interpretation of Royal Navy daguerreotypes through the period 1840 to 1860 are the uniform regulations which were published as part of the *Navy Lists* by the Admiralty for the years 1833, 1843, 1846, 1856 and 1860. The 1833 regulations establish the uniform worn at the very beginning of the daguerreian era. Revisions of the uniform regulations by *Admiralty Memoranda* can even further narrow the date of an image. Changes made in the ranking devices on a sitter's epaulettes, shoulder placement of the epaulettes, button devices, button placement, cap insignia, and the presence of specific naval decorations are just some of the details vital to dating an image and determining the rank of the individual portrayed – and will be discussed in detail. The uniform regulations of 1860 serve as an end point, since by then the ambrotype, tintype, and *carte-de-visite* had fairly well supplanted the daguerreotype image.

As a historic record, the daguerreotype provides an exacting visual reference of the naval uniforms actually worn. To research uniforms before 1839, scholars and researchers have to rely on artist's renderings such as portraits, miniatures on ivory, sketches, etchings and prints. A series of lithographic prints which often were privately published and accompanied the uniform regulations, were important reference material for an officer's tailors – to know the uniform specifications and patterns to be sewn. These uniform-detail prints are now an invaluable tool for studying the naval dress of this period.

Important resources for identifying uniforms are the collections of the National Maritime Museum in Greenwich, England, which houses an extensive array of original uniforms, prints, and artifacts from the period. Also the Portsmouth Royal Naval Museum which has more than seven thousand uniforms and insignia in its collection, covering from 1748 to modern times, as well as extensive collections of prints, images, and artifacts from the period. The collections of the National Portrait Gallery in London feature many prominent officers dressed in uniform. The Anne S. K. Brown Military Collection at Brown University is an excellent resource and contains a fine collection of Rudolf Ackermann lithographs from the mid-1800s, along with prints by other artists, such as C. H. Martin, J. Harris, and others who depicted the Royal Navy uniform.

British Royal Navy Uniform

The origin of the blue British Royal Navy officer's uniform dates to the year 1745, when a group of naval officers met at 'Wills Coffee House' in London to petition the Admiralty for a standardized naval uniform for Captains and Lieutenants. Until that time, the colour and cut of the uniform of a ship's commanding officer was pretty much up to his discretion. Because of their request, the Admiralty had various officers present themselves in their self-appointed naval dress. The anecdotal story goes that there was a preference toward blue and red, as these were the national colors, but that King George II determined they be blue with white facings after the seeing Duchess of Bedford riding in the park wearing a riding habit with those colors. For the next several years, however, there would be a wide differences on how the officers and their tailors would interpret the instructions. Dress and undress uniforms were introduced at this time with the undress uniform being a plain blue frock without any military distinction. In the dress uniform, an officer's rank would be determined by variations in the cut and embroidery of the lapels, cuffs and collars, and the placement of buttonholes on the lapel. It was not until 1795 that epaulettes were used to determine rank on officers' uniforms. By the Victorian period however, every aspect of the Royal Naval uniform was well regulated.

Naval Officers Uniform: On board the confines of a ship after long months at sea it was well known to the officers and crew who was who, and what rank they held. The naval uniform however reinforced the officer's authority and the chain of command, and quickly established who held an executive or military position, and who held a civil or staff position. It also quickly separated the warrant officers from the ratings under them. At a glance one could see if the coat was doubled breasted, as for executive officers; or single breasted, for those with the civil duties of surgeon, purser or secretary, which were further designated by the placement of buttons in groups of three, two, or in a single row, respectively. One could also look at the waist belt: if it were embroidered in an ornate pattern of oak leaves and acorns, they were dealing with a Flag Officer with a rank of Admiral or Commodore. If there were three gold lines circling the belt they were Captains or Commanders; two gold lines, they were Lieutenants, Masters or Mates. The belt plate with an anchor surmounted by Victoria's crown designated the wearer was a member of the British Royal Navy. In an instant any member of the crew or a member from any other ship immediately knew the relative status of anyone he met. While these aspects of the Royal Navy uniform would hold true throughout the period from 1840 to 1860, other details of the uniform and insignia of rank would go through various changes during this time, as seen in these examples.

Coat: The blue undress frock coat was most commonly worn while on ship or during off duty on land; whereas the full dress uniform was worn on special occasions such as Ceremonies of State and Court Martial. In the uniform regulations of 1843 the dress uniform's collars were changed from scarlet to white. The 1843 regulations also allowed greatcoats for officers with a stand and fall collar using the same button arrangement as the undress uniform, and to be worn with or without epaulettes. The 1846 uniform regulations abolished the blue undress frock coat, and the *Admiralty Memoranda* of 23 November 1847, allowed the undress 'surtout frock coat' for certain officers with the following distinctive marks: Admiral, with four rows five-eights-inch lace on the cuffs, with or without epaulettes; Captain, with three row of half-inch lace on the cuff without epaulettes; Commodore with two rows of lace on the cuff without epaulettes; Lieutenants and Masters with one row of lace on the cuff without epaulettes.

Trousers: The trousers of all Naval officers in full dress uniform were to be white between 23 April and 14 October, and blue between 15 October and 22 April. The 1846 uniform regulations also stipulated that white duck trousers be worn with the undress uniform in tropical climates and on the Home squadron during the summer months.

Epaulettes: The epaulettes were worn on both dress and certain undress uniform coats. The epaulette is usually braided with coils of gold bullion, though for certain ranks and in undress may be unbraided. The epaulette consists of a crescent, strap, and button for attachment on which are placed the various ranking devices: a Crown, Star, and/or Anchor. In 1846 the Crossed Baton and Sword was introduced as a device denoting the ranks of Admiral. The shoulder placement of epaulettes also changed through this period. Lieutenants wore a single epaulette on only the right shoulder until the 1843 uniform regulations. The use of a single epaulette was also used to distinguish Mates and Second Masters until 1856, and Surgeons until 1846. Assistant Surgeons did not wear any epaulettes until 1846, and then a second epaulette was added in 1856.

Buttons: After 1812 all Royal Navy and Marine buttons bore the crown cipher of the reigning monarch above the anchor, distinguishing them from buttons worn by the merchant navy. Buttons of all Admirals or Flag grade officers displayed the Queen's crown cipher above an anchor between two branches of laurel leaves and having a twisted rope border. All other officers in both executive and civil branches wore a button with an anchor and crown, but without the laurel leaves. The only exception was the Engineer officers, who wore a button depicting a crown above a steam engine from 1841 until 1853, when it was replaced by the same buttons as other officers: a crown and anchor and twisted-rope-bordered edge. Petty officers wore a flat button with the crown and anchor on a plain background but without a twisted-rope border.

Swords: The 1827 pattern officer's sword has a lion-head back piece, a solid half-basket guard with folding counter-guard, and raised bars and crown-and-anchor badge. The blade is slightly curved with pipe-back, 31¼ inches long with a double-edged spear point. The grip was covered in white fish skin for commissioned officers. In 1846 this pattern was slightly altered with a straight 'Wilkinson pattern' blade and a capstan rivet on the lion head pommel. Warrant Officers (i.e. Masters of the Fleet, Masters, Second Masters, Mates, Gunners, and Carpenters) had a sword of the same 1827 pattern but with black fish skin grips, and plain back-strapped handle with fluting around the top and down the back. In 1842 Flag Officers had the option of using a Mameluke hilt sword similar to those used by the General Officers of the Army until 1856. This sword has crowns at the ends of the cross quillons and the langet is embossed with a foul anchor. Midshipmen wore a shortened version of the 1827 pattern sword until 1856 when they were issued dirks instead of swords.

Scabbard: From 1833 to 1846 the sword scabbard distinguished the Flag Officers (i.e. Admirals and Commodores) from other officers by showing ornamental oak leaves in bas-relief on the top, middle lockets and upper portion of the chape (or drag) and a honeysuckle ornament at the tip. In 1846 the middle locket was removed but returns in the 1856 regulations. The scabbards of Captains and officers of lower ranks were ornamented with fluted threads and scrolls instead of oak leaves.

Headwear and Cap Insignia: A cocked hat was worn with both the Navy officer's dress and undress uniforms when worn with epaulettes while on shore, as per *Admiralty Memoranda* of 1847 and 1856. In the dress uniform, an Admiral's cocked hat was edged with gold lace and displayed a black silk cockade six inches wide, looped with six gold bullions, the two center loops being twisted. In both dress and undress uniforms, a Captain's was edged with black silk instead of gold lace and the cockade was looped with four gold bullions, with the two center loops twisted. A Lieutenant's cockade was looped with two gold bullion, both twisted. In the 1833, 1843, and 1846 uniform regulations, officers on board ship in undress uniform were allowed a round black hat with a narrow black silk band and black buckle, with a black silk or leather cockade; or a blue cloth cap with a band around it the same width and material as the lace on their coat. Officers with no lace on their coats would wear a one-inch band of gold lace around their caps. In 1847 a gold crown would be added above the gold band. This cap is replaced in with the 1856 uniform regulations by a blue cap with a leather peak and a black mohair band one-and-a-half inches wide. Upon the front of the band is placed an insignia of a crown embroidered in gold and silver, above a silver anchor surrounded by gold laurel branches for executive officers, and the same device embroidered in gold for civil officers. The leather peak of the cap was embroidered all around in gold for Admirals and Commodores of the First Class; along the front edge for Commodores of the Second Class, Captains, and Commanders; and without any embroidery for all other officers. In 1856, black round hats were only to be worn with undress uniform in bad weather while on board ship.

Sailor's Dress: Seamen in the various sea services and even foreign navies wore a similar style of dress, which developed over time based upon the purser's supplies, practicality, tradition, and the discretion of the ship's commanding officer. A member of the crew most often tailored these outfits, which are illustrated in contemporary images and prints. Sailors' wide blue collars date back to the late-1830s with variations in the decorative taping done to the sailor's taste. In 1845 Captain J. W. Washington of the HMS *Blazer* dressed his boat crew in a blue-and-white-striped jacket for review by the Queen. In 1827 Petty Officers, and eventually other ratings, were authorized a cloth badge to be worn on their left upper sleeve. Until 1860 these were worn in white on the blue uniform and in blue on the white uniform. In 1849 a Good Conduct badge for greater-than-five-years service was authorized to be placed on the left arm. In 1857 the dress of Royal Navy sailors was regulated, and it was stipulated that the square blue collar have three rows of white cloth tape with a black silk scarf. The sailor would wear a jacket and trousers of blue cloth or a white frock with white duck (untwilled cotton) trousers. A straw hat known as a 'sennet' hat was used by sailors even in the years before Lord Nelson and was later worn with the name of the ship in gold letters on a black band around the crown of the hat. A sailor's cap was like that of the blue officer's cap but without a peak and was also worn with a black ribbon bearing the name of the ship.

PORTFOLIO – 16 Plates

Since this article is intended as a research tool, the Editors have allowed military titles and offices to be capitalized for easier perusal. Images that are known to be reversed, such as most daguerreotypes, have been visually corrected (horizontally transposed) to allow comparison between British Navy regulations and the uniforms illustrated.

Plate 1
Richard Beard, Artist
Commander James Fitzjames, R.N. HMS Erebus.

Sixth-plate daguerreotype, 1845. Second original unknown location. One is in the collections of the Scott Polar Research Institute. Secondary copies at the National Maritime Museum, Greenwich and the Derbyshire County Archives, Matlock.

James Fitzjames entered the Royal Navy in 1825 as a First Class Volunteer on board HMS *Pyramus* and was present during the transport of the British Commissioner to Mexico, and later to Lisbon during Don Miguel's usurpation of the Spanish throne. In 1830 he joined HMS *Vincent* and as a Midshipman witnessed the revolution in Greece, and the occupation of the Palmedi at Nauplia by Russian, French and British forces. In 1833 he was on board HMS *Madagascar* while escorting King Otto and the Bavarian Regency from Trieste to Greece. Fitzjames passed his examination in 1833 and served as Mate on the HMS Steamer *Euphrates* in an expedition led by Col. Chesney to the Euphrates River. During the expedition he broke his leg and later is taken prisoner by Bedouin Arabs for ten days. Fitzjames was promoted in 1838 to Lieutenant on HMS *Excellent* for his actions and was later transferred to *Ganges* during the campaign in Syria in 1840. He was selected to distribute the proclamation of Sir Charles Napier to the Egyptian

COM: FITZJAMES. (CAPT. "EREBUS.")

soldiers at Beirut for which Soliman Pocha put a price on his head. He was present at the bombardment of Beirut, the operations at D'Journi, and the blockade of Alexandria. In 1841 Fitzjames joined HMS *Cornwallis* in China, earning him numerous mentions for directing the rocket attack on the heights of Segoon and Tsikie, Chapu, on the shore battle of Woosung and during the capture of Ching-Kang-Foo. He was present at the signing of the Treaty at Nanking. In 1842 he was promoted to the rank of Commander, and given command of HMS *Clio*. He was sent to the coast of Africa and returned to England in 1844. In 1845 he assumes command of HMS *Erebus*, Sir John Franklin's flagship for the Arctic Expedition to discover the Northwest Passage. Fitzjames was also in charge of the magnetic determinations connected with the expedition.

Uniform: Fitzjames wears the undress uniform of a Commander according to the 1843 uniform regulations. The epaulettes would have a silver anchor within the crescent (not visible in the image). He wears a blue cap with a band of gold lace around the crown and is holding a telescope.

Plate 2
Unattributed.
Captain Erasmus Ommanney, R.N. (1814-1904).
Stereo-daguerreotype in a Mascher's, Improved Stereoscope case, Patent, March 8, 1853. Collection of Timothy Lindholm.

Erasmus Ommanney was born the son of a Member of Parliament in 1814. He entered the Royal Navy in 1826, serving the following year at the Battle of Navarino in the Mediterranean. In 1836, he joined the

British Relief Expedition led by James Clark Ross, organized by the Admiralty to rescue the crews of whaling vessels stranded in the Davis Strait. Ommanney was promoted to commander in 1840 and served in the Mediterranean on HMS *Vesuvius* from 1841 to 1846. In 1846 he advanced to Captain and served during relief of the Irish famine. He returned to the Arctic as commander of HMS *Assistance* during the 1850-51 expedition in search of the Franklin Arctic Expedition. Ommanney discovered the first evidence that the Expedition had in fact reached the Canadian

Arctic. There were signs of a field camp at Cape Riley, Devon Island, and cairn (stones stacked to form a memorial or marker) and relics on Beechey Island which proved to be Franklin's 1845–46 winter quarters. After the expedition Ommanney commanded HMS *Euryice* in the White Sea during the Crimean War, and subsequently in North America and the West Indies. He also commanded the HMS *Hawke* in the Baltic. In 1857 while commanding HMS *Brunswick*, Ommanney was senior officer in Colon when American filibuster William Walker attempted to invade Nicaragua. Ommanney was promoted to Rear Admiral in 1864, retiring from the Royal Navy as an Admiral and was knighted in 1887. He died in 1904.

Uniform: Ommanney is shown wearing the undress uniform of Captain with epaulettes according to 1846 uniform regulation. Visible on his epaulettes are an anchor in the crescent and a nine-pointed star on the strap. Obscured by his lapel would be a crown surmounting the strap. Ommanney wears white duck trousers as were worn in tropical climates, or on the Home station in summer. He wears a signet ring on his right hand and his cap shows a crown insignia above a gold band as first seen with the 1846 uniform regulations.

Engraved telescope: The leather-covered telescope Ommanney is holding has a retractable brass sunshade over the lens, and a brass plate over the middle drawtube which is attached with sewn leather straps. The plate is richly engraved with signal flags in at least three visible vertical rows. Above the flags is a compass rosette with the letters 'E' and 'S' for East and South just barely visible. The compass needle points due North and extends above the dial and an arch of signal flags, above which lettering is visible, surmounts the compass dial.

Medals: Ommanney wears two medals: Navy General Service Medal and the Turkish Medal for Acre 1840.

Plate 3
John Jabez Edwin Mayall, The American Daguerreotype Institute, London.
Rear Admiral Sir Francis Beaufort, R.N. (1774-1857).
Half-plate daguerreotype, c. 1848. Collection of Shaun Caton.

Sir Francis Beaufort was born in County Meath, Ireland and began his naval career as a Volunteer at the age of thirteen on HMS *Colossus* stationed on the English Canal. He became a Midshipman in 1790 on HMS *Latona* where he began his life-long practice of maintaining a journal of meteorological observations. Five years later Beaufort is present at Cornwallis's Naval Retreat during the French Revolutionary Wars. He is promoted to Lieutenant in 1796, and as Mate of HMS *Phaeton* was instrumental in capturing the Spanish ship of war *San Josef*, earning him promotion to Commander. In 1803 he devotes the next year in setting up signal stations from Dublin to Galway. In 1805 Beaufort received his first command on board HMS *Woolwich*, conducting a hydrographic survey of the Rio de la Plata region of South America. He served on various stations and in 1810 was promoted to Post Rank. For the next couple years he was engaged in surveying the eastern Mediterranean coast but returned to England after receiving a near-fatal gunshot wound while rescuing a survey party that was attacked while making astronomical observations. Beaufort was next engaged in constructing a number charts from his surveys of the Black Sea and Eastern Mediterranean. In 1832 he was appointed Admiralty hydrographer where his duties were expanded to supervising the construction of nautical charts from various naval expeditions, including that of HMS *Beagle*. In 1835 Beaufort standardized weather notation and three years later introduced Beaufort's Wind Force Scale, to be used for all log entries by the British fleet. He was given Flag-rank as Rear Admiral in 1846 and received the title Knight Commander of the Bath two years later. He retired in 1855 after sixty-eight years of service in the Royal Navy, and died in 1857.

Uniform: Sir Francis Beaufort is shown in civilian dress.

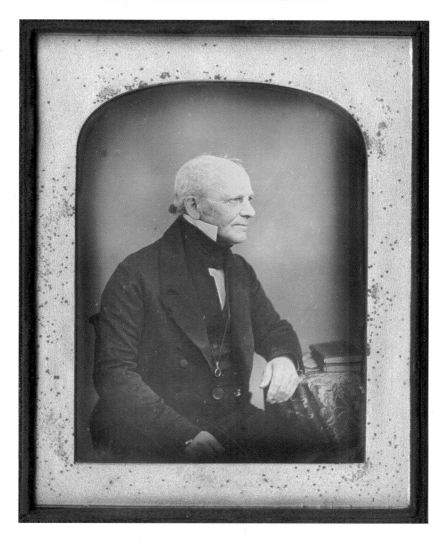

Plate 4

J.E. Mayall, 433 West Strand (with '224 Regent Street' overprint).
Unidentified Flag Officer Royal Navy.
Half-plate daguerreotype, c. 1850. Collection of Roger Tannenbaum.

Uniform: He wears the undress uniform of a Flag Officer according to the 1847 Admiralty Memoranda which introduced the surtout frock-coat. His coat is double breasted with four rows of distinction lace on the cuff and could be worn with or without epaulettes. The sword knot is of blue and gold cord according to the tinting instructions to the photographer found behind the image. His cap displays the Victorian crown above a gold lace band and rests upon an unfolded nautical chart on the table.

Medal: He wears a Naval General Service Medal.

Plate 5

W. Hulme, Birmingham England.
Unidentified Senior Captain, R.N.
Sixth-plate daguerreotype, c. 1847. Collection of the author.

Uniform: He is shown wearing the full dress uniform of a Senior Captain (Over Three Years Standing) according to the 1846 uniform regulations. His coat is of blue cloth, double breasted with two rows of ten buttons, three inches across the breast. He has a white collar tapered off in the front with one line of one-and-a-half inch gold lace along the top and front edges and one line of three-quarters-of-an-inch gold lace along the bottom edge of the collar. He wears slash flaps on his sleeves with one-and-a-half inch lace around his cuffs. Visible on his epaulettes are an anchor within the crescent, and a star on the strap surmounted by a crown. His black Morocco leather sword belt has three straight lines embroidered in gold, one at each margin edge and one down the middle. This distinguishes him from a Commodore or Flag Officer who would have worn a belt embroidered with gold oak leaves and acorns.

Medals: The Senior Captain wears two medals: a Navy General Service Medal and a First China Medal, 1842.

Plate 6

A. Claudet, 107 Regent Ste, Quadrant.
Commander Geoffrey Thomas Phipps Hornby R.N. (1825-1895).
Half-plate ambrotype, c.1854. Collection of the author.

Geoffrey Hornby was born in 1825, the son of Admiral Sir Phipps Hornby. He went to sea at the age of twelve and was present at the capture of Acre in November 1840. In 1852 he was promoted to the rank of Captain. In 1858 he was sent to China to take command of HMS *Tribune* to transport a company of Royal Marines to San Juan Island during a dispute with the United States dubbed the 'Pig War'. Partly due to his calming temperament as senior naval officer, a major incident was averted through the joint occupation of San Juan Island. His illustrious career would take him to the rank of Admiral of the Fleet.

Uniform: He wears a full dress uniform according to the 1846 Uniform Regulations with his epaulettes showing an anchor insignia in the crescent and a star on the strap denoting the rank of Commander. His black morocco leather sword belt has two straight lines embroidered in gold, one at each border edge as would be prescribed for a Lieutenant. His blue cap has a gold band surmounted by a crown cap badge, as was first prescribed in the 1846 uniform regulations.

Medals: He wears two medals: a Navy General Service Medal and a First China Medal, 1842.

Plate 7

Unattributed.

Lieutenant Herbert Philip de Kantzow.

Quarter-plate daguerreotype, 1849. Collection of Gary Landis.

Herbert Philip de Kantzow was promoted to Lieutenant in 1849 and during the Crimean War he served in the Baltic on HMS *Imperieuse*, commanded by Captain Rundle Burges Watson. Advanced to Commander in 1856 de Kantzow is made second in command on HMS *Conqueror* in the Mediterranean, commanded by Captain Hastings Reginald Yelverton. He attained the rank of Captain in 1862 and retired in 1870.

Uniform: De Kantzow wears the undress uniform of a Lieutenant according to the 1846 uniform regulations. Although not visible in the image his epaulettes would have an anchor within the crescent. He wears a white vest

and white duck trousers as were worn in tropical climates or while on Home station in summer. The guard of his 1827 pattern naval officers sword can be seen cradled at his right elbow.

Plate 8

Mr. Clarkington, 183 Strand, London.
Unidentified Mate or Second Master.
Quarter-plate daguerreotype, c. 1848. Collection of Robert Conley.

Uniform: He wears a double-breasted coat with a single epaulette on his right shoulder. According to the 1846 uniform regulations a Mate would wear one epaulette of the same pattern as a Lieutenant only smaller in size and with a smaller anchor device. A Second Master would wear the same uniform only the device on the epaulette would be a smaller version of the Master's crossed anchors.

Plate 9

Carlos D. Fredericks & Ca.
Catalina Stafford with unidentified Navy Mate or Second Master.
Quarter-plate daguerreotype, c. 1852. Collection of Carlos Vertansessian.

Uniform: He wears the undress uniform of a Mate or Second Master according to 1856 uniform regulations, with one row of quarter-inch braid around the sleeves instead of the Lieutenant's lace. He wears white duck pants as prescribed in a tropical zone and his cap dates to the 1846 pattern, showing the crown insignia over the gold band.

Medal Ribbons: Undetermined.

Plate 10

Unattributed.
Unidentified Navy Mate or Second Master.
Sixth-plate daguerreotype, c. 1852. Collection of Peter Buxtun.

Uniform: He wears the undress uniform of a Mate or Second Master according to 1856 uniform regulations, along with white duck pants indicating he was either in a tropical zone or at his Home station during the summer months.

Medals: He wears two medals: a Navy General Service Medal and the other is undetermined.

Plate 11

Unattributed.
Unidentified Boatswain.
Sixth-plate daguerreotype, c. 1850. Collection of the author.

Uniform: He wears the uniform of a Gunner, Boatswain or Carpenter according to the 1846 uniform regulations as having no epaulette. His blue cap has a crown insignia above the gold band.

Medal: He wears a Navy General Service Medal.

Plate 12
Unattributed.
Unidentified Boatswain and daughter.
Quarter-plate ambrotype, c. 1858. Collection of Robert Nofal.

Uniform: The Gunner, Boatswain or Carpenter's uniform has no epaulette, similar to earlier uniform regulations, but he wears the cap insignia introduced in 1856, a crown embroidered in gold and silver above a silver anchor surrounded by laurel leaves.

Medals: He wears two medals: a Naval General Service Medal and the other undetermined

Plate 13
Unattributed.
Unidentified Warrant Officer.
Quarter-plate ambrotype, c.1855.
Collection of Russell Falk.

Uniform: He wears a single-breasted
jacket with three buttons on the cuff and
white trousers. His cap has a single gold
band without insignia.

Plate 14
Unattributed.
Unidentified Midshipman.
Daguerreotype, c. 1852. Collection
of Charles Sangerman.

Uniform: He is shown wearing the
undress uniform of Midshipman.

Plate 15
Unattributed.
*Midshipman Charles Dickson Inglis,
R.N.*
Sixth-plate ambrotype. Collection of
Dr. Nicholas Skezas.

Written upon the case is 'C. D. Inglis
R.N. Midshipman of H.M. Ship
Amphitrite 25 guns Valpraraiso May
1854'. Charles Inglis entered the Navy
as a Midshipman on board HMS
Amphitrite on the West Indies station
and was commissioned a Lieutenant
on 14 January 1857.

Uniform: Inglis wears the uniform of
a Midshipman according to uniform
regulations of 1846.

Plate 16
Beard's Photographic Institute.
Assistant Surgeon Edward H. Cree R.N. (1814-1901).
Quarter-plate daguerreotype, 1846. Collection of the author.

Edward Cree was born on 14 January 1814 in Devonport, one of five children. He studied medicine at Dublin and Edinburgh Universities, graduating with a Licentiate of the Society of Apothecaries in 1837. In 1847 Cree received his MD and MRCS from Edinburgh University. He entered the Royal Navy as an Assistant Surgeon in 1837 to serve on the HMS *Royal Adelide* and at the Devonport Naval Hospital. He served briefly in the Mediterranean before departing for the Orient on the troop-ship HMS *Rattlesnake*. Cree was present at the attack on Chusan, China, 5 July 1840 at the start of the First China or Opium War. He made several excursions up the Canton River, witnessing several engagements and was present at the second taking of Chusan on 1 October 1841, and the taking of Chin-kiang-foo on 21 July 1842. Cree was also present at the ending of hostilities at the Nanking Conference on 28 August 1842. Aboard the HMS *Vixen* he saw action against Malayan pirates and was promoted to Surgeon in 1843. Going back to England in March 1846, Cree returned to the Orient in 1848 and to the Hai-nan Island area to again battle pirates. Returning to Plymouth, England, he married in 1852. During the Crimean War Cree witnessed the bombardments of the Russian towns of Brahestad, Bomersund and Gamla Carleby and the series of engagements that lead to the destruction of the docks at Sebastopol in February 1856. In 1858 he ended his sea duty on HMS *Russell*, then performing Coastguard service off Devonport. Promoted Staff Surgeon in 1862, Cree served at HM Dockyard Portsmouth from 1864 to 1869. He retired with the honorary rank of Deputy Inspector-General of Hospitals and Fleets.

Uniform: Cree wears the uniform of a Surgeon according to the uniform regulations of 30 June 1843; a uniform similar to a Masters but with nine buttons (three groups of three) and one epaulette on the right shoulder. The uniform regulations of 21 March 1846 would be revised to two epaulettes for Surgeons and one for Assistant Surgeons. In 1856 regulations will have both wear two epaulettes.

His cap with the gold crown surmounting a band of one inch gold lace was introduced in 1846, though individual officers may have worn it prior to its official use. He has the pattern 1827 Navy officers sword with white fish skin grips at his side.

Some Suggestions for Further Reading

British Royal Naval Uniforms

Rene Chartrand, *Canadian Military Heritage: Volume II, 1755-1871* (Montreal: Art Global, 1995).
Dudley Jarrett, *British Naval Dress* (London: J.M. Dent, 1960).
Robert Wilkinson-Latham, *The Royal Navy, 1790-1970* (London: Osprey Publishing, 1977).

Insignia

Ottley L. Perry, *Ranks and Badges in Her Majesty's Army and Navy* (London: n.p, 1887).
Major H.G. Parkyn, *Military Shoulder-Belt Plates and Buttons* (Aldershot: Gale and Polden, 1956).

Medals

Sir Bernard Burke, *The Book of Orders of Knighthood and Decorations of Honour of All Nations, etc* (London: Hurst and Blackett, 1858).
Major Lawrence L. Gordon, *British Battles and Medals, 1588-1946* (Aldershot: Gale and Polden, 1947).
Donald Hall, *British Orders, Decoration and Medals* (St. Ives: Balfour, 1973).
Paul Hieronymussen, *Orders, Medals and Decorations of Britain and Europe In Colour* (London: Blandford, 1967).
D. Hastings Irwin, *War Medals And Decorations* (London: Gill, 1890).
William Henry Long, *Medals of the British Navy and How They Were Won* (London: Norie and Wilson, 1895).
John Horsley Mayo, *Medals and Decorations of the British Army and Navy* (Westminster: Constable, 1897.
Vaclav Mericka, *The Book of Orders and Decorations* (London: Hamlyn, 1976).
Algernon Payne, *A Handbook of British and Foreign Orders, War Medals, and Decorations* (Sheffield: Northend, 1911).
Neville W. Poulsom, *The White Ribbon: A Medallic Record of British Polar Expeditions* (London: Seaby, 1968).
Alec A. Purves, *Collecting Medals and Decorations* (London: Seaby, 1968).
Earl of Sandwich, *British and Foreign Medals Relating to Naval and Maritime Affairs* (Greenwich: National Maritime Museum, 1937).
George Tancred, *Historical Record of Medals and Honorary Distinctions Conferred on the British Navy, Army, and Auxiliary Forces etc* (London: Spink, 1891).

British Naval Swords

P.G.W. Annis, *Naval Swords: British and American Naval Edged Weapons, 1660-1815* (London: Arms and Armour, 1970).
Henry T.A. Bosanquet, *The Naval Officer's Sword* (London: HMSO, 1955).
W.E. May and P.G.W. Annis, *Swords for Sea Service* (London: HMSO, 1970).
W.E. May and A.N. Kennard, *Naval Swords and Firearms* (London: HMSO, 1962).

British Daguerreotypists

Bernard and Pauline Heathcote, *A Faithful Likeness: The First Photographic Portrait Studios in the British Isles 1841 to 1855* (Nottingham: Technical Print Services, 2002).
Shaun Caton, 'A Meeting of Eyes: Reflections on the world of miniatures and metaphysics as seen in three daguerreotypes by John Jabez Edwin Mayall', *The Daguerreian Society Newsletter*, 15:3 (2003).
Robert B. Fisher, 'The Beard Photographic Franchise in England', *The Daguerreian Society Annual* (1992), pp. 73-95.
Michael G. Jacob, 'A Visit to Mr. Beard's', *The Daguerreian Society Annual* (1994), pp. 154-65.

Early Photography

George Gilbert, *Photography: The Early Years – A Historical Guide for Collectors* (New York: Harper and Row, 1980).
Mark Haworth-Booth, ed., *The Golden Age of British Photography, 1839-1900* (New York: Aperture, 1984).
Gerry Badger, *The Genius of Photography: How Photography Has Changed Our Lives* (London: Quadrille, 2007).

Alfred John West and the Trafalgar Centenary

David Clover

Living beside the historic harbour of Portsmouth with its great naval traditions and fame as a yachting centre, and with my own love of the sea which as a boy gave me a strong desire to join the Royal Navy and capture pirates, it was natural that in taking up photography I should grasp the opportunity that dry plates offered to obtain sea scenes.[1]

Alfred John West was born in 1857 into a Victorian working family with three brothers and two sisters. As he would describe in later years, it was the influence of the sea, as much his parents, which would be the shaping principle of his ambitions in life. His father George West of 55 High Street, Gosport in the County of Southampton (since 1959 simply 'Hampshire') was a skilled joiner. George made the transition from joiner to the studio photographic trade – the family later crediting this change of career, seemingly not unusual for the time, to his being able to make small and light proof camera boxes which could take photographs using the wet plate 'Collodion' process. By 1881, their photographic business was well established with the National Census returns for 97 High Street Gosport of that year showing George West (Senior), 65 years old and head of the family as 'Occupation – photographer', George West (Son), age 40 'Occupation – photographer', Mary West daughter, 38 'Occupation – photographer', William West, son 32 'Occupation – photographer', Maria West daughter 24 'Occupation – photographer', and Alfred West son 22, 'Occupation photographer'. By 1881, Alfred would have actually been 24 (the age written on the census return appears to be wrong) but there was no doubt at all that this was a family who had embraced the new art of photography. For a pioneering family business, it is remarkable how little is known about their activity. This article attempts to provide new insights into the business of this innovative technology and to introduce its most famous practitioner, Alfred West.

West was born some fifty-two years after the Battle of Trafalgar, still well within the living memory of some of the men, many local, who had been at close quarters in it. Forty-eight years later as a noted pioneer cinematographer, he took a principal part in the 1905 Centenary

Alfred John West, FRGS.
Courtesy David Clover.

commemoration of the Battle at the Albert Hall London. His active participation in, and presence at, the celebrations in 1905 was almost inevitable given the interests, dispositions and skills he had acquired in the first half of his life. His career spanned the transition from the days of sail and muscle, paint and print to the technological age of steam, mechanical and photographic reproduction and above all, into the age of global and rapid communication that we are still living in. His story makes us realise how rapid the pace of change was in this vibrant century. So much was different by 1905 – technologically, socially, politically – that life would have been completely incomprehensible to Nelson and his contemporaries. From our twenty-first century vantage point, I believe that we would probably have been more able to recognise and feel 'at home' in the world of 1905 than a person from that era would have felt in 1805.

Marine Photography

By 1881, it had indeed become possible to dispense with the messy and restrictive 'wet' process in favour of the new 'dry' plates that completely revolutionised photography and allowed it to become a mobile activity as opposed to a strictly studio-based one.[2] Dry plate, also known as gelatine process, was the first economically successful durable photographic medium. It was invented by Richard L. Maddox in 1871, and by 1879 it was so well introduced that the first dry plate factory had been established. By 1881, Alfred West had become a master not only of the technology, but of the much more useful art of pointing the camera at something interesting not just to himself, but to others. Always resourceful, and the son of a carpenter/joiner, he even invented his own instantaneous shutter release mechanism and camera stabilising device which enabled him to take award winning yachting photographs of a quality which astonished his peers and won him much fame in international photographic circles.[3] His chosen subject and profession from that time onwards was 'Marine Photography' at which he excelled for fifteen years before his major change of direction into the then very young art of Cinematography in 1897. In the course of his photographic career, he was awarded more than forty medals from competitions organised by photographic societies across the world. Some examples are shown below:

Medal awarded Messrs. West & Sons by Newcastle on Tyne and Northern Counties Photographic Association 'For Yachting Studies', 1883. Courtesy of Mr Simon West, Western Australia, curator of the 'West' medals.

Medal awarded Messrs. West & Sons by the Photographic Society of Ireland for 'Instantaneous Yachting Views', 1884. Courtesy of Mr Simon West, Western Australia, curator of the 'West' medals.

A picture of which West was most proud, and which neatly encapsulates his incomparable technique and love of the dramatic, was of the racing yacht Mohawk. His portrait of the vessel racing at the Royal Southampton Yacht Club Regatta in 1884 was awarded the gold medal at the St. Louis Convention USA for which nine other countries competed and the image later featured on many of his handbills and playbills. A print still hangs in the New York Yacht Club. The picture is wholly representative of his style and ability to portray as a still picture a subject that is so full of vitality and motion. We are fortunate that West sold his copyright and archive of yachting pictures to Beken of Cowes in 1916 where they can still be inspected. They have been conserved, scanned and catalogued and are maintained as an integral part of the Beken collection.

The yacht Mohawk. Courtesy David Clover. Copyright Beken of Cowes.

Moving Pictures

By 1897, West had amassed enough capital from his still and studio photography business to take up the new and expensive art of Cinematography that fascinated him intensely. He tells us that:

> *The developing was loosely done in a pan, and the films were hung over a line to dry like so much washing, while at first there were no spools and the film was wound into reels by hand. At that time I had not heard of acetone for joining together different lengths of film, so each subject was run through the projector separately, slides being shown during the threading process. The officers of H.M.S. 'Vernon' the torpedo depot ship, heard of what I was doing, and becoming interested invited me to take films of the explosion of mines and the firing of a Whitehead, an enlargement from which latter was framed and hung on board for many years.*[4]

Within a year, he had some fifty staff working for him, and he had started his 'Our Navy' Cinematographic business, based in 'The Anchorage' in Villiers Road, Portsmouth, which was directed largely at filming Naval activities with the full sanction of the Admiralty. It is not clear how he so rapidly gained the confidence of the authorities, but for a time he was granted an exclusive license to allow him to film and photograph a wide variety of naval subjects. Early lantern-slides exist showing mines and diagrams in chalk on a wall, probably taken under Admiralty contract at Gosport.[5] Amongst the first of his moving pictures were sequences of a mine explosion[6] and a Whitehead torpedo being fired (the film still surviving[7]), both of which he obtained aboard the hulks associated with the training ship HMS *Vernon* in Portsmouth Harbour.[8]

West witnessed at first hand the incident of the appearance at thirty-five knots of Charles Parson's experimental steam yacht *Turbinia* through the lines at the Queen's Diamond Jubilee Review in 1898. The Commander in Chief had granted him special permission to remain in the lines during the Royal Procession and from there he was able to photograph it – and the shot was so successful that Charles Parsons asked him to make moving and still pictures of her on the Tyne.[9]

West was rapidly extending his reach into narrative film making, based around promotion, through film, of the Royal Navy. He appears to have had very well-placed and influential contacts in the Navy and Navy League at

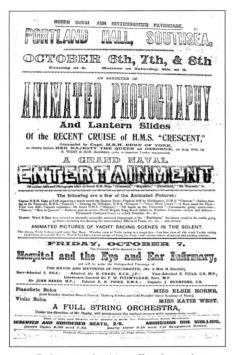

Early poster advertising a film taken on the Cruise of HMS Crescent. Courtesy Barnes Collection, Hove.

this time, possibly nurtured through Freemasonry.[10] This suggestion is supported by the recent discovery of a long but uncharacteristic film sequence of Freemasons in procession along Fawcett Road, Southsea, on 21 May 1902, which is undoubtedly the work of West.[11]

In 1898, he shipped aboard HMS *Crescent* to film and photograph events on the Royal cruise commanded by HRH Duke of York. He exhibited these films to the crew and then at Osborne House to Queen Victoria who was reported as being 'greatly pleased'.[12] These films formed the basis of his first and very popular public showings in Portsmouth and London and later through the country. From the start in 1898, the specialist press reported very favourably. An early show billed as 'A Grand Naval Entertainment' in 1898 at St James's Hall London during the second week of November was reviewed in *The Photogram* as follows:

> … the kinetograms can only be spoken of as wonderful in the variety and excellence of their subjects … It is true that certain technical defects in the films were somewhat plainly visible to those who sat close to the screen, but even these were insufficient to appreciably detract from the interest of the display.[13]

West himself provides us with a colourful description of a very early performance in his autobiography:

> The stage was profusely decorated, the screen being draped with the Union Jack and the White Ensign flanked by palms and banks of flowers. A large orchestra was engaged together with a professional

271

lady singer. The Hall was packed with an appreciative audience, which included some of the Lords Commissioners of the Admiralty, members of the Navy League, and many representatives of the Press ... Great applause greeted one particular film taken from the Warner lightship of yachts racing in rough weather. They came so close to the camera that, smothered in foam, they appeared to be sailing right out of the picture, and the effect on one member of the audience was so realistic that he was forced to leave suffering from acute sea sickness!

... Amongst the pictures was one of the Captains of the 'Crescent' mustering his crew, who marched past him in single file. Each one halted before the Captain and saluted whilst an officer by his side read from a large book the man's name and rank. It was a formal introduction, enabling the Captain to become personally acquainted with his crew, the naval term for the evolution being called 'Inspection by the Open List'. Other subjects included physical drill by the Midshipmen H.M.S. 'Crescent' leaving Portsmouth Harbour General Quarters Preparing for action working the guns – away boats' crew racing round the fleet dancing on the fo'c'sle The Hornpipe Firing torpedoes Attack and defence Cutlass drill. The series concluded with a remarkable shot of the 'Turbinia' steaming at 35 knots.[14]

Alfred West registered his organisation formally as 'Our Navy' in 1902 under Limited Company number: 72532.[15]

Exhibitions in London

After a few false starts caused by having to comply with increasingly stringent safety regulations imposed by the London County Council to protect the public from a series of disastrous fires caused by the explosive nitrate film stock used for the films, West rapidly developed his 'Our Navy' cinematographic shows at The Polytechnic in Regent Street through the early · 1900s and on the strength of these he became a very popular figure. Always a showman and always with the intention of promoting life in the Royal Navy through his entertainments, West used the device of 'seeding' on buses and public places small packets, ostensibly of Seltzer powders, which when unwrapped contained a small advertisement for his daily shows.

To further promote the business, he constructed a highly detailed, 13ft-long, model battleship named *King Edward VII* which was towed around London on a trolley as an advertisement. He was though eventually asked by the Police to desist as it was causing serious obstruction due to the crowds that surrounded it. Later he used the model as a filmic 'prop', destroying it with charges as part of a 'battle' sequence which he called 'Let Loose the Dogs of War!' Parts of this sequence survive, showing the destruction of the model on the beach at Whale Island and were very probably being shown in 1905 as an integral part of the 'Our Navy' performances. These would have become dramatic affairs as he polished his presentational techniques over many performances. West wrote:

> *I decided to act as compère myself and to introduce sound effects, as I considered that it would not do for the audience to see, for instance, a gun fired and hear no report, and so I arranged with someone behind the screen to hit a big drum at the right moment. With such effect was this done that it quite startled the audience, particularly the ladies, and caused roars of laughter. Sheets of coarse sandpaper rubbed together gave a realistic enough impression of the splashing of waves, and words of command delivered at the right juncture unknowingly anticipated the 'talkies' of today and added to the appreciation of the films.*[16]

Trafalgar Day in 1905

Alfred West was booked to create a show at the Albert Hall for the Trafalgar Centenary. It was to be a programme of the patriotic and nautical films that he had made over the previous few years, full of the 'accustomed zest and vigour' associated with the 'Our Navy' productions. We still have the full printed catalogue from the period, and we know that he would probably have wanted to show sequences selected from his 'Our Navy' entertainments.[17] These shows were based around subjects such as 'The Training of the Boy', featuring the tearful departure from his mother and home of a young recruit, his arrival at Greenwich, 'The Cradle of the Navy', and all the activities typically undertaken during training, The regular shows would have also featured scenes of sail drills and training aloft on the old ship *St Vincent*, of yacht racing, the *Turbinia* at speed ('showing the effects of foam'), realistic gunnery drills afloat and ashore, including some naïve 'Battle' scenes made up using models and film of real ships in Portsmouth Harbour intercut. A small, but telling, amount of this material is still extant in the National Film Archive.

The Trafalgar Centenary events were held in various provincial and London venues, and as well as the Albert Hall. His supporting films were shown in three London locations, the Regent Street Polytechnic, the Crystal Palace, and the People's Palace in the East End at Mile End Road.

However, the official tone of the 1905 celebrations was not to be over-triumphal, rather 'rejoicing over the part played by Nelson in securing the inestimable blessing of peace and of sorrow for the brave men who fell in battle at the hands of Nelson's men in 1805'.[18] To emphasise the point, wreaths 'bound up in French and Spanish colours' were laid at Trafalgar Square. The French Navy sent a squadron of ships to Portsmouth. Alfred West filmed an 'evolution' by the gunnery school at Whale Island, Portsmouth to celebrate the arrival of the French. This sequence was very probably included in the Albert Hall performance. He describes it as follows:

> ... H.M.S. 'Excellent', the gunnery school, provided a surprise when they arrived at Whale Island. It took the form of a special evolution for which the whole complement of the island was required ... On the top of a grassy hank bordering one side of the parade ground, nothing could be seen but a long row of straw hats. On a blast of a whistle, these straw hats immediately became animated, the sailors jumping up and, scattering themselves about the bank in a mixed crowd of moving objects. The whistle blew a second time, and this multitude suddenly formed themselves into letters, making the words 'Vive La France'.

> This evolution was greeted with intense enthusiasm by the French visitors. So large were the letters in the words that it took five men to form the full stop after 'France ... On the whistle being blown for a third time, the sailors broke up and dashed across the plateau in two lines, then forming fours they went off at the double amidst the cheers of the onlookers ...

> A special matinee was given to which 1,500 French officers and men were invited. They marched from their ships to the hall headed by the full band and pipers from the Royal Naval Barracks ... The programme and the title slides were printed in French, which was greatly appreciated by the guests. The excitement and enthusiasm was intense, and when a film was shown of a White Ensign and a Tricolour being hoisted side by side, whilst the Orchestra played the National Anthem and the Marseillaise, caps were thrown into the air, and the visitors stood up and shouted 'Vive l'Angleterre'.

It's likely therefore that Alfred West, somewhat inhibited by the spirit of the prevailing 'Entente Cordiale', would have had to moderate his normal programme for the event. It would certainly have been something a little more restrained than he had been accustomed to presenting in his regular afternoon and evening 'Our Navy' patriotic shows at the Regent Street Polytechnic.

Lantern Slide of HMS Victory in Portsmout Harbour.
Courtesy David Clover.

The main Albert Hall event on the afternoon of Saturday 21 October 1905, was attended by a large audience 'Under the Patronage of Their Majesties The King and Queen'.[19] Although they didn't attend in person, it seems from contemporary reports that they lent their Royal box seats to the organisers so that they could be let out at higher prices than the regular seats and boxes.[20] Regular ticket prices ranged from £2 12/6d for an evening box in the Grand Tier (though presumably rather more for the donated Royal Box seats) to 1/- for a promenade in the Gallery. The event was designed to raise money for the 'Nelson Centenary Memorial Fund' that had been set up by the British and Foreign Sailors Society (BFSS). The official handbill for the event concludes by offering a 'Nelson charm of copper from Victory presented with each programme', which the audience proudly took home with them.[21]

The programme and contemporary reports in *The Times* tell us that the event took place in the afternoon, coinciding with the exact time that Nelson died. It included a 'Unique Nautical Display involving an evolution with a Field Gun (a direct precursor of the 'Field Gun Competition' which started in 1907 and which was to become a major feature of the later Royal Tournament events at Earl's Court until 1999).[22] This was enacted by 'Miss Weston's Naval Boy's Brigade from

Portsmouth', who also made a 'Presentation of Victory souvenirs bearing His Majesty the King's initials'. The event started with an organ recital, singing of 'The Old Hundredth' and a prayer. Mrs Tree recited Kipling's poem 'Recessional' and the raising of the Union Jack on a specially constructed white flagpole preceded the presentation of the Nelson busts and mementoes. The Mayor of Paddington made a brief and unexpected speech of thanks for his, as did Captain Kaburaki of the Japanese Navy on behalf of Admiral Togo (who was not present). Mr Ben Davies sang 'The Death of Nelson', with the words 'O'er Nelson's Tomb, With silent grief oppress'd, Britannia mourns her Hero, Now at rest'.[23]

This ballad was performed dozens of times around the country by tenor singers at this time.[24] Other naval and military bands were also present along with the Artistes Miss Evangeline Florence, Miss Marie Brema (an opera singer who had worked with Wagner), Mrs Tree (wife of the actor Herbert Beerbohm Tree), Mr Ben Davies, Mr John Coates and the famous Welsh operatic baritone (later Professor) Mr David Ffrangcon-Davies.

And so the event progressed to the showing of Alfred West's films. *The Times* had reported in its preview the day before:

> *After this Mr Alfred West, well known for admirable kinematographic shows of a naval character, will give a novel one, illustrating the reception of the French Fleet.*[25]

So Alfred West and his assistants duly stepped forward and presented a film sequence which included footage of a very old seaman who had served with Admiral Hyde-Parker (one of Nelson's captains) on the quarterdeck of HMS *Victory*, showing a young boy the features of the ship – the ship's wheel, the memorial plaque 'Here Nelson Fell' and culminating in the laying of a wreath and much mopping of brows. Again, this charming sequence survives intact for us all to enjoy.[26] West wrote of this *Victory* sequence in his unpublished autobiography:

> *The year 1905 being the centenary of the battle of Trafalgar, a special programme was arranged introducing Our Navy of the past. One of the films obtained was of an old naval veteran, 92 years of age, then living in Portsmouth, who had served under Admiral Hyde Parker, one of Nelson's captains. He was a little feeble on his legs and rather deaf, but otherwise well and hearty, and he was not only willing, but eager to take part in the film I outlined to him. He was taken aboard the 'Victory', then lying at anchor in mid-stream, and accompanied*

by a Petty Officer from the Royal Naval Barracks and two Boys from the 'Royal Seamen and Marines' Orphanage'.

After climbing a gangway without assistance, a chair was placed for him to rest before proceeding to the Quarter Deck. Looking around, the old salt remarked that the ship was somewhat altered from when he was last aboard 72 years before. He seemed a little overcome as he saluted the Quarter Deck, and taking out his hand-kerchief to mop his face, he sat down to watch me act the part he was going to take. He understood what he had to do, and did it splendidly.

With one hand on one of the boys who were beside him, and the Petty Officer following behind, he slowly came to the spot where Nelson fell, and kneeling down with some difficulty he took he wreath which one of the boys was carrying, and placed it carefully and reverently over the tablet that marks the spot.

He had to be helped up by the Petty Officer, and then proceeding slowly to the poop, pointed out with his stick the famous words that are painted around the steering wheel:- 'England expects that every man will do his duty'.

Turning round, he points aloft, and the scene changes to the famous signal, which was hoisted for this occasion by the special permission of the Commander in Chief. Other films obtained included one of guns used at Trafalgar being worked by seamen in contemporary rig. These, together with lantern-slides of the battle and the death of Nelson were included in the Centenary programme.[27]

One of the boys mentioned and seen in the film is believed to be Frank Beggs from a Portsmouth Naval family, but the names of the others are not known.[28] All the filmed scenes, including the recent one from Whale Island celebrating the 'Entente Cordiale' would have been accompanied from behind the screen by large drums, shouted commands, whistle signals, explosions and patriotic music to give (as far as could be done) the illusion of reality to those watching. West continued the account in his autobiography:

A bust of Nelson made out of oak and copper from the 'Victory' was presented to me in recognition of my services in helping to organise and assist in the programme. Miss Weston's Naval Boys' Brigade from Portsmouth arrived with a field gun to give a display of drill, and a wreath sent from the Royal Sailors' Rest was placed upon another bust of Nelson and sent with it to Admiral Togo of the Japanese Navy from the boys of Britain. The Brigade, under Naval instructors, gave a unique display in the arena of the hall.

At 3 o'clock the vast audience stood up and sang the hymn 'All People that on earth do dwell', after which the Revd. Canon Barker, private Chaplain to the King, offered up an appropriate prayer. Mrs. Tree then recited Rudyard Kipling's much treasured 'Recessional'.

On the platform was the oak timber taken from the 'Victory' and presented by the Lords Commissioners of the Admiralty to the British and Foreign Sailors' Society. On it were the words in faded gilt:

'Here Nelson Died'.

By its side was a flagpole, and at the exact moment, when, one hundred years before, Nelson had breathed out his heroic soul in the 'Victory's cockpit, an English sailor boy hoisted the Union Jack to half mast; after a brief silence Mr. Ben Davies sang 'The Death of Nelson', and the flag was mast-headed.

Following this came an exhibition of films and lantern slides depicting 'Our Navy in 1805 and 1905'. Lord Brassey presided over the whole proceedings, and was supported by a number of Admirals. The Lord Mayor of London and the Mayors of many London Boroughs were present in their robes of office, as well as many other high dignitaries. The performance closed with the hoisting side by side of the Union Jack and Tricolour and the singing of the National Anthems of England and France.[29]

The Times correspondent present at the event itself (who incidentally discovered that his press pass didn't afford him a very good view of the proceedings) reported on the following Monday:

After this came Mr West's cinematograph display, very good as usual, full of Nelsonia and recent scenes in the Entente Cordiale ...[30]

A further and similar event was held at the Albert Hall in the evening of 21 October – though it seems it was poorly attended, described somewhat frostily by *The Times* reporter saying: 'The entertainment may be described as a concert of high merit, part only of which had any special reference to the occasion'.

A Lasting Memento

As a result of West's efforts, he, along with many others (including the Mayor of Paddington) was presented with a bronze bust of Nelson (which the family treasures to this day) – given by the British and Foreign Sailors Society (now 'Missions to Seamen'). The King, who took a great interest in the Society, had allowed his initials, E.R. VII, to be stamped on souvenirs sold by the fund including the busts.[31] Subscribers were also able to acquire medals and badges. 'Victory Copper', donated by the Admiralty was used to make the Nelson busts which were available for donations of £50 to the fund.[32] These busts continued to be sold well into the 1930s as presentation items. The upper section under Alfred West's presentation Nelson bust is inscribed as standard:

A bust of Nelson by the British and Foreign Sailors' Society presented to West 'in recognition of his valued services'. Courtesy David Clover.

NELSON
THIS BUST CONTAINS
VICTORY COPPER
FOR NELSON CENTENARY
OCTOBER 21 1905
PRESENTED BY
British & Foreign Sailors Society
E.R.VII

The personal inscription label on the plinth section reads:

'ENGLAND EXPECTS THAT EVERY MAN WILL DO HIS DUTY'
NELSON CENTENARY MEMENTO
OAK & COPPER FROM HMS *VICTORY*
Given by Lords of the Admiralty
TO BRITISH & FOREIGN SAILORS' SOCIETY
Patron VICE ADMIRAL H.R.H. THE PRINCE OF WALES K.G.
AND PRESENTED TO MR ALFRED J WEST F.R.G.S
In recognition of his valued services at the
CENTENNIAL CELEBRATION OF THE Death of Nelson
AT THE ROYAL ALBERT HALL October 21st 1905
ER VII

After 1905

West was a Fellow of the Royal Geographic Society and travelled widely with his camera in the Colonies, expanding the 'Our Navy' shows to include 'Our Army', 'Our Colonies' and other themes. His sons took his shows to Canada, New Zealand and Australia, and descendants of the family still live in those places. He appears to have added little to the collection after 1912, and in 1916, well aware of the newly developing competition at the cinema for the attention of the public, he sold the businesses. The yachting plates went to Beken of Cowes, and the film stock to a 'Glasgow Firm' who never paid for them, though he tells us intriguingly that he 'kept the negatives'. They were however almost certainly recycled for nitrate munitions in the First World War – a fitting if ignominious end for material that had borne such dramatic witness to patriotism and preparation for conflict. West concludes his own account by saying:

> *When the great struggle that lasted for four weary years had at last ended, I found myself no longer eager to conquer fresh fields in photographic discovery, but content to spend the rest of days in quiet retirement, sitting back and watching others make new discoveries along the path where I had been the pioneer.*[33]

---

[1] A.J. West, 'Sea Salts and Celluloid' (hereafter 'SS&C'), 1935 (unpublished) p. 1. It is available for free PDF download at http://bit.ly/a6DiD URL current as at 25/09/2009). A great amount of useful information may be found at the 'Our Navy' website: http://www.ournavy.org.uk. The Barnes Collection, Hove Museum houses ephemera including playbills and other material relating to Alfred West and his photographic and film career. It is available to view by appointment. The author of this article, David Clover (1949-), was introduced to the 'Our Navy' archive at an early age by his grandmother, and was instrumental in locating John Barnes at his St. Ives museum during a family holiday in the late 1960's. With his father, Antony Scott Clover, he arranged for photocopies of the ephemera to be supplied to Barnes. Although the original archive was later destroyed, that early contact ensured the survival of much of the content of the West material and led to the extensive research by John Barnes, which has placed Alfred West in his correct historical context. In his late teens, he was, for several summers, an officer aboard the TS *Foudroyant* moored in Portsmouth, just across the harbour from HMS *Victory*. He is currently IT Development Manager in the Faculty of Mathematics, Computing and Technology at the Open University in Milton Keynes. Although he is a keen choral singer, he has never sung 'The Death of Nelson'. He celebrated the bicentenary of the Battle of Trafalgar by singing in a performance of Haydn's 'Nelson Mass' at Radley College near Oxford. Fittingly the performance was illustrated by a series of projected slides related to Nelson's origins, his career, the Battle of Trafalgar and the eventual apotheosis of Nelson as a national hero. Email: d.a.clover@open.ac.uk

[2] C.E. Kenneth Mees, *From Dry Plates To Ektachrome Film: A Story of Photographic Research* (Ziff-Davis Publishing Company: New York, 1961). See also John Barnes, *Pioneers of the*

British Film: The Beginnings of the Cinema in England, 1894-1901. Volume 3: 1898, The Rise of the Photoplay (London: Bishopsgate Press, 1983), pp. 45-53; *Who's Who of Victorian Cinema*, edited by Stephen Herbert and Luke McKernan (London: British Film Institute, 1996), pp. 149-150.

[3] http://bit.ly/Ex4Gt – relates to technical inventions developed by AJ West (URL current as at 25/09/2009).

[4] SS&C, p. 188.

[5] Barnes Collection, Hove Museum.

[6] http://bit.ly/172CE (requires 'Real Player' software).

[7] http://bit.ly/11e5r5, http://bit.ly/J8uet, http://bit.ly/yqJq3, http://bit.ly/172CE, http://bit.ly/110n4t, http://bit.ly/PFaHf (URL current as at 25/09/2009 – all clips require 'Real Player' software).

[8] http://bit.ly/2krxp. HMS *Vernon* continued its work as a floating and shore establishment for mine warfare and countermeasures until 1995

[9] The moving pictures have unfortunately been lost except for two frames, but the classic still photograph captured by West remains the defining image of *Turbinia* at speed, even today.

[10] The aims of the Navy League were to promote an awareness in the British public on the dependency of the country on the sea and that the only safeguard was to have a powerful navy; to convince the public of the justification for adequate expenditure and maintenance of the navy to enable them to fulfil their role; that naval issues required continuity and should not be interfered with through differing party politic; education of the public and young people about the need of a strong navy through publications and lectures. In 1901, the League had a membership of 14,000 and continued to grow until 1914 when over 100,000 people were members. http://www.royalnavalmuseum.org/info_sheets_navy_league.htm

[11] The original is curated by the Wessex Film and Sound Archive at Winchester from which copies can be obtained.

[12] *The Optician*, 1 September 1898.

[13] *The Photogram*, 5:60, December 1898, p. 397

[14] SS&C, pp. 33-34.

[15] National Archives Kew – Piece details BT 31/9737/72532.

[16] SS&C, p. 33.

[17] British Library Catalogue Entry: 'WEST, Alfred, F.R.G.S. *A Synopsis of the Life-Work of Alfred West ... Depicting Cinematograph Scenes of Life in our Navy and our Army, our Mercantile Marine, our Colonies, our Pleasure Fleet & Our Homeland. An Illustrated and Descriptive Catalogue.* Wessex Press; Portsmouth, [1912.]. pp. vii. 81; 4 Shelfmark 8829.k.34.' Available for PDF download at: http://bit.ly/SwBsr (URL current as at 25/09/2009).

[18] *The Times*, 21 October 1905.

[19] A facsimile of the poster for this event is available at: http://tinyurl.com/oyjur3 (URL current as at 25/09/2009).

[20] *The Times*, 20 October 1905.

[21] http://bit.ly/15AwJg (URL current as at 25/09/2009).

[22] A film made by Alfred West of this evolution is available at: http://bit.ly/1a7PBu (requires Real Player).

[23] http://bit.ly/h1MnU (URL current as at 25/09/2009).

[24] At an early performance of this piece, Lady Hamilton had to be taken out of the performance in a fit of hysterics. Critics have suggested that her reaction was related more to the musical setting than to the words.

[25] *The Times*, 20 October 1905.

[26] Real Media video available online at: http://bit.ly/TjYHs and also from Wessex Film and Sound Archive – http://www3.hants.gov.uk/wfsa.htm Ref: AV56/1.

[27] SS&C, p. 76.

[28] *Portsmouth News*, 25 March 1996. The Beggs family faithfully re-enacted the scene on *Victory* with their own grandchildren in 2005 to commemorate the bicentenary, establishing what they hope to become a dynastic tradition to be repeated every one hundred years thereafter.

[29] SS&C, p. 80.

[30] *The Times*, 23 October 1905.

[31] Illustration: http://bit.ly/lJZtl (URL current as at 25/09/2009).

[32] Some of the copper used for the medallions was probably taken from the materials salvaged from the *Foudroyant* in order eke out the supply. *Foudroyant* had been Nelson's flagship in 1799-1800, and was sold out of service by the Admiralty in 1891. She had broken her moorings in a storm and was subsequently wrecked at Blackpool opposite the Hotel Metropole in June 1897 whilst being towed north for exhibition and proposed restoration as a floating training ship by Geoffrey Wheatley Cobb (d.1931), a Welsh industrialist of Caldicot Castle.

[33] SS&C, p. 212.

Acknowledgements: The author would particularly like to acknowledge John Barnes (1920-2008), film historian and collector, Barnes Museum of Cinematography; Antony Scott Clover (1917-1998), Alfred West's grandson, who encouraged Alfred West to write his autobiography in 1936, and who kept the ephemera archive, passing photocopies of it to the Barnes Collection now at Hove Museum for posterity to use and enjoy; Gladys Marian Clover (Neé West) (1887-1966), West's daughter who curated the 'Our Navy' archive after West's death in 1937; and David Lee, Wessex Film and Sound Archive Winchester, for locating and curating extant film.

'The Greatest Reserve of the Imagination': The Naval Theatre in the Age of Empire

Jan Rüger

When Michel Foucault described ships as 'the greatest reserve of the imagination', as 'heterotopias' that symbolically unite spaces or sites that would otherwise be seen as incompatible, he did not think of the British or German battlefleets in the age of empire.[1] Yet these fleets were precisely that: powerful cultural symbols that reconciled otherwise divergent ideas of nationhood and belonging. It is this symbolic quality that this essay is engaging with. The navies of Wilhelmine Germany and Edwardian Britain have been in the focus of historians ever since the end of the First World War. Yet this attention has been almost entirely about technology, strategy and warfare, about administration, personalities and politics. The two fleets' symbolic dimension, in contrast, has remained largely unexplored. This is surprising, given the undeniable prominence that battleships enjoyed as cultural symbols in the decades before 1914. The dreadnoughts of both countries drew huge crowds at public displays. They were embraced by popular culture, entertainment and advertising. Whatever their real strategic value might have been, they turned into public symbols, located at the intersection of cultural and political contexts.

Questions of Nationhood

This came at a time when ideas about nationhood and national identity were the subject of continuous debates, both in the United Kingdom and Germany. In the case of the *Kaiserreich* this tension was felt particularly acutely. The construct of a German nation-state, put on the European map in 1871, faced competing ideas of tradition, loyalty and belonging. Indeed, Bismarck's foundation challenged traditional ideas of German nationhood as much as it offered a solution to them. Not only did the German-speaking parts of the Austro-Hungarian Empire pose a reminder of the *großdeutsche* alternative that had been at the heart of much thinking about German nationhood, but challenges to the Prussian-dominated idea of a *kleindeutsche* nation-state existed also within the new *Kaiserreich*. The states that formed Imperial

Germany continued to exert considerable power as separate entities, both culturally and politically. Some of them – Bavaria, Baden, Württemberg and Saxony in particular – had fought with Austria against Prussia only five years before unification. A number of recent studies have explored regional and local Germany in the late nineteenth century and its relationships with the more distant vision called *Kaiserreich*. The picture that emerges shows a Germany that was, despite unification, deeply fragmented.[2]

This fragmentation was reinforced by a high degree of regional autonomy, especially where culture and education were concerned, and by confessional division. While Prussia and the German Emperor were staunchly Protestant, roughly a third of the Kaiser's subjects, mostly in the West and in the South, were Catholic. And although Catholicism in itself did not necessarily imply an opposition to the *kleindeutsche* nation-state, its loyalty to a supra-national institution was not easily reconciled with the Prussian-Protestant national project. What made matters worse was the *Kulturkampf*, a conflict that went beyond the question of what role the Catholic Church should play in German public life. As Helmut Walser Smith has argued, the *Kulturkampf* amounted to a 'strategy for nation-building', an attempt to impose by state means a Protestant-Prussian vision of 'the nation', which ultimately failed.[3] It left a divisive legacy for ideas of German nationhood, which had reverberations long after the conflict between the Prussian state and the Catholic Church had been laid to rest. In short, there were many reasons why, as Alon Confino has put it, 'in spite of the unification of the nation-state, German nationhood continued to exist as a patchwork of regions and states'.[4]

The idea of the nation was just as contentious an issue in the United Kingdom.[5] After the first Act of Union, new manifestations of 'Britishness' had developed alongside, and in competition with, English, Scottish and Welsh ideas of nationhood. Yet, the four 'sub-nations' had continued to exert a strong influence.[6] With the incorporation of Ireland into the United Kingdom and the expansion of the empire questions of nationhood were complicated further. Mounting Anglo-Irish tensions and the fierce debate about Home Rule meant that by the end of the century this was 'already a disunited kingdom'.[7] The conflict about Home Rule was the strongest factor, but by no means the only one. In parallel to the continuing crisis about the future of Ireland, the awakening of Scottish and Welsh nationalisms produced a growing articulation of uncertainty about British identity.[8] Notions of nationhood were similarly challenged from outside the United Kingdom. The empire, an important source of a shared vision of 'Britishness', seemed heavily stretched. The South African War, in particular, exposed the 'weary titan'.[9] It severely tested the imperial construct, and simultaneously galvanized particularist and anti-imperialist movements, especially in Ireland.[10] Threats to the British command of the sea also undermined senses of national identity, closely connected as they were to naval superiority in this period. All this meant that a strong sense of unresolvedness characterised the issue of nationhood in the United Kingdom of the late nineteenth century, a kingdom that was increasingly struggling to accommodate its four nations and define what their common purpose was. Moreover, this came at a time when the monarchy was still facing the effects of its transformation into an institution with limited political power and therefore a heightened need to convince national and international audiences of it continued relevance.

The Navy as Symbol

In both countries the navy and the sea were highly relevant for the processes in which these challenges were negotiated. The Royal Navy was one of the most important agents of national sentiment in the Victorian and Edwardian era. While the army was bound, by tradition as well as recruitment, to regional allegiances, the navy offered itself ideally for a British, unionist and imperial emphasis.[11] The Imperial Navy too presented a remarkably well-suited vehicle for a national emphasis. Unlike the army, which remained fragmented in structure, the navy was an imperial institution.[12] It unequivocally symbolised the new united Germany. As the Kaiser explained to Prime Minister Arthur Balfour in 1902 on a visit to the United Kingdom:

> *[…] the young German Empire needed institutions that embodied the unitary Reichs idea. The Navy was such an institution. The Kaiser was its only commander. The Germans from all counties rushed towards it, and it was a constant living example of the unity of the Reich. For this reason alone, the navy was necessary and found a warm supporter in His Majesty.*[13]

No wonder, then, that the fleet was paraded in an ever more spectacular fashion towards the end of the nineteenth century. Fleet reviews, launches of warships and a range of related rituals became more elaborate and professionally stage-managed, and they took place more often now and on a larger scale than at any time since the late eighteenth century.[14] The most conclusive way of illustrating this is by looking at the rising costs involved in this public theatre.

Between 1887 and 1911, expenditure on Spithead fleet reviews rose almost tenfold.[15] Alarmed by this rise, the Treasury engaged the Admiralty in a behind-the-scenes battle that continued until 1914. In June 1912 the Secretary of the Treasury wrote an internal memorandum about what he saw as the excessive costs of naval celebrations. The forthcoming 'parliamentary inspection' of the fleet at Spithead seemed particularly wasteful. He complained that the Admiralty had asked for 'an enormous sum for this "picture"'. 'I can conceive of no reason at all', he continued, 'why it should take place this year – which has neither a Coronation or Colonial Office Celebration'.[16] In a letter to the Admiralty, the Secretary of the Treasury objected strongly to the 'altogether excessive' use of funds.[17] Yet faced with pressure in the cabinet, the Chancellor of the Exchequer footed the bill for the unprecedented spectacle. Only in June 1914 did he succeed in reining in the Admiralty's expenditure on this public theatre. Sir John Bradbury, permanent secretary to the treasury, argued the case in a scathing memorandum. Referring to the planned fleet review and an elaborate scheme for the entertainment of special guests, MPs, and the press, he wrote:

> *The last picnic of this character was two years ago, the one before three years before that. It will no doubt soon become ... annual. As will be seen from the papers herewith these entertainments have given rise in the past to parliamentary criticism and in 1912 the Treasury attempted without success to cut down the amount accounted for.*[18]

The rise of the naval theatre caused similarly unprecedented expenditure in Germany. In November 1908, the German Imperial Audit Office reprimanded the naval leadership, lamenting the massive increase in the cost of launch celebrations. Originally, in 1876, when regulations for the launching of battleships had first been set up, these had been regarded as low-key affairs without much pomp or ceremony. Now, wrote the Audit Office, 'costs for such celebrations, which had formerly never been considerable' had reached 'very substantial heights'.[19] Local authorities struggled to keep costs at bay too, especially in Hamburg and Bremen. In 1909, the Bremen Senate topped all records with the cost of festivities created around the launching of HMS *Thüringen*. It put on a dinner for Prince Eitel Friedrich, the duchess of Saxony-Altenburg, and a host of 'high guests', costing a staggering 10,000 Marks. Realizing that such a sum was not to be found in the city's coffers, the burgomaster rushed an amendment through the Senate and the Bürgerschaft, the lower chamber. He did so by evoking paragraphs 49 to 51 of the Bremen constitution, extraordinary instruments reserved for moments of crisis that empowered the Senate to speed up the legislative process if the 'welfare of the state' (*das Staatswohl*)

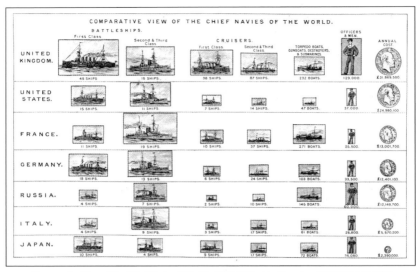

Comparative View of the Chief Navies of the World. Published in Harmsworth's Universal Atlas and Gazetteer, London, 1909. Courtesy Warwick Leadlay Gallery.

was under threat.[20] To keep all this from public scrutiny, the Senate obliged the members of the Bürgerschaft to treat the budget amendment as top secret and the official printer was instructed to destroy all references to the amendment.[21] These were remarkable financial and political manoeuvres, undertaken for the celebration of a warship. They demonstrated how far these rituals had come since the 1870s when naval ceremonial had aimed at avoiding 'all costly elaborations'.[22]

Given these figures, there is little doubt that the celebration of the navy was an arena in which monarchs and governments were busy projecting their power. Yet it would be wrong to explain the rise of this public theatre merely as an exercise in the 'invention of tradition'.[23] By the end of the century, monarchs and governments had to contend with new actors and new audiences that lay outside their direct control, yet had a key influence on the character of public ritual. Modern transport and tourism brought a dramatically widened radius of direct participation, turning naval ceremonies into mass events. Cinema, *Flottenschauspiele* and other forms of urban entertainment celebrated the navy and the sea in places that were distant from the coast. Yet the impact of mass culture and commercial initiatives went considerably beyond simply 'popularising' the navy. Popular culture represented new sources of power and participation. The 'opening' of private aspects of ritual to the public, the intrusion of mass participation into the core of royal ceremonies, the changing spatial character of naval rituals, the increasingly prominent role that 'the crowd' played in stagecraft and choreography: these were important new features brought about by mass media and popular culture. It is thus not simply government initiative or propaganda, but its intersection with the new forces of the 'age of the masses' that explains why the navy turned into such a powerful symbol in this period.

Icons of Modern Technology

But why, to come back to the initial quote by Michel Foucault, was the navy so well suited as a 'heterotopia'? Here it is necessary to look more closely at the cultural context in which the Edwardiand and Wilhelmine fleets operated. What was it that made battleships so 'strikingly impressive', as one journalist put it at the launch of the Dreadnought in 1906?[24] Crucial was their role as icons of modern technology. Like the zeppelin and aeroplane the modern fleet was at the forefront of technological advance, provoking admiration and curiosity. It embodied innovation and progress; it was an icon of the rationality and efficiency of the machine age. Moltke the younger, the German general, was captivated by the character of modern dreadnoughts as 'machine organisms':

> *A ship like this has its own brain and its own nerves, just like a human being. The electric connections control every limb; and the ship moves its gigantic guns to the right and the left, upwards and downwards, and starts its machines with the same ease with which we stretch a leg or move an arm.*[25]

Such fascination was not only for what these instruments of war could do, but how they did it, as high-tech organisms that operated with the overriding goals of efficiency and rationality. They mirrored important aspects of modernity in that they expressed a new relationship between individual and machine, offered new experiences of space and time, and involved new forms of risk.[26]

Importantly, the fleet was not only an icon of modern technology; it also made it possible to represent power in new ways. Perhaps the most impressive example of this is to be found in the searchlight displays that so many naval celebrations involved. The use of powerful light beams for public displays was not, as is often assumed, born out of the use of anti-aircraft searchlights. It was the fleet with its naval searchlights, which pioneered this public theatre in the decade before 1914. In a distinctly modern fashion, the

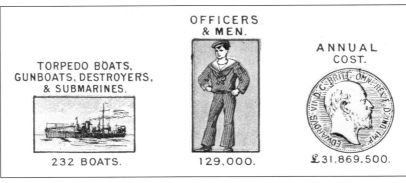

OFFICERS
& MEN.

TORPEDO BOATS,
GUNBOATS, DESTROYERS,
& SUBMARINES.

ANNUAL
COST.

232 BOATS.

129,000.

£31,869,500.

Comparative View of the Chief Navies of the World. Published in Harmsworth's Universal Atlas and Gazetteer, London, 1909. (Detail: Annual British expenditure). Courtesy Warwick Leadlay Gallery.

representation of technology and power merged in these light displays. This was all the more effective since it coincided with innovations in the reproduction of images, in particular moving images. Photography and film captured the monsters of steel and might and reinforced their visual impact.[27]

Yet the navies in both countries projected not only a striking imagery of technology, novelty and power. They also evoked nostalgic or romanticised notions about adventure, 'overseas' and man's battle with nature. In popular culture they appeared as instruments of imagined chivalry and tradition as much as a high-tech symbols of efficiency and progress. Indeed, in its public representation and popular appropriation, the navy seemed to reconcile the contradictions and challenges that modern technology brought about. What made it so fascinating was that it brought together the new feasibilities with older ideas of adventure, heroism and chivalry. It combined the traditional 'story of the sea' with the unprecedented possibilities offered by new technology.

What made this all the more appealing was that this spectacle of technology and power could be experienced in an entertaining fashion. Audiences could 'play the naval game' in a range of activities in which the representation of power and technology, adventure and risk, came together with fun and amusement. Fleet reviews and mock battles in particular afforded the opportunity to watch representations of power, violence and battle as entertainment. Here, rivalry and antagonism could be performed in isolation from the complexities of international affairs and the secret diplomacy of cabinets and courts. This game was so fascinating precisely because it brought together play and war. It allowed audiences to approach violence and aggression, otherwise supposed to be 'serious', as something playful and entertaining. At its heart was the continuous ambiguity between *Spiel* and *Ernst*, between play and seriousness. It was the performative 'as if', the opportunity to experience conflict while not having to engage with its reality that made the naval game so appealing: in this theatre you could play war without having to want it.[28]

A Circumstance of Male Pomp

The symbolic value of the Wilhelmine and Edwardian fleets was further heightened by strongly gendered associations. Official representation stressed that the working of this machinery of steel and technology was a male prerogative. The 'one vast machine' that was the navy was a realm of masculinity in which 'guns and men' came together.[29] Ships and men alike were to show bravery, discipline, stamina, willpower and the readiness to die for the nation. In Wilhelmine Germany the gendered representation of the navy went further than in Britain. A remarkable demarcation between men and women existed at public rituals such as warship launches, a demarcation that was not only informed by ideas about separate gender spheres, but also about the divide between military and civilian society. The separation of 'the ladies' from the male actors and special guests, who were in the vast majority, was minutely planned and strictly adhered to, both at government and private yards.[30] It was a key mechanism by which the Wilhelmine naval theatre constructed the 'the nation' along gender lines. While this demonstrative demarcation between men and women was a uniquely Wilhelmine phenomenon, the naval theatre projected a strongly gendered image of 'the nation' in both countries. At a time when traditional gender images were profoundly contested, this celebrated the 'hegemonic masculinity' that was expressed in the navy.[31]

No wonder, then, that some could not resist ridiculing the navy as a prime symbol of male pomp. In February 1910 a party of six Bloomsbury literati, amongst them Virginia Woolf, announced themselves to the Commander of the Home Fleet by telegram as 'Prince Makalen of Abbysinia [sic] and suite'.[32] Disguised with brown face powder and false beards, they were promptly received with royal honours and shown all over the *Dreadnought*, the flagship of Admiral Sir William May. As the Admiralty's internal report put it, the officers attending 'never detected anything' about the party that 'consisted of four dark skinned persons in Oriental costumes and two Europeans'.[33] The press had a field day when the story was revealed, while at the Admiralty 'the question of what should be done about that wretched hoax was still a matter of perplexity', as its Secretary admitted in a private letter to Admiral May ten days later.[34]

What made the incident so 'wretched' is explained by the gender politics involved.[35] The Admiralty were particularly incensed at the inclusion of a cross-dressed woman. A decision was taken that the males of the group should be 'beaten' by naval officers. In the end, only two 'beatings' took place – two male hoaxers were briefly abducted by naval officers and taken to secluded spots. But as it turned out, the beating was no more than a ceremonial tap on the bottom with a cane – apparently just enough to avenge the honour of the navy. The farce of these events clearly made a deep impact on Virginia Woolf, vividly bringing home to her the 'ludicrous points of honour and formalised revenges' of homosocial institutions such as the navy. It apparently left her permanently sensitive to the 'masculine absurdities' of the establishment.[36] As Quentin Bell put it, 'she came out of it with a new sense of the brutality and silliness of men.'[37]

The Great Naval Game

In short, the navy and the sea were powerful cultural symbols that merged some of the most important sources of Wilhelmine and Edwardian self-understanding: technology, gender and war, as well as monarchy, empire and 'the nation'. Importantly, all of this took place in an arena that was at once national and international. 'The other' was, directly or indirectly, always present in the public staging of the fleet. Not only because of the Anglo-German naval race itself, but more generally because of the culture of deterrence that unfolded in this period. Creating an image, a visual and emotional impression of threat was critical. For intimidation to work, it had to be felt, the source of threat had to be shown and exercised. For Sir John Fisher, impressing and intimidating were what naval strategy in the Dreadnought era was all about. In a 1903 memorandum he said boldly: 'The word intimidate is used since the history of the world points to intimidation being the greatest safeguard against hostile operations'.[38] There was therefore a strong need for the display of deterrence. The public staging of the fleet and the celebration of the sea catered to this need, emphasising that this was a national as much as an international symbol.

It is thus the coming together of intensely political and cultural contexts that explains best why the Wilhelmine and Edwardian navies turned into such potent symbols. The intersection of government initiative with voluntary and commercial agendas; the rapid rise of mass media, leisure and entertainment; the attractiveness of the naval stage for the projection of local, regional, national and imperial loyalties; the curious combination of modern and traditional themes offered by the fleet as an instrument that acted at once as the pioneer of technological advance and as an arbiter of the nation's past; finally its obvious role in international rivalry and the Anglo-German antagonism: these are the main factors that explain the unique symbolic value that the Imperial and Royal Navy had in this period.

---

[1] Michel Foucault, 'Of Other Spaces', *Diacritics*, 16 (1986), 25-27.

[2] Celia Applegate, *A Nation of Provincials: The German Idea of Heimat* (Berkeley: University of California Press, 1990); Alon Confino, *The Nation as a Local Metaphor: Württemberg, Imperial Germany, and National Memory, 1871-1918* (Chapel Hill: University of North Carolina Press, 1997); Abigail Green, *Fatherlands: State-Building and Nationhood in Nineteenth-Century Germany* (Cambridge: Cambridge University Press, 2001).

[3] Helmut Walser Smith, *German Nationalism and Religious Conflict: Culture, Ideology, Politics, 1870-1914* (Princeton: Princeton University Press, 1995), p. 14.

[4] Confino, *The Nation as a Local Metaphor*, p. 14.

[5] J. G. A. Pocock, 'British History: A Plea for a New Subject', *Journal of Modern History*, 47 (1975), pp. 601-28; Hugh Kearny, *The British Isles: A History of Four Nations* (Cambridge: Cambridge University Press, 1989); J. C. D. Clark, 'English History's Forgotten Context: Scotland, Ireland, Wales', *Historical Journal*, 32 (1989), pp. 211-28.

[6] Linda Colley, *Britons: Forging the Nation, 1707-1837* (New Haven: Yale University Press, 1992); Kearny, *British Isles*, pp. 230–62; Keith Robbins, *Great Britain: Identities, Institutions and the Idea of Britishness* (London: Longman, 1998), pp. 262–94; Adrian Hastings, *The Construction of Nationhood: Ethnicity, Religion and Nationalism* (Cambridge: Cambridge University Press, 1997), pp. 1–95.

[7] Peter Clarke, *Hope and Glory: Britain 1900-1990* (London: Harmondsworth, 1996), p. 1.

[8] Kearny, *British Isles*, ch. 10; John S. Ellis, 'Reconciling the Celt: British National Identity, Empire, and the 1911 Investiture of the Prince of Wales', *Journal of British Studies*, 37 (1998), pp. 391-419; Paul Readman, 'The Place of the Past in English Culture c.1890-1914', *Past & Present*, 186 (2005), pp. 147-99. For a range of other responses, see also Paul Ward, *Britishness Since 1870* (London: Routledge, 2004); Simon Dentith, *Epic and Empire in Nineteenth-Century Britain* (Cambridge: Cambridge University Press, 2006); Christopher Harvie, *A Floating Commonwealth: Politics, Culture and Technology on Britain's Atlantic Coast, 1860-1930* (Oxford: Oxford University Press, 2008); Marjorie Morgan, *National Identities and Travel in Victorian Britain* (Basingstoke: Palgrave, 2001); Steve Attridge, *Nationalism, Imperialism and Identity in Late Victorian Culture: Civil and Military Worlds* (New York: Palgrave Macmillan, 2003); Jonathan Parry, *The Politics of Patriotism: English Liberalism, National Identity and Europe, 1830-1886* (Cambridge: Cambridge University Press, 2006); Duncan Bell, *The Idea of Greater Britain: Empire and the Future World Order, 1860-1900* (Princeton: Princeton University Press, 2007).

[9] Joseph Chamberlain coined the phrase of the 'weary titan' staggering 'under the vast orb of its fate' at the colonial conference in 1902; see James L. Garvin and Julian Amery, *The Life of Joseph Chamberlain* (London: Macmillain, 1969), v, p. 30. The financial and military weakness that the war uncovered is analysed in detail by Aaron L. Friedberg, *The Weary Titan: Britain and the Experience of Relative Decline, 1895-1905* (Princeton: Princeton University Press, 1988).

[10] Donal Lowry, '"The Boers were the Beginning of the End"?: The Wider Impact of the South African War', in *The South African War Reappraised*, edited by Donal Lowry (Manchester: Manchester University Press, 2000), pp. 231-36; Geoffrey Searle, '"National Efficiency" and

the "Lessons" of the War', in *The Impact of the South African War*, edited by David Omissi and Andrew S. Thompson (Basingstoke: Palgrave, 2002), pp. 194-211.

[11] Colin Matthew has stressed this point in his introduction to the *Short Oxford History of the British Isles: The Nineteenth Century* (Oxford: Oxford University Press, 2000), p. 22. See also Max Jones, *The Last Great Quest: Captain Scott's Antarctic Sacrifice* (Oxford: Oxford University Press, 2003), ch. 6.

[12] For the regionally fragmented character of the German army see Stig Förster, 'The Armed Forces and Military Planning', in *Imperial Germany: A Historiographical Companion*, edited by Roger Chickering (Westport: Greenwood Press, 1996), pp. 454-88, here 473.

[13] Politisches Archiv des Auswärtigem Amtes, Berlin, R 5772: Metternich to Bülow, 9 November 1902.

[14] For a detailed account see Jan Rüger, *The Great Naval Game: Britain and Germany in the Age of Empire* (Cambridge: Cambridge University Press, 2007), ch. 1.

[15] In 1887 the Admiralty footed a bill of £3,500 for the accommodation and entertainment of visitors and an additional, unspecified amount for illuminations and fireworks. The National Archives, Kew (hereafter TNA), ADM 1/6871: Treasury to Admiralty, 9 June 1887). By 1911 the expenses had risen to a record £31,800. This included the entertainment of guests, the hire of vessels, messing on board steamers, and extra pay for police officers, but excluded the illumination of the fleet, the cost of which was carefully distributed across a labyrinth of naval votes, heads, subheads, and local dockyard accounts (TNA, ADM 1/8230: Director of Stores to Controller, 17 May 1911; Ibid., Memorandum by Accountant General, 23 May 1911; Ibid., Admiral Superintendent of Portsmouth Dockyard to Controller of the Navy, 19 Septtember 1911; Ibid., Controller of the Navy to Portsmouth Dockyard, 3 May 1912).

[16] TNA, T 1/11642: Minutes, 15 June 1912.

[17] TNA, ADM 1/8317: Secretary of the Treasury to Secretary of the Admiralty, 17 June 1912; ibid. Secretary of the Admiralty to Secretary of the Treasury, 20 June 1912.

[18] TNA, T 1/11642: Minute by Sir John Bradbury, 26 June 1914. See also ibid. Bradbury to Secretary of the Admiralty, 3 July 1914.

[19] Bundesarchiv-Militärarchiv, Freiburg, RM 3/118, fos. 99–100: Imperial Audit Office to State Secretary of the Imperial Treasury, 17 October 1908.

[20] *Verfassung der Freien Hansestadt Bremen* (Bremen: Schunemann, 1854), 8–9.

[21] Staatsarchiv (hereafter StA) Bremen, 3-B.16, fo. 20: Sonderprotokoll. Vertraulich. Mitteilung des Senats vom 5.11.1909. Stapellauf des Linienschiffes 'Ersatz Beowulf'; ibid., 20a: Senatssekretär an die Carl Schünemannsche Druckerei, 6 November 1909, streng geheim.

[22] *Marineverordnungsblatt*, 7 (1876), 15.

[23] Eric Hobsbawm, 'Mass-Producing Traditions: Europe, 1870-1914', in *The Invention of Tradition*, edited by Eric Hobsbawm and Terence Ranger (Cambridge: Cambridge University Press, 1983), pp. 263-308; David Cannadine, 'The Context, Performance and Meaning of Ritual: The British Monarchy and the "Invention of Tradition", c.1820-1977', in *The Invention of Tradition*, pp. 101-164.

[24] *Portsmouth Evening News*, 10 February 1906.

[25] Helmuth von Moltke, *Erinnerungen, Briefe, Dokumente, 1877-1916*, edited by Eliza von Motke (Stuttgart: Der Kommende Tag A-G Verlag, 1922), p. 357 (22 July 1910).

[26] For this context see Stephen Kern, *The Culture of Time and Space 1880-1918* (London: Weidenfeld and Nicolson, 1983); Bernhard Rieger, *Technology and the Culture of Modernity in Britain and Germany, 1890–1945* (Cambridge: Cambridge University Press, 2005) and Carolyn Marvin, *When Old Technologies Were New: Thinking About Electric Communication in the Late Nineteenth Century* (Oxford: Oxford University Press, 1988).

27 For an analysis of the relationship between film and the 'modern wonders' of technology see Rieger, *Technology and the Culture of Modernity*, ch. 4.

28 Johan Huizinga, *Homo Ludens: A Study in the Play-Elements in Culture* (London: Maurice Temple Smith, 1980), ch. 5; Victor Turner, *From Ritual to Theatre: The Human Seriousness of Play* (New York: Performing Arts Journal Publications, 1982); Richard Schechner, *Essays on Performance Theory, 1970-1976* (New York: Drama Book Specialists), pp. 98-103. See also the section on theatricality and war games in ch. 2.

29 *Daily Express*, 19 July 1909; *Official Programme of the Coronation Review, Spithead, June 24th, 1911: All About the Ships: All About the Guns and Men* (London: Gale and Polden, 1911).

30 For a detailed account see Rüger, *Great Naval Game*, ch. 4.

31 John Tosh, 'Hegemonic Masculinity and the History of Gender', in *Masculinities in Politics and War: Gendering Modern History*, edited by Stefan Dudink, Karen Hagemann and John Tosh (Manchester: Manchester University Press, 2004), pp. 41-60. For an illuminative case study see Lucy Delap, '"Thus Does Man Prove His Fitness to Be the Master of Things": Shipwrecks, Chivalry and Masculinities in Nineteenth and Twentieth-Century Britain', *Cultural and Social History* 3, (2006), pp. 45-74. On the wider challenges to traditional gender roles, see Sally Ledger, 'The New Woman and the Crisis of Victorianism', in *Cultural Politics at the Fin de Siècle*, edited by Sally Ledger and Scott McCracken (Cambridge: Cambridge University Press, 1995), pp. 22-44; Leonore Davidoff, *Worlds Between: Historical Perspectives on Gender and Class* (Cambridge: Cambridge University Press, 1995); *Manful Assertions: Masculinities in Britain Since 1800*, edited by Michael Roper and John Tosh (London: Routledge, 1991).

32 TNA, ADM 1/8192: Telegram purporting to be from Sir Charles Hardinge, Foreign Office, but sent by Horace Cole, to Commander-in-Chief Home Fleet, 7 February 1910.

33 TNA, ADM 1/8192: Admiral Sir William May to Secretary of the Admiralty, 17 February 1910, confidential.

34 TNA, ADM 1/8192: W. Graham Greene, Secretary of the Admiralty, to Admiral Sir William May, 16 February 1910, private. For an account by one of the participants see Adrian Stephen, *The 'Dreadnought' Hoax* (London: L and V Woolf, 1936) and for a flavour of the press coverage: *Daily Express*, 12 February 1910, front page: 'Amazing Naval Hoax: Sham Abyssinian Princes Visit the Dreadnought: Bogus Order'; *Globe*, 12 February 1910: 'Bogus "Princes" on the Dreadnought' and *Daily Mirror*, 16 February 1910.

35 For an excellent analysis see Lucy Delap, 'The Woman's Dreadnought: Maritime Symbolism in Edwardian Gender Politics', in *The Dreadnought and the Edwardian Age*, edited by Robert Blyth, Andrew Lambert and Jan Rüger (Aldershot: Ashgate, 2009).

36 Adrian Stephen, *The Dreadnought Hoax*, p. 16.

37 Quentin Bell, *Virginia Woolf: A Biography* (London: Hogarth Press, 1972), p. 52.

38 TNA, ADM 116/942, appendix A. For Fisher's interest in displays of deterrence compare *Fear God and Dread Nought: The Correspondence of Admiral of the Fleet Lord Fisher of Kilverstone*, edited by Arthur J. Marder (London: Cape, 1952), i, p. 278; Jon Tetsuro Sumida, *In Defence of Naval Supremacy: Finance, Technology and British Naval Policy, 1889-1914* (London: Routledge, 1993), p. 259; and Nicholas Lambert, *Sir John Fisher's Naval Revolution* (Columbia: University of South Carolina Press, 1999), pp. 73-94.

Editors' Note: Jan Rüger's fine book *The Great Naval Game: Britain and Germany in the Age of Empire* has recently been published in paperback by Cambridge University Press.

The Cecil Isaacson Lecture, 2009

Riot and Rap – The 1743 Portsmouth Dockyard Strike: Management Failure or Excess of Duty?[1]

Ann Coats

> *By the last Post, I acquainted you with the irregular Proceedings of the Shipwrights, &c:[a] yester Morning; between which time, and Noon, they had drank very freely, and were so Resolute that many of the People, who were inclinable and willing to come to their Duty, at ½ past 1 of the Clock, were prevented, by the most forward in this Riot; who appear, to be Principally Servants. As there was no possibility of appeasing them, I sent to the Mayor of Portsmouth, who came and Order'd the Riot Act to be Read; notwithstanding which, it was a long time, before they dispersed. This morning they assembled again, and behave in the same Riotous manner; they'l not permit any of the People to come to their Duty, nor are they to be prevailed on.[2]*

Striking shipwrights closed Portsmouth Dockyard for ten days in January 1743. Trained as a naval commander to use his initiative, Resident Commissioner Richard Hughes was in charge of one of the largest industrial sites in Western Europe, in wartime, at a busy time of year. Portsmouth Dockyard was the largest of the six, with 1,943 employees out of the total dockyard workforce of 7,952.[3] His actions to improve productivity precipitated the strike, civil powers were undefined and his actions drew Admiralty criticism. Like a mutiny, a strike exposes the dynamics of management. ADM106 Navy Board In-Letters contain detailed reports of events in Portsmouth Dockyard the first year of the war, the 1743 strike and its conclusion. They also record workforce language, which is encountered rarely elsewhere, apart from legal depositions. 'Riot' was applied to a strike or actions or disturbances against authority; 'Rap' was a smart blow of punishment.[4]

War meant more business for both navy and dockyards. It also gave the dockyard workforce more bargaining power. The start of the 1739 War of

Jenkins' Ear (1739-43), which continued into the War of Austrian Succession (1742-48), led to a spate of strikes in all the dockyards.[5] The 1743 Portsmouth strike was, however, caused by Hughes's campaign of stopping two days' wages for one day's absence during 1742. The right to time off work depended on status. Dockyard officers could have leave for ill health or 'private business'. In 1746 the lowest ranking dockyard officer, Porter William Woodrow, obtained leave from Hughes for his 'Privet affairs' and while in London requested another fortnight's leave from the Navy Board, which was granted.[6] But the workforce could not be absent without paying beforehand in fees for permission, or afterwards in fines.

Richard Hughes 1674-1756.
Courtesy Robin Wager.

Portsmouth Dockyard in the Eighteenth Century

In 1729 Captain Stephen Martin described Portsmouth harbour as 'certainly one of the finest in the world, safe and commodious for shipping, and secure against an enemy.' He asserted that it 'contains near one-third of the British navy, and is so conveniently situated for fleets or convoys to annoy the enemy and protect our trade.'[7] According to Dan Baugh, 'In the war of 1739-1748 Portsmouth was plainly the most important of the dockyards.' In the preceding twenty-five years its facilities had been enlarged and streamlined, and its officers claimed they could maintain two-thirds of the fleet.[8] By 1747 Hughes considered that 'for every Ship that goes out of the Harbour, I think, two others come in.'[9]

Richard Hughes's naval service between 1688 and 1729 was impressive.[10] In 1729 he became Commissioner for Portsmouth Dockyard.[11] For Baugh, 'Portsmouth yard was unmistakably under the command of its vigorous Commissioner.'[12] Confrontation with naval officers and the Admiralty was implicit. The process of docking and undocking could only occur at spring tides and prior unrigging and unloading of ships' guns was necessary so that ships sat higher in the water for docking.[13] However, incoming sea officers often left their ships without supervising this process adequately, and were often reluctant to leave harbour when their ships were ready.[14] Docking was also delayed because ships were not brought earlier into harbour for seamen to assist in the unrigging, but kept at Spithead for fear of their desertion. Hughes's 'line managers' were the other Navy Board Commissioners; above them was the Admiralty Board; and in Portsmouth were the Mayor, JPs, the navy and army.

In the six months of January-June 1740 Hughes's correspondence covered coals for the smithery, the difficulty of working with New England tar; contracts for POWs, small beer, treenails, oars, shovels, Portland stone and limestone; the accidental death of horses belonging to the yard teams, naval deserters, complaints about *Royal William's* purser, and daily coordination of the dockyard officers.[15]

Number of Artificers employed in each of His Majesties Yards, January 1742[3]. Courtesy the National Archive, ADM49/159.

Portsmouth officers aimed to improve productivity at the beginning of the war. On 24 January 1740 the Master Shipwright and his Assistants requested an increased allowance of apprentices to make up the complement of shipwrights building the 'new Fortysix' ordered in August 1739. They were still eighteen short, and:

it would be an Advantage to the Service if as many Servants were Enter'd, to Shipwrights, as the Establishment of the Navy allows off, when our Complement of Men is full, which would be Eighteen in Number, who would soon earn more than their Wages, & therefore more Workmen be rais'd of our Own for his Majesties Service, as well as enable us to give the deserving Men the Encouragement of Servants.[16]

This was the traditional way of 'breeding up' new shipwrights. It was also the only means, apart from overtime, of retaining shipwrights in the yard rather than losing them to private shipbuilders. Shipwright pay rates of 2s 1d a day could not be raised without an act of Parliament, but having an apprentice increased a shipwright's income, as he received his pay for seven years.[17] Apprentice pay rates rose from 14d a day to 22d a day over seven years.[18] They could also do much of the hard physical work.

In February 1740 Hughes forwarded another proposal of the Master Shipwright, Joseph Allin, to make the most of winter daylight:

for the quicker dispatch of the Ships fitting out at this Port, that the Workmen Employ'd on them, should come to their Duty, at one of the Clock P: M... Half an Hour's Day Light, may be improved, to the Advantage of the Crown, and more Work be performed, than in double that time, by Candle Light.[19]

At the time Hughes had sixteen ships at Spithead and ten in the harbour or dock.[20] A serious problem was that increased wartime dockyard stores tempted workers who knew there was a ready market for all items in private yards. On 10 February 1740 Hughes reported that:

John Heaton, a Riggers Labourer belonging to this His Majesties Yard, was detected, on Saturday the 2.d Instant, by William Bucket Warder, and John Jennings Watchman, upon his returning from his Duty, just as he was going to pass the Gate, with Three Old iron Bolts, Secreted under his Coat, which he intended to Embezzle.[21]

Embezzlement involves taking or misusing someone else's money or goods in violation of trust or duty. Hughes directed that Heaton be held for trial in Portsmouth Sessions:

'tis expected he will receive Corporal Punishment, for his Offence, which will have a greater influence on, and may deter such Villains,

(if such there be), as now belong to the Yard, and may hereafter attempt to Embezle His Majesties Stores, especially, as it will be inflicted in the Place, where the Crime was committed, and before all the workmen Employ'd in the Service.[22]

The bolts weighed 'ab:t Ten Pounds…of the Value of Ten Pence'.[23] William Buckett gave evidence that 'on Saturday last in the Afternoon' he saw Heaton coming out of the Dockyard and observed his coat 'to stick out at the Side bigger than usuall & suspecting he had something tied under it he stopt him'. Buckett and Scavenger John Jennings 'found in the Side of his Coat the Three old Iron Bolts' and believed 'he would have carryed the Same out of the s.d Dock if he had not been stopt ... for that they were concealed under his Coat in a clandestine Manner'.[24] Heaton admitted to the Mayor both the offence and his intention to sell the bolts.[25] On 25 April 1740 the Portsea solicitor, George Augustus Prosser, informed Hughes that Heaton had been convicted at the Sessions the day before, commenting:

As the Punishment for these Offences, the more Publikly 'tis inflicted may have probably the greater effect; I therefore moved the Court that the Offender's Sentence might be to have the three Bolts hung about his Neck and that he might be Whipt at the Dock Gates just as the Artificers were coming from Work to the end that those amongst them as have such an Ungratefull turn of Mind may be deterr'd from future Practices of this Kind by the Example before them; w:^{ch} Punishment will be Executed at a Cart's Tail Exactly at 12 o' clock to Morrow.[26]

On 5 June 1740 Hughes suggested alterations to the 1658 Double Dock:

… as there is at High Water, always Two foot Water less in the Double Dock, than there is in the Great Dock; I can't help thinking, if the former was to be Divided in the Middle, with Gates, to be in Three parts, as they were formerly made, (which in my Opinion may be done, with very little Expence to the Crown) it wou'd be attended with an Advantage, and be of great Service: because, the Fore part of the said Dock, may then be applied, to make good the Works of all such Ships, as it will be capable of receiving, and may require a considerable Repair; the after part may then be kept Open; and will serve to Clean &c:ᵃ those that shall be Order'd, from Sixty Guns downwards.[27]

The Navy Board ordered Portsmouth officers to comment and give 'an Estimate of the Charge' and specify the smallest class of ship that could go

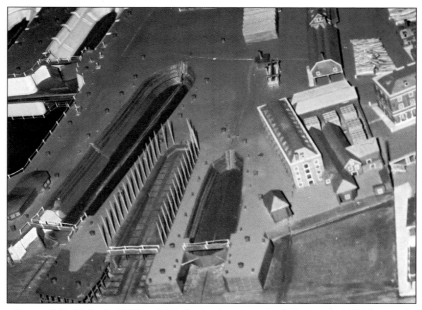

Portsmouth Double Dock of 1658 on the left showing the narrower head. Photograph of 1774 Portsmouth Dockyard Model, National Maritime Museum. Courtesy the Author.

into the Dock and its head. Also, 'whether if Gates should ever bee found Usefull it will be advisable to putt them up 'till the Dock is Lengthened At the head, which has long been designed to be done, as soon as the North Dock is Compleated.'[28] Hughes was clearly thinking proactively to maximize his facilities and increase productivity. Unfortunately he was hindered in completing repairs on the North Dock because he was waiting for limestone from Plymouth.

1743 Strike

The 1743 strike occurred in the winter period, when although work was hindered by short days and inclement weather, fewer ships at sea meant that more ships were being repaired. Portsmouth employees in January 1743 numbered 1,943, whereas in June 1743 there were 1,911 and in July, 1,924.[29] The men were working part of their tides[30] (overtime) in their dinner break to make the most of daylight[31] and Hughes had fined them two days' wages for every call missed or day absent. His view was that:

> *Many of the workmen, labourers and others, assume to themselves an unaccountable liberty of leaving the works of the Yard, to follow their own inclinations of assisting merchant builders and harvesting as well as other sorts of labour, for the prospect of some little advantage to their wages,....without considering the constancy of their employ here, or whether the service can spare them or indeed asking leave of me or their proper officers.*[32]

Others dealing with the strike were Sir Charles Hardy, Commander in Chief, Portsmouth burgess and MP;[33] Mayor William Rickman, merchant and dockyard contractor of beer and Portland stone and agent for Spanish prisoners-of-war,[34] and Colonel Edmondston who brought in extra soldiers. The Navy Board, Board of Admiralty and Secretary for War were also involved. The Mayor and 'thriving, prosperous Corporation'[35] lived in Portsmouth, separated from the dockyard by the Millpond, now the United Services Ground. Hughes lived in the middle of the yard in the Commissioner's House that lay north of the long Ropehouse. The Naval Academy was and is in the south-east corner. Defoe wrote in 1724-5:

> *These docks and yards are now like a town by themselves, and are a kind of marine corporation, or a government of their own kind within themselves; there being particular large rows of dwellings, built at the public charge, within the new works, for all the principal officers of the place.*[36]

Portsmouth Dockyard was enclosed to the east and south by Portsmouth Common (later named Portsea) where dockyard housing had begun in the 1690s. It was originally part of Portsmouth's field system. Its tenous borough and parish governance was controlled by the largest occupational group, the shipwrights. By the eighteenth century the workforce lived in Portsea or across the harbour in Gosport. To supplement their work in the dockyard they had been accustomed for decades to working short term contracts in private yards (which paid higher wages in wartime) and working in the fields which occupied most of Portsea Island at harvest-time.[37] The number of Portsea county freeholder voters already outstripped Portsmouth's by 1713: 605 to 580.[38] By 1725 16 streets, containing 422 houses, had been built in Portsea.[39] In 1743 1,943 men worked in the yard, 833 of them shipwrights, the largest single occupational group.

The strike began on Friday 31 December 1742. Hughes reported that 'the Service is at a stand', warning that 'should they (at this time) gain their Point,

I apprehend, there will be no such thing as Discipline, or even a possibility of carrying on the Service, for the future: for, in such Case, they must, and always will be Masters'. On Saturday 1 January 1743 the 'Shipwrights, &c:ᵃ, continued very Riotous all day'. One rioter had been taken, but three shipwrights, Henry Bennett, George Shepherd and Samuel Sheffield, and caulker Richard Griley 'forc'd into the Yard... & Rescu'd the Person that was in Custody'. Hughes had the 'Names of Three of the Principals concerned therein; as well as a 'List of some of the forward

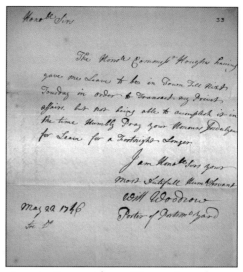

Letter from Portsmouth Porter William Woodrow requesting further leave, 22 May 1746. Courtesy the National Archive, ADM 106/1023, fo. 33.

Mutineers, who dispersed about 11 of the Clock last night, and remain very quite this Day'.⁴⁰ In the evening they threatened the men who had been working:

> ... as they went out of the Wicket; (for the Great Gates they had Barricaded up with two Boats, (one of them being Nail'd to the Gates) & a Waggon Load of Hay; all w:ᶜʰ we have Cleared this Morning) to prevent any mischief, they were kept all Night in the Yard, & as the poor Fellows were Employd, without Victuals, all day on the Woolwich, (tho' it Raind a great part of it) I wrote to Capt:ⁿ Smith of the Pr:ˢ Mary for two Bags of bread, & a Quantity of Cheese, for their Sustenance: for the Rioters had placd Posseys at Gosport, the Point, Dock Gates, & the New Buildings, to attack them, should they go out of the Yard, or Land at any of those places.⁴¹

Sir Charles Hardy related graphically to Thomas Corbett, Secretary to the Admiralty, how on the same night, at about 11 o'clock, carpenters 'begun to knock at the Gate as if they intended to break it open, but hearing the Marines Bayonets rattle in the Muzles of their peices they retir'd'. On Sunday 2 January he described how, one quarterman,⁴² Mr. Varlo:

> *... attempted himself this morning at the head of some of the Shipwrights, to the Number of a hundred and fifty, to get into the Dock to work; one of the Rioters who he knew not clap'd a pistoll to him & told him if he valued his Life, or Family, he had best desist from any further Attempt, and he was Oblig'd to retire.*[43]

He also reported that Mr. Varlo 'beleives there are four hundred of the Rioters arm'd with Pistols, musquetts, axes, & Addices' and that 'at least Fifty Country ffellows at the Dock gates; with long staffs had joyn'd the Rioters'. He heard them say 'there would be five hundred more joyn them; and had sworn not to disperse 'till the workmen had Justice done them.'[44] Possibly Varlo recognized his assailant, but as a senior shipwright in charge of twenty others he was only one step up from them and would not risk harming his family. Hardy ordered sixty-two marines from Spithead to the Yard to protect the Magazines.

On Monday 3 January Hughes consulted the Mayor, who read a Navy Board Proclamation:

> *... but while it was reading, they were so Outrageous, that with much difficulty the Gent:^{n} returned to the Town, so that it had no Effect; for they still continue in their Tumultious Behaviour, to so great a degree, that they not only oppose all Persons, that would come into the Yard, but has likewise provided themselves with Arms; and are so Obstinate they will not give Ear to the Propositions made by me & S:^{r} Cha:s Hardy: w:^{ch} was, that they should disperse themselves, and depute any Persons to lay their Grievances before me, in Order (if in my Power) to Redress them, but had no Effect.*[45]

Hardy reported 'There cannot be less than Five hund:^{d} men without the yard Gate half drunk.'[46]

The Board of Admiralty considered the 1715 Riot Act the solution to the problem.[47] From 3 January they repeatedly urged Hardy to call upon the Mayor to read it 'and if they do not disperse in the time prescribed by Parliament, you are to put in execution the Powers given by that act, which they recommend to you to peruse'.[48] But the Mayor and Justices told Hughes and Hardy 'they would not order the troops to fire', and Hughes considered he had no 'authority to order the troops to fire without the yard except the rioters had made an attack upon his Majesty's dock'. Hardy and Hughes reported to the Admiralty the doubts of the Mayor and Justices, who believed 'the act did not empower either mayor, or Justice of the peace, to order the Military Forces to Fire upon the Rioters; only to command their Assistance, in seizing some of them; and leave the Officers of the Troops to act as they thought proper.'[49]

However, 'Their Lordships' replied that they could see no 'doubt about the way of putting that act in Execution, which must necessarily be left to the discretion of the Civil and Military Power, to act as the exigences of the Case shall require.'[50] The Secretary for War, Sir William Yonge, was informed of the situation on 4 January because the Yard was 'totally at a stand'. His authorisation was required to call out the Portsmouth Garrison and send for Colonel Cholmondley's regiment from Salisbury.[51]

On 4 January some shipwrights sent a petition setting out their grievances, but Hughes was unreceptive:

> ... *several of them have behaved in such a Mutinous daring Insolent manner I realy think one or more of the Principal Agressors shou'd be Prosecuted with the utmost severity of the Law and some others Discharg'd, & not on any Account Entertaind in this or any other of his Maj:^ties Yards, because they will always expect their Demands to be Complied with they will Act in all respects just as they please without any Comptrol & every thing that happens in the future if it is not Consonant to their own Sentiments will be Attended with Riots, Mobs & Disturbances Proceedings that greatly tend to the Prejudice of his Maj:^ties Service.*[52]

He reported that 'out of the Number but 52 came into the Yard of Shipw:^ts & Caulkers & 158 of the other People Riggers, Masons &c:^a which (as all the works are still at a stand) I send by Express.' The shipwrights' petition complained if they were 'requiring or Neglecting a day for their Private Business or should lose their Call by any means whatever' they lost two day's pay, and that:

> ... *when Your Petitioners apply for Relief the Master Shipwright tells your Petitioners that he will make them as humble as Doggs and glad to work for Eighteen Pence a day which great Oppressions to Your Petitioners will render them unable to Support their Families and Oblige Your Petitioners to seek their Bread in other Places.*[53]

Hughes had targeted and penalised workers who took other jobs.[54] This was confirmed by shipwright William Yateman on 29 January. At a suggestion that they should have approached Commissioner Hughes for redress of their grievances before rioting, 'the said Alexander Pullen replied, why, will you be such Fools? do you think he does not (meaning the Commissioner) know, what the Builder has done?'[55] The Builder (Master Shipwright) also stopped two days' pay for one day's absence.

The shipwrights ended their petition by requesting that 'in Case they should Lose their first Call they may not lose their Extra but may be allowed a Second Call and go to work' and prayed 'that no Shipwright might be reduced to a Labourer', or be 'Injured on Account of the late Disturbance', in return for agreeing to go back to work. The Navy Board asked Hughes 'to Enquire into the allegations of the Petition'[56] and to investigate another petition from workmen 'not concerned in the present Riot, representing the hardships they are under from the expence they are put to, when they apply for leave to be absent in their private occasions.'[57] They had to pay a shilling at each of the offices of the Commissioner, Master Shipwright, and Clerk of the Cheque.[58] If 'the poor Men have been subject to such an unreasonable Imposition', Hughes was 'strictly' charged 'to put an immediate end to it, and to prevent the like Oppression & Exaction for the future.'[59] The Admiralty Secretary

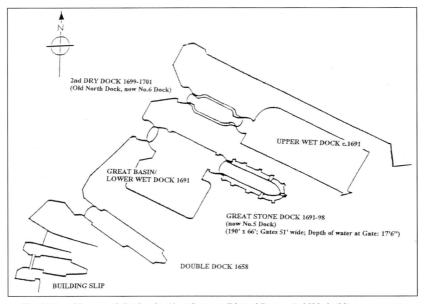

Sketch Map of Portsmouth Docks after Navy Surveyor Edmund Dummer's 1690s building programme.
Courtesy the Author.

criticised Hughes further: 'the Excuse made by your Clerk is trifling & evasive & they wander that you could send it for an Excuse'.[60]

Hughes reported to the Navy Board that at noon on Tuesday 4 January:

> *I went to the Gate as usual, attended by the Officers to Invite the Workmen, (Assembled there) into the Yard, to their duty but they still Absolutely deny'd my request and Continued there all the afternoon Rioting with Clubs & other Weapons Opposing every Person that offerd to come in at the Gate.*[61]

On Wednesday 5 January:

> *... this Morning they Assembled themselves in the same Mutinous manner as before and the few People that do pass the Gate whether belonging to the Yard or not are not Permitted without giving them Money for their Passage. They told me this Morning that they were determined not to come to their duty till all their Checques were taken off.*[62]

After consultation with Hughes and the civil and the military authorities on 6 January, Hardy considered that the 200 marines in the yard plus the Garrison, 'young and good for nothing', were 'not sufficient to reduce the Rioters by Force', and requested troops from Winchester and Salisbury.[63] Only 324 workmen had mustered, 1,466 were absent. In the Ropeyard 95 mustered, 17 were absent.[64] On 7 January a further 148 men mustered, with another six mustering in the Ropeyard.

A week into the strike two-thirds of the workforce were still absent and 'the Rioters still continues at the Dock Gates'. But on Sunday 9 January Hughes reported the end of the strike: 'Colonel Edmonds, with the Mayor, Yesterday Afternoon, made a speech to the Rioters at the Gate, on w:ch they presently dispersd: & told them, they wou'd come to Work a Monday.'[65] On Monday 10th he reported that 'the Workmen of this his Maj:ties Yard, came to, & attended their Duty this Morning, very Peaceably'.[66] The list of absentees on Tuesday 11 January revealed just seventy-eight men missing, of whom the greatest proportion (twenty-seven), were shipwrights.[67] Baugh considers that the strike 'was broken',68 but evidence suggests that the shipwrights had made their point and were ready to return to work.

In a highly critical letter, the Admiralty Board did not 'approve of the conduct' of Hughes and Hardy, sending a 'Rap, for not acting according to their orders' and being 'extremely remiss'. They could not 'conceive how you could suffer such a disgrace',

> *instead of making use of the Force you had to repell them, you suffer'd them to break into the Yard, and rescue one of their Number ... contenting yourselves with making smooth speeches to them, which could tend to nothing but to aggravate & inflame the disorder.*[69]

They considered there had been sufficient armed force to be more assertive: 'Their Lordships are no less surprised at hearing, that Col.° Edmonston has been at the Dockyard, to perswade the Rioters to disperse themselves, without either of yourselves being in his Company.'[70]

Aftermath

Hughes prepared for a troublesome aftermath and held troops in readiness when the ringleaders were discharged on 24 January. The Mayor and JPs were ready 'to assist with the Civill Power', but at 5 pm the discharged rioters 'went quietly out of the Yard'.[71] However,

> *at a quarter after Eight, a Mob assembled themselves together, at the Dock Gates, and began to cut through them; but immediately dispers'd themselves, as soon as the Watch of the Yard could get down to the Gates; on which the Mayor, Magistrates, Millitary Officers, & Soldiers, were desired, and directed to go forthwith to the Dock Gates, and fix a Guard there ... Then the Mob beginning to Multiply, the Riot Act was read to them; after which the Grenadiers seiz'd and brought five men into their Ranks, for severall Speeches, and Circumstances of Behaviour tending to raise, and Foment, Trouble, and disturbance; which men (in conjunction with the Mayor, and magistrates, of this place) we are now going to examine.*[72]

The next day, however, the 'rest of the Workmen went all quietly in to their Duty.'[73] Hughes's initial suspicion that the rioters were principally servants (apprentices) was confirmed after the disturbance from his records.[74] It is probable they included the extra recruited apprentices of 1740. The gravity with which the Admiralty and Navy Boards regarded the riots is shown by the military reinforcements which they pressed on Hughes and Hardy, criticism of their actions, and their determination to prosecute the ringleaders. Hughes identified Alexander Pooling and Edward Atwick, shipwrights, as the 'Ringleaders, first Proposers and Abettors of the Riot', with eleven others active, four of whom were servants. Alexander Pullen had incited the shipwrights to action:

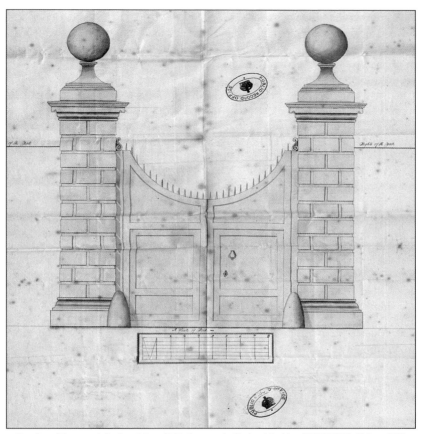

Drawing of Portsmouth Dockyard Gate 1711. Courtesy the National Archive, ADM106/667, 29 June 1711. The Navy Board directed that piers should be plain, cheaper than these rusticated ones drawn by the Officers.

> *... by telling them that he belonged to Woolwich Yard when the Shipwrights Rioted there and that he ... then advised the Men and Boys that were (then) present in order to prevent any of the Boats coming from Gosport to Bore Holes in them or to turn them loose ... And ... Edward Atwick another Shipwright now belonging to the said Yard (and who did belong to one other of His Majesties Yards at the very time a Riot was there committed) not only spirited up but at the same time perswaded them to Act as Pullen advised ...*[75]

The fact that they were from Thames yards, with concentrated numbers of dockyard and private shipwrights, may have made their leadership more forceful, but the grievance must have been felt strongly for the workforce to have struck so unanimously (although many may have stayed away from physical intimidation). Hughes's case rested on the evidence of shipwright, William Yateman, 'Examin'd by me',[76] two lieutenants and a sergeant-major from Colonel Cholmondley's regiment, called out on 24 January, Clerk of the Cheque George Atkins, and Porter William Woodrow.[77] These testified to numbers ranging from '10 or 12 men arm'd with Addiz's and hangers close to the great Gate' and 'about a hundred more standing off', to 'Persons to the Number of Five Hundred at Least', and 'a great Number of People riotously & unlawfully assembled ... about the Number of Twenty or more'.[78]

Hughes and Hardy had faced a complex and delicate situation. They had little latitude for changing the operating systems: pay rates, overtime rates; numbers and quality of men or junior management. As Baugh declared, in 'emergencies, the Commissioner was expected to act first and seek approval later.'[79] The London Boards, sending a stream of advice, were conveniently distanced and at no personal risk of physical danger or friction from overstepping legal bounds or conventions. Although the Riot Act was read on two occasions, 31 December 1742 and 24 January 1743, when troops were present, shots were never fired on the shipwrights who dominated the Portsea community.

The Master Shipwright, his Assistants and the Clerk of the Cheque were asked how they 'came to suffer any of the workmen of this yard to be idle and very idle'. They replied: 'being determined to remedy this evil', they have 'mulcted [fined] a day's pay for a day's idleness; and this is the very reason they give for this their late outrageous behaviour'.[80] As the main cause of the strike was Hughes's policy of fining two day's pay for a missed call, only outside agents: the Mayor and Colonel Edmondston, could resolve the dispute. The ringleaders were dismissed and prosecuted by the civil powers.

Hughes displayed empathy and humanity towards the non-striking workforce, and was prepared to 'exert' himself on their behalf, but expected commitment and obedience in return. In vain, he requested the Navy Board not to enter into another dockyard the five prosecuted shipwrights who requested their discharge from Portsmouth in March 1743, as:

> *their view in requesting it, is, only to go into some other of His Majesties Yards, where Extra is at this Time wrought; or, to work on some of the Ships, that are Building for His Majesties Service, by Contractors; where, they may receive greater Wages, then they now make, at a Single Days Pay.*[81]

He argued:

> *they make use of the Kings Yard, only as it Sutes their Inclination and Advantage; where during the Winter Season, little work can be performed; owing to the Shortness of the Days, and badness of the weather...yet, they have their full Pay: and, when the Days are long, the weather fine, and it may be reasonably expected, His Majesty may reap some Benefit from their Labour, they then, more for their own Interest, request their Discharge.*[82]

He was 'sorry to see' that they were allowed to enter Sheerness Dockyard.[83] As resident Commissioner, Hughes's duty to the Navy Board was paramount. He supported the workforce when they demonstrated commitment to his concept of duty and deserved redress; but would not compromise his perception of duty, enshrined in the Duke of York's Instructions of 1673.[84] To Hughes, duty meant physical presence, disciplined and diligent obedience. He or the Porter could have time off with no loss of pay, but the workmen suffered financial penalties for absence. Although the Navy Board discharged workmen at the end of each war, and paid wages at least six months in arrears, it demanded constant attendance from those on their books. The workforce resented this and felt justified and confident in striking in wartime. The strike did not change Hughes's management style – the workforce tested power relations by asserting their right to work elsewhere, but the balance of power was maintained.

---

[1] This article is developed from the 1805 Club Cecil Isaacson Memorial Lecture, delivered in Greenwich on 25 April 2009.

[2] The National Archive (TNA), ADM 106/975, 1.1.1742[3]. Square brackets modify dates between 1 January and 25 March, when the Old Style Julian New Year began. Where the original document acknowledges the New Year (1742/3), this has been retained.

[3] TNA, ADM 49/159, January 1742[3]. The six dockyards were Deptford, Woolwich, Chatham, Sheerness, Portsmouth and Plymouth.

[4] *Oxford English Dictionary:* Riot: wanton, dissipated unrestrained behaviour, actions against authorities for redress of grievances, disturbance of the peace. Rap: to hit a smart blow, to rap someone's fingers or knuckles in punishment.

[5] See Ann Coats, 'The Œconomy of the Navy and Portsmouth: A Discourse Between the Civilian Naval Administration of Portsmouth Dockyard and the Surrounding Communities, 1650 to 1800' (DPhil, University of Sussex, 2000), Chapter 5 for a fuller description of the strike.

[6] TNA, ADM 106/1023 fo. 33, Navy Board In-Letters, W. Woodrow to Navy Board, 22 May 1746.

[7] C. Markham, ed., *Life of Captain Stephen Martin, 1666-1740* (London: NRS, 1895), pp. 211-12.

[8] D. A. Baugh, *British Naval Administration in the Age of Walpole* (Princeton: Princeton University Press, 1965), pp. 272-73.

[9] Quoted, Baugh, *British Naval Administration*, p. 273.

[10] See Robin Wager, 'From Quarterdeck to Quill – A Study of the Hughes Family and the Navy 1674-1812' (MA Maritime Studies, University of Portsmouth, 2003), Chapter 1. My thanks to Robin for permission to use the data in Table 1. and the picture of Richard Hughes.

[11] Admiralty Library, Portsmouth, Royal Naval Museum, MSS 247, 'Captains and Ships 1688-1777'.

[12] D. A. Baugh, ed., *Naval Administration, 1715-1750* (Navy Records Society, 1977), vii, p. 263.

[13] Higher tides every fortnight, which gave greater depth of water at the dock gates.

[14] Baugh, *British Naval Administration*, pp. 334-39 and p. 212.

[15] Pronounced trennel or trunnel, the wooden cylindrical pins of up to 5 feet (1.5 metres) long which were the principal fasteners for ships' timbers.

[16] TNA, ADM 106/920, Joseph Allin, Tho Fellowes and John Poole to Navy Board, 24.1.1739[40].

[17] TNA, ADM 42/1215; Baugh, *Naval Administration*, p. 265 and p. 268.

[18] For instance, TNA, ADM 42/220, Chatham Extra, 1774; ADM 42/221, Chatham Extra 1775; ADM 42/222, Chatham Extra 1776.

[19] TNA, ADM 106/920, R. Hughes to Navy Board, 5.2.1739[40]], fo. 61.

[20] Ibid. At Spithead: *Namur, Russell, Princess Caroline, Buckingham, Grafton, Orford, Kent, Bristol, Dunkirk, Pearl, York, Rippon, Weymouth, Centurion, Defiance, Lenox. In harbour: Princess Amelia, Rochester, Ludlow Castle, Chester, Argyle, Severn, Lark, Eltham, S͠: Castle, S͠: Albans.*

[21] Ibid., fo. 68. R. Hughes to Navy Board, 10.2.1739[40].

[22] Ibid.

[23] Ibid., enclosed copy of order of Geo. Huish, JP, to the Constable and the Keeper of Portsmouth Gaol, 4.2.1739[40].

[24] Ibid., fo. 70, R. Hughes to Navy Board, 10.2.1739[40], enclosing a copy of Portsmouth Mayor John White's Deposition, 4.2.1739[40]. The language is likely to be that of George Huish, as the Mayor notes the witnesses' marks in his deposition.

[25] Ibid., fo. 71, R. Hughes to Navy Board, 10.2.1739[40], enclosing a copy of Heaton's statement to Mayor John White, 4.2.1739[40]. Heaton signed his name, so is assumed to be literate.

[26] Ibid., fo. 202A, George Augustus Prosser to R. Hughes, 25.4.1740.

[27] Ibid., fo. 276, R. Hughes to Navy Board, 5.6.1740.

[28] Ibid., fo. 276, 6.6.1740 Navy Board turnover note on reverse of R. Hughes to Navy Board, 5.6.1740.

[29] TNA, ADM 49/159, June, July 1743.

[30] One and a half hour's overtime, paying 7½d a tide.

[31] Baugh, British Naval Administration, p. 311 and p. 327.

[32] Ibid., 311, citing Macleod, Unpublished extracts, 5 August 1730.

[33] Sir Charles Hardy was aged about 63, a Rear Admiral of the Blue, D. Syrett and R. L. DiNardo, *The Commissioned Sea Officers of the Royal Navy 1660-1815* (Aldershot: NRS, 1994), p. 200; Baugh, *Naval Administration*, p. 306; R. East, *Extracts from Records in the Possession of the Municipal Corporation of the Borough of Portsmouth and from other*

documents relating thereto (Portsmouth, 1891), p. 381. He died in November 1743. R. Sedgewick, *The History of Parliament, the House of Commons, 1715-54* (History of Parliament Trust, HMSO, 1970), ii, p. 109.

34 TNA, ADM 106/920, 1740; N. W. Surry & J. H. Thomas, Book of Original Entries 1731-1751 (Portsmouth Record Series, 3, City of Portsmouth, 1976), lvii, 90, pp. 116-18; TNA, SP 42/26.

35 D. Defoe, *A Tour Through the Whole Island of Great Britain* (London: Everyman, 1962), p. 150.

36 Ibid., 151.

37 B. McLaren Ranft, 'Labour Relations in the Royal Dockyards in 1739', *Mariner's Mirror*, 47 (1961), p. 286; Baugh, *British Naval Administration*, p. 311. See D. Hodson, *Maps of Portsmouth before 1801* (Portsmouth Record Series, 4, City of Portsmouth, 1978).

38 Ann Coats, 'The Œconomy of the Navy and Portsmouth: A Discourse Between the Civilian Naval Administration of Portsmouth Dockyard and the Surrounding Communities, 1650 to 1800' (DPhil, University of Sussex, 2000), Appendix 3.4: Portsmouth and Portsea freeholder votes in eighteenth century Hampshire pollbooks.

39 Portsmouth Museums Records Service (PMRS), Portsea Rate Book 1700-1725 81A/3/21/1.

40 TNA, ADM 106/975, 1.1.1742/3. Caulker Richard Griley was also discharged, ADM 106/2558.

41 TNA, ADM 106/975, 2.1.1742[3]. *Woolwich* and *Princess Mary* were both in the harbour.

42 Quartermen were in charge of a shoal (gang) of usually 20 shipwrights, selected at the beginning of each year. Baugh, *Naval Administration*, p. 264; Baugh, *British Naval Administration*, pp. 313-16.

43 TNA, ADM 1/907, 3.1.1742[3].

44 Ibid.

45 Baugh, Naval Administration, pp. 305-306; TNA, ADM 106/975, 3.1.1742[3].

46 TNA, ADM 1/907, 3.1.1742[3].

47 See S. Palmer, 'Calling out the troops', *Journal of the Society for Army Historical Research*, 56: 228 (1978), pp. 198-214; W. Holdsworth, *A History of English Law* (London: Methuen, 1931), viii, pp. 330-31; Ibid., xiii, p. 566; J. Burke, ed., *Jowitt's Dictionary of English Law* (London: Sweet and Maxwell, 1977), ii, p. 1585; M. Harrison, *Crowds and History: Mass Phenomena in English Yowns, 1790-1835* (Cambridge: Cambridge University Press, 1988), 37, pp. 286-87; G. Holmes and D. Szechi, *The Age of Oligarchy, 1722-1783* (London: Longman, 1993), p. 185; E. Williams, *The Eighteenth-century Constitution* (Cambridge: Cambridge University Press, 1960), p. 409.

48 TNA, ADM 2/478, 3.1.1742[3].

49 TNA, ADM 1/907, 6.1.1742[3].

50 TNA, ADM 2/478, 3.1.1742/3, 8.1.1742/3.

51 TNA, ADM 1/907, 6.1.1742[3].

52 TNA, ADM 106/975, 4.1.1742[3].

53 Ibid.

54 Baugh, *British Naval Administration*, p. 311, p. 326, and pp. 330-32; Baugh, *Naval Administration*, p. 264 and pp. 304-08.

55 TNA, ADM 106/975, 1.2.1742[3] and see Baugh, *Naval Administration*, p. 307. Master Shipwright, see Baugh, *British Naval Administration*, pp. 294-295.

56 TNA, ADM 106/975, 4.1.1742[3].

57 TNA, ADM 2/478, 5.1.1742[3].

58 Ibid.

59 Ibid.

60 Not traced. TNA, ADM 3/46, 4.1.1742/3, 5.1.1742[3]; ADM 2/478, 10.1.1742[3].

61 TNA, ADM 106/975 5.1.1742[3]

62 Ibid. 'Checques' – fines or stoppage of wages for being absent.

63 TNA, ADM 1/907, 3.1.1742[3], 6.1.1742[3].

64 TNA, ADM 106/975, 7.1.1742[3].

65 Ibid.; ADM 1/907, 10.1.1742[3].

66 TNA, ADM 106/975, 10.1.1742[3].

67 TNA, Ibid, 9.1.1742[3], 10.1.1742[3], 11.1.1742[3].

68 Baugh, *British Naval Administration*, p. 326.

69 TNA, ADM 2/478, 10.1.1742[3].

70 Ibid.

71 TNA, ADM 1/907, 25.1.1742[3].

72 TNA, ADM 106/975, 26.1.1742[3].

73 TNA, ADM 106/975, 25.1.1742[3].

74 TNA, ADM 106/975, 1.1.1742[3], 9.1.1742[3], 29.1.1742[3].

75 TNA, ADM 106/975, 1.2.1742[3].

76 Ibid.

77 Ibid., 27 & 28.1742[3].

78 Ibid,. 27.1.1742[3].

79 Baugh, *British Naval Administration*, p. 289.

80 Baugh, *Naval Administration*, p. 297.

81 TNA, ADM 106/975, 20.3.1743.

82 Ibid.

83 TNA, ADM 7/633 13.6.1673.

Ship Yard.

Contributors' Biographies

Jennifer Bodie completed her undergraduate degree in History and Languages at King's College London in 2008, with a focus on the Early Modern period and the history of London. A gap-year spent in the Prints and Drawings department of the British Museum instilled a love for the eighteenth century and the history of print culture. Originally from the United States, she is proud to be a naturalized British citizen and enjoys travelling around the UK and abroad. She currently works in the financial industry.

Joseph F. Callo is a retired U.S. Navy Reserve rear admiral and award-winning television producer. His latest book *John Paul Jones: America's First Sea Warrior* won the Naval Order of the United States Samuel Eliot Morison Award. Admiral Callo's other books include *Nelson in the Caribbean: The Hero Emerges, 1784-1787* (Naval Institute Press, 2002), *Nelson Speaks: Admiral Lord Nelson in His Own Words* (Naval Institute Press, 2001), and *Legacy of Leadership: Lessons from Admiral Lord Nelson* (Hellgate Press, 1999). He also was US editor/author for *Who's Who in Naval History* (Routledge 2004). He currently is writing a memoir about the influence of the sea on his life.

David Clover spent several summers as an officer aboard the TS *Foudroyant* in Portsmouth, just across the harbour from HMS *Victory*. On graduating in Politics and Economics from Oxford Polytechnic in 1973, he entered a career as a college and university administrator. He is currently IT Development Manager in the Faculty of Mathematics, Computing and Technology at the Open University in Milton Keynes. He celebrated the bicentenary of the Battle of Trafalgar by singing in a performance of Haydn's 'Nelson Mass' at Radley College near Oxford.

Dr Ann Coats completed her doctoral thesis 'The Economy of the Navy and Portsmouth: Discourse between the Civilian Naval Administration of Portsmouth Dockyard and the Surrounding Communities, 1650 to 1800', at the University of Sussex in 2000. Since then she has taught on the MA Maritime Studies and MSc Heritage and Museum Studies at the University of Portsmouth and is currently its Course Leader. Ann jointly founded the Naval Dockyards Society in 1996 and since 1997 has been its Secretary. The Society has published five volumes of *Transactions* of NDS Conference Proceedings to date. In 1997, she was joint organiser of two conferences, two exhibitions and edited the conference papers on *The 1797 Naval Mutinies* (forthcoming). She has jointly published three books as a maritime publisher and has written articles on naval administration, dockyards, convicts and mutiny. Her latest article, 'Bermuda Naval Base: Management, Artisans and Enslaved Workers in the 1790s: The 1950s Bermudian Apprentices' Heritage', appeared in *Mariner's Mirror* in May 2009.

Terry Coleman is an historian, novelist, and journalist. As roving reporter for *The Guardian* he reported from eighty countries. He has interviewed eight British prime ministers, was New York correspondent, and was named Journalist of the Year in the British Press Awards. His historical novel *Southern Cross* was a worldwide bestseller. His most recent publications have been biographies of Nelson and Laurence Olivier. He is working on a biographical study of George III.

Dr David Cordingly was Keeper of Pictures and then Head of Exhibitions at the National Maritime Museum, Greenwich, where he organised displays including 'Captain James Cook, Navigator', 'The Mutiny on the Bounty', and 'Pirates: Fact and Fiction'. He read Modern History at Oxford and has a doctorate from the University of Sussex. His publications include *Life Among the Pirates*, and the much praised *Billy Ruffian: The Bellerophon and the Downfall of Napoleon* (broadcast as Book of the Week on BBC Radio 4). His most recent book is *Cochrane the Dauntless: The Life and Adventures of Thomas Cochrane*.

Anthony Cross is Director of Warwick Leadlay Gallery in Greenwich, London, specialists in antique maps, prints and fine art. He is President of Greenwich Historical Society, Editor of *The Trafalgar Chronicle* and an authority on Nelsonian iconography.

Chris Holt served in the Royal Engineers 1995-2005 retiring as a Major. He spent much of his career as a Bomb Disposal Officer, but was fortunate enough to meet the Royal Navy whilst qualifying as a commando and an Army Diver. He has a keen interest in underwater exploration and British military history. Chris is a Director of a risk management consultancy and lives with his family in North Somerset.

Professor Tamara L. Hunt is chair of the History Department at the University of Southern Indiana. She is the author of *Defining John Bull: Political Caricature and National Identity in Late Georgian England* (Ashgate, 2003) and a number of articles on caricatures during the reign of George III. She is the co-editor of *Women and the Colonial Gaze* (Palgrave, 2002). Professor Hunt is currently working on a biographical study of two early eighteenth-century women in the London publishing trades.

Professor Andrew Lambert is Laughton Professor of Naval History in the Department of War Studies at King's College, London. His work focuses on the naval and strategic history of the British Empire between the Napoleonic Wars and the First World War, and the development of naval historical writing. His work has addressed a range of issues, including technology, policy-making, regional security, deterrence, historiography, crisis management and conflict. He presented the acclaimed television series 'War at Sea' for BBC2 in 2004. His latest book, *Franklin: Tragic Hero of Polar Navigation*, was published by Faber in June this year.

Dr Huw Lewis-Jones is a historian and Curator of Art at the Scott Polar Research Institute, University of Cambridge. His book *Face to Face: Polar Portraits* (Cambridge, 2008) was released to critical acclaim last year. A second English edition has just been published (Conway, 2009), in addition to others in foreign languages. Supported by the Heritage Lottery Fund, Huw is currently building a national collection of Inuit art, whilst working on a number of new book projects. He is also Editor of *The Trafalgar Chronicle* and Editorial Director of the independent publishing company Polarworld.

Dr Keith Mercer is a post-doctoral fellow at the Gorsebrook Research Institute for Atlantic Canada Studies at Saint Mary's University in Halifax, Nova Scotia. This article stems from his doctoral thesis on impressment in the North Atlantic world, which he is currently preparing for publication.

Matthew McCarthy is currently engaged in an AHRC-sponsored PhD project at the Maritime Historical Studies Centre, University of Hull. His thesis will investigate the character of piracy and privateering in the early nineteenth century, its impact on British trade and shipping, and the effectiveness of the British government's efforts to suppress prize-taking activity in this period.

Professor Scott Hughes Myerly is a cultural and military historian and is the author of *British Military Spectacle From the Napoleonic Wars through the Crimea* (Harvard, 1996), which was a finalist in the Longman/*History Today* book of the year competition. He has been a professor at several American universities and has published articles on the cultural impact of military dress in the early nineteenth century. He is currently working on a number of projects, including a study of American attitudes towards Arabs and Islam prior to 1860.

Dr Roland Pietsch is currently writing a book *The Real Jim Hawkins* (Seaforth Publishing), exploring the lives of eighteenth-century ships' boys in the Royal Navy. He has previously written on maritime history, the history of youth culture, and on the philosopher Niccolo Machiavelli. He also worked as a historian for TV documentaries, both for popular formats, such as the BBC series

Who Do You Think You Are?, as well as for feature films like the award-winning *Life Goes On: The Last Propaganda Film of the Third Reich*. Dr Pietsch is lecturing history at Queen Mary, University of London. Previously, he was a manager of London's music venue The Spitz.

Justin Reay is Tutor in Naval History for the University of Oxford's International Programmes, and a Fellow of St Bede's Hall, Oxford where he is Tutor in the History of Art and Architecture. He is a senior manager at the Bodleian Library and is editing the Bodleian's collection of Samuel Pepys' naval papers for publication in 2010. A Fellow of the Society of Antiquaries, Justin is reading for a Doctorate in Maritime History at the University of Exeter; his history of the Admiralty buildings and people will be published in 2010.

Professor N.A.M. Rodger is a Senior Research Fellow of All Souls College Oxford, and Visiting Professor of Naval History at the University of Exeter. Two volumes of his 'Naval History of Britain' have already been published, *The Safeguard of the Sea* in 1997 and *The Command of the Ocean* in 2004, and he is at work on the third.

Dr Jan Rüger teaches modern history at Birkbeck, University of London. His research focuses on the history of Britain and Germany in the nineteenth and early twentieth centuries. He was a convener in the 'Capital Cities at War' project, a comparative cultural history of London, Paris and Berlin in the First World War. His recent book, *The Great Naval Game: Britain and Germany in the Age of Empire* has just come out as paperback (Cambridge).

Dr William J. Schultz graduated from The Ohio State University, received his medical degree from the University of Texas at Houston, and holds a graduate degree in Neurobiology and Anatomy from Colorado State University. He was honoured as the Ohio Family Physician of the Year in 2000. Collecting and studying daguerreotypes for more than twenty-five years, his stunning collection focuses on military, occupational and surveyor images, along with rare portraits that capture the American experience. Schultz has authored numerous articles, notably 'Silver Shadows Before the Storm: The American Military Daguerreotype' for the *Daguerreian Annual* (2002-03), 'Exploring the American Frontier: Legacy of the Land Surveyor in the Daguerreian Era', *Daguererian Annual* (2004), and 'Images of Colonial Empire: British Military Daguerreotypes – The British Sea Services', *Daguerreian Annual* (2005).

James Taylor studied at the Universities of St Andrews and Manchester. Formerly Head of Victorian Paintings at Phillips Fine Art Auctioneers, he was for ten years curator of paintings, drawings and prints, and exhibition organiser at the National Maritime Museum. From 1999 he has been a freelance art consultant, exhibition organiser and author. His publications include *Marine Painting* (Studio Editions, 1995), *Yachts on Canvas* (Conway, 1998), and most recently *The Voyage of the Beagle* (Conway and Naval Institute Press, 2008).

Peter Warwick has been chairman of The 1805 Club since 2004 and has served on the Council for 13 years. He is also a member of the Official Waterloo Committee, chairman of the Nelson Legacy Conference Series, and one of the permanent crew for HMS *Victory's* Cutter, tender to the flagship of the Second Sea Lord and C-in-C Naval Home Command. After graduating in Economics from Hull University, Peter spent 20 years working in the City and is a founder member of the Society of Property Researchers. In the early 1990s he became a Member of the Chartered Institute of Public Relations and established himself as an independent marketing and communications consultant. He recently assumed the chairmanship of Thames Alive 2012.

Professor Glyn Williams is Emeritus Professor of History at Queen Mary, University of London. He is a former President of the Hakluyt Society, and the author of numerous books on the exploration of the Pacific and the Arctic. His most recent books are *The Death of Captain Cook: A Hero Made and Unmade* (Profile Books, 2008) and *Arctic Labyrinth: The Quest for the Northwest Passage* (Allen Lane, 2009).

Notes for Contributors

The Trafalgar Chronicle is published annually by The 1805 Club. As well as preserving maritime monuments and memorials, the Club's aim has always been to promote and publish research into the Royal Navy of the Georgian period. *The Trafalgar Chronicle* is a rapidly expanding journal, with an international profile and a discerning readership, and its continued success is dependent upon original, engaging, and high-quality submissions. While the emphasis is on maritime and naval history, the journal welcomes articles which reflect other approaches, or which offer new interdisciplinary insights.

The Trafalgar Chronicle invites academics, graduate students, public history professionals, and club members to offer papers for the consideration of the Editors. Articles should be addressed to: The Editors, *The Trafalgar Chronicle*, 5 Nelson Road, Greenwich, London, SE10 9JB. Articles should be submitted in English and should normally be between 2,000 and 5,000 words, although shorter research notes will also be considered. All articles must be submitted on a CD-ROM, or as an MS Word attachment together with two hard copies. Articles should be typed and double spaced, accompanied by an abstract of no more than 100 words, and a short biography of the contributor. Articles may include endnotes, and authors are asked to follow the Modern Humanities Research Association Style Guide to ensure 'clarity and consistency in matters of style and presentation'. Further guidance is available at *www.mhra.org.uk*, or at the Club's website *www.admiralnelson.org*. All contributions must be submitted by 1 August, though the Editors accept articles throughout the year.

Articles that include illustrative material are welcomed but they must be of publishable quality and not subject to copyright restrictions. The Editors may also be able to assist in sourcing appropriate imagery to accompany submissions. Submission of an article to *The Trafalgar Chronicle* will be taken as an assurance that it has not been published and is not being considered for publication elsewhere. No payment is made for contributions, but authors will receive a free copy of the journal. The Editors will attempt wherever possible to provide authors with a decision on publication within eight weeks of receipt of an essay, and their decision on publication is final.